LONELY PLANET PUBLICATIONS

D0391527

BECKY OHLSEN

SEATTLE
CITY GUIDE

INTRODUCING SEATTLE

It's raining again, but you don't mind. This is your cue to duck inside for another latte. Maybe you'll chase it with a local beer, then tackle the Space Needle before rocking the Crocodile Café.

Welcome to Seattle, whose perpetually cloudy skies mean that if the sun peeks out for a second, everyone drops whatever they're doing and gears up to take their kayaks or bicycles out. They can do this because they're part-time baristas, freelance IT consultants, club bookers or chefs at all-organic small-plates restaurants. They're as likely to drink PBR as IPA, but they'd rather die than sip truck-stop coffee or down a Quarter Pounder with cheese. They always recycle. They've been on skid road, and they know Alki has nothing to do with the drinking habits of barflies in Pioneer Square. If you ask them, they'll tell you it really doesn't rain that much around here.

They might also tell you to watch the 'flying fish' at Pike Place Market early in the morning, visit the brand-new Olympic Sculpture Garden on a sunny afternoon and take an evening ferry ride to Bainbridge Island. Most likely they'll say not to bother with the Space Needle unless the weather is brilliant. If you're game for a bar crawl, they might take you to Georgetown, the neighborhood for drinkers in the know. If you're arty, it might be an opening at an edgy Belltown gallery instead.

CITY LIFE

Seattle is the largest metro area in the Pacific Northwest, with a population of about 3.3 million (580,000 in the city proper). It's a bookish, well-educated place, but also a dynamic and inventive urban center – most of the city's recent economic growth has been fueled by technology, both high-tech and the old-school, engine-parts variety. And it seems to be working: a London-based market-research company (TNS Global) recently reported that King County has 68,000 millionaires.

Two of those also happen to be the city's two largest public figures, Bill Gates and Paul Allen. And they symbolize a certain aspect of the city's contradictory attitude toward its own success. Both undeniably ambitious and indisputably successful, Gates and Allen are seen simultaneously as points of civic pride and shameless capitalists who are totally alien to the prevailing Seattle culture.

And speaking of culture, you'll be forgiven for thinking Seattle's is mostly white – at least if you hang out in hipster coffee-shops or go to indie-rock shows in Belltown – but Seattle has a rich multicultural history and is home to Native-American, African-American, Asian and growing Ethiopian populations. The city ranks 23rd of the 30 largest US cities in African-American population, at 8.4% – higher than every West Coast city except Los Angeles. It also has the largest concentration of Native Americans in the Pacific Northwest. The largest group in urban Seattle are the Duwamish people, the Native Americans that lived on the shores of Elliott Bay originally.

It's been a neighborhood-centric city for most of its history, but Seattle now sits on the verge of major structural and demographic change. The area expects 40% population growth in the next two decades and the regional transportation board has put together a mass-transit plan that some say will alter the city's landscape radically. Many locals see their home as suddenly being on the brink of major-city status. It's an exciting time to visit an always exciting place.

Marching girls parade through Seattle's International District (p59)

HIGHLIGHTS

DOWNTOWN & FIRST HILL

Downtown Seattle is the functional business heart of the city, with a jungle of office buildings and an electric weekday buzz. It's also home to many of the city's main hotels, as well as the Seattle Art Museum. Head to First Hill for the architecturally impressive Seattle Public Library.

❶ Seattle Art Museum
Eye up eclectic art in cool surroundings (p49)

❷ Seattle Public Library
Find peace and prose at this stylish library (p52)

❸ Sorrento Hotel
Dabble in decadence at the Sorrento Hotel (p52)

PIONEER SQUARE & INTERNATIONAL DISTRICT

Pioneer Square is the birthplace of Seattle, and its redbrick buildings and plazas give it a historic, film-set feel. It's also popular for its restaurants, bars and independent shops, which are well worth a visit. The International District is home to Seattle's Chinatown and the Wing Luke Asian Museum.

1 Zeitgeist
Perk up on coffee in arty surrounds (p140)

2 Wing Luke Asian Museum
Absorb yourself in Pan-Asian history (p59)

3 Pioneer Square Park
Step back in time to Seattle's early days (p56)

PIKE PLACE MARKET & WATERFRONT

One of Seattle's best-loved attractions, Pike Place Market is a labyrinthine fish and produce market that oozes theatricality. Find yourself entertained amid 'flying fish', buskers, tourists and locals before stepping out along the Waterfront, where scenic views of Puget Sound and the Olympic Mountains await.

❶ Seattle Aquarium
Spy the underwater world of Puget Sound (p66)

❷ Waterfront
Catch the flavor of a major seaport (p63)

❸ Pike Place Market
Watch the world go by at this loud, lovable market (p62)

BELLTOWN

The alternative scene in Belltown may have mellowed slightly, but this neighborhood can still be classed as cool. Watch a band at the Crocodile Café before taking an easy stroll to other offbeat bars in the area. Belltown is also home to the impressive Olympic Sculpture Park.

1 Shorty's
Play pinball and drink beer (p142)

2 Crocodile Café
Start in the café, end up in the mosh pit (p70)

3 Olympic Sculpture Park
Feel small amid giant sculptures (p70)

4 Ace Hotel
Be fascinated by bedtime reading at this hipster hotel (p179)

SEATTLE CENTER & QUEEN ANNE

Seattle Center is a 1960s vision of the future, making it an endearingly retro place to visit. As well as the Space Needle, it contains numerous museums and attractions, including the Experience Music Project. Rising up on the hill above Seattle Center is the dignified Queen Anne neighborhood.

1 **Experience Music Project**
See Kurt Cobain's handwritten lyrics (p72)

2 **Queen Anne**
Pose by perfectly manicured lawns (p75)

3 **International Fountain**
Get wetter in this sci-fi fountain in Seattle Center (p74)

4 **Space Needle**
Zoom to the top for incredible views (p72)

LAKE UNION, CAPITOL HILL & VOLUNTEER PARK

Lake Union hums with the sound of seaplanes, but you can have fun skirting the edge on a bike or boat. Nearby Capitol Hill is an artsy and diverse neighborhood, where you'll find cafés, galleries and street theater. If you need a break from kayaks and counterculture, stop at the Volunteer Park Conservatory.

❶ Jimi Hendrix Statue
Follow the trail of rock legends (p81)

❷ Lake Union
Paddle around this Y-shaped lake (p78)

❸ Volunteer Park Conservatory
Brush past palms in Seattle's tropical corner (p81)

❹ Wall of Sound
Flip through racks of music (p116)

9

FREMONT & WALLINGFORD

Fun-loving Fremont has coffee shops, pubs and some of the oddest public art that you'll ever see, making a visit to this neighborhood a must. Pleasant Wallingford is on the route of the Burke-Gilman cycle trail and its main draw is Gas Works Park.

1 Fremont Troll
Hunt the troll and see him gobble up a VW Beetle (p90)

2 Gas Works Park
Find yourself drawn inexplicably to a strange maze of pipes (p93)

3 Lenin Statue
Consider adding art to your collection (p90)

BALLARD & DISCOVERY PARK

Ballard is a Scandinavian-influenced neighborhood that lies just over Ballard Bridge. It seems a world away from urban Seattle and is known for its down-to-earth bars and live-music venues, as well as the interesting Fish Ladder. Neighboring Discovery Park is 534 acres of urban wilderness.

❶ Ballard Fish Ladder
Spot salmon on their way to spawn (p99)

❷ Nordic Heritage Museum
Learn more about Ballard's heritage (p97)

❸ Discovery Park
Walk the trails and escape the city (p100)

GREEN LAKE & PHINNEY RIDGE

If you like zoos, parks, rose gardens and low-key neighborhoods then you'll love Green Lake and Phinney Ridge. Green Lake Park is a perfect place for sunbathing in summer or walking in fall, and Woodland Park Zoo is one of Seattle's greatest tourist attractions.

❶ Seattle Rose Garden
Smell the scent of 5000 roses (p96)

❷ Woodland Park Zoo
Monkey around at the zoo (p96)

❸ Green Lake Park
Bike or skate by the lake (p95)

AROUND SEATTLE

Situated in a stunning part of the Pacific Northwest, Seattle is within easy reach of mountain ranges, the ocean, hundreds of islands and a temperate rainforest. This makes Seattle a perfect hub for getting out and exploring the natural world.

❶ Mt Rainier National Park
Climb the highest peak in the Cascades (p193)

❷ Ferry across Puget Sound
Ride the waves and look back at Seattle's famous skyline (p187)

❸ San Juan Islands
Kayak around breathtaking islands (p189)

❹ Hoh River Rain Forest
Hike in a mossy temperate rainforest (p197)

CONTENTS

Continued from previous page.

THE AUTHOR

BECKY OHLSEN

Originally drawn to the Pacific Northwest 12 years ago by a hopeless crush on Mudhoney singer Mark Arm, Becky Ohlsen didn't even make it all the way up to Seattle on her first try. Instead she settled in Portland, Oregon, biding her time, until one day the promise of unlimited pinball games and high-altitude trespassing drew her to the Emerald City to work on the previous edition of this book. Since then she's spent enough time mooching around the city to have seen it from the water, the gutter and the tops of numerous buildings, with wildly varying degrees of clarity. She has yet to leave any impression whatsoever on Mark Arm.

BECKY'S TOP SEATTLE DAY

When I'm in Seattle I like to wake up uncharacteristically early and go straight to Pike Place Market (p62). The scene here is fascinating any time of day, but it's best in the morning, when most of the customers are locals getting their shopping done. It's a nice place for a walking breakfast, too, with options ranging from fresh fruit to coffee and pastries to a hefty *hum bao* (steamed pork bun) big enough to power you through the whole day. After exploring the labyrinth of weird little market shops, I'll browse the progressive literature at Left Bank Books (p113) to keep myself honest and bolster hope. Afterwards, a short stroll down toward Elliott Bay gives me a panoramic view of the mountains from the new Olympic Sculpture Park (p70).

Of course I can't be in Seattle without spending some time digging around the creaky shelves at Elliott Bay Book Company (p57), and as long as I'm this close I might as well grab a meaty sandwich at Salumi (p123) for lunch.

I'll spend the rest of the afternoon soaking up culture at the new Seattle Art Museum (p49), abandon it for happy hour at the Nitelite Lounge (p142), then probably squander the evening and whatever's left in my pockets on pinball and beer in the back room of Shorty's (p142).

Other than finding accommodation, Seattle doesn't require a huge amount of pre-planning. Most of the can't-miss sights are clustered around downtown within easy walking distance of each other. If you bring a decent map, book accommodations in advance and have some sort of plan for transportation – whether it's a car and an idea of where you'll park overnight, or a public-transport schedule – you'll be fine. Keep in mind that the city is hillier than it looks on maps and – if you're driving – many streets in the city center are one-way only.

Once you're there, getting around is relatively easy. Driving and parking are the main annoyances and if you can avoid them, you'll be happier. Luckily this is easy to do. Buses connect to most neighborhoods of interest to visitors, although they stop running too early to be of much use for nightlife exploration. But then, that's why mother nature gave us taxi cabs (see Transportation chapter, p203).

For more help with advance planning, visit Seattle's Convention and Visitors Bureau (Map p50; ☎ 206-461-5888, 866-732-2695; www.visitseattle.org; 701 Pike St; ☺ 9am-5pm Mon-Fri, also Sat & Sun Jun-Aug). The website has a schedule of events, a few discount coupons and a form for ordering a visitor-information packet. Also among the bureau's services is the Citywide Concierge Center, a free service for visitors that will book you a table, a tour or transportation and answer questions about events going on while you're in town.

WHEN TO GO

Unless you're a skier or snowboarder – or *really* interested in aquatic life – Seattle in the winter makes for a pretty dreary holiday. The city receives 65% of its precipitation from November to March. But in spring the relentless downpour frequently lets up to provide gorgeous days that are well worth the wait.

April and May are best for enjoying the fruits of all that gloomy winter rain: suddenly everything is supernaturally green and covered in flowers. Summer – June, July and August – is the high season and can usually be relied upon for sunny days, warm weather and lots of people saying things like 'I thought you said it rained all the time here.' Fall, the season of Bumbershoot and Oktoberfest, is the favorite of beer lovers and music fans.

FESTIVALS

January

CHINESE NEW YEAR

☎ 206-382-1197; www.cidbia.org
Beginning towards the end of January or the start of February and lasting for two weeks, the year's first big ethnic festival takes place in the International District; you can contact the Chinatown/International District Business Improvement

Association for information. The first day of the New Year festival is celebrated with parades, firecrackers, fireworks and plenty of food.

February

NORTHWEST FLOWER & GARDEN SHOW

☎ 800-229-6311; www.gardenshow.com; Washington State Convention & Trade Center
Usually held the second week of February, this popular event includes lectures and seminars, demo gardens and samples, and children's activities.

top picks

OFFBEAT SEATTLE FESTIVALS

- Bumbershoot (p18) A cultural buffet of music, theater, artwork and poetry on 25 stages.
- Fremont Street Fair (opposite) Celebrate one of Seattle's quirkiest corners.
- Winterfest (p18) A celebration of all that's cold, furry and white.
- Trolloween (in Fremont on Halloween; p18) Just in case regular Halloween isn't weird enough for you.
- Moisture Festival (opposite) Performances by oddball artists both local and international.

March

MOISTURE FESTIVAL
☎ 800-838-3006; www.moisturefestival.com;
Hale's Palladium, 4301 Leary Way NW; tickets $5-20
With regular performances held between
March 15 and April 1, the Moisture Festival has developed from a little-known
quirkfest into something that locals look
forward to each year. It has retained a
laid-back, casual vibe and usually features
random appearances by folks like Artis
the Spoonman, Circus Contraption and
The Bobs.

ANTHONY'S OYSTER GAMES
☎ 206-297-7002; www.pugetsoundkeeper.org;
Anthony's Homeport on Shilshole Bay
Watch local celebs slurp oysters – and
enjoy some fruits of the sea yourself – at
this annual festival, which also includes
live music, raffles, a fashion contest (?), art
exhibits, beer and wine.

ST PATRICK'S DAY
March 17 is the day the patron saint of
Ireland is honored by all those who have
Irish in their blood, and by those who
want to have Irish beer in their blood.
Everyone wears green (otherwise you
risk getting pinched). Irish bars such as
Kells serve green beer, and even bars
that haven't an Irish trinket in sight get
swamped with revellers. Catch the parade
going from City Hall to Westlake Center
along 4th Ave.

April

CHERRY BLOSSOM & JAPANESE CULTURAL FESTIVAL
☎ 206-684-7200; www.seattlecenter.com; Seattle
Center
Usually held in mid-April, this celebration of
Japanese heritage includes performances
of music, dance and drama.

May

CINCO DE MAYO
May 5 commemorates the day the Mexi-
cans wiped out the French Army in 1862.
Now it's the day all Americans get to eat
lots of Mexican food and drink margaritas.
Seattle celebrates with an annual parade
and exhibitions of Hispanic artwork.

OPENING DAY OF YACHT SEASON
☎ 206-325-1000; www.seattleyachtclub.org
Held the first Saturday in May at various
locations on Lakes Washington and Union,
this Seattle original starts with a blessing of
the fleet. It features scull racing and a boat
parade through the canals.

SEATTLE INTERNATIONAL CHILDREN'S FESTIVAL
☎ 206-684-7338; www.seattleinternational.org;
Seattle Center
Held in mid-May, this cultural extravaganza
includes a wide variety of performances
and activities for kids.

NORTHWEST FOLKLIFE FESTIVAL
☎ 206-684-7300; www.nwfolklife.org; Seattle
Center
This festival – the largest of its kind in
North America – takes over Seattle Center
during Memorial Day weekend. More
than 5000 performers and artists from
over 100 countries present music, dance,
crafts, food and activities in celebration
of the rich cultural heritage of the Pacific
Northwest.

SEATTLE INTERNATIONAL FILM FESTIVAL
☎ 206-324-9996; www.seattlefilm.com
Held from late May to mid-June, this festival
brings nearly a month's worth of international film premieres to Seattle. Screenings
take place at several theaters. Check the
website for a detailed schedule.

June

FREMONT STREET FAIR
☎ 206-649-6706; www.fremontfair.com
Off-kilter Fremont is just the place you'd
want to be for a street fair. This one has live
music and other entertainment, food and
crafts and the overtly artsy Solstice Parade.
It takes place adjacent to the ship canal,
usually in mid-June.

SEATTLE PRIDE FESTIVAL
☎ 206-684-7200; www.seattlepride.org; Seattle
Center
Seattle's lesbian- and gay-pride event
usually falls on the last Sunday in June and
includes a film festival, art exhibit, parade
and the requisite food and entertainment.

July

BITE OF SEATTLE

☎ 425-283-5050; www.biteofseattle.com; Seattle Center

This culinary celebration is usually held the second weekend in July. For a single entry fee, guests can sample food from dozens of Seattle-area chefs and taste local beer and wines. The evening ends with live music.

SEAFAIR

☎ 206-728-0123; www.seafair.com

A month-long extravaganza, Seafair is a civic celebration that began as a hydroplane race on Lake Washington. It's now the city's biggest festival, with all manner of festivities extending across Seattle. Events include a torchlight parade, an air show, lots of music, a carnival and even the arrival of the naval fleet. Lodging is in short supply in Seattle on Seafair weekends and traffic becomes hopelessly tangled thanks to closed bridges and the influx of visitors, so plan accordingly.

September

BUMBERSHOOT

☎ 206-281-7788; www.bumbershoot.org

Seattle's biggest arts and cultural event takes over Seattle Center on Labor Day weekend (the first Monday in September). Hundreds of musicians, artists, theater troupes and writers come from all over the country to perform on the festival's two dozen stages. It's hard not to find something you like. There's also a crafts street fair and lots of good food from local vendors.

SEATTLE AIDS WALK

☎ 206-329-6923; www.nwaids.org

This festive and friendly event, held in late September, grows every year. It's a 10km or 5km walk. Locations vary, so check the website for details. The walk benefits the Lifelong AIDS Alliance.

FREMONT OKTOBERFEST

☎ 206-632-1500; www.fremontoktoberfest.org

There are versions of Oktoberfest held all over town, but this one's a good introduction to the concept as well as the neighborhood. It includes crafts, a car show, live entertainment and, of course, beer tasting.

October

SEATTLE LESBIAN & GAY FILM FESTIVAL

☎ 206-323-4274; www.seattlequeerfilm.com

Held in the third week of October, this film festival brings both mainstream and underground queer films to various theaters around town.

HALLOWEEN

On October 31, kids and adults dress up in scary costumes. In the safer neighborhoods you're likely to see children out 'trick-or-treating' door-to-door for candy. The gay and lesbian bars are especially wild places on Halloween, and Fremont has its own version, Trolloween (named after the Fremont Troll). It features a candlelit procession of costumed locals on Halloween night, followed by a public dance.

December

WINTERFEST

☎ 206-684-7200; www.seattlecenter.com

Seattle Center holds a month-long celebration of holiday traditions from around the globe, starting with Winter Worldfest, a massive concert and dance performance, and continuing with exhibits, dances, concerts and ice skating.

NEW YEAR'S EVE

☎ 206-443-2111; www.seattlecenter.com

The place to be on the 31st is Seattle Center, where festivities are focused on the Space Needle. Most people celebrate by dressing up and drinking champagne, or staying home and watching it all on TV. The following day people stay home to nurse their hangovers and watch college football.

COSTS & MONEY

As in most large cities, expenses in Seattle can vary depending on your interests and means. With a little strategizing, it's possible to scrape by on a backpacker's budget. Accommodations are the main sticking point here. Cheap sleeps are limited, but always easier to find if you book in advance. Planning to visit during the off-season will also ensure lower rates, even at midrange and top-end hotels.

A dorm bed in a downtown youth hostel runs at about $25; a double room in one of Seattle's European-style hotels will go for $50 to $65. Midrange doubles are between $80 and $150, usually including a free continental breakfast. Also see the Sleeping chapter (p174) for details about Seattle Super Saver hotel discount packages.

To get the best value out of meals, eat in the bar section of a restaurant rather than the main dining room. Seek out happy-hour food specials; or share a few starters or small plates rather than going for a full entree. Several of the nicest Seattle restaurants are handily designed to work this way already, allowing diners to sample a wider variety of dishes.

For discounts on sights and entertainment, consider buying a Go Seattle card (www.goseattlecard .com) or a Seattle CityPass (www.citypass.net), both of which offer free or discounted admission to a number of the city's top attractions. See the Neighborhoods chapter (p54) for details.

INTERNET RESOURCES

The following websites may be helpful in planning your travels.

dailycandy.com The Seattle edition digs up new and fun things to see, do or buy each day.

hankblog.wordpress.com Insider art-related news and views from the folks at the Henry Art Gallery.

lineout.thestranger.com *The Stranger*'s music blog – a great way to get plugged into the scene quickly.

seattle.metblogs.com Metroblogging, Seattle style.

seattlenma.org Want to know what your bartenders are talking about? This is the home of Seattle's Nightlife and Music Association.

slog.thestranger.com A frequently updated blog by the staff of *The Stranger* newsweekly.

www.seattlediy.com A great source of information on underground events and house shows.

www.seattlest.com An interesting but less-savvy-than-the-*Stranger* blog about various news and goings-on in and around Seattle.

www.sustainableseattle.org Though it's a bit academic, this site has thorough information on ecofriendly projects and initiatives in Seattle.

www.visitseattle.org Seattle's Convention and Visitors Bureau site.

www.vrseattle.com If you just can't wait until you get there, check out this site for 360-degree views of various Seattle sights, shops and hangouts.

SUSTAINABLE SEATTLE

Nature is a huge part of the Seattle experience and it should come as no surprise that the city is good at being green. So what can visitors do to help?

International flights are pretty much unavoidable, so consider contributing to a carbon offset organization like www.carbon fund.org, www.terrapass.com, www.native energy.com or www.driveneutral.org, where your money is transformed into support for sustainable practices. Or, if you're close enough, plan to travel on a biodiesel bus (p205) or on a train (p206).

Once you've arrived in Seattle, you can easily get by without having a car. Local bus networks are good, and biking is a great option (rentals abound). Walking and using the public transportation system are also good earth-friendly options. And if you do need a car, think about making use of www .flexcar.com, a car-sharing program. Some car-rental agencies offer hybrid vehicles, so be sure to ask around. Also, take a look at www.craigslist.com, an online bulletin board where you can find regional rideshares (look under 'community'), ie folks who are looking for people to carpool and share the cost of gas.

In hotels, save energy by requesting that your sheets and towels not be laundered every day. Shut off lights, the TV and air-con when you're not in the room. And consider not using those inefficient little travel-sized sundries.

Hostels are another option – their high-density dormitories use less space and energy. The adventurous can check www .couchsurfing.org, where you sleep on other

HOW MUCH?

Adult ticket up the Space Needle $16

Cover charge at the Crocodile Café $5-15

Gallon of gasoline $3.50

Late-night burrito from a taco cart $3.50

Liter of bottled water $1.50

Pint of local microbrewed beer $3.50

Room at the hip Ace Hotel $99

Single-shot latte at Starbucks $2.65

Souvenir T-shirt $20

Taxi from airport to Pike Place Market $33

ADVANCE PLANNING

As in any large American city, planning ahead will let you spend more of your time enjoying Seattle. Things like car rental, accommodations and tours should be booked in advance, not only because it saves money, but also because, if you show up without a hotel booking in peak season, you might find yourself stranded.

Train tickets to Seattle may need to be booked in advance, as some trains do sell out. Make reservations at amtrak .com or by phone at ☎ 800-872-7245.

If you're hoping to see a particular performance or game, whether it's the Mariners or the opera, it's wise to buy tickets in advance. See individual listings chapters for price ranges and information on how to book (for sporting events, see p165; for theater and other performance events, see p159).

Some restaurants recommend or require booking a table in advance, and these are noted in the Eating chapter (p120). For most places in Seattle, booking a day or two ahead is enough, unless it's a holiday.

The Seattle CityPass (www.citypass.net), which offers discounts on Seattle museums and other attractions, can be ordered in advance on its website. The website dailycandy.com produces a 'weekend guide' to Seattle; it's worth subscribing to the mailing list before a trip.

It's useful to read up on what's happening in town via The Stranger's savvy and entertaining online blogs, Slog (for news) and LineOut (for music and nightlife) at www.thestranger.com. Rabid menu-readers will appreciate the Seattle Times' archive of restaurant reviews, available online at www.seattletimes.com.

Seattle's Citywide Concierge Center (☎ 206-461-5888; www.visitseattle.org; 701 Pike St) can help with advance bookings of almost anything you'll need, including accommodations, tours and the CityPass.

member's couches all around the world – exchanging cultures, saving money and using hopefully fewer resources.

When you're out and about, keep the environment in mind as you spend your travel dollars: carry reusable cloth grocery bags instead of plastic, avoid excessive packag-ing and consider eating in restaurants that emphasize locally sourced, organically grown ingredients, such as Tilth (p134), the Globe (p132) or Chaco Canyon Cafe (p133). Support local businesses rather than national chains. And, of course, recycle as much as you can.

BACKGROUND

HISTORY

For a major US city, Seattle's civic history begins very late in the chronicle of the nation. While the rest of the country was establishing firm roots, most of today's Seattle was covered in deep forest that was perennially drenched in rain. Though native groups lived here long before, colonialist settlement didn't reach Puget Sound until 1851. The history of Seattle as a city is itself only about 130 years long, but in that time it's become the cultural and economic center of the Pacific Northwest. Not that the city would ever brag about that status itself, mind you.

Despite its achievements and importance to the region, Seattle still has the mellow sense of modesty and self-deprecation that characterizes the Northwest. This dates back to its laid-back origins as 'New York Pretty Soon' (see p23). The attitude peaked in the 1950s and '60s, with the wild antiboosterism of newspaper columnist Emmett Watson (who wrote things like 'Have a nice day – somewhere else' and 'Our suicide rate is one of the highest in the nation. But we can be No 1!'). And it colored the way the nation perceives Seattle with the popularization of the antiglamourous in the form of grunge, a trend whose fame seemed to mortify the city. Then there was the city's naive excitement at being selected to host the 1999 World Trade Organization (WTO) conference and many residents' shock at the resulting fallout. Seattle always seems to have an uncomfortable relationship with the success it has struggled to achieve.

NATIVE PEOPLES OF PUGET SOUND

When the accumulated ice of the great polar glaciers of the Pleistocene Epoch lowered sea levels throughout the world, the ancestors of Native Americans migrated from Siberia to Alaska via a land bridge across the Bering Strait. By this reckoning, the present tribes of Puget Sound arrived here 11,000 or 12,000 years ago, before the glaciers receded.

Unlike the Plains Indians living further inland, who were primarily nomadic hunter-gatherers, the first inhabitants of the Pacific Northwest were intimately tied to the rivers, lakes and sea. The tribe living on the site of today's Seattle was called the Duwamish. They and other tribal groups along Puget Sound – notably the Suquamish, Coast Salish and Chinook – depended on catching salmon, cod and shellfish. On land, they hunted deer and elk, more for their protective hides than for their flesh. Though each group had its own dialect, coastal natives communicated through a language called Lushootseed, which natives today struggle to keep from extinction.

Summer and fall were dedicated to harvesting the bounty of the sea and forest. Food was stored in massive quantities to carry the tribes through the long winter months, when the most important ancient legends and ceremonies were handed down to the younger generations. In terms of artistic, religious and cultural forms, the Northwest coastal Indians reached a pinnacle of sophistication unmatched by most Native American groups. Ornately carved cedar canoes served as transportation, and extensive trading networks evolved between the permanent settlements that stretched up and down the coast and along the river valleys.

TIMELINE

1804–06	1845	1851
Meriwether Lewis and William Clark set out on their famous expedition across the Louisiana Territory, covering 8000 miles in two years, with the help of Shoshone Indian translator Sacagawea.	The first US settlement in Washington is established at Tumwater. For the next 15 years, some 53,000 settlers will migrate across the 2000-mile-long Oregon Trail.	The Denny party arrives at Alki Point and settles in Puget Sound, already home to the Duwamish people. A year later, thanks to rough tides that made pier-building impossible, the settlement moves to Seattle proper.

Extended family groups lived in cedar longhouses, which were constructed over a central pit-like living area. The social structure in these self-sustaining villages was quite stratified, with wealth and power held by an aristocratic class of chiefs. Social and religious rituals were dominated by a strict clan system. Wealth was measured in goods such as blankets, salmon and fish oil. These items were consumed and to some degree redistributed in ceremonial feasts in which great honor accrued to the person who gave away valued items.

Puget Sound natives evolved complex cultural, social, and economic structures, which the invasion of Euro-American settlers in the mid-1800s almost erased. Today tribes struggle for survival, respect and renewal (see boxed text, p24).

EARLY EXPLORATION

Puget Sound and the Pacific Northwest in general were among the last areas of the Americas to be explored by Europeans. In fact, almost 300 years passed between the arrival of white explorers in America and their 'discovery' of Puget Sound.

The first white expedition to explore the Puget Sound area came in 1792, when the British sea captain George Vancouver sailed through the inland waterways of the Straits of Juan de Fuca and Georgia. In the same year, the USA entered the competition to claim the Northwest when Captain Robert Gray reached the mouth of the Columbia River.

The major reason for European and American eagerness to claim this forested and well-watered corner of the map was its immense wealth in furs. The region's waterways were especially rich in beavers and otters, the pelts of which were a highly valued commodity in Europe and Asia and thus an important article of trade.

None of these exploration or trade expeditions led directly to a pioneer settlement or even a permanent trading post. This development came with the powerful fur-trading companies, especially the British Hudson's Bay Company (HBC). From Fort Vancouver, the HBC – and hence Britain – controlled all trade in the Pacific Northwest. The Puget Sound area was linked to the fur-trading fort by the Cowlitz River. Because of its strict code of conduct, the company had legal authority over the area's few whites, mostly French Canadian and Scottish trappers. The HBC also policed trade relationships between the whites and the region's native inhabitants.

top picks

SEATTLE HISTORY BOOKS

- **Divided Destiny: A History of Japanese Americans in Seattle, David A Takami (1999)**
  Originally created to accompany an exhibition at the Wing Luke Asian Museum, this richly illustrated book documents 100-plus years of Seattle's Japanese American community.
- **The Good Rain, Timothy Egan (1991)**
  The *New York Times* correspondent sheds light on the Northwest and its inhabitants.
- **Seattle and the Demons of Ambition: A Love Story, Fred Moody (2003)**
  A former *Seattle Weekly* editor, Moody puts a personal spin on Seattle's complex economic, political and cultural history.
- **Vanishing Seattle: Images of America, Clark Humphrey (2006)**
  A collection of vintage photographs of city landmarks that have either disappeared or been radically altered.
- **Stepping Westward, Sallie Tisdale (1991)**
  In this critical memoir, Tisdale casts a keen eye on the often contentious relationship between humans and nature in the Pacific Northwest.

1854–55	1885	1889
US treaty grants 2600 acres of reservation in return for two million acres of prime real estate. Warfare erupts between tribes and white settlers. Chief Sealth delivers his masterful address.	A group of white settlers establishes the Anti-Chinese Congress, setting a deadline by which all Chinese must leave Seattle. About 500 stay, and the mob's attempt to remove them leads to riots the following year.	The Great Fire sweeps through the city, gutting its core and destroying the mostly wooden storefronts and log homes on stilts. This in turn leads to a new brick-and-stone city centre built on regraded streets.

The first US settlers straggled overland to the Pacific Northwest in the 1830s on the rough tracks that would become the Oregon Trail. The HBC chief factor, Dr John McLoughlin, sought to restrict American settlement to the region south of the Columbia River, in Oregon. In doing so, he kept the prime land along Puget Sound from settlement. McLoughlin sensed that one day the USA and Britain would divide the territory; if US settlement could be limited to the area south of the Columbia, then Britain would have a stronger claim to the land north of the river. It worked. When the settlers in Oregon voted in 1843 to become a US territory, present-day Washington remained in British hands.

American settlers continued rolling in to the Pacific Northwest. Between 1843 and 1860 some 53,000 settlers migrated across the 2000-mile-long Oregon Trail. As they pushed northward into land controlled largely by the HBC, boundary disputes between the USA and Britain became increasingly antagonistic. The popular slogan of the 1844 US presidential campaign was 'Fifty-four Forty or Fight,' which urged US citizens to occupy territory in the Northwest up to the present Alaskan border, including all of Washington state and British Columbia. Finally, in 1846, the British and the Americans agreed to the present US–Canadian border along the 49th parallel.

'NEW YORK PRETTY SOON'

Arthur and David Denny were native New Yorkers who, in 1851, led a group of settlers across the Oregon Trail with the intention of settling in the Willamette Valley. On the way, they heard stories of good land and deep water ports along Puget Sound. When the Denny party arrived in Portland in the fall, they decided to keep going north. The settlers staked claims on Alki Point, in present-day West Seattle. The group named their encampment Alki–New York (the Chinookan word *Alki* means 'pretty soon' or 'by and by'). After a winter of wind and rain, the group determined that their fledgling city needed a deeper harbor and moved the settlement to the mudflats across Elliott Bay. The colony was renamed Seattle for the Duwamish chief Sealth (pronounced *see*-aalth, with a guttural 'th' being made up of a hard 't' and an 'h' that's almost a lisp off the end of the word), who was the friend of an early merchant (p24).

The attitudes of Seattle's first settlers established it as a progressive, budding community. Traversing the Oregon Trail was an arduous and costly adventure. The Pacific Northwest was not settled by penniless wanderers, but earnest young men and women, mostly in their twenties, who had the wherewithal to make the six-month trip and were determined to establish farms, businesses and communities.

BIRTH OF THE CITY

Still, early Seattle was hardly a boomtown. The heart of the young city beat in the area now known as Pioneer Square. Although there was a small but deep harbor at this point in Elliott Bay, much of the land immediately to the south was mudflats, ideal for oysters but not much else. The land to the north and east was steep and forested. The early settlers (whose names now ring as a compendium of street names and landmarks: Denny, Yesler, Bell, Boren) quickly cleared the land and established a sawmill, schools, churches and other civic institutions. From the start, the people who settled Seattle never doubted that they were founding a great city. The original homesteads were quickly plaited into city streets, and trade, not farming or lumbering, became the goal of the little settlement.

1897	1910	1932
The Klondike Gold Rush is sparked by the arrival of the ship *Portland*. Along with general economic growth, the gold rush leads Seattle's small businesses to make quick fortunes over the next decade. The city's population doubles by 1900.	Seattle begins to grow up. Its population has now reached a quarter million, making it a clear contender for the preeminent city of the Pacific Northwest.	A Depression-era shantytown called 'Hooverville', after president Herbert Hoover, forms south of Pioneer Square. Made up of lean-tos, shacks and cardboard boxes, it houses hundreds of unemployed squatters.

TODAY'S DUWAMISH PEOPLE

Seattle took its name from Chief Sealth (1786–1866), anglicized to 'Seattle', the leader of the Duwamish tribe who initially welcomed members of the Denny party when they arrived in 1851. Now, some 160 years later, the Duwamish tribe has more than 560 enrolled members and holds monthly meetings and annual gatherings.

In 1983 the tribe established Duwamish Tribal Services, a nonprofit organization devoted to ensuring the social, cultural and economic survival of the Duwamish tribe. The tribe has yet to receive federal recognition; efforts to do so are continuing. For more information, visit www.duwamishtribe.org.

Chief Sealth's impact on the mindset of Seattle's population isn't difficult to see. The following lines from his most famous speech became a cornerstone in the New Age, environmental-preservation philosophy that is almost the default belief in the Pacific Northwest.

'The earth does not belong to human beings; human beings belong to the earth. This we know. All things are connected like the blood that unites one family. All things are connected. Whatever befalls the earth befalls the sons and daughters of the earth.'

In many ways, the interactions between white settlers and the natives who lived on the land for thousands of years before they arrived have been ugly, conflicted, and rife with violence and unfairness. But if the people who settled in the Pacific Northwest have absorbed anything from the pre-existing Indian cultures, it's a sense of reverence for nature and the surrounding wilderness, even though that reverence is frequently ineffective and often comes across as hypocritical in the light of history. 'How can you buy or sell the sky, the warmth of the land?' Chief Seattle asked in his most famous speech, delivered at a gathering of natives and white settlers, which included territorial governor Isaac Stevens, who was attempting to purchase Puget Sound land from the area's native inhabitants. This 1855 address is considered one of the masterpieces of Native American oratory, although the standard text of the speech was penned 30 years later from notes by a literary-minded surgeon who attended the event. Oral history is vital to the Duwamish culture.

Since it was a frontier town, the majority of Seattle's male settlers were bachelors. One of the town's founders (and sole professor at the newly established university), Asa Mercer, went back to the East Coast with the express purpose of inducing young, unmarried women to venture to Seattle. Fifty-seven women made the journey and married into the frontier stock, in the process establishing a more civilized tone in the city.

Seattle's early economic growth came from shipping logs to San Francisco, a city booming with gold wealth. At the time, loggers had to go no further than the bluffs above town, now First and Capitol Hills, to find hundreds of acres of old-growth fir forest. As the sawmill was located on the waterfront, the logs had to be transported down the steep hillside. A skid road was developed on which horses and mules pulled the logs down a chute of ever-present mud. This skid road later became Yesler Way, the prototype of the term 'skid road' or 'skid row.'

THE BATTLE FOR RAILROADS

The Northwest's first rail link was the Northern Pacific Railroad, which linked Portland to Chicago in 1883. The young towns of Puget Sound – Seattle, Tacoma, Port Townsend and Bellingham – believed their dreams of becoming major trade centers depended on luring a

1942	1949	1954
Japanese Americans are ordered to evacuate Seattle, sent to a 'relocation center,' or internment camp, in Puyallup, then on to another camp in Idaho, where they are detained under prison conditions for the duration of the war.	Port of Seattle dedicates Seattle-Tacoma International Airport. First opened in 1944, it takes over the bulk of the city's commercial flight traffic from the original Boeing Field.	Boeing Air Transport, launched 40 years prior when William Boeing designed and produced the pontoon biplane and already a pioneer in commercial airline flight, announces production of the 707.

Stories contain the collective wisdom of the tribe, lessons from the past about how to behave. 'Without them,' the tribe's website says, 'we are thought to be bound in a state of psychological poverty.' The website contains a list of oral histories that current tribal members have remembered and recorded.

At the time of the Denny party's arrival, the peaceful Duwamish culture was deeply linked to the salmon that made seasonal runs on the Green and Duwamish Rivers. White settlers received permission from the Duwamish to build their first structures on the site of a summer camp that the area's native inhabitants called Duwamps – the name that the settlers applied to their little town as well. Chief Seattle urged peaceful coexistence between the people of his tribe and the whites, and he encouraged the Duwamish to work side by side with the settlers building houses, cutting trees and laying out streets.

Relations with other tribes along Puget Sound were not as good. To address growing hostilities, the US government drew up a treaty in 1854 granting area tribes $150,000 in goods and 2600 acres of reservation land in return for vacating two million acres of prime real estate in western Washington, including the present-day Seattle area. Distrust and anger soon broke out, and in 1855 warfare erupted between the natives and white settlers.

Chief Seattle persuaded the Duwamish not to become involved in the conflict, but the settlement at Duwamps was besieged by a group of hostile Indians, forcing the settlers to take shelter in the town's small stockade. A visiting navy sloop, the *Decatur*, fired its cannons into the forest above the little town to frighten the Indians away. In retaliation, the Indians burned and looted nearly all of the settlements on Puget Sound. In the end, the settlers prevailed and one of the Indian rebel leaders, Leschi, was captured, tried and hanged for murder.

The Duwamish were moved to the Port Madison Reservation in 1856, despite their peaceable history. In part to recognize Chief Seattle's aid and pacifist efforts, the settlers renamed their town in the chief's honor. Apparently Chief Seattle was not exactly pleased with the honor. According to Duwamish beliefs, if someone utters a dead person's name, the soul of the deceased is denied everlasting peace.

national rail line to link them to the east. Land speculators especially profited when railroads like the Northern Pacific and the Great Northern came shopping for a Puget Sound terminus. Seattle lost out to Tacoma when the Northern Pacific built its shipyards there, but it later became the terminus for the Great Northern Railroad and the Milwaukee Rd.

ANTI-CHINESE RIOTS OF 1886

Because of the region's many railroad and mining companies, and Seattle's position on the Pacific Rim, a large number of Chinese immigrants settled in the city. The fact that Asian laborers worked at jobs that most white Americans shunned didn't prevent the perception that these 'foreign' workers were taking jobs away from 'real Americans' and then, as now, it didn't prevent episodes of ugly racism.

As anti-Chinese sentiment grew in outlying communities around the Pacific Northwest, more and more Chinese moved to Seattle, where the multitude of employment opportunities offered them continued security and led to a sense of community. The area south of Yesler Way was considered Chinatown, where most of the new arrivals made their homes; today it has a more varied population, including 'Little Saigon,' and is known as the International District.

1959	1960	1962
While researching malaria in the Congo, University of Washington medical geneticist Dr Arno Motulsky collects a blood sample of the first documented case of HIV, the virus that causes AIDS.	The population of King County tops one million and one in 10 people work for Boeing. The '60s are a tumultuous decade in Seattle as in most of the country. Civil rights struggles shake the establishment.	The World's Fair in Seattle takes place. The headliner on opening night is singer John Raitt. His 12-year-old daughter, Bonnie, holds his sheet music.

The first recorded clash between the Chinese minority and white settlers came in 1885, when a Chinese immigrant was knifed to death. That year, a group called the Anti-Chinese Congress – primarily composed of radical labor unions – used fear tactics and mob assent to establish a date by which all Chinese would be forced to leave the Puget Sound area. Between 750 and 1000 Chinese workers left. But about 500 Chinese continued to live and work in Seattle. In February 1886, a mob entered Chinatown and attempted to forcibly remove the remaining Chinese, driving them onto ships. State and city officials tried to mediate, but violence erupted. Five people were shot. One white protester died from his wounds. Federal troops were called in to restore order.

The Chinese population plummeted, especially in light of court rulings that barred Chinese men from sending for their wives in China. This restriction was a result of the Chinese Exclusion Act, which was finally repealed in 1943 when China became a US ally during WWII.

THE GREAT FIRE & THE REGRADING OF SEATTLE

Frontier Seattle was a thrown-together village of wooden storefronts, log homes and lumber mills. Tidewater lapped against present-day 1st Ave S, and many of the buildings and the streets that led to them were on stilts. No part of the original downtown was more than 4ft above the bay at high tide, and the streets were frequently a quagmire.

On June 6, 1889, a fire started in a store basement on 1st Ave and quickly spread through the young city: the boardwalks provided an unstoppable conduit for the flames. By the end of the day, 30 blocks of the city had burned, gutting the core of downtown.

What might have seemed a catastrophe was in fact a blessing, as the city rebuilt immediately with handsome structures of brick, steel and stone. This time, however, the streets were regraded, and ravines and inlets filled in. This raised the new city about a dozen feet above the old. In some areas the regrading simply meant building on top of older ground-level buildings and streets.

The sense of transformation inspired by the Great Fire also fueled another great rebuilding project. One of Seattle's original seven hills, Denny Hill, rose out of Elliott Bay just north of Pine St. Its very steep face limited commercial traffic, though some hotels and private homes were perched on the hilltop. City engineers determined that if Seattle's growth was to continue, Denny Hill had to go. Between 1899 and 1912, the hill was sluiced into Elliott Bay. Twenty million gallons of water were pumped daily from Lake Union and sprayed onto the rock and soil. Under great pressure, the water liquefied the clay and dislodged the rock, all of which was sluiced into flumes. Existing homes were simply undercut and then burned.

KLONDIKE GOLD RUSH

Seattle's first real boom came when the ship *Portland* docked at the waterfront in 1897 with its now-famous cargo: two tons of gold newly gleaned from northern Yukon goldfields. The news spread quickly across the USA; within weeks, thousands of fortune seekers from all over the world converged on Seattle, the last stop before heading north. That summer and fall, 74 ships left Seattle bound for Skagway, Alaska, and on to the goldfields in Dawson City, Yukon.

In all, more than 40,000 prospectors passed through Seattle. The Canadian government demanded that prospectors bring a year's worth of supplies, so they wouldn't freeze or starve to death midway. Outfitting the miners became big business in Seattle. The town became the

1973	1975	1980
Seattle's 'one percent for art' rule is established, specifying that 1% of the city's capital improvement project funds go toward the commission, purchase and installation of public artworks.	Bill Gates and Paul Allen start Microsoft, giving home-computer users everywhere an infinite supply of things to complain about and ensuring the livelihoods of antitrust lawyers for the foreseeable future.	Mt St Helens blows her top, spreading ash through five states and killing 57 people. The eruption leaves a horseshoe-shaped crater atop the mountain.

banking center for the fortunes made in the Yukon. Bars, brothels, theaters and honky-tonks in Pioneer Square blossomed.

Many of Seattle's shopkeepers, tavern owners and restaurateurs made quick fortunes in the late 1890s. Far more so than most of the prospectors. Many who did make fortunes in Alaska chose to stay in the Northwest, settling in the thriving port city on Puget Sound.

Seattle grew quickly. The Klondike Gold Rush provided great wealth, and the railroads brought in a steady stream of immigrants, mostly from Eastern Europe and Scandinavia. Seattle controlled most of the shipping trade with Alaska and increasingly with nations of the Pacific Rim. Company-controlled communities like Ballard sprang up, populated almost exclusively with Scandinavians who worked in massive sawmills. A new influx of Asian immigrants, this time from Japan, began streaming into Seattle, establishing fishing fleets and vegetable farms.

At the height of the gold rush in 1900, Seattle's population reached 80,000, double the population figure from the 1890 census. By 1910, Seattle's population jumped to a quarter million. Seattle had become the preeminent city of the Pacific Northwest.

THE WAR YEARS

Seattle's boom continued through WWI, when Northwest lumber was in great demand. The opening of the Panama Canal brought increased trade to Pacific ports, which were free from wartime threats. Shipyards opened along Puget Sound, bringing the shipbuilding industry close to the forests of the Northwest.

One of the significant events in Seattle history occurred in 1916 when William Boeing, a pioneer aviator, designed and produced a pontoon biplane. Boeing went on to establish an airline, Boeing Air Transport (later United Airlines). But it was WWII that really started the engines at Boeing. The factory received contracts to produce the B-17 and B-29 bombers, which led in the US air war against Axis nations. Huge defense contracts began to flow into Boeing and by extension into Seattle, fueling more rapid growth and prosperity.

WWII brought other, less positive, developments to Seattle. About 7000 Japanese residents in Seattle and the nearby areas were removed forcibly from their jobs and homes. They were sent to the nearby 'relocation center,' or internment camp, in Puyallup, then on to another camp in Idaho where they were detained under prison conditions for the duration of the war. This greatly depleted the Japanese community, which up to this point had built a thriving existence farming and fishing in Puget Sound. In all, an estimated 110,000 Japanese across the country, two-thirds of whom were US citizens, were sent to internment camps. Upon their release, many declined to return to the homes they'd been forced to abandon.

Meanwhile, the boom in aircraft manufacturing and shipbuilding brought tens of thousands of new workers to the region. Because of Boeing, and the shipyards at Bremerton, Puget Sound became a highly defended area, which led to the building of several military facilities in the region. These bases also brought in thousands of new residents. By the end of the war, Seattle had grown to nearly half a million people.

THE SHAPE OF THE CITY

Seattle's population hit 565,000 in 1965 before economic realities began to draw baby boomers out of the city center and into the cheaper housing available in the suburbs. By 1970, the population of the rest of King County had passed Seattle's. It's still twice as large today.

1991	1993	1996
The formerly underground style of music known as grunge goes mainstream, with Pearl Jam's *Ten* and Nirvana's *Nevermind* hitting record store shelves. Three years later, Nirvana front-man Kurt Cobain commits suicide.	Gary Locke becomes the first Asian American to be elected King County Executive. The Chinese American politician becomes governor of Washington in 1997.	The Sound Transit plan clears a second vote, opening the door to a series of much-needed upgrades to Seattle's mass transportation system and extending its coverage to outlying neighborhoods.

DIGGING BENEATH THE SURFACE

Want to delve into underground Seattle – literally? Local historian Bill Speidel's Underground Tour (p211) will take you there. Leaving daily from Doc Maynard's Public House, the slightly cheesy but entertaining tour prowls the streets beneath the streets of Pioneer Square, evoking the past by digging down to the olden days.

While there's not actually much to *see* on the 90-minute tour except dirty passageways and decayed plumbing from the 1890s, the story of why there is an underground in the first place is pretty interesting. Despite its prime location on Elliott Bay, early Seattle wasn't exactly conducive to urban development. The area lacked an ideal foundation upon which to build; the land was either hilly and steep or shallow and wet. Many of the storefronts in the Pioneer Square area were built upon soggy tideflats and actually dropped below sea level at high tide. When it rained hard (and it rained hard a lot), the streets bloated into a muddy soup, sewage backed up at high tide and things got pretty messy. As you can imagine, the smell wasn't so great either.

When an apprentice woodworker accidentally let a boiling pot of glue spill over onto a pile of wood chips in a shop on 1st Ave and Madison St, he did Seattle a great favor. It was June 6, 1889, and the ensuing flames swept up the town's wooden houses and storefronts faster than a pioneer could swig a pint of beer. The Great Fire gutted the city and gave city planners a chance to lift the town out of its waterlogged foundation. They decided to regrade the streets first. Great piles of dirt were propped up with retaining walls, and streets were raised up to 12ft higher than they originally were. People had to cross deep trenches to get from one side of the street to another. Buildings were constructed around the notion that the first floor or two would eventually be buried when the city got around to filling in the trenches. Storefronts from the old ramshackle town that were once at street level effectively became basements and, later, passageways for the Underground Tour.

Tours are first come, first served, so plan to arrive a half-hour early in the busy summer months. They leave from Doc Maynard's Public House (Map p57; ☎ 206-682-4646; www.undergroundtour.com; 608 1st Ave) roughly every 30 minutes between 11am and 5pm; tickets for an adult/senior/child cost $14/12/7. You can see bits of the underground by yourself in the Pioneer Square Antique Mall in the Pioneer Building and on the bottom floor of the Grand Central Arcade.

In an attempt to win people back from the suburbs, downtown businesses dreamed up so-called 'urban renewal' projects such as razing Pioneer Square and Pike Place Market to build apartment towers and parking garages. Not many people liked this idea, of course, and the public banded together to preserve these and other historic landmarks. Around the same time, activists used new environmental-protection laws to defeat proposals for two local freeways and scale down an expansion plan for Interstate 90. With this new interest in its preservation, downtown's vitality gradually started to return.

By 1972, voters had approved an all-bus transit system. In 1990 Metro Transit opened a bus tunnel beneath downtown. Voters gave rail transit the nod in 1996. One year later, voters also approved a new monorail system, but inadequate funding meant it never happened. Later came new stadiums for the Mariners and Seahawks, as well as voter-authorized funding for park improvements and new libraries.

The city is currently about to be reshaped yet again, and probably quite dramatically. The Alaskan Way Viaduct between the city and the Waterfront, generally considered an eyesore, will most likely be torn out and replaced (plans were still being formulated at the time of research). Rail transit is set to be expanded, and a planned new bio-tech center and surrounding neighborhood on the southern shore of Lake Union will be served by the city's first streetcar in 65 years. And, for the first time in recent history, Seattle's population is growing again.

1999	2000	February 28, 2001
Seattle is rocked by the World Trade Organization riots. The same year, Microsoft is declared a monopoly and enters into lengthy negotiations over the future of its business.	In a spectacular implosion that is the result of an engineering feat, the Kingdome is collapsed, making way for the new Qwest Field, home of the Seattle Seahawks National Football League team.	An earthquake measuring 6.8 on the Richter scale hits Seattle, toppling several historic buildings and causing more than $2 billion in damage to the city.

BOEING

The Boeing Airplane Company, started in 1917, was founded and named by William E Boeing and his partner, Conrad Westervelt. (Boeing tested his first plane, the *B&W*, in June 1916 by taking off from the middle of Lake Union.) For years, Boeing single-handedly ruled Seattle industry. After WWII, the manufacturer diversified its product line and began to develop civilian aircraft. In 1954, Boeing announced the 707, and the response was immediate and overwhelming. The world found itself at the beginning of an era of mass air travel and Boeing produced the jets that led this revolution in transportation. By 1960, when the population of Seattle topped one million, one in 10 people worked for Boeing, and one in four people worked jobs directly affected by Boeing.

But the fortunes of Boeing weren't always to soar. A combination of overstretched capital (due to cost overruns in the development of the 747) and a cut in defense spending led to a severe financial crisis in the early 1970s, known as the 'Boeing Bust.' Boeing was forced to cut its work force by two-thirds; in one year, nearly 60,000 Seattleites lost their jobs. The local economy went into a tailspin for a number of years.

In the 1980s, increased defense spending brought vigor back to aircraft production lines, and expanding trade relations with China and other Pacific Rim nations brought business to Boeing too. But just a few days after Seattle was rattled by a mighty earthquake, the city received a blow that rocked it even more. Boeing head honcho Phil Condit announced in March 2001 that the world's largest airplane manufacturer, the company as synonymous with Seattle as rain, was blowing town. Boeing, he said, would relocate at least 50% of its headquarter staff to bigger and brighter digs in Chicago in September 2001.

At that time, the company employed 78,400 people in the Seattle area and 198,900 people worldwide. Only the headquarters was moved to Chicago; the company's major production center remains in the Seattle area. But the announcement, followed by several stages of layoffs, left Seattleites more than a little concerned about what the future would hold.

The company later took a beating in the economic slump that swept the US – and especially the Northwest – during the early 2000s.

Things were beginning to look up in early 2004, as Boeing announced it would build the major new 7E7 plane in Everett, Washington, and promised that its new business strategy would avoid its previous pattern of massive hiring followed by large-scale layoffs.

MICROSOFT

Starbucks aside, the biggest story in Seattle's economic history is the business behemoth of Microsoft. Springing onto the scene in the mid-1970s and '80s, it was a force that would change Seattle forever. After tinkering around with a little notion called BASIC (a programming language for the world's first microcomputer), local boy Bill Gates joined up with his childhood chum Paul Allen to start Microsoft in 1975. Though the software giant, located in Redmond across Lake Washington, never achieved quite the total control over the Seattle economy that Boeing once had, it became increasingly hard to find someone who wasn't a contractor, caterer or car dealer for the Microsoft crowd. Microsoft also attracted other high-tech companies to the area, making the city particularly vulnerable to the high-tech slump that hit the country during its recent economic crisis.

Microsoft's heyday hit something of a capitalist brick wall in the late 1990s, when the federal government began a very long and politically hot suit against Microsoft. The Justice Department accused the company of monopolistic practices and alleged that it used – and

2001	2003	2006
Boeing relocates its headquarters to Chicago. This removal of a financial linchpin shakes the city's confidence in its overall economy, even though Boeing keeps a substantial portion of its operations in the area.	Seattle voters say no to a proposed 10-cents-a-cup coffee tax. Starbucks Corporation purchases Seattle's Best Coffee and Torrefazione Italia, making it even more difficult to avoid the growing chain's coffee shops.	The Seattle Seahawks reach the Super Bowl, battling favorites the Pittsburgh Steelers to an exciting finish, but ultimately losing the National Football League championship with a score of 10 to 21.

abused – its prodigious market power to prevent any competition from getting in its way. Microsoft's reputation for bullying other players on the technological playfield was deemed legally unfair.

In April 2000, Judge Thomas Penfield Jackson ruled that Microsoft had violated antitrust laws by 'engaging in predatory tactics that discourage technological competition.' The judge ruled that Microsoft needed to divest the company. Microsoft launched a barrage of appeals, which resulted in various settlements with the federal government and several states. Then, in 2004, the European Commission found that Microsoft had violated antitrust laws, slapping it with a €497 million ($657 million) fine. The company appealed, and at the time of research was awaiting a ruling from the EC's second-highest court stating whether the EC may continue to pursue the case or pull back and let Microsoft continue its business practices. The ruling was set for September 17, 2007.

SEATTLE FACTS

- City Center area 83.9 sq miles
- Population 578,700
- Metro area 4424.9 sq miles
- King County area 2126.1 sq miles
- King County population 1.8 million
- Freshwater shoreline 147.52 miles
- Saltwater shoreline 53.38 miles
- Puget Sound 500 sq miles of water, 300 islands

Through the 1990s, internet start-up companies – often financed by the young, affluent millionaires that Microsoft's early days spawned – sprouted like weeds and attracted a younger, more educated population than Seattle had ever seen. It seemed too good to be true and, in fact, it turned out that way. The 'dot-com' fiasco was the economic equivalent of a candy bar, providing a major rush followed by a depressing crash.

MUSIC & ARTS

When you think of Seattle, what leaps to mind (after rain and coffee) is probably something music-related – whether it's Jimi Hendrix, Nirvana, Pearl Jam, Soundgarden, the burgeoning hip-hop scene, or KEXP radio. Glance through either of the city's weekly papers and it becomes obvious that music makes up the bulk of 'alternative' popular culture. But there are a lot of other things going on in the field of arts, as well.

A city of readers (with more bookstores per capita than any other US city), Seattle is also home to a stable of internationally recognized writers, among them Tom Robbins, Jonathan Raban and Sherman Alexie. The city's visual arts are also dynamic, as its cultural strands – from Native American and Asian to contemporary American – meet and transfuse on canvas, in glass and in sculpture. For more information on venues for the arts, see the Arts chapter (p158).

MUSIC
Indie Rock

Seattle has long had an active music scene, even if its vibrancy has tended to wax and wane. One year there will be hardly any good clubs, then two years later there are twice as many. Right now, Seattle is blessed with a decent number of live-music venues, particularly for indie rock and its subcategories. A burgeoning hip-hop scene has locals excited, particularly because Seattle seems to produce a more socially conscious brand of hip-hop than most other places. Jazz and blues, though not as epic as they were in the days when Quincy Jones was sneaking into Pioneer Square clubs, are still swinging. There are also small but thriving music scenes in Bellingham to the north (Jon Auer and Ken Stringfellow started the Posies in a Bellingham basement, and Death Cab for Cutie was formed there) and in Olympia, home of the riot grrl movement (and the sadly-no-more Sleater-Kinney, Two Ton Boa, Old Time Relijun and others).

You've almost certainly heard or heard of a few Seattle bands, whether you've realized it or not. Pioneering Northwest rock bands like the Kingsmen, the Sonics and Seattle's own legendary Jimi Hendrix helped define rock 'n' roll in the '60s. Local groups like Heart and the Steve Miller Band made it big in the '70s. Blues musician Robert Cray and saxophonist Kenny G gained notoriety during the '80s. The media represented none of these as Seattle musicians per se. Not until the city's grunge boom in the '90s did the world turn to Seattle as the origin of a unique sound.

Grunge, a guitar- and angst-driven derivative of punk, grew out of garage rock, where dudes with nothing else to do jammed in their garages because, before grunge, there weren't that many places to rock out in Seattle unless you were already a headlining band. These days, there's still a very active local rock scene, though it no longer has the cohesive sound that characterized most of the bands that made it big during the grunge years.

In the wake of grunge, the hipster core of Northwest music moved slightly south, to Olympia, home of riot grrls, indie rock and renowned music scribe Greil Marcus' favorite band, Sleater-Kinney. Outlying areas also produced a number of great bands that are close enough to being Seattle bands to be thought of as such. Another big name in indie rock, Modest Mouse, formed in Issaquah, Washington. Bellingham band Death Cab for Cutie front-man Ben Gibbard went on to form The Postal Service, whose album *Give Up* became the best-selling release for Seattle's Sub Pop label since Nirvana's *Bleach*.

Seattle hip-hop in recent years has successfully crossed over and infiltrated the indie-rock universe and begun to make a serious impact. This is partly thanks to influential radio station KEXP making a habit of adding local hip-hop artists into the mix at all hours. But it's mostly due to the fact that the work coming out of the Pacific Northwest is overwhelmingly high quality and, as befits the region, generally positive and socially conscious. Seattle hip-hop artists to look out for include the Blue Scholars (*Blue Scholars, The Long March*), Specs One (*Mega, Return of the Artist*), Silent Lambs Project (*Soul Liquor*), Grayskul (*Deadlivers*) and the Boom Bap Project (*Reprogram*).

Jazz & Blues

A lot of people may not be aware that Seattle was home to a thriving jazz and blues scene back in the day. You could find raging clubs all along Jackson St in Pioneer Square in the 1930s and '40s, and the young (*too* young, legally speaking, but scrappy and talented enough to get away with it) Quincy Jones and his pal Ray Charles would hustle their way into all the clubs and

---

SOUND OF SEATTLE

What most people think of as the definitive Seattle sound can be grasped pretty easily by a quick spin of these landmark grunge-era records:

- *Superfuzz Bigmuff* (Sub Pop), Mudhoney – released in 1988, the catchy debut single, 'Touch Me I'm Sick,' became an instant classic. Singer Mark Arm is allegedly the guy who came up with the term 'grunge,' although he intended it as a diss, not a marketing label destined to become pandemic.
- *Bleach* (Sub Pop), Nirvana – the melodic-punk band's first album.
- *Nevermind* (Geffen), Nirvana – grunge anthem 'Smells Like Teen Spirit' became, and remains, one of the most-analyzed singles in the history of rock.
- *Ten* (Epic), Pearl Jam – the first studio album by one of rock's biggest groups took a while to peak but contained three hit singles.
- *Badmotorfinger* (A&M), Soundgarden – the hair-metal side of grunge.

But don't stop there. A huge variety of sounds can be found in Seattle, even if you stay within the boundaries of rock. All of the following artists – whose styles vary wildly – have their roots in Seattle, and many of them still play there frequently. Dig around online, ask questions at record stores and flip through the local papers for more.

- Murder City Devils – now-defunct band that split into the also defunct but also great Pretty Girls Make Graves and Dead Low Tide, as well as Big Business.
- Queensryche – the band everyone forgets is from Seattle (well, Bellevue) because they're unironic prog-metal.
- The Gits – awesome punk band that fell apart when singer Mia Zapata was brutally murdered.
- Foo Fighters – Nirvana drummer Dave Grohl's band.
- Melvins – the heaviest of sludge.
- Supersuckers – punkers turned cowpunkers led by Eddie Spaghetti.
- Spits – frequently costumed garage-punk maniacs.
- Zeke – one-minute songs about girls, drugs and cars.
- Fastbacks – pioneering NW band with an all-star cast and about 15 different drummers.
- The Trashies – born to play basements (that's a compliment).

ROCK PILGRIMAGES

The dark side of Seattle music history holds a morbid fascination for many fans. The city and its surroundings are home to several sites that might be of interest to rock 'n' roll pilgrims.

Jimi Hendrix (November 27, 1942 – September 18, 1970) is buried in Greenwood Memorial Park in Renton, Washington. His original headstone included a drawing of a Stratocaster guitar, although it's the traditional right-handed setup, not left-handed as Hendrix played it. The guitarist's increasing popularity raised concerns that nearby graves were being disturbed by visiting fans, so in 2002, Hendrix's remains and those of his father and grandmother were moved to a separate burial site. The memorial is a large pedestal over his grave, supported by three columns, and incorporating the original gravestone. There's also a statue of Hendrix playing guitar on Broadway in Capitol Hill (p81).

Nirvana front-man Kurt Cobain (February 20, 1967 – April 5, 1994) was born at Grays Harbor Community Hospital in Aberdeen, Washington. He spent his early childhood in a house at 1210 E 1st St, had an apartment at 404 N Michigan St, made a brief foray onto the rooftop of a building at 618 W Market St as an intoxicated teen, and in 1986 rented a dilapidated house at 1000½ E 2nd St.

Not having a whole lot else going for it, Aberdeen has embraced its lost son and the musical pilgrims who visit seeking landmarks of Cobain's youth. A sign at the entrance to the city reads 'Welcome to Aberdeen – Come As You Are' as a tribute to Cobain, and the city museum has set up a Kurt Cobain self-guided tour (www.aberdeen-museum .org/kurt.htm). The nonprofit Kurt Cobain Memorial Committee also plans to build a Kurt Cobain Memorial Park and a youth center in Aberdeen.

Cobain's body was cremated so he has no gravesite, but fans visit Viretta Park, near Cobain's former Lake Washington home, to pay tribute – particularly on the anniversary of his death.

Keeping up the mortality theme, Green River, the seminal band that included future members of Pearl Jam and Mudhoney, is named after serial killer Gary Ridgway. Known as the Green River Killer, Ridgway was still at large when the band was formed. He was arrested in 2001 in Renton and later pleaded guilty to 48 counts of aggravated murder. It is estimated that he killed at least 50 women in the Seattle-Tacoma area, most of them prostitutes or runaway teens.

Decidedly less gloomily, hair-metal grunge band Soundgarden are named after a wind-channeling pipe sculpture, the *Sound Garden*, in Seattle's Magnuson Park (Map p48).

play as much as they could. Nothing of that caliber exists in Seattle any more, but you can still manage to hear some good jazz and blues, either in Pioneer Square clubs like the New Orleans Creole Restaurant (p123) or at places like Tula's (p155), the Paragon (p154) and Dimitriou's Jazz Alley (p155).

Classical

Seattle offers a full array of classical music, including well-respected professional symphony and opera companies. The Seattle Symphony is regarded as a major regional orchestra, and its downtown performance hall, the Benaroya Concert Hall (p49), is as gorgeous as it is acoustically exquisite. The Northwest Chamber Orchestra is the Northwest's only orchestra that focuses on period chamber music; the group gives performances at various venues throughout the city.

The Seattle Opera is another major cultural focus in Seattle. Although it's a regional company, it isn't afraid to tackle weighty or nontraditional works. Productions of Philip Glass and a summer Wagner's *Ring* cycle have given opera lovers a lot to mull over. However, the company is perhaps most noted for its unconventional staging of the traditional repertoire. The Seattle Men's Chorus, a 180-member gay chorus, delights audiences with its 30 concerts each year.

For more information see p161.

LITERATURE

The pioneers of early Seattle had city building on their minds, and didn't exactly fill libraries with weighty tomes. Nonetheless, some of the city's first settlers took time to record chronicles. In 1888 Arthur Denny, one of the founders of Seattle, wrote *Pioneer Days on Puget Sound* (1908). James Swan wrote *The Northwest Coast* (1869) and *Indians of Cape Flattery* (1870) during the

1850s. *The Canoe and the Saddle* (1863) by Theodore Winthrop recounts a young man's trip across Washington on his way to Seattle in 1853.

One of the most prolific Seattle writers in the early 20th century was Archie Binns. Of his many novels, *The Land is Bright* (1939), the story of an Oregon Trail family, is still read today. A socio-economic chronicle of Seattle, *The Northwest Gateway* (1941) provides a good, if dated, introduction to Seattle's attitudes toward itself. Meanwhile, Murray Morgan's *Skid Road: An Informal Portrait of Seattle* (1951) enables the quirky characters of pioneer Seattle to come to life. Many of these older books, of course, are out of print, but it's worth asking at libraries and antiquarian bookshops if you're interested in tracking one down.

In the 1960s and '70s, western Washington attracted a number of counterculture writers. The most famous of these (and the best!) is Tom Robbins, whose books, including *Another Roadside Attraction* (1971) and *Even Cowgirls Get the Blues* (1976), are a perfect synthesis of the enlightened braininess, sense of mischief and reverence for beauty that add up to the typical mellow Northwest counterculture vibe.

Having, among other things, a fondness for the Blue Moon Tavern in common with Robbins, poet Theodore Roethke taught for years at the University of Washington, and along with Washington native Richard Hugo (see boxed text p159) he cast a profound influence over Northwest poetry.

Raymond Carver, the poet and short-story master whose books include *Will You Please Be Quiet, Please?* (1976) and *Where I'm Calling From* (1988), lived near Seattle on the Olympic Peninsula. Carver's stark and grim vision of working-class angst has profoundly affected other young writers of his time. Carver's last wife, Tess Gallagher, also from Port Angeles and a UW alum, is a novelist and poet whose books include *At the Owl Woman Saloon* (1997).

Neal Stephenson, a sci-fi writer who initially rose to fame with *Snow Crash* (1992) and most recently published his three-volume, eight-book Baroque Cycle (2003–04), also lives in Seattle and is enough of a local that his original manuscripts now reside in Paul Allen's Science Fiction Museum (see p73).

Ivan Doig writes of his move to Seattle in *The Sea Runners* (1982). In *Winter Brothers* (1980), Doig examines the diaries of early Washington writer James Swan, who lived among the Makah Indians on the northern tip of the Olympic Peninsula. Noted travel writer Jonathan Raban, who lived in Seattle for years, then left only to return recently, has written such books as *Coasting* (1987), *Hunting Mister Heartbreak* (1990) and *Badlands* (1996). His recent novel *Waxwings* (2003) is a fictionalized account of two families of Seattle immigrants. Annie Dillard, essayist and novelist, wrote about the Northwest in *The Living* (1992).

Sherman Alexie (see boxed text p35) writes from a Native American perspective. His short-story collection *The Lone Ranger and Tonto Fistfight in Heaven* (1993) was among the first works of popular fiction to discuss reservation life. In 1996, he published *Indian Killer,* a chilling tale of ritual murder set in Seattle, to great critical acclaim. David Guterson writes about the Puget Sound area and the internment of Japanese Americans during WWII in *Snow Falling on Cedars* (1994).

top picks

SEATTLE BOOKS

- Heavier than Heaven, Charles Cross (2001)
  Editor of the defunct music zine the *Rocket,* Cross uses his nearly unrestricted access to paint a moving portrait of Nirvana's Kurt Cobain.
- Come as You Are: The Story of Nirvana (1993)
  Local journalist Michael Azerrad interviewed the band for his rock bio, recording something like 25 hours of audiotape.
- Indian Killer, Sherman Alexie (1996)
  In Alexie's most controversial book, a series of scalping murders of white men threatens to destroy the Indian community.
- Waxwings, Jonathan Raban (2003)
  Elegant travel writer Raban illuminates Seattle's recent high-tech boom in a novel that tells the parallel stories of two immigrants.
- The Terrible Girls, Rebecca Brown (1992)
  One of Seattle's most prominent writers dissects the complicated hearts of women in this experimental collection of short stories about lesbian relationships.
- Another Roadside Attraction, Tom Robbins (1971)
  A mainstay of the Pacific Northwest counterculture, Robbins' wacky word carnival imagines Jesus alongside a flea circus at a pit stop.

BACKGROUND MUSIC & ARTS

The misty environs of western Washington is a fecund habitat for mystery writers. Dashiell Hammett once lived in Seattle, while noted writers JA Jance, Earl Emerson and Frederick D Huebner currently make the Northwest home.

Local historian Bill Speidel, he of the famous Underground Tour (p28), has written a couple of enthusiastic histories dealing with Seattle's early characters, such as *Doc Maynard: The Man who Invented Seattle* (1978) and *Sons of the Profits* (1967). In *Stepping Westward* (1991), Sallie Tisdale relates her experiences of growing up in the Northwest, with insights into the culture of the region. Timothy Egan's *The Good Rain* (1991) is an insightful discussion of the Northwest and its people by the local *New York Times* correspondent. Seattle preacher Robert Fulghum made it big as an inspirational writer with *All I Really Need to Know I Learned in Kindergarten* (1988). And more recently, Fred Moody, former managing editor of the *Seattle Weekly*, synthesized the city's complex history and uncomfortable relationship with its own gradual success in his engaging history-memoir, *Seattle and the Demons of Ambition: A Love Story* (2003).

Local music critic Charles Cross caused a sensation with *Heavier than Heaven* (2001), his intimate biography of Nirvana's Kurt Cobain, and won even greater critical acclaim for his 2005 biography of Jimi Hendrix, *Room Full of Mirrors*. Fearless grunge photographer Charles Peterson, with cooperation from musicians including Mudhoney's Steve Turner and Pearl Jam's Eddie Vedder, has published a great book of photos from the heydays of grunge, named after the Mudhoney song *Touch Me I'm Sick* (2003).

One peculiar phenomenon is the relatively large number of cartoonists who live in the Seattle area. Lynda Barry *(Ernie Pook's Comeek, Cruddy)* and Matt Groening (creator of *The Simpsons)* were students together at Olympia's Evergreen State College. Gary Larson, whose *Far Side* animal antics have netted international fame and great fortune, lives in Seattle. A good number of underground comic book artists live here, too, among them the legendary Peter Bagge *(Hate),* Jim Woodring (*The Frank Book),* Charles Burns (*Black Hole),* and Roberta Gregory (*Naughty Bits).* It could well have something to do with the fact that Fantagraphics, a major and influential publisher of underground comics and graphic novels, is based here.

VISUAL ARTS

Museums and galleries in Seattle offer a visual-arts experience as varied as the rest of the city's culture. The newly expanded Seattle Art Museum (p49) has a substantial European art collection, a range of modern art that's well suited to its new exhibition spaces, and an impressive collection of native artifacts and folk art, especially carved wooden masks. There are also a number

top picks

SEATTLE ART GALLERIES

- Roq la Rue (p70)
  Devoted to showing counterculture art, this Belltown gallery is anything but stodgy.
- Center on Contemporary Art (p100)
  A major force in the Seattle art scene, this artist-run collective makes a point of putting on high-energy, envelope-pushing shows.
- Greg Kucera Gallery (Map p57; ☎ 206-624-0770; 212 3rd Ave S)
  Kucera has been around for 20-plus years and frequently hosts big names – cult filmmaker John Waters, for example – as well as supporting unknown artists in his large gallery.
- McLeod Residence (Map p69; ☎ 206-441-3314; mcleodresidence.com; 2209 2nd Ave)
  Art gallery and lounge in Belltown, with fashion shows, lectures, live music and exhibits. The place promotes itself as 'a home for extraordinary living through art, technology, and collaboration.' At the time of research, exhibits included 'A Brief History of Outlaws: Portraits of the American Badass.'
- BLVD Gallery (Map p69; www.blvdart.com; 2316 2nd Ave)
  Started by the folks behind Roq la Rue and the War Room, among others, BLVD is the champion of urban contemporary art, ie graffiti and skateboards.
- Lawrimore Project (Map p57; ☎ 206-501-1231; www.lawrimoreproject.com; 831 Airport Way S)
  A no-holds-barred modern art space, the Lawrimore Project is a big, pliable warehouse-like gallery that consistently has some of the most inventive exhibitions you'll see in Seattle.

of exhibition spaces around the city devoted to contemporary Native American carvings and paintings. A considerable Asian art collection is located at the Seattle Asian Art Museum (p81) in Volunteer Park. More experimental and conceptual art is displayed at the University of Washington's Henry Art Gallery (p84) and the Frye Art Museum (p51).

A specialty of the Puget Sound area is glassblowing, led by a group of inventive and influential artisans known as the Pilchuck School. The most famous of these is Dale Chihuly, whose flamboyant, colorful and unmistakable work is on display at the Benaroya Concert Hall and in a number of galleries.

Pushing the envelope of contemporary art is the specialty of several younger galleries around town, notably Belltown's Roq la Rue (p70) and BLVD (see boxed text opposite) and the Center on Contemporary Art (p100), which also now has a new Belltown gallery space (at 2721 1st Ave). These unconventional spaces display provocative, boundary-distorting artwork of all kinds, usually by unknown or underground artists. They also regularly host rock shows, theatrical performances and film screenings. Check the local weeklies for listings.

SHERMAN ALEXIE

Sherman Alexie is a 6ft 2in Spokane-Coeur d'Alene Indian with an even-larger-than-life sense of humor and an un-shakeable but hard-earned confidence. He grew up on the Spokane Indian Reservation in Wellpinit, Washington. Born hydrocephalic, he wasn't expected to live; at six months of age he had brain surgery and doctors expected he would either die or be mentally handicapped.

What happened was the exact opposite. Alexie became an unstoppable reader and, in his 30s, a he became celebrated writer. He was named one of Granta's '20 Best American Novelists Under the Age of 40,' and he has won masses of critical acclaim for his novels, short stories and poetry. Recently he's been writing a number of screenplays; he wrote the screenplay for fellow Native American director Chris Eyre's fantastic *Smoke Signals*, and he wrote and directed *The Business of Fancydancing*.

Alexie's readings are the stuff of legend and no one should miss a chance to attend one. Not interested in dry recitals of static texts, Alexie memorizes whatever piece he plans to read, then performs it dramatically, much to the crowd's delight. One of the fascinating things about his public speaking appearances is that, although there's a lot of buried anger in what he says, he is also outrageously funny, which means he can, for example, throw a bunch of scathing lines about crazy, clueless white people to an audience full of white people and make them love it.

Alexie dismisses the idea that his comic presentation might distract listeners from the serious aspects of his work. 'Did Richard Pryor let people off the hook?' he asks. 'Did Lenny Bruce? I'd argue the reverse. I think the reason liberals have so little power is because we're so earnest and the reason the conservatives kick our asses is because they're funny…Give me a right-wing redneck over a vegan any time! Give me Rush Limbaugh over an Earth First-er any night of the week.'

Politics are integral to Alexie's life and work. Whether he likes it or not, he's been saddled with the role of Official Native American Spokesman. You get the idea that sometimes he likes it and sometimes he doesn't at all. 'I'm just who I am,' he says. 'I'm an individual. If anything I hope what I do gets *everybody* to question authority, to be eccentric, to get rowdy, to create art, to follow their dreams. In the end all I hope is that I've celebrated eccentricity.'

Alexie's first short-story collection, *The Lone Ranger and Tonto Fistfight in Heaven*, was published in 1993. In the decade since then, he says, the cultural milieu of Seattle has seen some changes. 'There's a lot more white-collar Indians. There's now what you would call a Native American elite. It's a very visible Indian elite. Because Seattle's so white, we stand out more.'

On the other hand, he says, day-to-day racism is seldom a problem – at least within city limits. 'In Seattle it mostly amounts to getting looked at, and not even that, necessarily. This is a liberal city. I deal with very little overt racism. Once you get outside the Seattle boundaries, that changes. In Seattle you deal with institutional racism. Outside of Seattle you deal with people who might have a gun.'

As for Seattle's literary scene, it continues to thrive. 'It's the only place in the world, I think, where writers are super-stars. I get recognized every day.' When he went to the Department of Motor Vehicles to renew his driver's license, he says, they called out his name and he ended up signing autographs. 'I don't think the same thing would happen in Manhattan's DMV.' If anything, he says, the city's literary bent has intensified. There are a lot of young people getting involved in readings and events, and there are cultural resources like the Richard Hugo House (p159).

'If you love books and want to be in a book town and want to go to a reading every night of the week,' Alexie says, 'you can.'

PUBLIC ART

Seattle is also known for its interesting and plentiful public art. A King County ordinance, established in 1973, stipulates that 1% of all municipal capital-improvement project funds be set aside for public art. The 'one percent for art' clause, which other cities across the nation have since adopted, has given Seattle an extensive collection of artworks ranging from monumental sculpture and landscape design to individualized sewer hole covers.

Fremont (p88) is a good place to start looking for examples of off-beat and often inspired public art in Seattle. Fremont boasts, among other things, the *Waiting for the Interurban* sculpture, a community centerpiece often decorated with politically pointed costumes and trappings.

All of the county's public artwork is commissioned through a public process. A panel of artists and project and city planners gets together to choose an artist out of thousands of applicants. Keep your eyes open and your art radar on high. You'll find public art throughout Seattle, in the metro bus tunnels, in public parks, on building walls and embedded in the sidewalks.

CINEMA & TELEVISION

Seattle has come a long way as a movie mecca since the days when Elvis starred in the 1963 film *It Happened at the World's Fair,* a chestnut of civic boosterism. Films with Seattle as their backdrop include the *Tugboat Annie* (1933); *Cinderella Liberty* (1974), a steamy romance with James Caan and Marsha Mason; and *The Parallax View* (1974) with Warren Beatty. Jessica Lange's movie *Frances,* about the horrible fate of outspoken local actor Frances Farmer (she was jailed on questionable pretenses, then institutionalized for years and eventually lobotomized), was shot here in 1981. Debra Winger's hit, *Black Widow* (1986), shows many scenes shot at the University of Washington.

John Cusack starred in *Say Anything* (1989), Michelle Pfeiffer and Jeff Bridges did it up in *The Fabulous Baker Boys* (1989), and Sly Stallone and Antonio Banderas flopped in *Assassins* (1995), all partly filmed in and around Seattle. Recently, horror hit *The Ring* and J.Lo vehicle *Enough* both had a few scenes shot in Seattle and on local ferries.

Perhaps the two most famous Seattle movies happened when the city was at the peak of its cultural cachet in the '90s: *Singles* (1992), with Campbell Scott, Kyra Sedgwick, Matt Dillon and Bridget Fonda, captured the city's youthful-slacker vibe. (Incidentally, both *Singles* and *Say Anything* were directed by Cameron Crowe, who is married to Seattle rock band Heart's Nancy Wilson.) But no film shot in Seattle garnered as much attention as *Sleepless in Seattle,* the 1993 blockbuster starring Tom Hanks, Meg Ryan and, perhaps more importantly, Seattle's Lake Union houseboats.

Sherman Alexie, having brought mainstream national attention to the city as a literary center, has expanded into the realm of filmmaking as well. *Smoke Signals* (1998), which Alexie wrote based on one of his short stories, starred Adam Beach and was directed by Chris Eyre. An entirely Native American effort, it was a huge success. For his follow-up, *The Business of Fancydancing* (2002), Alexie both wrote the screenplay and directed the film.

Some interesting documentaries have also been produced here. *Dragon: The Bruce Lee Story* follows the career of the one-time Seattle resident. *Hype!* (1996) is a documentary about the explosion of underground music in the Northwest and the resulting fallout, with lots of interviews and great live-music footage. On the other end of the spectrum is the always controversial English rabble-

top picks

SEATTLE FILMS

- Sleepless in Seattle (1993)
  Meg Ryan and Tom Hanks are irresistibly adorable in this riff on *An Affair to Remember*.
- Singles (1992)
  Attractive slackers deal with apartment life and love. Look for cameos by Pearl Jam's Eddie Vedder, Soundgarden's Chris Cornell and other local celebrities.
- Twin Peaks: Fire Walk with Me (1992)
  David Lynch rolls his warped eye toward the dark underbelly of the Northwest.
- Say Anything (1989)
  John Cusack instantly became everyone's dream boyfriend with his boom-box serenade.
- Hype! (1996)
  An excellent time capsule of the grunge years.

TOTEM POLES OF THE NORTHWEST COAST

Though Puget Sound tribes did not typically carve them, totem poles are found along the Northwest Pacific Coast, roughly between northern Washington state and Alaska. Carved from a single cedar log by the Haida, Tlingit, Tsimshian and Kwakiutl tribes, totem poles identify a household's lineage in the same way a family crest might identify a group or clan in Europe, although the totem pole is more of a historical pictograph depicting the entire ancestry. Like a family crest, totem poles carry a sense of prestige and prosperity.

Totems serve a variety of functions: freestanding poles welcome visitors to a waterfront or village; a memorial pole is often erected outside a deceased chief's home; mortuary poles are implanted with a box of the honored individual's decomposed remains. Incorporated into the design of a house, totem poles also appear as house posts and front doors. Shame poles, carved with upside-down figures denoting social or ritual transgressions, were temporary fixtures and are found only in museums today. Traditional poles vary greatly in height, though rarely exceed 60ft. Modern poles can be much taller. The world's tallest totem pole at Alert Bay in British Columbia is 173ft.

Despite the saying 'low man on the totem pole,' the most important figures are usually at eye level; figures at the bottom usually have an integral, grounding function that supports the rest of the pole. Figures can represent individuals, spirits, births, deaths, catastrophes or legends.

Unless you're an expert, it's not so easy to identify what's what on a totem. Here are a few rules of thumb. Birds are always identified with a pronounced beak: ravens have a straight, mid-sized beak; eagles have a short, sharp, down-turned beak; hawks have a short, down-turned beak that curls inward. Bears usually have large, square teeth, while beavers have large incisors and a cross-stitched tail. A few animals appear as if viewed from overhead. For example, killer whales' fins protrude outward from the poles as if their heads face downward. Long-snouted wolves also face downward, as do frogs. Pointy-headed sharks (or dogfish), with grimacing mouths full of sharp teeth, face upward, as do humpback whales.

Though totem symbols are usually interconnected and complex, these animals possess certain undeniable characteristics:

beaver – industriousness, wisdom and determined independence

black bear – a protector, guardian and spiritual link between humans and animals

eagle – intelligence and power

frog – adaptability; ability to live in both natural and supernatural worlds

hummingbird – love, beauty and unity with nature

killer whale – dignity and strength; often a reincarnated spirit of a great chief

raven – mischievousness and cunning; the perennial trickster

salmon – dependable sustenance, longevity and perseverance; a powerful symbol

shark – ominous, fierce and solitary

thunderbird – strong, supernatural; the wisdom of proud ancestors

rouser Nick Broomfield's 1998 film *Kurt & Courtney*, which delves without restraint into the troubled lives of Seattle's king and queen of rock.

More recently, the locally filmed *Zoo* (2007) is a documentary co-written by *Stranger* columnist Charles Mudede about a community of, ahem, extreme animal lovers that was inspired by news reports of a man's death after an unusually close encounter with a horse. The excellent and critically acclaimed documentary *Iraq in Fragments*, shown at Sundance, was filmed in Iraq and directed by Seattle filmmaker James Longley. Due out in late 2007 was *Battle in Seattle*, a locally filmed feature about the WTO riots starring Charlize Theron, Woody Harrelson, Ray Liotta and Michelle Rodriguez.

TV's *Northern Exposure*, filmed in nearby Roslyn, Washington, and *Frasier* both did a lot to boost Seattle's reputation as a hip and youthful place to live. The creepy, darker side of the Northwest was captured in the moody *Twin Peaks: Fire Walk with Me*. And let's not forget, of course, MTV's *The Real World: Seattle*.

THEATER

Seattle has one of the most dynamic theater scenes in the country. There are reportedly more equity theaters in Seattle than anywhere in the US, except New York City. This abundance of venues provides the city with a range of classical and modern dramatic theater. Check out the Arts chapter (p159) for detailed listings.

In addition to quality professional theater, the city offers a wide array of amateur and special-interest troupes, including both gay and lesbian theater groups, puppet theaters, children's theater troupes, cabarets and plenty of alternative theaters staging fringe plays by local playwrights. The arts and culture sections of local papers will have the most up-to-date listings and recommendations.

DANCE

Seattle is home to the nationally noted and famously well-attended Pacific Northwest Ballet, considered one of the nation's five best ballet companies. It's justifiably renowned for its performance of *The Nutcracker,* which it has been doing since 1983.

Seattle is a springboard for dancers. The modern dance pioneer Merce Cunningham was born and raised in nearby Centralia and was trained at Cornish College in Seattle. Choreographer Mark Morris, known for his fusion of classical and modern dance, is native to Seattle and has worked everywhere from small opera houses to Broadway and now works mostly in Europe. New York–based avant-garde dancer Trisha Brown is originally from Aberdeen, Washington, and classical ballet choreographer Robert Joffrey hails from Seattle.

Keep an eye out for UW's annual World Series (☎ 206-543-4880, 800-859-5342; www.uwworldseries .org) of music, performance and dance from all over the world. Smaller dance groups, such as On the Boards (www.ontheboards.org), which performs at the Behnke Center for Contemporary Performance (☎ 206-217-9888), bring an exciting, experimental edge to the city's dance scene.

ARCHITECTURE

Seattle is as notable for what is missing as for what remains, architecturally. The Great Fire of 1889 ravaged the old wooden storefronts of downtown, which were replaced by the stone and brick structures around the city's old center in Pioneer Square. Architect Elmer Fisher is responsible for more than 50 buildings erected immediately after the fire. Any Victorian places that escaped the Great Fire did not escape the Denny Regrade (1899–1912), which flattened a steep residential hill in order to make room for more downtown commercial properties.

Seattle's next big building phase came in the early decades of the 20th century. The beaux arts and art-deco hospitals that fill the skyline on First and Beacon Hills are good examples of the civic buildings of that era. Smith Tower (p58), near Pioneer Square, was built in 1914, and with 42 stories it was for many years the tallest building in the world outside of New York City. The campanile-like tower of white terra-cotta brick is still one of the city's beauties. Also during this time, Capitol and Queen Anne hills were filled with homes of the popular Georgian, Federal, English, and Arts and Crafts styles.

More recent additions to the downtown skyline include the West Coast's tallest building, the Bank of America Building (formerly the Columbia Seafirst Center), a monolith with no other distinction than its 76-story shadow. Six others rise higher than 50 stories. Only the Washington Mutual Building, with its plaid-like facade and turquoise glass, makes a pleasant impression.

As the architectural icon of Seattle, no other modern structure comes close to the Space Needle (p72). Built for the 1962 World's Fair, its sleek but whimsical design has aged amazingly well. The newest and most controversial addition to Seattle architecture is the Frank Gehry–designed Experience Music Project (p72), which has a curvy metallic design that caused quite a commotion. The city's sparkliest architectural jewel at the moment, though, is the brand-new and almost universally admired Seattle Public Library (p52).

ENVIRONMENT & PLANNING

Environmental issues in many ways dominate life in the Pacific Northwest. Seattle was founded on resource-extracting industries. The city's first major employer was a sawmill and the ability to export the area's wealth in timber was key in the city's development. Fishing Puget Sound and the area's rivers for salmon was also a major source of employment, especially for immigrant workers from Japan and Scandinavia. Today, endangered fish runs, especially of seagoing salmon, top the list of environmental concerns. While jet manufacturing and software dominate

Seattle's present economy, the older resource-based industries continue to be an active feature of the city's economic and political landscape.

Seattle sits right alongside the Cascadia Subduction Zone, one of the earth's most active seismic regions. Beneath the Strait of Juan de Fuca, two tectonic plates – the North American Plate and the Juan de Fuca Plate – struggle against each other, grinding away as the North American Plate slides underneath, causing pressure to build and the earth to rumble. The most recent of these rumblings happened on February 28, 2001, when an earthquake measuring 6.8 on the Richter scale rocked the Seattle area. The quake caused one death, rang up more than $2 billion in damages and caused some dramatic geological change. The earthquake narrowed the Duwamish River by a few inches, shifted Seattle about a fifth of an inch to the south-southwest and pushed the Eastside about a third of an inch further east.

A snapshot of this area taken 60 million years ago would show a vista of jumbled offshore islands, low coastal mountains and marine marshlands invaded by the shallow Pacific. Plants and animals thrived in the tropical climate, which extended inland unobstructed by mountains. Coastal sediments and offshore islands started wedging together, forming today's Olympic Range and setting the stage for three intense periods of volcanic activity, which would utterly change the face of the region. The line of volcanoes that shot up as the Cascade Range caused enormous explosions of lava, ash and mud. The region's most recent volcanic activity drew worldwide attention in 1980 when Mt St Helens, just 150 miles south of Seattle, blew her top, killing 57 people and spreading ash through five states and three Canadian provinces. Volcanic activity continues in the region.

The land on which Seattle now stands was once dense forest, and the waters of Puget Sound and the freshwater lakes that surround the city once teemed with wildlife. While metropolitan Seattle hardly accounts for a natural ecosystem, you don't have to go far from the center of the city to find vestiges of the wild Pacific Northwest.

GREEN SEATTLE

In keeping with its 'green' reputation, Seattle has one of the most comprehensive curbside recycling programs in the USA. Depending on where Seattleites live, their recycling is picked up either weekly or monthly. The cost is included in the price of regular garbage collection. Recycling here is easy. As such, you won't find anyone chucking a tin can or ditching a plastic bottle. Coffee drinkers basically boycott Styrofoam, and don't be surprised if somebody scolds you for littering.

Even if you're just visiting and don't have access to curbside recycling, it's easy to find a place to recycle the cans, bottles and papers that accumulate as you travel. Most public areas and food courts will have separate recycling bins for various kinds of products. See the Getting Started chapter (p19) for more on how you can contribute to the city's eco-friendliness.

Other contentious environmental issues that get locals' ire up include the history and continued practice of logging in old-growth forests, the fate of endangered salmon, and the much-publicized protection of the endangered spotted owl and its natural habitat.

URBAN PLANNING & DEVELOPMENT

Seattle's spectacular economic and population growth during the '90s altered the city's political landscape in ways that still cause problems. Partly due to the explosive growth of Microsoft – and the sudden young millionaires its stock options created – Seattle faced outrageous real estate bidding wars and a glut of traffic.

Transportation is still one of the city's thorniest issues. With the Puget Sound area's population growing fast, the transportation infrastructure simply isn't holding up. Traffic jams are often horrendous, due partly to topography but also to the lack of effective planning for public transport. Voters continually swing back and forth in support of funding light-rail commuter trains, but inevitably a glitch keeps the construction at bay. Things are looking up. In May 2007, the Sound Transit board gave final approval to a set of long-range plans that will add some 50 miles of light-rail extensions around the city.

The skyrocketing cost of housing in Seattle is also a major political and social concern. Seattle is playing catch-up with urban growth and land-use planning. The city's rapid growth, especially on the Eastside, has turned thousands of acres of farmland into anonymous tract developments, and the suburbs are rolling up to the foothills of the Cascades. In the Bellevue suburb of Medina, where Bill Gates built his 48,000-sq-ft mansion, a limit is now enforced on how many 'mega houses' are allowed. For an example of creative and artistic land-use, check out the new Olympic Sculpture Park (p70) tucked between high-rises and a highway at the edge of Belltown.

GOVERNMENT & POLITICS

Seattle is governed by a mayor and a nine-person city council. All city council members are elected to four-year terms on an at-large basis, meaning they are not assigned to a specific council district. Although city posts are nonpartisan, political ideology in Seattle dependably veers to the left-leaning side of the Democratic Party.

Greg Nickels was elected mayor in 2001 and won a second term in 2005. During his time in office he's strengthened the role of the mayor and has made transportation a top priority.

MEDIA

Seattle's major daily newspapers are the *Seattle Post-Intelligencer* (usually called the *P-I*) and the *Seattle Times.* They run under a joint-operating agreement, meaning that all advertising, production, marketing and circulation operations, as well as most business functions for both papers, are managed by The Seattle Times Company, while the news and editorial operations of the two newspapers are separate and competitive. After a four-year legal battle over the agreement, the two newspapers reached an agreement in April 2007 that essentially served to confuse everyone involved – but the upshot is that Seattle will continue to be a two-newspaper town for the time being.

The city also has a lively alternative publishing scene, led by one of the best alt-weeklies in the nation, *The Stranger.* Started by Tim Keck, formerly of the *Onion,* it's a valuable source for an irreverent take on politics, underground culture, film and music information and is a great guide to the clubs. It's edited by 'Savage Love' columnist Dan Savage.

The *Seattle Gay News,* referred to mostly as *SGN*, covers the gay and lesbian scene. The *Seattle Weekly* is the baby-boom generation's alternative news. It has full listings of arts and entertainment and investigative pieces exposing city hall's bad guys.

It's hard to mention Seattle radio without a shout-out to KEXP (90.3 FM), one of the best radio stations in the country. It used to be the UW station, but has taken off and become internationally known online, particularly for its promotion of world music (see opposite).

The University of Washington's news-oriented National Public Radio (NPR) affiliate is heard on KUOW at 94.9 FM (which also carries the BBC World Service). See the Directory chapter (p212) for a list of Seattle's favorite commercial radio stations.

Although the local chapter is no longer active, it was Seattle that initiated the grassroots internet media phenomenon that is Indymedia.org, which now has open-publishing branches set up all over the world. Founded by activists and alternative media folks in 1999 to provide independent coverage of the World Trade Organization (WTO) protests in Seattle, the Indymedia website served as a source of constantly updated dispatches, photos, audio and video footage. The information collected via the website was also used to make documentary films, a newspaper and audio clips distributed by internet radio.

FASHION

Once upon a time, Seattle ruled the freak-fashion world. Even as late as the early '90s, youth culture was marked by bizarre, usually homemade, always parent-upsetting fashion creations that expressed...*something,* whether it was angst, sexuality, gloom or simple frustration. Then came grunge, the fashion that ate itself. It's odd to imagine that an aesthetic so absent of effort would be so easily and instantly co-opted by the mainstream, but it was. Very soon after Nirvana hit it big, major fashion designers were dressing catwalk models in ripped clothes, long johns and unwashed hair. It's almost no wonder Seattle has opted for more of a Banana Republic-Nordstrom brand of chic over anything new that might call attention to itself.

LISTENING TO SEATTLE *Darek Mazzone*

Darek Mazzone was born in Poland, where he lived until age nine; then he moved to Boston and, in 1992, Seattle. He ended up here by accident, when his and a friend's van broke down after a long road trip. 'The funny thing is I was listening to KEXP when it happened,' he says. He's now a KEXP world-music presenter and an advertising consultant.

How has the local music scene changed over the years?
Well, it's always got an eyeball on it, internationally. I do a lot of travel and any time I say I'm from Seattle – it depends on the person I'm talking to, how old they are – sometimes they'll go 'Jimi Hendrix,' others they'll go 'grunge.' There's always something new that's bubbling up in Seattle. Right now it's Modest Mouse and Death Cab for Cutie. But it's interesting to see it from a perspective of being *in* the city, because right now the most interesting thing that's bumping in Seattle is hip-hop. There are some phenomenal bands – like Blue Scholars. Hip-hop is the most popular music in the world. It's great music and it needs something like Blue Scholars, desperately. They're conscious, they sing about the war and about what's really going on. They do a lot of really good work.

But there's other stuff too. We've got a great jazz scene, we've got a really funky reggae scene and one of the best Balkan groups in the world, Kultur Shock. There's always something interesting going on. It's a good town for collaboration.

What neighborhood do you live in?
Capitol Hill. This place has gone nuts. How many cranes did you see? But change is good. I rent. I'd love to buy here but there's no way I could afford it. But it's a great, vibrant scene here, it's a great part of town.

Favorite thing about Capitol Hill?
I love being in the center of everything. I love walking. I'm desperate for the light-rail, which is going to transform the city dramatically. This is my favorite city in the world and I love coming back to it. But I would love to take off for five years and come back and just see it transform.

Where do you take visitors?
If it's family? Space Needle, Pike Place Market. If they're hip, I take them to Georgetown, which I love, and Nine Pound Hammer. It's such a cool neighborhood. I take friends to places that I know there's no way they would experience otherwise. I take them to farmers markets. This is a foodie kind of town, it's amazing. Fremont's always fun; that's changed, too, but it still has that commie/hippie vibe. Seattle's the west coast, so there's a few subcultures here. There's a pretty significant Burning Man community, there's a great heritage in amazing jazz, we've got Garfield High School, which has some of the greatest jazz players in the world coming out of it. Music plays an integral part in this town.

Any only-in-Seattle moments?
There are a lot of only-in-Capitol Hill moments. This is where the freaks live. This is where you're gonna see a 60-year-old fetish couple walking down the street with leashes. You're going to see a wide range of really interesting fashion choices. I know millionaires and billionaires who live here, so, you know, you're at the espresso stand, and there's the billionaire, there's the rock star, there's the crusty, and there's the tourist. And there really isn't the separation that you'd find in other cities, because nobody gives a fuck. That really is the definitive Seattle moment.

The default Pacific Northwest outfit, of course, still consists of outdoorsy, rain-friendly REI practicality. People wear yoga pants, Teva sandals and polar fleece to dinner. But it's still easy to find pierced, dyed and tattooed specimens here, mostly in Capitol Hill, Georgetown and the U District. The young and hip will dress to the nines to go out on the town: whether that means satin and heels, plaid zippered bondage pants or a perfectly aged, faded-black vintage Aerosmith T-shirt. And there are a number of young, hip fashion designers selling their wares at chic boutiques around town. Go to the Shopping chapter (p110) for more.

LANGUAGE

English is spoken by the overwhelming majority in Seattle. But there are a number of Asian languages spoken, particularly in the International District, where signs on shop fronts frequently don't include an English translation. Several Native American languages are also spoken and taught here, such as the Duwamish dialect Lushootseed, a branch of the Salishan language family. Many tribes in the region have devoted themselves to the preservation and growth of these endangered languages.

top picks

- **Seattle Art Museum** (p49)
  The new, expanded SAM looks businesslike on the outside but holds some exciting new works within.
- **Pike Place Market** (p62)
  One of those mandatory sights – everybody does it, but there's a good reason for that.
- **Woodland Park Zoo** (p96)
  A classic family outing and one of the nicest zoos in the country.
- **Seattle Asian Art Museum** (p81)
  An extensive collection in an interesting space.
- **Henry Art Gallery** (p84)
  Small but impeccably curated university gallery.

NEIGHBORHOODS

In Seattle, neighborhood is everything. Though the city is in fact very compact, each area has its own distinct feel, and the different parts of town often feel worlds apart. This is most likely because of the disconnected terrain: before bridges and ferries made it easy to navigate the canal and lakes, most people just stayed close to home, resulting in the outlying neighborhoods being pretty isolated. That's why Ballard still feels like a Scandinavian fishing village, Chinatown feels like Chinatown and Capitol Hill could be its very own artsy, freewheeling universe. Today, though, it's easy to get around the city, and it's fun to compare and contrast the various neighborhoods beyond the downtown core. The primary hassle will be finding a parking place, so it's highly recommended that visitors use public transport to reach sights within the city center. See the Transportation chapter (p203) for details about how to get around the city using public transportation.

Of course, that's not to say visitors should neglect downtown itself. Downtown Seattle sits on a long isthmus between Lake Washington and Elliott Bay. Short-term visitors will spend most of their time here. North of Seattle's downtown area is another freshwater lake, Lake Union. The lakes are linked to Puget Sound by the canals and locks of the Lake Washington Ship Canal. Although Seattle is a major Pacific port, the ocean is 125 miles away, which can be a little confusing because there's water everywhere. It's a good idea to look at a map to see how all the bodies of water connect, and trace the long route that ships must sail from Seattle to the open seas.

The downtown area butts up against Elliott Bay and encompasses the financial and shopping areas, First Hill, Pioneer Square, Pike Place Market, the Waterfront and Belltown. Seattle Center, with many of Seattle's cultural and sports facilities and attractions, including the Space Needle, is just north. West of Seattle Center is funky Lower Queen Anne, which is connected to Upper Queen Anne by Seattle's steepest hill. East of Seattle Center is gritty Capitol Hill, the city's gay quarter and hub of youthful urban culture. The Central District, Madison Valley, Madison Park and Madrona are residential neighborhoods on the east side of the Seattle peninsula.

Lake Union and the Lake Washington Ship Canal divide the city into northern and southern halves. The northern neighborhoods include the U District, named for the University of Washington campus, Wallingford, Fremont and Ballard. Each of these areas has a lively commercial center filled with restaurants, shops and bars. Just north of Fremont and Wallingford is Green Lake, the focal point of a large park area that also contains the city zoo.

To the west of Seattle, across Elliott Bay, is another peninsula, appropriately named West Seattle. This is where the original pioneer settlers founded Seattle.

It's worth noting that four bridges (besides the freeway bridges) cross the ship canal. The University and Montlake Bridges connect neighborhoods south of the canal with the U District. West of Lake Union, the Fremont Bridge crosses from Queen Anne to Fremont. The westernmost, Ballard Bridge, links the neighborhood of Magnolia, west of Queen Anne, with Ballard.

STREETWISE

Seattle street addresses are confusing, and few visitors will have time to figure out how the system works. It's easier to use neighborhoods to indicate where things are found: '10th Ave on Queen Anne' indicates which 10th Ave is being referred to; likewise '1st Ave in Wallingford' as opposed to 1st Ave downtown. So it's important to get a working knowledge of Seattle's neighborhoods. With so many different numbering systems, it's the only easy way to make sense of the city.

Downtown is in the middle of the hourglass part of Seattle; Pioneer Square is to the south of it. Capitol Hill lies to the northeast, and the Central District/Madrona area to the east. The U District is north of Capitol Hill, across Lake Washington. Belltown, Seattle Center and Queen Anne are slightly northwest of downtown. Fremont, Wallingford and Green Lake are north, across Lake Union, and Ballard is off to the northwest. Georgetown is south, and West Seattle – well, that's easy.

Generally speaking, avenues run north and south, and streets run east and west. Yesler Way near Pioneer Square is the zero street for numbering addresses on downtown avenues; Western Ave is the zero street for addresses on streets. Usually Seattle's avenues have a directional suffix (6th Ave S), while its streets have directional prefixes (S Charles St); however, downtown streets and avenues have neither.

ITINERARY BUILDER

The following planner should help you narrow down what to do when you find yourself in one of Seattle's neighborhoods. Hole in your pocket? Scroll down the Shopping column. Got the munchies? Prowl through Eating. When you find your target, turn to the page number listed for a review.

NEIGHBORHOODS ITINERARY BUILDER

AREA	ACTIVITIES Sights	Eating	Shopping
Downtown	Seattle Art Museum (p49) Seattle Public Library (p52) Frye Art Museum (p51)	Dahlia Lounge (p121) FareStart (p122) Top Pot Donuts (p123)	Bon-Macy's (p110) Nordstrom (p111) North Face (p111)
Pioneer Square	Elliott Bay Book Company (p57) Klondike Gold Rush National Park (p55) Pioneer Square Park (p56)	Salumi (p123) Zaina (p124) Bakeman's (p124)	Bud's Jazz Records (p112) Elliott Bay Book Company (p112) Pioneer Square Antique Mall (p111)
International District	Wing Luke Asian Museum (p59) Hau Hau Market (p60) Hing Hay Park (p60)	House of Hong (p125) Pho Bac (p125) Tamarind Tree (p125)	Kinokuniya (p112) Uwajimaya (p112) Viet Hoa (p61)
Pike Place Market & Waterfront	Pike Place Market (p62) Seattle Aquarium (p66) Odyssey Maritime Discovery Center (p67)	Café Campagne (p127) Steelhead Diner (p126) Athenian Inn (p127)	Left Bank Books (p113) Made in Washington (p113) Metsker Maps (p113)
Belltown	Olympic Sculpture Park (p70) Roq la Rue (p70) Crocodile Café (p70)	Flying Fish (p128) Black Bottle (p129) Shiro's Sushi Restaurant (p128)	Patagonia (p114) Singles Going Steady (p114) Elliott Bay Bicycles (p114)
Seattle Center & Queen Anne	Space Needle (p72) Experience Music Project (p72) Pacific Science Center (p74)	Canlis (p129) Paragon Bar & Grill (p130) 5 Spot (p130)	Channel 9 Store (p114) Mountaineers (p114) Queen Anne Books (p114)
Capitol Hill	Seattle Asian Art Museum (p81) Jimi Hendrix Statue (p81) Richard Hugo House (p81)	Café Septieme (p131) Coastal Kitchen (p131) Globe Café & Bakery (p132)	Babeland (p115) Sonic Boom (p116) Wall of Sound (p116)
U District	Henry Art Gallery (p84) Burke Museum (p84) Suzzallo Library (p86)	Cedars Restaurant (p132) Flowers (p133) Agua Verde Café (p133)	Bulldog News & Expresso (p117) Hardwick's Hardware Store (p116) Recycled Cycles (p116)

Drinking p140, Eating p121, Shopping p110, Sleeping p175

Downtown Seattle is a bit of an anomaly. Instead of being the beating heart of the city, it's a fairly quiet, functional business district between Seattle's twin hearts, Pike Place Market and Pioneer Square. What most people mean by 'downtown' is the collection of office buildings, hotels and retail shops between 2nd and 7th Aves. It's best to visit on a weekday, when throngs of people are working and shopping in the area. At night and on weekends, this part of town feels rather desolate.

Flanked to the south by Pioneer Square and to the north by Belltown (also referred to sometimes as the Denny Regrade), today's city center is bordered to the east by First Hill, where Seattle's pioneer elite built elaborate mansions with views of downtown and Elliott Bay. The jungle of high-rises teetering on Seattle's steep streets makes downtown look very imposing when viewed from a distance. The city seems especially daunting on the incoming ferry ride from Puget Sound or when you first glimpse it from I-5. The actual core, however, is quite compact. No part of downtown is more than a brisk 20-minute walk from another, and the multiple transit options make it easy to get around.

Downtown is home to much of the city's important charming architecture – it's worth following the 'Downtown Architecture' walking tour (p52) for a closer look. The big hit here, though, is the newly revamped Seattle Art Museum. Be warned that parking around here is pure hell – instead take one of a dozen or more buses that serve downtown, stopping at 3rd Ave and Union St and several other stops; any bus that says 'downtown' on the front will get you here.

Seattle's retail heaven extends from the corner of 5th Ave and Pike St two or three blocks in all directions. A block north, on 5th Ave at Pine St, is the flagship store of Nordstrom, the national clothing retailer that got its start in Seattle. Just to the west of Nordstrom is Westlake Center, the veritable pumping heart of the retail district.

Across Pine St, a pedestrian plaza called Westlake Park is a popular people-watching haven and a great place to plop down on a bench and eat lunch or sip coffee on sunny days. Skateboarders and bike messengers careen through crowds of trench-coat-clad professionals and shoppers teetering under the weight of their bags. Buskers pipe out songs, entrepreneurs hawk T-shirts, and preachers bellow fire and brimstone. Don't miss artist Robert Maki's water sculpture, which you can walk through without getting wet.

It's worth remembering that Seattle has some *very* steep streets, something that needs to be considered for both drivers and pedestrians. If you are going to spend a significant chunk of time downtown, leave the car at home or park it in one of the outlying neighborhoods. Abrupt uphill or one-way streets and expensive and limited parking make driving downtown a little hectic. It's even less tempting a venture when you consider that the buses available in the downtown core are free.

First Hill, with its commanding position directly to the east and above downtown, became the foremost status neighborhood for early Seattleites. Throughout the area you'll still find traces of the early glory, including a few magnificent old mansions and some excellent examples of early Seattle architecture. But most mansions of the once mighty have long since been torn down and replaced by hospitals. Now nicknamed 'Pill Hill,' First Hill is home to three major hospitals. With the accompanying research and support facilities, it can seem that practically everything up here is related to the medical industry. But there's also a good museum and a historic hotel worth visiting.

To reach First Hill, catch bus 2 on the west side of 3rd Ave downtown and get off at the Swedish Medical Center. First Hill is out of the Ride Free Area, however, so be prepared to pay up if you take the bus from here. On foot First Hill is a short walk uphill from downtown. From Westlake Center, head over to University St and walk uphill through Freeway Park or, if you're in the business district, walk straight up Madison St to Terry Ave, and you will be at the Sorrento Hotel.

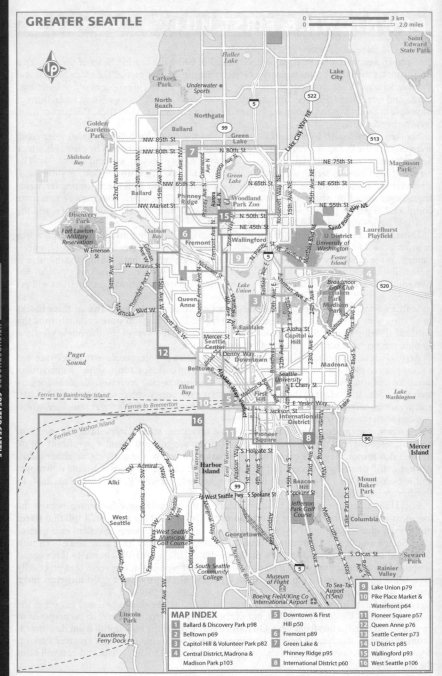

GREATER SEATTLE

lonelyplanet.com

MAP INDEX

DOWNTOWN

SEATTLE ART MUSEUM

Map p50

SAM; ☎ 206-654-3100; 1300 1st Ave; adult/senior/student/child $13/10/7/free, admission free on first Thu of month; 10am-5pm Tue-Sun, 10am-9pm Thu & Fri;

One of the most talked-about developments in the downtown area is the expansion and 2007 reopening of the Seattle Art Museum. With more than twice as much gallery space as before, the museum can now display its eclectic collections in a way that makes some narrative sense, rather than being, as it used to call itself, 'a collection of collections.' There's also a lot of new art to show off – to the tune of about $1 billion worth of gifts and 1000 new acquisitions.

The original Robert Venturi–designed building of limestone and ornamented terra-cotta – with Jonathan Borofsky's enormous moving sculpture, *Hammering Man,* at its front door – contains 150,000 sq ft of space. Architect Brad Cloepfil's design expands the museum into the adjoining Washington Mutual building, adding 118,000 sq ft, including a number of new spaces that are free to the public.

Although many people have criticized the new section for having a cold, clinical feel, it's difficult not to be struck by the sense of excitement palpable from the museum's entrance up to the main floors. Above the ticket counter hangs Chinese artist Cai Guo-Qiang's *Inopportune: Stage One,* a series of white cars exploding with neon. (Yes, actual cars. It's a big room – some say too big.) Between the two museum entrances (one in the old building and one in the new) is now the 'art ladder,' a free space with various art installations cascading down a wide stepped hallway. And, while the new public spaces are taking some heat for being too cold and airy, practically everyone likes the galleries themselves.

Two of the first things that you will see upstairs are Andy Warhol's painting of Elvis and an enormous sculpture by Korean artist Do-Ho Suh, *Some/One,* a cloak made of thousands of dogtags. Nearby is a room that's dedicated to the work of Harlem Renaissance painter Jacob Lawrence, who spent his last 30 years in Seattle, and to Gwendolyn Knight, his wife and fellow painter. There are also now dedicated spaces for the museum's impressive collections of masks, canoes and totems from Northwest coastal Indian tribes, as well as the museum's collection of Australian Aboriginal art and its American and Native American textiles. There's a huge glass and porcelain showroom, and, on the top floor, the Italian Room – an entire reassembled room of carved wood and leaded glass from Chiavenna, Northern Italy, originally built around 1600. And, of course, there's also now a chic new museum restaurant.

BENAROYA CONCERT HALL

Map p50

☎ 206-215-9494; 200 University St;

With a hefty bill of almost $120 million in construction costs, it's no wonder the Benaroya Concert Hall, Seattle Symphony's primary venue, oozes luxury. From the minute you step into the glass-enclosed lobby of the performance hall you're overwhelmed with views of Elliott Bay; on sunny days you might be lucky enough to see the snowy peaks of the Olympic Range far in the distance. Even if you're not attending the symphony, you can walk through the foyer and marvel at the 20ft-long chandeliers, specially created by Tacoma glassmaker Dale Chihuly.

top picks

IT'S FREE!

- **Frye Art Museum** (p51) First Hill's small but well-stocked art museum.
- **Olympic Sculpture Park** (p70) Al fresco artwork overlooking the Olympic Mountains and Elliott Bay.
- **Volunteer Park Conservatory** (p81) This Victorian greenhouse is the park's crowning jewel.
- **Fremont Sunday Market** (p89) You don't have to spend a dime to enjoy this bustling marketplace in the city's quirkiest quadrant.
- **Ballard Fish Ladder** (p99) Betcha didn't know fish could climb ladders.

BANK OF AMERICA TOWER
Map p50

☎ 206-386-5151; 701 5th Ave; observation deck $5; ⏲ 8:30am-4:30pm Mon-Fri

Formerly the Columbia Seafirst Center, this striking structure is also known as the 'Darth Vader' building. Catch a breathtaking view from the observation deck on the 73rd of its 76 floors.

SEATTLE TOWER Map p50
1218 3rd Ave

Formerly the Northern Life Tower, this 26-story art-deco skyscraper, built in 1928, was designed to reflect the mountains of the Pacific Northwest. The brickwork on the exterior blends from dark at the bottom to light on top, the same way mountains

appear to do. Check out the 18-karat-gold relief map in the lobby.

1001 FOURTH AVE PLAZA Map p50
Built in 1969, this was one of the city's first real skyscrapers. At the time, 1001 Fourth Ave Plaza was a darling of the architectural world, though nowadays the 50-story bronze block looks dated. Locals nicknamed it 'the box that the Space Needle came in.' In the plaza outside is the Three Piece Sculpture: Vertebrae, a sculpture by Henry Moore – a result of Seattle's 'one percent for art' clause.

ARCTIC BUILDING Map p50
700 3rd Ave at Cherry St

The Arctic Building, completed in 1917, is unique for its intricate terra-cotta orna-

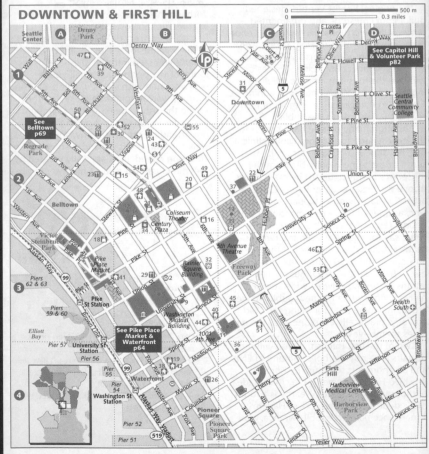

DOWNTOWN & FIRST HILL

mentation and 25 walrus heads peeking off the building's exterior. Though the walruses' tusks were originally authentic ivory, an earthquake in the 1940s managed to shake a few of them loose to the ground. To protect passersby from the unusual urban hazard of being skewered by falling tusks, the ivory was then replaced with epoxy.

TIMES SQUARE BUILDING
Map p50
Olive Way & Stewart St
This terra-cotta and granite structure, guarded by eagles perched on the roof, was designed by the Paris-trained architect Carl Gould (who also did the Seattle Asian Art Museum and the UW's Suzzallo Library). It housed the *Seattle Times* from 1916 to 1931.

WASHINGTON STATE CONVENTION & TRADE CENTER Map p50
☎ 206-447-5000; 7th Ave & Pike St (main entrance)
It's hard to miss this gigantic complex decked out with ballrooms, meeting rooms, space for exhibitions and a visitors center (☎ 206-461-5840; 800 Convention Pl; ☑ 9am-5pm Mon-Fri). An arched-glass bridge spans Pike St between 7th and 8th Aves, with

what looks like a giant eye in the middle of it.

WESTLAKE CENTER
Map p50
4th Ave & Pine St
This shopping center is the veritable pumping heart of the retail district. One of the Rowse Company developments found in practically every sizable US city (notably Atlanta's Peach Tree Plaza, Boston's Faneuil Hall and Portland's Pioneer Place), Westlake Center is filled with national boutique chains (see Shopping, p111) and has a top-floor food court. This is also where the monorail stops and starts on its 1.2-mile trip to and from Seattle Center. The courtyard-like area outside Westlake Center has become a favorite place for activist gatherings and political protests.

FIRST HILL
FRYE ART MUSEUM
Map p50
☎ 206-622-9250; 704 Terry Ave; admission free; ☑ 10am-5pm Tue-Sat, noon-5pm Sun, 10am-8pm Thu; ☒ 64, 303, 941, 942 & others
This small museum on First Hill preserves the collection of Charles and Emma Frye.

DOWNTOWN & FIRST HILL

The Fryes collected more than 1000 paintings, mostly 19th- and early 20th-century European and American pieces, and a few Alaskan and Russian artworks. If this inspires a stifled yawn, think again. Since its 1997 expansion, the Frye has gained a hipness that it once lacked; fresh ways of presenting its artwork, music performances, poetry readings and interesting rotating exhibits from traveling painters to local printmakers, make the museum a worthwhile stop.

SORRENTO HOTEL
Map p50

900 Madison St; 🚌 **64, 303, 941, 942 & others**
This grand working hotel located on First Hill is a fine example of Italian Renaissance architecture. Built in 1909 by a Seattle clothing merchant, the Sorrento was one of the first hotels designed to absorb the crowds of prospectors journeying through town on their way to Alaska in search of gold; see p175 for more information on the hotel.

STIMSON-GREEN MANSION
Map p50

☎ **206-624-0474; 1204 Minor Ave;** 🕑 **by appointment only;** 🚌 **64, 303, 941, 942 & others**
One of the first homes on First Hill, the baronial Stimson-Green Mansion is an English Tudor-style mansion completed in 1901 by lumber and real-estate developer CD Stimson. Built from brick, stucco and wood, this stately home is now owned by Stimson's granddaughter and used for private catered events such as weddings and themed dinners. The interior rooms are decorated to reflect the different design styles popular at the turn of the 20th century.

DOWNTOWN ARCHITECTURE
Walking Tour

1 Arctic Building Start this walk on the south end of downtown at the Arctic Building (p50). Crane your neck to get a look at the walrus heads on the building's exterior. Then walk up Cherry St and take a left onto 4th Ave.

2 Bank of America Tower The Bank of America Tower (p50), formerly the Columbia Seafirst Center, takes up the block between 4th and 5th Aves and Columbia and Cherry Sts. This is the tallest building on the West Coast. If you have time, check out the observation deck on the 73rd floor.

3 1001 Fourth Ave Plaza Follow 4th Ave to Madison St, to the 1001 Fourth Ave Plaza (p50), one of the city's first real skyscrapers, built in 1969. Locals call it 'the box that the Space Needle came in.' In the plaza outside is Henry Moore's *Three Piece Sculpture: Vertebrae.*

4 Seattle Tower Continue north on 4th Ave to University St and take a left, walk half a block and look up. Formerly the Northern Life Tower, the Seattle Tower (p50), an art-deco skyscraper built in 1928, was designed to reflect the mountains of the Pacific Northwest.

SEATTLE PUBLIC LIBRARY

As much as architecture types have carped about the new Seattle Art Museum building (p49), they've universally raved about the new Seattle Public Library (☎ 206-386-4636; 1000 4th Ave; 🕑 10am-8pm Mon-Wed, 10am-6pm Thu-Sat, 1-5pm Sun). Designed by Rem Koolhaas and LMN Architects, the $165.5 million building of glass and steel was designed to suit the functions it would need to serve: a community gathering space, a tech center, a reading room and, of course, a whole bunch of book storage. The entry-level floor is a 'living room,' with a teen center, shop and coffee stand. There's an underground level for parking ($10.50 for two hours). Near the top is the Seattle Room, a 12,000-sq-ft reading room with 40ft glass ceilings. It has amazing light, nice views of downtown and seating for up to 400 people.

But the importance of the building's function certainly hasn't cost it anything in the form department. In short, it looks awesome, as striking as any other building in the city including the Space Needle. The overall style of the place is as far from stodgy as you can possibly get – sort of like when that sexy librarian finally takes her spectacles off. Lemon-yellow escalators, hot pink chairs and zippy wi-fi connections make for a modern, tech-friendly experience. There are also 132 research computers available in the 'Mixing Room,' as well as roving librarians happy to answer questions. And the Book Spiral, spanning several floors, organizes books by the Dewey Decimal System with numbers marked on small mats on the floor.

There's an 18-karat-gold relief map in the lobby.

5 Washington Mutual Tower Continue down University St across 3rd Ave. The beauty of the Seattle skyline is the blue-and-cream Washington Mutual Tower at 3rd Ave at Seneca St, which changes colors with the clouds and sunsets. Don't be shy; enter off 3rd Ave to explore the building's stunning interior.

6 Benaroya Concert Hall Cross University St to Benaroya Concert Hall (p49). Walk into the glass-enclosed lobby of the performance hall, where you can take in excellent views of Elliott Bay. Check out the 20ft-long chandeliers.

7 Seattle Art Museum Since you're this close, continue along University to get an eyeful of the new Seattle Art Museum (p49). It may not be one of the seven wonders of the architecture world, especially from the outside, but it is a clever solution to the problem of finding more and better gallery space in a downtown area without much available real estate.

8 Cobb Building Walk back up University St, across 3rd Ave to the corner of 4th Ave. Look up at the 1910 Cobb Building and see remnants of an older Seattle. Peering out from the building is the dour terra-cotta head of a Native American chief.

9 Rainier Tower & Fairmont Olympic Hotel Continue on University St across 4th Ave to Rainier Tower. Taking up an entire block between 4th and 5th Aves and University and Union Sts is Rainier Square, a shopping center connected to the top-heavy tower. Cross University St and gaze in wonder at the Fairmont Olympic Hotel (p175), undoubtedly one of the classiest remnants of Seattle's early-20th-century heyday. The block-square building looks sober and unrevealing on the outside, but journey through the revolving doors to discover a sumptuous lobby dominated by chandeliers, marble walls and exotic carpets. Take a peek into the Georgian Room to see a dining room right out of a stylish 1930s film.

10 Freeway Park Continue northeast on University St past 6th Ave; look ahead to Freeway Park. Meander through it, then follow signs to the Washington State Convention & Trade Center (p51), and the visitors center inside.

Leave the convention center through its front doors on Pike St. Follow Pike south (you'll see Pike Place Market at the end of the street) to 5th Ave.

11 Coliseum Theater You won't be able to miss the imposing Banana Republic store

WALK FACTS

Start Arctic Building
End Westlake Center
Distance 2 miles
Duration 1 hour
Fuel stops Georgian Room

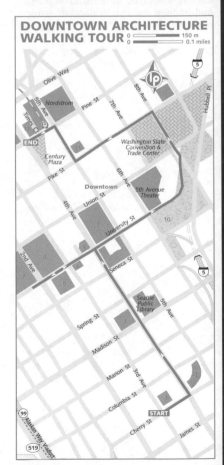

DOWNTOWN ARCHITECTURE WALKING TOUR

DISCOUNT PASSES

If you're going to be in Seattle for a while and plan on seeing its premiere attractions, you might want to consider buying a CityPass (adult/child aged 3-12 $39.50/24). Good for nine days, the pass gets you entry into the Pacific Science Center, Seattle Aquarium, Argosy Cruises' Seattle Harbor Tour, the Museum of Flight and the Woodland Park Zoo. You wind up saving 50% on admission costs and you never have to stand in line. You can buy one at whichever of the sfivenuves you visit first or online at www.citypass.com/city/seattle.html.

Another option is the Go Seattle card (www.goseattlecard.com; adult $55-149, child $39-105) that offers free or discounted admission to a long list of sights and entertainment. Available in one-, two-, three-, five- and seven-day versions, the cards get you in free to a number of the city's top attractions.

at the corner of 5th Ave and Pike St. It is located in the wonderful old terra-cotta-faced Coliseum Theater, a film palace dating back to 1916. In its heyday, the theater filled its 1700 seats with eager moviegoers. The theater suffered from neglect over the years until it was saved by Banana Republic's multimillion-dollar rehabilitation project, completed in 1985.

12 Westlake Center Take a right on 5th Ave to Pine St; turn left. You can't miss the steel-and-glass vision of Westlake Center (p51). Stop for a latte and park yourself in front of Westlake Center for some people-watching.

From here you can shop at the upscale boutiques, go to the top of the mall and catch the monorail to Seattle Center, or head back south along 4th Ave to Cherry St.

PIONEER SQUARE

Drinking p140, Eating p123, Shopping p111, Sleeping p177

Browsing the Pioneer Square Historic District is rather like visiting a movie set of early 20th-century Seattle, except that the food and the shopping are better. This is the birthplace of Seattle, and the redbrick district of historic buildings and totem-lined plazas is still a real crossroads of the modern city.

Seattle's first town-site at Pioneer Square is an enclave of handsome old buildings and shaded squares. The area is also full of restaurants and cafés and some of the best non-chain store shopping in the city, with great bookstores, antique markets, art galleries and gift shops. Even die-hard antishoppers should stop at a couple of the old storefronts. The Grand Central Arcade (214 1st Ave S between S Washington & S Main Sts) has a good bakery-café, plenty of tables, a cozy fire and staircases leading to the underground shopping arcade. You can walk straight through here to Occidental Park (p56). At night, Pioneer Square pubs and clubs kick up an energetic party scene that offers quantity, if not quality (p140).

In the early days of Seattle, Pioneer Square was a haphazard settlement of wooden storefronts, log homes and lumber mills. The Great Fire of 1889 leveled 30 blocks – the original town – but the city rapidly rebounded: almost all of the buildings that now stand in the Pioneer Square area were constructed between 1890 and 1905. As many as 50 of these structures were designed by one architect, Elmer Fisher. As part of this massive rebuilding project, city planners took the dramatic step of regrading Denny Hill, one of Seattle's original seven steep hills that rose sharply out of Elliott Bay. This raised the new city about a dozen feet above the original settlement. Back in the good old days, the underground tunnels that remained were used as opium dens and speakeasies (p211).

Many post-fire buildings were built in the grand Romanesque Revival style already popular in Boston and Chicago, which displayed wealth and prosperity to the pioneers. Plus, no one wanted to see the town go up in flames again – brick, stone and steel are a lot less likely to burn.

Pioneer Square fell on hard times for years – amazingly, there were plans to level the area in the late 1960s to make room for parking lots and office buildings. But alert citizens banded together to rescue the city's atmospheric core. Eventually, bank loans, cheap rents and Historic Register status brought in businesses, art galleries, antique shops and interior-design stores. These days, many Pioneer Square restaurants play up the frontier image while serving notably good food. Pioneer Square is also a major center for live music and nightlife.

Perhaps mirroring its early days when this was a rough-and-tumble frontier town, Pioneer Square still sees some rowdiness; there's often a juxtaposition of drunken tourists and Seattle's homeless hanging around the bar scene. Though the ruckus may be a little unnerving, especially at night, there's not much to worry about beyond drunken frat-boy brawls and some pan-handling.

This is the oldest part of town, full of historic buildings and fun just to wander around in. It's also likely to be the first part of town you see if you arrive in Seattle by train. As you meander through the neighborhood, be on the lookout for informative signs on statues and plaques on historic buildings.

Pioneer Square is a few short blocks from the heart of downtown, meaning that any of the city buses that stop in downtown will get you pretty close.

KLONDIKE GOLD RUSH NATIONAL PARK
Map p57

☎ 206-553-7220; Jackson St & 2nd Ave S; admission free; ⏰ 9am-5pm

In an early example of Seattle civic boosters clamoring to put the city 'on the map,' the Seattle *Post-Intelligencer* trumpeted the news that a ship full of gold had arrived in town on July 17, 1897. Masses of gold-fevered unfortunates swarmed the city on their way to the Klondike River area in the Yukon Territory, and local merchants made a killing. Seattle's seminal position as the outfitting and transportation hub for the Alaskan and Yukon Gold Rush is recognized at Klondike Gold Rush National Park, one of the USA's few indoor national historical parks. It's easy to miss, but worth seeking out. Exhibits, photos and news clippings document the era and give an idea of how much gear, food and true grit were necessary to stake a claim in the Klondike. Gold panning is demonstrated by park rangers, and you can sit down and view a slide presentation about the gold rush.

KING STREET STATION Map p57
303 S Jackson St
The old Great Northern Railroad depot is now in use as an Amtrak station. This onetime jewel of a train station – built in 1906 by Reed & Stem, who also designed New York City's Grand Central Station – has been blighted since the 1960s by a horrible ceiling-lowering revamp, but the fabulous old Italianate plasterwork and detailing are still there. The old depot's stately brick tower has long been an integral (though now dwarfed) piece of the downtown skyline. Continuing renovations to the building are being planned to restore and reveal its original architecture as well as improving its practical functions.

OCCIDENTAL PARK Map p57
Between S Washington & S Main Sts, just off 1st Ave S
Notable in this cobblestone plaza are the totem poles carved by Duane Pasco, a nationally respected Chinookan carver and artist from Poulsbo on the Kitsap Peninsula. The totems depict the welcoming spirit of Kwakiutl, a totem bear, the tall Sun and Raven and a man riding on the tail of a whale. For more on the art and purpose of totem poles, see p37.

Also eye-catching is the Firefighters' Memorial, featuring life-size bronze sculptures of firefighters in action. Engraved on the granite slabs surrounding the sculpture are the names of Seattle firefighters who have been killed in the line of duty since the department's inception after the Great Fire. The artist is Hai Ying Wu, a University of Washington graduate.

OCCIDENTAL SQUARE Map p57
S Main & S Jackson Sts
Occidental Square, with its cobblestone plaza flanked by unusually handsome Victorian buildings, is one of the nicest places in this area. Visit Glass House Studio (☎ 206-682-9939; 311 Occidental Ave S) to see local artists' impressive works of blown, cast and lamp-worked glass. If you need a shot of caffeine or a chance to catch your breath, make the pilgrimage to Zeitgeist (Map p57). This groovy coffeehouse is a local haunt of artists and architects. Along S Jackson St you'll find an excellent concentration of antique stores and some of the city's most prestigious galleries.

PIONEER BUILDING Map p57
606 1st Ave S
Built in 1891, this magnificent structure facing Pioneer Square Park is one of the finest Victorian buildings left in Seattle; many mining companies had offices here during the Klondike Gold Rush years. It was designed by Elmer Fisher, whose fingerprints are all over Pioneer Square. Resting on the site of Henry Yesler's original home, the building now houses, in part, Doc Maynard's Public House (below), a handsome old bar and restaurant, and the ticket office for Bill Speidel's Underground Tour (p28). Be sure to peek in at the Italian marble in the lobby.

PIONEER SQUARE PARK Map p57
Cherry St & 1st Ave S
The original Pioneer Square is a cobblestone triangular plaza where Henry Yesler's sawmill cut the giant trees that marked Seattle's first industry. Known officially as Pioneer Square Park, the plaza features a bust of Chief Seattle (Sealth, in the original language), an ornate pergola and a totem pole. Some wayward early Seattleites, so the story goes, stole the totem from the Tlingit natives in southeastern Alaska in 1890. An arsonist lit the pole aflame in 1938, burning it to the ground. When asked if they could carve a replacement pole, the Tlingit took the money offered, thanking the city for payment of the first totem, and said it would cost $5000 to carve another one. The city coughed up the money and the Tlingit obliged with the pole you see today.

The decorative pergola was built in the early 1900s to serve as an entryway to an underground lavatory and to shelter those waiting for the cable car that went up and down Yesler Way. The reportedly elaborate restroom eventually closed due to serious plumbing problems at high tide. In January 2001, the pergola was leveled by a wayward truck; it has been restored and was put back where it belongs the following year, looking good as new.

DOC MAYNARD'S PUBLIC HOUSE Map p57
☎ 206-682-4646; 610 1st Ave S
This atmospheric pub transports you back to the old days of pioneer Seattle. It's named after Doc Maynard, one of the city's founding fathers and quite a character. An Ohio native, Maynard was divorced when

he arrived in the city and was out for a good time; he was vivacious and generous and he liked his liquor. This combination led him to give away cash or land to almost anyone with a promising idea, and he died essentially landless and broke (the rather revealing epitaph on his second wife, Catherine's, tombstone reads, 'She did what she could'). The gorgeous carved bar here was shipped over from Chicago. Doc's is also the starting point of Bill Speidel's Underground Tour (p28).

ELLIOTT BAY BOOK COMPANY Map p57

☎ 206-624-6600; 101 S Main St; ⏰ 9:30am-11pm Mon-Sat, 11am-6pm Sun

Seattle's premier bookstore and literary gathering place, and the original home of the Globe Hotel, built in 1890. The place is made for browsing, with its high ceilings, peculiar

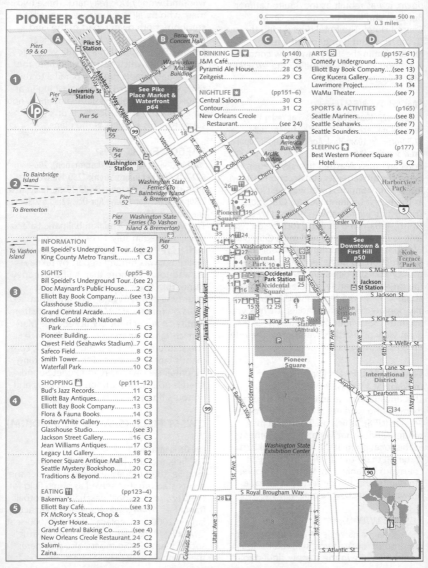

PIONEER SQUARE

0 — 500 m
0 — 0.3 miles

DRINKING 🍸	(p140)
J&M Café	27 C3
Pyramid Ale House	28 C5
Zeitgeist	29 C3

NIGHTLIFE ★	(pp151-6)
Central Saloon	30 C3
Contour	31 C2
New Orleans Creole Restaurant	(see 24)

ARTS 🎭	(pp157-61)
Comedy Underground	32 C3
Elliott Bay Book Company	(see 13)
Greg Kucera Gallery	33 C3
Lawrimore Project	34 D4
WaMu Theater	(see 7)

SPORTS & ACTIVITIES	(p165)
Seattle Mariners	(see 8)
Seattle Seahawks	(see 7)
Seattle Sounders	(see 7)

SLEEPING 🛏	(p177)
Best Western Pioneer Square Hotel	35 C2

INFORMATION	
Bill Speidel's Underground Tour	(see 2)
King County Metro Transit	1 C3

SIGHTS	(pp55-8)
Bill Speidel's Underground Tour	(see 2)
Doc Maynard's Public House	2 C2
Elliott Bay Book Company	(see 13)
Glasshouse Studio	3 C3
Grand Central Arcade	4 C3
Klondike Gold Rush National Park	5 C3
Pioneer Building	6 C2
Qwest Field (Seahawks Stadium)	7 C4
Safeco Field	8 C5
Smith Tower	9 C2
Waterfall Park	10 C2

SHOPPING 🛍	(pp111-12)
Bud's Jazz Records	11 C3
Elliott Bay Antiques	12 C2
Elliott Bay Book Company	13 C3
Flora & Fauna Books	14 C3
Foster/White Gallery	15 C3
Glasshouse Studio	(see 3)
Jackson Street Gallery	16 C3
Jean Williams Antiques	17 C3
Legacy Ltd Gallery	18 B2
Pioneer Square Antique Mall	19 C2
Seattle Mystery Bookshop	20 C2
Traditions & Beyond	21 C2

EATING 🍴	(pp123-4)
Bakeman's	22 C3
Elliott Bay Café	(see 13)
FX McRory's Steak, Chop & Oyster House	23 C3
Grand Central Baking Co	(see 4)
New Orleans Creole Restaurant	24 C2
Salumi	25 C2
Zaina	26 C2

multilevel bookshelves and funny niches and corners. Downstairs is a snug little café (p124).

GRAND CENTRAL ARCADE Map p57

☎ 206-623-7417; 214 1st Ave S

This lovely meeting point was originally Squire's Opera House, erected in 1879 by Watson Squire, who became one of Washington's first senators after it achieved statehood. When the Opera House burned down, it was rebuilt as the Squire-Latimer Building and later became the Grand Central Hotel. The hotel died during the Depression, but it underwent a major restoration in the 1970s and now contains two floors of shops, including the excellent Grand Central Baking Co.

SMITH TOWER Map p57

☎ 206-622-4004; 506 2nd Ave S at Yesler Way; observation deck adult/senior & student/child $7.50/6/5; ⏱ 10am-dusk Apr-Oct, 10am-3:30pm Sat & Sun Nov-Mar

You can't miss Seattle's first skyscraper. For half a century after its construction in 1914, the 42-story Smith Tower was well known as the tallest building west of Chicago. The distinctive tower was erected by LC Smith, a man who built his fortune on typewriters (Smith-Corona) and guns (Smith & Wesson). Smith died during the building's construction, so he never got to see the beauty that still bears his name. Walk into the onyx- and marble-paneled lobby, step aboard one of the brass-and-copper manually operated elevators and let it whisk you up to the 35th-floor observation deck for a great view of Seattle's Waterfront. The ride up is as exciting as the view.

WATERFALL PARK Map p57

Cnr S Main St & 2nd Ave S

This unusual park is an urban oasis commemorating workers of the United Parcel Service (UPS), which grew out of a messenger service that began in a basement at this location in 1907. The artificial 22ft waterfall that flows in this tiny open-air courtyard is flanked by tables and flowering plants. This is a perfect spot to eat a brown-bag lunch or to rest weary feet.

YESLER WAY Map p57

Seattle claims its Yesler Way was the coining ground for the term 'skid road' – logs would 'skid' down the steeply sloped road

linking a logging area above town to Henry Yesler's mill. With the decline of the area, the street became a haven for homeless people. Soon the nickname 'skid road' or 'skid row' was being used for equally destitute areas around the country, sort of the opposite to 'easy street.'

As for Arthur Yesler himself, local historians paint him as an ambitious business zealot who clashed frequently with the wild-and-woolly Doc Maynard. These two men, who by all accounts were equally stubborn, both owned part of the land that would eventually become Pioneer Square. This resulted in a highly symbolic grid clash, in which Yesler's section of the square had streets running parallel to the river, while Maynard's came crashing in at a north-south angle. Yesler maintained, not unreasonably, that Doc was drunk when he submitted his portion of the plans.

SAFECO FIELD Map p57

☎ 206-346-4241 (general information), 206-622-4487 (ticket information); 1250 1st Ave S; adult/child $8/6; 1hr tours ⏱ 10:30am, 12:20pm & 2:30pm on nongame days Apr-Oct; 12:30 & 2:30pm Tue-Sun Nov-Mar

The Mariners' $517 million ballpark, Safeco Field, opened in July 1999. The stadium, with its retractable roof, 47,000 seats and real grass, was funded in part by taxpayers and tourists; more than half the money came from taxes on food sold in King County restaurants and bars, and from taxes on rental cars. Money also came from profits on scratch-lottery tickets. The Mariners coughed up most of the difference. The stadium's unique design means it commands fantastic views of the surrounding mountains, downtown and Puget Sound. There's no 2:30pm tour on game days and no tours if the game is before 6pm.

QWEST FIELD (SEAHAWKS STADIUM) Map p57

800 Occidental Ave S

The late, mostly unlamented Kingdome, long Seattle's biggest eyesore, was once the sports stadium that served as home field for the city's professional baseball and football franchises. Then it was imploded spectacularly in 2000 and replaced by the 72,000-seat Qwest Field, or Seahawks Stadium. Seattle's soccer team, the Sounders, also play here; the Mariners now play at Safeco Field.

INTERNATIONAL DISTRICT

Drinking p140, Eating p123, Shopping p111, Sleeping p177

Not far from Pioneer Square, but feeling worlds away, is the International District, Seattle's China-town, where Asian groceries and restaurants line the streets. The updated moniker reflects both Seattle's tendency to be politically correct and the gradual diversification of the area. The Chinese were among the first settlers in Seattle in the late 1800s (the original Chinatown was around 2nd Ave and Washington St), followed by Japanese, Filipinos, Vietnamese, Laotians and others. Later immigrants settled just to the east of present-day Chinatown, in an area known as Little Saigon.

Although 'International District' seems a pretty useful term for this mix of races and cultures, it is in fact a relatively recent and controversial moniker, fashioned in the early 1970s. The Chinese grew resentful of the term when the renaming left 'Chinatown' a seemingly dirty word, but other Asian groups welcomed representation. Scuffles about who the neighborhood belongs to continue as they have throughout the area's history. Many Seattleites still refer to the area as Chinatown or simply 'the ID.'

Asian immigrants had an important presence in Seattle pretty much from the beginning. The muscle behind this early Asian settlement was the Wa Chong Company, labor contractors who brought in Chinese workers for timber, mining and railroad jobs in the 1860s and 1870s. After the anti-Chinese riots of 1886 (p25), the population of Chinatown dropped from an estimated 1500 to about 500; large numbers of Chinese immigrants didn't start coming back to the area until after the Great Fire of 1889. At that point, Chinatown shifted to where it is now, around the King St and Jackson St area.

Immigrants from Japan settled the area in the later 1800s and remained the largest minority group until WWII. 'Japantown' was just to the north of Chinatown; the Japanese population at one point was about 6000. From the 1920s to '40s, this was a bustling place, thriving with Asian markets and other businesses that were built and patronized by the country's highest concentration of Japanese and Chinese Americans. African Americans and Filipinos also moved in, but the area remained a veritable Japantown, with Japanese newspapers, schools, banks and restaurants.

The neighborhood took another massive hit during WWII, when all inhabitants of Japanese descent were forcibly moved out and interned at labor camps in the US interior. The once-bustling shops were boarded up. When released, few of those who had been in the internment camps chose to return here to their old homes; those who did return, including the Moriguchis who founded the Uwajimaya store, made quite an impact on the future development of the neighborhood.

When I-5 pushed through the heart of the district, destroying many blocks of housing, the area became even more blighted and its identity even more divided. The arrival of Vietnamese immigrants in the 1970s and '80s, and more recently, an influx of immigrants from Hong Kong and mainland China, have breathed new life into the city's Asian community.

The renovation of Union Station, new sports stadiums and nearby office and condo developments around the International District have led to fears of homogeneity in a district already rife with boundary issues. Throughout the USA, major cities boast Chinatowns, Japantowns and other neighborhoods that embody a specific ethnicity. In Seattle, it's all crowded into one small neighborhood whose boundaries are threatened every time a land-use application shows up at City Hall. District activists strive to keep the area vital by stressing anti-crime measures and maintaining a strong community voice in housing and commercial development.

The 'ID' has all of the trappings of a multiethnic neighborhood, from bustling markets to fun import shops to amazing places to eat. There's also a lot of history here, as explained most thoroughly in the Wing Luke Asian Museum. As you explore the nooks and crannies of the neighborhood, keep your eyes peeled for hidden treasures, like that sketchy pet shop straight out of *Gremlins* tucked away in a back alley.

WING LUKE ASIAN MUSEUM Map p60

☎ 206-623-5124; 407 7th Ave S; adult/child/student $4/3/2; ☉ 11am-4:30pm Tue-Fri, noon-4pm Sat & Sun; 🚌 7, 14, 36

This Pan-Asian museum is devoted to Asian and Pacific American culture, history and art. Named after the first Asian elected official in the continental US, it examines the often difficult and violent meeting of Asian and Western cultures in Seattle. Particularly fascinating are the photos and displays on Chinese settlement in the 1880s and the retelling of Japanese American internment during WWII. It has received enough funding to move to its planned new location a block away, in the East Kong Yick Building, where it expects to reopen in 2008.

DANNY WOO INTERNATIONAL DISTRICT COMMUNITY GARDENS
Map p60
Walk up S Main St from 6th Ave S
The Danny Woo International District Community Gardens are a 1.5-acre plot reserved for about 120 older and low-income International District residents, who grow a profusion of vegetables and fruit trees. Visitors can wander along the gravel paths and admire both the tidy gardens and the Seattle skyline, as well as good views of Elliott Bay. Unfortunately, while you take in the view you'll have about 17 lanes of I-5 traffic right at your back.

UWAJIMAYA Map p60
☎ 206-624-6248; 600 5th Ave S; ☼ 9am-10pm
Founded by Fujimatsu Moriguchi, one of the few Japanese to return here from the WWII internment camps, this large department and grocery store – a cornerstone of Seattle's Asian community – has everything from fresh fish and exotic fruits and vegetables to cooking utensils, and you'll come face-to-face with those dim sum ingredients you've always wondered about. The current location is a brand-new 'community' that includes living quarters and occupies a whole block. There's a food court in addition to the grocery store. It's a great place to browse. Sharing the same building as Uwajimaya, the giant Kinokuniya bookstore has an excellent collection of books about Asia and by Asian writers as well as import CDs and DVDs.

HAU HAU MARKET Map p60
☎ 206-329-1688; 412 12th Ave S
Hau Hau is a modern and bustling Chinese and Vietnamese food market where you can get cheap produce, specialty meats such as pork ears and chicken feet, fireworks, and Asian gifts and knickknacks.

HING HAY PARK Map p60
Maynard Ave S & King St
If you need a tranquil spot to rest while wandering the ID, Hing Hay Park lends a

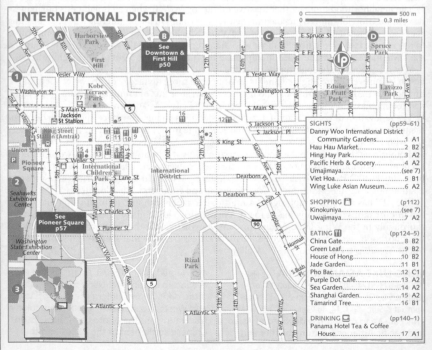

INTERNATIONAL DISTRICT

SIGHTS	(pp59–61)
Danny Woo International District Community Gardens	1 A1
Hau Hau Market	2 B2
Hing Hay Park	3 A2
Pacific Herb & Grocery	4 A2
Umajimaya	(see 7)
Viet Hoa	5 B1
Wing Luke Asian Museum	6 A2

SHOPPING	(p112)
Kinokuniya	(see 7)
Uwajimaya	7 A2

EATING	(pp124–5)
China Gate	8 B2
Green Leaf	9 B2
House of Hong	10 B2
Jade Garden	11 B1
Pho Bac	12 C1
Purple Dot Café	13 A2
Sea Garden	14 A2
Shanghai Garden	15 A2
Tamarind Tree	16 B1

DRINKING	(pp140–1)
Panama Hotel Tea & Coffee House	17 A1

little green to the otherwise austere district. The traditional Chinese pavilion was a gift from the people of Taipei.

INTERNATIONAL CHILDREN'S PARK
Map p60
S Lane St & 7th Ave
If the kids aren't up for exploring the Asian markets or sitting still for a dim sum brunch, bring them here to work off some energy by playing on the bronze dragon sculpture, designed by George Tsutakawa.

PACIFIC HERB & GROCERY
Map p60
☎ 206-340-6411; 610 S Weller St, btwn 6th & Maynard Aves S
A good place to get a sense of Chinatown is along S Weller St. Apart from the many restaurants, there's Pacific Herb & Grocery, where the herbal-medicine specialists can tell you all about the uses of different roots, bones, flowers and teas. The shop next door is a great place to buy tofu at low prices – you can even watch them make it on the premises.

UNION STATION Map p60
401 S Jackson St
Another landmark that benefited from restoration fever is Union Station, the old Union Pacific Railroad depot (1911). Until 1999, it had been unoccupied since 1971, when the last train chugged out of the station. The restoration project included the preservation of the original tile floors, clocks and windows. More than 90 years of build-up was hand-scrubbed off the exterior brick. The Great Hall, half the size of a football field, remains an impressive space.

VIET HOA Map p60
7th Ave S at S Jackson St
The Viet Hoa market (look for the 'Chinatown Market-Seafood & Meat' sign) has a greengrocer in one building and a fish and meat market in the other. Both display foods and cuts of meat you may have never seen before. The big tank of live turtles at the door and the buckets of fish that look like they're one splash away from coming back to life assure you that this market carries only the freshest ingredients.

PIKE PLACE MARKET & WATERFRONT

Drinking p141, Eating p125, Shopping p112, Sleeping p177

These two neighborhoods are perhaps Seattle's most visited areas. They're divided by the Alaskan Way Viaduct, but linked by several corridors and stairways, and it's easy to thoroughly explore both in the same day. The best bet is to hit the market early in the morning, relax in a waterfront park at midday, then stroll the shops along the boardwalk in the afternoon and watch the sun set over Elliott Bay while you munch a seafood dinner.

This area of town rewards early birds. It's particularly important to get to the market early if you want to avoid that cattle-truck feeling. Weekdays and before 10am on weekends are best. The waterfront is more weather-dependent; a sunny weekend afternoon finds it swarming, while on a misty weekday morning you'll have the place pretty much to yourself.

At the time of research, the historic Waterfront Streetcar line was closed due to various construction projects along the waterfront; its future was uncertain as plans for solving the problem of the Alaskan Way Viaduct (the problem being, mainly, its existence, but also its decrepitude) were being discussed.

PIKE PLACE MARKET

One of the best ways to fall in love with Seattle is to wake up early and head down to Pike Place Market, stroll around and watch people do what they do. Grab a coffee and a pastry, sit in a café window and listen to the elderly couple next to you debate whether or not they regret certain choices they made early in their lives. Watch a business-suit guy pacing the cobblestones and saying things like 'the gist of the strategy is this whole USB thing' into his cell phone while other suited guys rush past him, porting coffee in paper cups. A girl walking a puppy passes by a despondent-looking man on the corner selling *RealChange* newspapers. An Indian with long braids goes by on one crutch. A hipster couple with matching turquoise hair walks by, intertwined. Tourists line up to photograph the singing fish throwers; one joker throws a stuffed plush-toy fish right into the crowd, provoking giggles. An ancient black busker sings 'Mamas, Don't Let Your Babies Grow Up to Be Cowboys.'

The market is one of Seattle's most popular tourist attractions, as much for its exuberant theatricality as for its fish and produce market. The lively, always bustling buildings that make up the market fill daily with the bounty of local farms, rivers and the sea. Add in arts and crafts, loads of restaurants and cafés and buskers and other performers, and you'll discover why this mazelike market is Seattle at its irrepressible best. It sees about 40,000 visitors a day, and a good portion of them are locals out shopping for groceries.

The market features some of the most boisterous fishmongers in the world, whose daredevil antics with salmon merge gymnastics, theater and cuisine. Despite the tourist-tickling showiness, the market maintains a down-home authenticity; real people work and buy here. A tip: don't eat before you go. This is one of the hotbeds of Seattle snacking and dining. You can get everything from a freshly grown Washington apple to a pot sticker, or even a seven-course French meal. Some of Seattle's favorite watering holes are also tucked into unlikely corners of the market buildings – for more details, see the Eating (p125) and Drinking (p141) chapters.

Pike Place Market is the oldest continuously operating market in the nation. It was established in 1907 to give local farmers a place to sell their fruit and vegetables and bypass the middleman. Soon, the greengrocers made room for fishmongers, bakers, ethnic groceries, butchers, cheese sellers and purveyors of the rest of the Northwest's agricultural bounty. The market wasn't exactly architecturally robust – it's always been a thrown-together warren of sheds and stalls, haphazardly designed for utility – and was by no means an intentional tourist attraction. That came later.

An enthusiastic agricultural community spawned the market's heyday in the 1930s. Many of the first farmers were immigrants, a fact the market celebrates with annual themes acknowledging the contributions of various ethnic groups; past years have featured Japanese Americans, Italian Americans and Sephardic Jews.

By the 1960s, sales at the market were suffering from suburbanization, the growth of supermarkets and the move away from local, small-scale market gardening. Vast tracts of agricultural land were disappearing, replaced by such ventures as the Northgate Mall and the Sea-Tac airport. The internment of Japanese American farmers during WWII had also taken its toll. The entire area became a bowery for the destitute and a center for prostitution and peep shows.

In the wake of the 1962 World's Fair, plans were drawn up to bulldoze the market and build high-rise office and apartment buildings on this piece of prime downtown real estate. Fortunately, public outcry prompted a voter's initiative to save the market. Subsequently, the space was cleaned up and restructured, and it has become once again the undeniable heart and soul of downtown; some 10 million people mill through the market each year. Thanks to the unique management of the market, social services programs and low-income housing mix with market commerce, and the market has maintained its gritty edge. These initiatives have prevented the area from ever sliding too far upscale. A market law prohibits chain stores or franchises from opening up shop and ensures all businesses are locally owned. The one exception is, of course, Starbucks, which gets away with its market location because it marks the coffee giant's first (it opened in 1971).

Pike Place is made up of several buildings, covering about eight labyrinthine blocks at the top of the bluff overlooking the Waterfront. It's easy to get lost here – in fact, experiencing a slight sense of mayhem and dislocation is part of the charm of your initial acquaintance with the market. Don't let the sometimes seedy nature of the neighborhood bother you; the streets around the market are still dotted with sex shops and off-putting vagrancy, but there's very little real danger in the area. To help you find your way around, pick up a copy of *Welcome to the Pike Place Market,* a brochure with a map and directory of market shops. It's available throughout the market and at the information booth (see right).

If you're coming from downtown, simply walk down Pike St toward the Waterfront; you can't miss the huge Public Market sign etched against the horizon. Incidentally, the sign and clock, installed in 1927, constituted one of the first pieces of outdoor neon on the West Coast. From the top of Pike St and 1st Ave, stop and survey the bustle and vitality of the market: buskers strum and sing, baguettes stick out of shoppers' backpacks, towers of artichokes loom in market stalls and bouquets of flowers bloom in the arms of passersby. Walk down the cobblestone street, past perpetually gridlocked cars (don't even

DIY SEATTLE

Carrying a map around the Pike Place Market will only make you dizzy, so here's our advice: ditch the map, put this guidebook down and go exploring on your own. The market labyrinth holds surprises around every corner; even if you end up walking in circles, you're likely to see something new with each lap. So start at one corner, browse without an agenda or a timeline, stop wherever you feel like it, and see what happens.

think of driving down to Pike Place) and, before walking into the market, stop and shake the bronze snout of Rachel the Market Pig, the de facto mascot and presiding spirit of the market. This life-size piggy bank, carved by Whidbey Island artist Georgia Gerber and named after a real pig, collects about $6000 each year. The funds are pumped back into market social services. Nearby is the market information booth (☎ 206-682-7453; Pike St & 1st Ave), which has maps of the market and information about Seattle in general. It also serves as a Ticket/Ticket booth (p158), selling discount tickets to various shows throughout the city.

Pike Place Market is on the western edge of downtown, off 1st Ave. Buses 15, 18, 21, 22 and 56 run up and down 1st Ave from Pioneer Square. You can also take any bus along 3rd Ave and get off at the University Street Station, then walk west, toward the water. Along the Waterfront Streetcar route, Pike St Station is the stop for Pike Place Market; from there you need to climb the hill to the market itself. On foot, the market is just minutes from most downtown hotels. Walk down Pike, Pine or Stewart Sts toward the Waterfront and you're there.

WATERFRONT

This area faces dramatic change in the next few years, at least if the city's tentative plans to do away with the Alaskan Way Viaduct are put into effect. The viaduct, completed on April 4, 1953, is an elevated section of Washington State Route 99 that parallels the waterfront. It was damaged in the 2001 earthquake, and the question now is whether to repair, replace or remove it. After seemingly endless debate and a couple of public-opinion votes to test the waters, city planners finally acknowledged in mid-2007 that Seattleites, understandably, don't want a gigantic highway dividing their downtown from their playground. Early improvements and safety measures have been started, with removal of the viaduct scheduled for 2012. The impact this will have on the waterfront depends on how the design turns out – will it be a tunnel? another elevated system? etc – but it's certain to bring radical change to this historic neighborhood.

The waterfront is indelibly tied to Seattle's beginnings. Thousands of Klondike fortune hunters left from here on ships for Alaska in 1897 to seek gold, many returning with the wealth that served to boom the town into one of the foremost cities along the Pacific Rim. Seattle's waterfront is still a busy place, although today tourist facilities far outnumber actual port activities. Most of Seattle's considerable traffic in containers and imports is handled at the port area south of the historic waterfront.

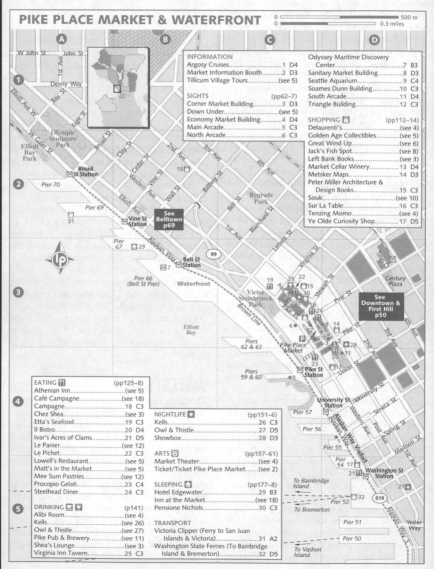

PIKE PLACE MARKET & WATERFRONT

INFORMATION
Argosy Cruises...........................1 D4
Market Information Booth.........2 D3
Tillicum Village Tours...............(see 5)

SIGHTS   (pp62–7)
Corner Market Building..............3 D3
Down Under.............................(see 5)
Economy Market Building..........4 D3
Main Arcade..............................5 C3
North Arcade.............................6 C3

Odyssey Maritime Discovery
   Center....................................7 B3
Sanitary Market Building............8 D3
Seattle Aquarium.......................9 C4
Soames Dunn Building..............10 C3
South Arcade...........................11 D4
Triangle Building.......................12 C3

SHOPPING   (pp112–14)
Delaurenti's............................(see 4)
Golden Age Collectibles..........(see 5)
Great Wind Up........................(see 6)
Jack's Fish Spot......................(see 8)
Left Bank Books......................(see 3)
Market Cellar Winery................13 D4
Metsker Maps..........................14 D3
Peter Miller Architecture &
   Design Books.......................15 C3
Souk......................................(see 10)
Sur La Table............................16 C3
Tenzing Momo.........................(see 4)
Ye Olde Curiosity Shop............17 D5

EATING   (pp125–8)
Athenian Inn...........................(see 5)
Café Campagne.......................(see 18)
Campagne.............................18 C3
Chez Shea.............................(see 3)
Etta's Seafood.......................19 C3
Il Bistro................................20 D4
Ivar's Acres of Clams.............21 D5
Le Panier..............................(see 12)
Le Pichet..............................22 C3
Lowell's Restaurant................(see 5)
Matt's in the Market...............(see 5)
Mee Sum Pastries..................(see 12)
Procopio Gelati.....................23 C4
Steelhead Diner....................24 C3

DRINKING   (p141)
Alibi Room............................(see 4)
Kells....................................(see 26)
Owl & Thistle........................(see 27)
Pike Pub & Brewery...............(see 11)
Shea's Lounge.......................(see 3)
Virginia Inn Tavern................25 C3

NIGHTLIFE   (pp151–6)
Kells.....................................26 C3
Owl & Thistle.........................27 D5
Showbox................................28 D3

ARTS   (pp157–61)
Market Theater.......................(see 4)
Ticket/Ticket Pike Place Market.....(see 2)

SLEEPING   (pp177–8)
Hotel Edgewater.....................29 B3
Inn at the Market...................(see 18)
Pensione Nichols....................30 C3

TRANSPORT
Victoria Clipper (Ferry to San Juan
   Islands & Victoria)...............31 A2
Washington State Ferries (To Bainbridge
   Island & Bremerton).............32 D5

Visitors can catch the flavor of a major seaport by walking along the Seattle Waterfront. This is also a fun, if tacky, place to eat seafood and shop for souvenirs. Most of the piers are now enclosed with endless tourist shops and clam-chowder venues. If you're looking for that 'I Heart Seattle' T-shirt, a souvenir coffee mug or a mass-produced trinket, this is the place.

The Port of Seattle has redeveloped much of the Waterfront area to the north of Seattle Aquarium. Pier 66, also known as the Bell Street Pier, is now home to the Bell Harbor International Conference Center and new Odyssey Maritime Discovery Center (p67), as well as some of the city's better seafood restaurants.

Take a break from the carnival atmosphere of the Waterfront by walking north on Alaskan Way, past Pier 71, to Myrtle Edwards Park, a fringe of lawn and trees along Elliott Bay, and the adjacent, brand-new Olympic Sculpture Park (p70). The path is a favorite of joggers and power-walkers pursuing lunchtime fitness. In warm weather, the linked parks, with stupendous views over the Sound to the Olympic Mountains, make a good place for a picnic.

Along the length of the Waterfront – amid the horse-drawn carriages, pedicabs and cotton-candy vendors – are a number of companies that offer harbor tours and boat excursions – see the Directory chapter (p211) for details.

The Waterfront is relatively cut off from the rest of downtown Seattle, although the nicely landscaped Hillclimb Corridor (at the end of Pike St) serves as a handy people-funnel between the Waterfront and Pike Place Market. Still, the steep hillsides make access problematic for some; it can be as much as an eight-story descent down open stairways from 1st Ave to Alaskan Way. And until something actually happens to the Alaskan Way Viaduct, it remains a psychological barrier that's hard to ignore. While it in no way infringes upon getting from one place to the other, Alaskan Way is incredibly noisy and the parking areas under the freeway can be scary at night. Be sure not to leave anything valuable in your car if you park here.

The main tourist areas of the Waterfront are between Piers 52 and 59. Waterfront Park is the name given to Pier 57; it's just a boardwalk on the pier, but at least you can get out onto the Sound and get a feeling for the area. It's also the best place to tote your corn dogs and fish and chips from the adjacent piers, then take a seat on a waterside bench. Keep your eyes on your fries, however, as Waterfront seagulls can resemble a pack of hungry bears.

Piers 54, 55 and 56 are devoted to shops and restaurants, including novelty venues such as the 100-year-old Ye Olde Curiosity Shop (p113), a bizarre cross between a cornball old-time museum and a souvenir shop.

Though it was on hiatus due to construction work at the time of research, the Waterfront Streetcar normally runs along Alaskan Way, the Waterfront's main thoroughfare. The trolleys are more for show than for transport, although they do go from near Seattle Center (from the base of Broad St), along the Waterfront (including near Pike Place Market) and on to Pioneer Square and the International District. Still, if you're anywhere downtown, it's just as easy to walk to the Waterfront.

Washington State Ferries operates transportation to Bainbridge Island and Bremerton from the piers, while privately owned ferries travel to the San Juan Islands and Victoria, BC. For more information on ferry operators and routes, see the Transport (p204) and Excursions (p187) chapters.

CORNER & SANITARY MARKET BUILDINGS Map p64
Pike Pl & Pike St
Across Pike Place from the Main Arcade is the 1912 Corner Market Building and the Sanitary Market Building, so named because it was the first of the market buildings in which live animals were prohibited. It's now a maze of ethnic groceries and great little eateries, including the Three Girls Bakery, which has a sit-down area (it's always packed) and a take-out window with some of the best breads and sandwiches around. This is also the home of Left Bank Books (p113), an excellent source for all your radical reading needs.

DOWN UNDER Map p64
As if the levels of the market that are above ground weren't labyrinthine enough, below the Main Arcade are three lower levels called the Down Under. Here you'll find a fabulously eclectic mix of pocket-size shops, from Indian spice stalls to magicians' supply shops and military-button booths.

ECONOMY MARKET BUILDING Map p64
1st Ave & Pike St
Once a stable for merchants' horses, the Economy Market Building on the south side of the market entrance has a wonderful Italian grocery store, DeLaurenti's – a great place for any aficionado of Italian foods to browse

and sample. There's also Tenzing Momo, one of the oldest apothecaries on the West Coast, where you can pick up herbal remedies, incense, oils and books. Tarot readings are available here on occasion. Look down at the Economy Market floor and you'll see some of the 46,000 tiles that line the floor. The tiles were sold to the public in the 1980s for $35 apiece. If you bought a tile, you'd get your name on it and be proud that you helped save the market floor. Famous tile owners include *Cat in the Hat* creator Dr Seuss and former US president Ronald Reagan.

MAIN & NORTH ARCADES Map p64
Western Ave
Rachel the Market Pig marks the main entrance to the Main and North Arcades, thin shed-like structures that run along the edge of the hill; these are the busiest of the market buildings. With banks of fresh produce carefully arranged in artful displays, and fresh fish, crab and other shellfish piled high on ice, this is the real heart of the market. Here you'll see fishmongers tossing salmon back and forth like basketballs (many of these vendors will pack fish for overnight delivery). You'll also find cheese shops, butchers, tiny grocery stalls and almost everything else you need to put together a meal. The end of the North Arcade is dedicated to local artisans and craftspeople – products must be handmade to be sold here. The Main Arcade was built in 1907, the first of Frank Goodwin's market buildings.

POST ALLEY Map p64
Between the Corner Market and the Triangle Building, tiny Post Alley is lined with more shops and restaurants. Extending north across Stewart St, this street offers two of the area's best places for a drink: the Pink Door (p126), an Italian hideaway with a cool patio, and Kells (p141), an Irish pub. In Lower Post Alley beside the market sign is the LaSalle Hotel, the first bordello north of Yesler Way; it was originally the Outlook Hotel, but was taken over in 1942 by the notorious Nellie Curtis, a woman with 13 aliases and a knack for running suspiciously profitable hotels with thousands of lonely sailors lined up nightly outside the door. (She's the namesake for the Pike Place Pub & Brewery's equally tempting Naughty Nellie's Ale.) The building, rehabbed in 1977, now houses commercial and residential space.

SOUTH ARCADE Map p64
1411 1st Ave
If you continue past DeLaurenti's, you'll come into the South Arcade, the market's newest wing, home to upscale shops and the lively Pike Place Pub & Brewery (p141).

TRIANGLE BUILDING Map p64
Pike Pl & Post Alley
All in a row in the Triangle Building are Mr D's Greek Deli, Mee Sum Pastries (try the great pork bao), a juice bar and Cinnamon Works – all great choices for a quick snack.

SEATTLE AQUARIUM Map p64
☎ 206-386-4300; 1483 Alaskan Way at Pier 59; adult/child $15/10; 🕙 9:30am-5pm
Probably the most interesting site in the Waterfront area, this well-designed aquarium offers a view into the underwater world of Puget Sound and the Pacific Northwest coast. In 2007 the pilings that support the building were found to be rotten, so they were replaced and the aquarium added a café, gift shop and two new exhibits. 'Window on Washington Waters' is a look at the sea floor of the Neah Bay area, where rockfish, salmon, sea anemones and more than 100 other fish and invertebrate species live. 'Crashing Waves' uses a wave tank to show how marine plants and animals cope with the forceful tides near shore.

Other exhibits include re-creations of ecosystems in Elliott Bay, Puget Sound and the Pacific Ocean, including tide pools, eelgrass beds, coral reefs and the sea

top picks

YOU KNOW: FOR KIDS!

Children will enjoy accompanying their parents on many of the activities described in this book, but a few places are keyed specifically to the short-pants set. Here are some of the best:

- Children's Museum (p74) in Seattle Center.
- Children's Park (p61) in the International District.
- Experience Music Project (p72) in Seattle Center.
- Odyssey Maritime Discovery Center (opposite) and Seattle Aquarium (above).
- Pacific Science Center (p74) in Seattle Center.
- Burke Museum (p84) in the U District.
- Alki Beach (p105) in West Seattle.

floor. The centerpiece of the aquarium is a glass-domed room where sharks, octopi and other deepwater denizens lurk in the shadowy depths. The passages eventually lead outdoors to a salmon ladder and a pool where playful sea otters and northern fur and harbor seals await your attention. Combination tickets with Argosy Tours are available at each site in different combinations. If you're tired of lugging all your Waterfront purchases around, you can rent a locker at the aquarium for 50 cents.

ODYSSEY MARITIME DISCOVERY CENTER Map p64

☎ 206-374-4000; www.ody.org; 2205 Alaskan Way at Pier 66; adult/senior/child $7/5/2; ⊗ 10am-3pm Tue-Thu, 10am-4pm Fri, 11am-5pm Sat & Sun

This unique museum in Waterfront Park is part of the Bell Street Pier, a huge complex that also houses convention space, restaurants and a marina. A haven for boat enthusiasts, the Discovery Center is also a wonderful place for families. The four galleries and more than 40 hands-on exhibits include a simulated kayak trip around Puget Sound, a chance to navigate a virtual ship through Elliott Bay and a visual recreation of the cruise up the Inside Passage to southeast Alaska. You can find out about boat construction and high-tech contributions to boating, learn about oceanography and environmental issues and hear audio simulations of ocean animals. One section of the museum is devoted to fishing and another to ocean trade. Anyone with a nose for the nautical should check this place out.

VICTOR STEINBRUECK PARK Map p64

Western Ave & Virginia St

When you've had enough of the market and its crowds, wander out the end of the North Arcade and cross Western Ave to Victor Steinbrueck Park, a grassy area designed in 1982 by Steinbrueck and Richard Haag. You'll find benches, a couple of totem poles designed by Quinault tribe member Marvin Oliver, a few shuffling vagrants and great views over the Waterfront and Elliott Bay. Rallies and political demonstrations are often held here.

BELLTOWN

Drinking p141, Eating p128, Shopping p114, Sleeping p178

Belltown is a textbook illustration of the progress of the urban ecosystem. A featureless area of warehouses and low-slung office buildings, this formerly scruffy and edgy-in-a-bad-way neighborhood was dismissed by many in the 1970s. But one of city planning's greatest mysteries is the way seedy, low-rent neighborhoods tend to be spawning grounds for raw musical and artistic talent – and so become cool, then gradually more expensive, and then 'ruined' by the influx of cash-slinging yuppies. Eventually, the cachet wears off and the neighborhood settles into a comfortable balance between the funky, artsy people who made it cool in the first place and the new crowd of condo-buying salary earners who keep the chic restaurants and boutiques in business, thereby drawing visitors. This is the stage Belltown seems to have settled into.

The area is also sometimes referred to as the Denny Regrade, for the massive sluicing project that reduced what was Denny Hill to a more convenient flat grade, intended to open up Belltown for a business explosion and rapid economic growth. It didn't exactly work; the area languished for years. Yet this allowed underground musicians and artists to move in and become part of an explosion of creative ferment that catapulted Seattle to international noteworthiness in the early 1990s: the grit and grime of Belltown were crucial ingredients in grunge music.

After that, the area went seriously upscale, making Belltown one of the hottest neighborhoods for new clubs and restaurants and a couple of chic hotels. These days, that vibe has calmed down somewhat, and the string of bars along Belltown's main drag has instead been discovered by Seattle's young mainstream, the post-college, ex-fratboy party crowd. One or two grubby punk dives still dot the neighborhood though, as well as grunge-era landmarks like the Crocodile Café (p153).

Meanwhile, warehouses are being converted to lofts and designer boutiques are now common. You're as likely to see businesspeople in suits as you are itinerant artists with nose rings. Many locals thought this neighborhood was 'over' a few years back. But the tenacity of places such as Shorty's (p142), Singles Going Steady (p114) and the Crocodile Café (p70), and the air of excitement among the people crowding the streets, restaurants and clubs every night, indicate that reports of Belltown's death have been exaggerated.

Belltown is long on entertainment but relatively short on tourist attractions – at least until recently. The neighborhood is now home to the Seattle Art Museum's ambitious new Olympic Sculpture Park, an outdoor sculpture and botanical garden that anchors the neighborhood and should serve as a major draw for visitors.

ART IN THE PARK

The eagle has landed. Or maybe it's about to take off. Hard to say, but it's certainly impossible to ignore. The 'Eagle,' of course, is Alexander Calder's 39ft-tall red steel creation from 1971 and it happens to be the crowning jewel of the Seattle Art Museum's new Olympic Sculpture Park. The thing probably weighs about a ton, but from where it's positioned, it looks like it's about to launch itself off the top of the hill and into the distant mountains.

The sculpture park is an excellent lesson in how to make the most out of limited urban space. Its Z shape slinks back and forth between Belltown, busy Elliott Ave, and the edge of the bay, rescuing three parcels of land and filling them with art and plant life.

Starting from the bottom, Tony Smith's *Wandering Rocks* zigzag up the hill in the Ketcham Families Grove, described on signage as 'a deciduous forest of quaking aspen' – well, eventually. It's sort of in the sprout stage now, but still pretty. More than 20 large pieces of sculpture dot the landscape, including the inevitable traffic hazard that is Claes Oldenburg and Coosje van Bruggen's *Typewriter Eraser, Scale X*, with its weird blue sprouts bristling over Elliott Ave.

The glass building at the top of the park contains a small café, restrooms and some hanging net sculptures that kids can climb into and play in.

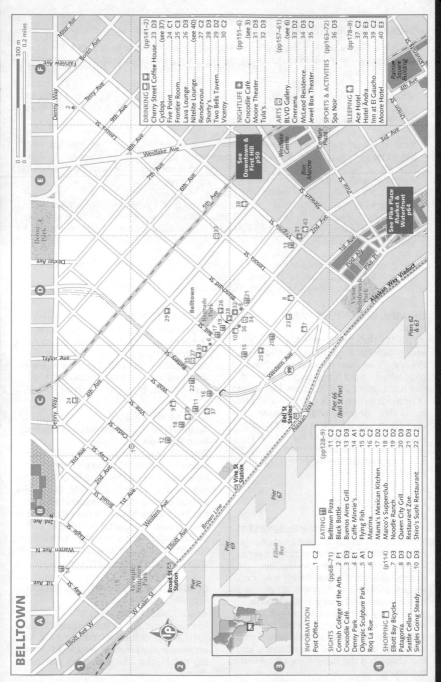

BELLTOWN

300 m
0.2 miles

DRINKING 🍸🍺 (pp141–2)
Cherry Street Coffee House...23 D3
Cyclops.................................24 C1
Five Point............................(see 37)
Frontier Room......................25 C3
Lava Lounge.........................26 D3
Nitelite Lounge...................(see 40)
Rendezvous..........................27 C2
Shorty's................................28 D3
Two Bells Tavern................29 D2
Viceroy.................................30 C2

NIGHTLIFE ⭐ (pp151–6)
Crocodile Café...................(see 3)
Moore Theater.....................31 D3
Tula's....................................32 D3

ARTS 🎭 (pp157–61)
BLVD Gallery.......................33 D2
Cinerama..............................34 D3
McLeod Residence..............35 C2
Jewel Box Theater...............36 D3

SPORTS & ACTIVITIES (pp163–72)
Spa Noir..............................36 D3

SLEEPING 🛏 (pp178–9)
Ace Hotel.............................37 C2
Hotel Ándra.........................38 E3
Inn at El Gaucho.................39 C2
Moore Hotel........................40 E3

INFORMATION
Post Office.............................1 C2

SIGHTS (pp68–71)
Cornish College of the Arts....2 F1
Crocodile Café.......................3 D3
Denny Park.............................4 E1
Olympic Sculpture Park.........5 A1
Roq La Rue.............................6 C2

SHOPPING 🛍 (p114)
Elliott Bay Bicycles................7 D3
Patagonia...............................8 D3
Seattle Cellars.......................9 C2
Singles Going Steady...........10 D3

EATING 🍴 (pp128–9)
Belltown Pizza......................11 C2
Black Bottle..........................12 C2
Buenos Aires Grill................13 D3
Caffe Minnie's......................14 A1
Flying Fish............................15 C3
Macrina.................................16 C3
Mama's Mexican Kitchen......17 D2
Marco's Supperclub.............18 D2
Noodle Ranch......................19 D2
Queen City Grill...................20 D3
Restaurant Zoe.....................21 D3
Shiro's Sushi Restaurant......22 C2

See Downtown & First Hill p50

See Pike Place Market & Waterfront p64

SCULPTING THE FUTURE *Cara Egan*

Cara Egan has lived in Seattle for nine years and worked as communications manager at the Seattle Art Museum's Olympic Sculpture Park (below) for six years. 'It was great to be part of it from the beginning concept to its reality in January 2007,' she says.

What's your favorite thing about the park? It embodies everything that is great about Seattle. This is a park with a setting like no other; views of the Olympic Mountains and Mt Rainier, a path and beach that connect with Elliott Bay, a vibrant urban setting that is integrated with art and landscape.

Best thing about your neighborhood? I live in West Seattle and I love the fact that it feels like you are far away from the city but only a 10-minute drive to downtown. Lincoln Park is great for hiking and picnicking. Alki Beach has some great little seafood restaurants and amazing views of the islands and the skyline. It's the Seattle equivalent to Venice Beach.

What season do you like best here? Summer is my favorite season in Seattle. Seattleites love the outdoors year-round but during the summer everyone literally lives outside soaking up the sun. I love to kayak, bike, garden and shop. I love to go to Fremont, Ballard and Wallingford and discover independent book and record stores, boutiques, coffee shops and restaurants.

Have you had any only-in-Seattle moments? Kayaking in Lake Union at twilight, among all the houseboats and float planes, with the Space Needle overhead.

OLYMPIC SCULPTURE PARK
Map p69

☎ 206-654-3100; 2901 Western Ave; admission free; ⏰ 6am-9pm May-Sep, 7am-6pm Oct-Apr
Hovering over train tracks in an unlikely oasis between the water and busy Elliott Ave is the brand-new, 8.5-acre, $85 million Olympic Sculpture Park. Worth a visit just for its views of the Olympic Mountains over Elliott Bay, it's still in that awkward youthful phase – many of the planned vegetation has yet to fill in, etc – but it has a lot of potential. See the boxed text p68 for more.

CROCODILE CAFÉ
Map p69

☎ 206-441-5611; 2200 2nd Ave; admission $5-15
This club is a landmark of '90s rock and its stage has showcased virtually every important Seattle band during the grunge years and since. Bands it hosted included, of course, Nirvana. It has become one of the best rock clubs in the country and the ever-present lines of people waiting to get to the bar are a who's who of Seattle's music scene; and if you get bored of looking at them, you can check out the indie-rock art tacked to the walls.

DENNY PARK Map p69
This park was originally designated as a cemetery – but that status ended up being rather temporary, and the land was re-dedicated as parkland. The park was later flattened in the Denny Regrade of 1910, over protests by preservationists.

ROQ LA RUE Map p69
☎ 206-374-8977; 2312 2nd Ave; ⏰ 1-6pm Wed, Thu & Sat, 1-7pm Fri
This Belltown gallery has secured its reputation by taking risks: the work on view here skates along the edge of urban pop-culture. Since opening in 1998, the gallery, owned and curated by Kirsten Anderson, has been a significant force in the Pop Surrealism field, frequently featured in *Juxtapoz* magazine. It also has an entertaining blog about the undercurrents of Northwest art, at thataintart.blogspot.com.

CORNISH COLLEGE OF THE ARTS
Map p69

☎ 800-726-2787; 1000 Lenora St
The south campus of the ornamental Cornish College of the Arts, built in 1921, has survived many bouts of debt and is now a top-notch school for music, art, dance and drama.

THE BELLTOWN HUSTLE
Walking Tour

1 Two Bells Tavern Start the tour by fueling up with an enormous Swiss-mushroom burger at the Two Bells Tavern (p142) on 4th Ave between Bell and Battery Sts. If the weather's nice, have your burger and a beer in the garden out back; otherwise, enjoy the conviviality of the main room, full of people who all seem to know and like each other.

2 Crocodile Café Wander down 4th Ave toward Blanchard St. Take a right on Blanchard and walk down to 2nd Ave. On the corner of 2nd Ave at Blanchard St, you'll see the snake-skin-green sign of the Crocodile Café (p153), one of the best rock clubs in the country and a key venue in the rise of the grunge movement. Many an up-and-coming band has rocked the crowd here. During the day it's a decent greasy-spoon café. Check its windows for upcoming shows.

3 Shorty's Next to the Crocodile is Tula's, a great local jazz venue. If that sounds good, stop in and hear some of Seattle's best-kept secrets. If you're after more active pursuits and you're thirsty, keep walking. Right in the middle of the block, you'll find Shorty's (p142), otherwise known as pinball heaven. Grab a cheap beer or a slushy blue cocktail and head straight to the back room to test your reflexes.

4 Lava Lounge When the pinball wears you out or simply beats you into submission, hop next door to the Lava Lounge (p142), another groovy nightspot. Its comfy wooden booths and tiki décor will soothe your battered ego.

5 Singles Going Steady On your way out, peek across the street at Singles Going Steady (p114), an excellent punk-rock record store.

6 Rendezvous Continue on past legendary nosh spots the Noodle Ranch and Mama's Mexican Kitchen. In the next block is Rendez-vous (p142), a classy place with a curvilinear bar and an adorable, recently gussied-up jewel-box theater in the back. Head back a block,

WALK FACTS

Start Two Bells Tavern
End Cyclops
Distance 1 mile
Duration One hour to whole evening
Fuel stops Noodle Ranch & Mama's Mexican Kitchen

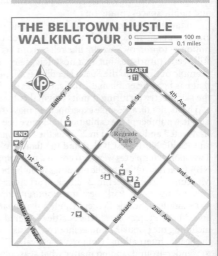

THE BELLTOWN HUSTLE WALKING TOUR

then up Bell St toward 3rd Ave to Regrade Park, where you'll usually find an unfortunate lot enjoying brown-bag beverages.

7 Frontier Room Walk back down Bell St to 1st Ave: you'll see the gloriously flashing neon sign of the Frontier Room (p142), a perfect symbol of Belltown's evolution – formerly a no-frills whiskey joint where you stood at the bar and didn't ask too many questions, it now seems to be an obnoxious fratboy hangout. Still looks great, though.

8 Cyclops Head toward the corner of 1st Ave and Wall St, where you'll find Cyclops (2421 1st Ave), half restaurant, half bar and a prime location for observing the street's late-night dramas. If you're lucky enough to be staying at the Ace Hotel (p179), you can chill at the Cyclops until your eyes match the bleary, bloodshot one hanging over the door, then stumble upstairs and fall into bed. End of tour.

SEATTLE CENTER

Drinking p143, Eating p129, Shopping p114, Sleeping p179

In the early 1960s, Seattle was confident and ready for company. And the 1962 World's Fair gave the city the perfect opportunity to display its self-assured, high-tech vision of itself and of the future. The fair, also known as 'Century 21 Exposition,' was a summer-long exhibition that brought in nearly 10 million visitors from around the world. A 74-acre warehouse area north of downtown was leveled; a futuristic international enclave of exhibition halls, arenas and public spaces sprang up.

Today, that 74-acre site has been set aside as the Seattle Center, a mecca for museums, entertainment and cultural venues. Varnished by time, the place now evokes a distinctly 1960s notion of tomorrow's world; like relics from World's Fair expos everywhere, the buildings here still seem 'futuristic,' but in a nostalgic, science-fiction, *Jetsons*-esque way. There's no better example of this than the Space Needle (below), the 520ft-high observation tower and restaurant that has become emblematic of Seattle. If you think it looks otherworldly now, spiking out of the skyline, try picturing it in its original color of bright orange.

The monorail, a 1½-mile experiment in mass transit, was another signature piece of the 1962 fair. Like it, a number of the exhibition halls have been adapted for civic use, such as the Opera House (renovated and reopened in 2003 as the Marion Oliver McCaw Hall, home of the Seattle Opera and Pacific Northwest Ballet) and the Bagley Wright, Intiman and Seattle Children's Theaters. Two sports complexes were also created, including the Key Arena, home of the Seattle Supersonics NBA franchise. Other public buildings include the Pacific Science Center and the Seattle Children's Museum. Various other museums and art spaces are also remnants of the World's Fair. The Fun Forest Amusement Park, near the monorail stop, is replete with carnival rides.

Additions to Seattle Center include a skateboard park, a public basketball court and the Experience Music Project (below). The Seattle Center also hosts many of the city's major annual events, including the popular Bumbershoot (p18) music festival, the Northwest Folklife Festival (p17) and the Seattle International Children's Festival (p17). On a nice day, Seattle Center is a pleasant place to wander around, and no matter what season you're here, there's always a lot going on.

The unofficial fun center of Seattle, this area is ground zero for good times, especially if you're a kid or are traveling with any. The most entertaining way to get back and forth to Seattle Center is by monorail (automatically fun). This service provides frequent transportation between downtown's Westlake Center, at Pine St and 4th Ave, and Seattle Center; cars run about every 10 minutes. Seattle Center contains more museums and attractions per square foot than probably any other part of the city. Smart visitors will pack a lunch or snacks, as the food available here can be of the overpriced carnival type.

SPACE NEEDLE Map p73

☎ 206-905-2100; www.spaceneedle.com; adult /senior/child $16/14/8; ☯ 9am-midnight
Seattle's signature monument, the Space Needle (originally called 'The Space Cage') was designed by Victor Steinbrueck and John Graham Jr, reportedly based on the napkin scribblings of World's Fair organizer Eddie Carlson. The part that's visible above ground weighs an astounding 3700 tons. The tower takes advantage of its 520ft-high observation deck – offering 360° views of Seattle and surrounding areas – to bombard visitors with historical information and interpretive displays. On clear days, zip to the top on the elevators (43 seconds) for excellent views of downtown, Lake Union, Mt Rainier and the Olympic Range mountains way across Puget Sound; don't bother spending

the cash on cloudy days. If you're coming up to take aerial photos, be forewarned that there's fencing around the observation deck's perimeter, making clear shots impossible. Its revolving restaurant, Sky City (p129), is, in line with the views, astronomically expensive. Reservations in the dining room do, however, give you a free ride up the elevator.

EXPERIENCE MUSIC PROJECT Map p73

EMP; ☎ 206-367-5483; www.emplive.com; 325 5th Ave N; adult/student & senior/child $19.95/15.95/14.95; ☯ 9am-6pm Sun-Thu, 9am-9pm Fri & Sat Jun-Aug; 10am-5pm Sun-Thu, 10am-9pm Fri & Sat Dec-Feb
The Experience Music Project (EMP) is worth a look for the architecture alone; whether it's worth the admission price is

SEATTLE CENTER

another story. The shimmering, abstract building – designed by Frank O Gehry – was inspired by Microsoft cofounder Paul Allen's passion for Jimi Hendrix's music and was initially intended as a tribute to Hendrix alone. It now houses 80,000 music artifacts, including handwritten lyrics by Nirvana's Kurt Cobain and a Fender Stratocaster that Hendrix demolished. There's also Janis Joplin's pink feather boa, the world's first steel guitar and Hendrix's signed contract to play at Woodstock.

Appropriately, the best exhibits are the Hendrix Gallery, a major tribute to Jimi; the Northwest Passage, displaying everything from Ray Charles' debut album (recorded in Seattle) to Heart's stage apparel; and a long hallway that details the evolution of grunge. Upstairs is the Sound Lab, a futuristic studio that lets you lay down vocal tracks and play guitars, drums and keyboards. Kids will love it, as will anyone obsessed with Northwest music, but others may find themselves yawning. If you're on the fence about paying the $20 admission, the Sky Church theater, Revolutions bar and Turntable restaurant are accessible free of charge.

SCIENCE FICTION MUSEUM
Map p73

☎ 206-724-3428; www.sfhomeworld.org; 325 5th Ave N; adult/child $15/12; ⏰ 10am-8pm Jun-Aug, 10am-5pm Wed-Mon Dec-Feb, free 1st Thu each month 5-8pm

Barnacled onto the hull of the EMP is this nerd paradise, a collection of costumes, props and models from various sci-fi movies and TV shows. Highlights include the actual alien queen from the movie *Aliens* (1986) – never fear, she's behind Plexiglas in the cargo bay – and the only 3D model of the Death Star made for *Star Wars: Episode 4*. Lowlights include a bedraggled Twiki costume from the *Buck Rogers* TV series. Rare books and manuscripts – including Neal Stephenson's handwritten *Baroque Cycle,* stacked as tall as the ET figure next to it – lend the display credibility. But mostly it just makes you want to go rent *Blade Runner* again.

CHILDREN'S MUSEUM Map p73

☎ 206-441-1768; www.thechildrensmuseum
.org; 305 Harrison St; adult & child/grandparent
$7.50/6.50; ☺ museum 10am-5pm Mon-Fri, 10am-
6pm Sat & Sun

In the basement of Center House near the monorail stop, the Children's Museum is a learning center that offers a number of imaginative activities and displays, many focusing on cross-cultural awareness and hands-on art sessions. The play area includes a child-size neighborhood, a play center and an area dedicated to blowing soap bubbles. Also nearby is the Seattle Children's Theater (☎ 206-441-3322; www.sct.org), a separate entity with summer performances in the Charlotte Martin and Eve Alvord Theaters.

PACIFIC SCIENCE CENTER Map p73

☎ 206-443-2001; www.pacsci.org; 200 2nd Ave N;
adult/child 6-12/child 3-5 $11/8/6, Imax Theater &
Laserium with general admission $3 extra, without
general admission $8/7/6; ☺ 10am-6pm

This interactive museum of science and industry once housed the science pavilion of the World's Fair. Today, the center features virtual-reality exhibits, a tropical butterfly house, laser shows, holograms and other wonders of science, many with hands-on demonstrations. Also on the premises is the vaulted-screen Imax Theater (☎ 206-443-4629), a laserium and a planetarium.

INTERNATIONAL FOUNTAIN
Map p73

☎ 206-684-7200; 305 Harrison St; ☺ call for
light-show times

This is the place to be on sunny days. With 287 jets of water (recycled, of course) pumping in time to a computer-driven music system, the International Fountain at the heart of the Seattle Center is a great place to rest your feet or eat lunch on a warm day. On summer nights, there's a free light-and-music show.

Drinking p143, Eating p129, Shopping p114, Sleeping p179

Rising above Seattle Center, Queen Anne is an old neighborhood of majestic redbrick houses and apartment buildings, sweeping lawns manicured to perfection and gorgeous views of the city and Elliott Bay. It has some of the most prestigious addresses in Seattle and a generally quiet, dignified atmosphere – not quite stodgy, but not exactly Capitol Hill, either.

Queen Anne Hill was one of the original seven hills of Seattle. At 456ft, it's also the steepest and highest, rising precipitously above Elliott Bay and Lake Union. Named for the prominent Queen Anne-style houses first built on the neighborhood's lower slopes, the area attracted affluent folks looking for views of the city. But unlike the First Hill neighborhood, whose residents dripped with money when they got here, Queen Anne was open to new wealth, too. As such, when walking around, you'll see a mix of architectural styles reflecting the varying tastes and incomes of the neighborhood's first residents. Most of the original Queen Anne houses are gone or have been divided into duplexes and apartments to absorb the neighborhood's quickly growing population, but there are still plenty of fabulous historic homes to gawk at.

Spend a little time here and it will become clear that the Queen Anne neighborhood has two distinct sides – roughly speaking, the bluebloods live up top and the young urbanites down below. Funky Lower Queen Anne (or as it's more evocatively known, the Bottom of Queen Anne) flanks Seattle Center to the west and butts up against Belltown on the other side of Denny Way. This area has a pleasant, old-fashioned and lived-in quality despite its busy urban locale. The old redbrick apartment buildings house a generally youthful population that spends its time on Queen Anne Ave N between Mercer and W Harrison Sts.

Because of their proximity to Seattle Center, the bars and restaurants in Lower Queen Anne get quite a workout before and after home games at Key Arena or when there's a performance at the Opera House.

Upper Queen Anne, on top of the hill, has lots of pretty gingerbread houses, excellent views of the city and some great restaurants. This part of the neighborhood has a grownup vibe and sense of the establishment and old money. Public ordinances decree that no-one should sit or lie down on public sidewalks, so if you're thinking about it, make sure there's a bench between you and the curb. Laws like this, combined with Upper Queen Anne's position as something of a destination (you don't just stumble upon it), make the absence of panhandlers obvious. Upper Queen Anne is also quite a restaurant hub, especially for upscale Asian and Spanish food; it may sound a bit snooty, but the shops and restaurants are patrician without being too pretentious.

Other than to eat, the main reason to visit Upper Queen Anne is to check out the old mansions and spectacular views. Top to bottom, the whole neighborhood has a quaint feel, thanks to its well-preserved architecture and mostly small businesses.

GABLE HOUSE Map p76
1 W Highland Dr at Queen Anne Ave N
This 14-gabled house was built in 1905 by Harry Whitney Treat, a friend of William F 'Buffalo Bill' Cody. Treat also built the Golden Gardens Park (p100).

KERRY PARK Map p76
211 W Highland Dr
This is where to go if you want to get postcard-perfect photos of the Seattle skyline, Mt Rainier and the Space Needle. Kerry Park, along the stroll-friendly and prestigious Highland Drive, has one of the three best views in town (the others are from Gas Works Park near Wallingford and Duwamish Head in West Seattle). It's a magical vista, especially at night or sunset. Going a little further along W Highland Dr will take you to the lesser-known Betty Bowen Park, an excellent spot for views across Puget Sound to the Olympic Mountains. Across the way, check out Parsons Garden, a public garden that's especially popular for summer weddings.

QUEEN ANNE COUNTERBALANCE Map p76
Queen Anne Ave N, north of W Roy St
The streetcar that chugged up and down the steep grade along Queen Anne Ave started operating on overhead-wire electricity in 1900, but it still needed some help to manage the hill. So engineers

designed a system of counterweights – a 16-ton train that ran in a tunnel beneath the street would go up when the cable car went down and vice versa. The cable cars were retired in 1943, but the underground tunnels are still there.

TURRET HOUSE Map p76
W Halladay St & 6th Ave W
This adorable castle-like building, with gables and (appropriately enough) turrets galore, was once the home of the Love Israel Family, an ex-hippie commune turned religious cult. Love Family members were famous for huffing noxious gasses, refusing to cut their hair and believing they were each part of the body of Jesus Christ. At one point the Seattle clan numbered some 400 members in 15 houses in this area. The Turret House has since been converted to apartments.

LAKE UNION

Eating p130, Shopping p114, Sleeping p180

Lake Union isn't quite the neat-and-tidy neighborhood that's typical of the rest of Seattle. For one thing, it's mostly afloat; Lake Union is known for having the largest houseboat population in the US. The Y-shaped lake's waters lap up against the shores of many traditional neighborhoods, including Fremont, southern Wallingford, Eastlake and the eastern slopes of Queen Anne. What ties this area together is the number of restaurants, lodgings and recreational facilities clustered around the lake. Lake Union is also a transportation hub for flights by seaplane to the San Juan Islands (p189) or Victoria, BC (p195).

South Lake Union is perennially in the news, as its heretofore relatively undefined nature makes it deeply attractive to developers. It has mostly been left to its own devices, kind of a backyard neighborhood, full of unglamorous storefronts and low-income housing. Then came an effort to raze many of this area's small businesses and transform 61 acres of land into Seattle Commons park. The neighborhood – aka the people whose houses would've been squashed to make room for the park – voted down the plan in 1995 and '96. But the park initiative led to some interesting results. Microsoft cofounder Paul Allen wound up owning 11 acres here, and Allen's company, Vulcan, spent about $200 million buying up land bit by bit over the intervening years. Allen's vision, to be completed over the next 15 years, has already started taking shape. The plan calls for much of the land to be developed as a biotech research center and residential community, with 10 million sq ft of offices, apartments, condos, hotels, restaurants and shops. And new plans are in the works to extend streetcar service to the area, which is likely to radically alter the whole neighborhood in the next decade or so.

A couple of resources for being active and outdoorsy in Seattle can be found in Lake Union. The area is on the verge of undergoing radical change, with thousands of new jobs (mainly in biotech) coming in to the neighborhood and new public transit options planned. Stay alert!

CENTER FOR WOODEN BOATS Map p79

☎ 206-382-2628; www.cwb.org; 1010 Valley St; small sailboat weekday/weekend $20/30, large sailboat $30/45; rowboat weekday/weekend $15/25; beginner sailing course $330

If you have an interest in the history and craft of wooden boats, then you'll definitely want to visit the Center for Wooden Boats. This museum and enthusiast's center features vintage and replica boats, and offers sailing lessons and classes on sail repair and boat building; you can also rent sailboats and rowboats here (see p167).

REI

Map p79

☎ 206-323-8333; 222 Yale Ave N; ☺ 9am-9pm Mon-Sat, 10am-7pm Sun

As much an adventure as a shopping experience, this giant REI store has its own climbing wall. You can check out the rain proofing of various brands of gear by entering a special rainstorm shower; or road-test hiking boots on a simulated mountain trail. REI also rents various ski packages, climbing gear and camping equipment – call for daily and weekly rates.

LAKE UNION

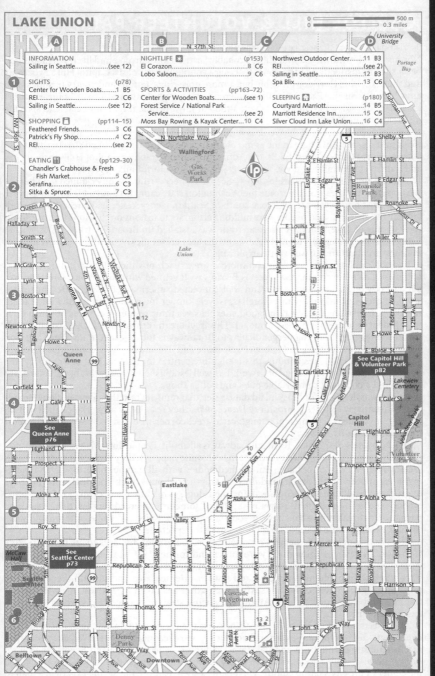

INFORMATION	
Sailing in Seattle	(see 12)

SIGHTS	(p78)
Center for Wooden Boats	1 B5
REI	2 C6
Sailing in Seattle	(see 12)

SHOPPING	(pp114–15)
Feathered Friends	3 C6
Patrick's Fly Shop	4 C2
REI	(see 2)

EATING	(pp129–30)
Chandler's Crabhouse & Fresh Fish Market	5 C5
Serafina	6 C3
Sitka & Spruce	7 C3

NIGHTLIFE	(p153)
El Corazon	8 C6
Lobo Saloon	9 C6

SPORTS & ACTIVITIES	(pp163–72)
Center for Wooden Boats	(see 1)
Forest Service / National Park Service	(see 2)
Moss Bay Rowing & Kayak Center	10 C4

Northwest Outdoor Center	11 B3
REI	(see 2)
Sailing in Seattle	12 B3
Spa Blix	13 C6

SLEEPING	(p180)
Courtyard Marriott	14 B5
Marriott Residence Inn	15 C5
Silver Cloud Inn Lake Union	16 C4

CAPITOL HILL & VOLUNTEER PARK

Drinking p144, Eating p131, Shopping p115, Sleeping p180

Northeast of downtown, Capitol Hill is probably Seattle's most diverse and lively neighborhood because of its distinctly edgy personality. Long a counterculture oasis, Capitol Hill's Broadway and the Pike–Pine Corridor probably boast more nose rings, tattoos and poetry readings than anywhere else in the Pacific Northwest. Trendy young students and urban homeless street kids share the sidewalks and café tables, although most people might not be able to spot the difference immediately.

East of Broadway, on 15th Ave E, is a more subdued commercial area. Some of the city's wealthiest residents live here in the grand old mansions along the tree-lined streets; this is also where some of the city's best B&Bs are. Add to these demographics Capitol Hill's thriving gay and lesbian community, and you have a very lively and colorful mix of residents.

When Capitol Hill was still thick forest, Seattle pioneer Arthur Denny claimed land here in the hope that the area would become the Washington state capital. Though his hope was never realized (that honor went to Olympia, south of Seattle), Henry Yesler had already set to work logging the area and soon people were building elaborate mansions on the slope that overlooks the east side of Lake Union. A streetcar route was installed up Broadway from Yesler Way to City Park, later renamed Volunteer Park, and the area grew quickly. Some fantastic vestiges of the early architecture are well worth exploring.

Capitol Hill boasts three major commercial areas, each of which attracts a different kind of crowd. The main commercial street is Broadway. It is lined with coffeehouses, restaurants, bars, trendy boutiques, bookstores and well-concealed supermarkets. Dilettante Chocolates (p115), decked out in pink with umbrellas, is well known for confection truffles and 'adult' milkshakes. All along Broadway are good, inexpensive ethnic restaurants, many of which cater to a student or long-haul traveler's budget. This is where the crowds are thickest and the vitality most engaging. Running perpendicular to Broadway is the so-called Pike–Pine Corridor. With most of the city's gay and lesbian bars, dance and live-music clubs, coffeehouses, record stores and fashionable restaurants, this is nightlife central for Seattle. East of Broadway, the quieter business district along 15th Ave E has well-established restaurants, book and record stores, and a couple of comfortable pubs and coffee shops.

As you wander, look for brass inlaid dance-step diagrams set into the sidewalk along Broadway – inventively called *The Broadway Dance Steps,* they're a public artwork designed by Jack Mackie. If you decide to attempt a tango on a street corner, you assuredly won't be the most unusual sight on Broadway.

In fact, a sense of spectacle is what Broadway is all about. People don't visit here for the food or the shopping (though you can indulge in both quite happily), they visit for the scene. You'll see any and every color of hair, semi-clothed bodies with all manner of tattooing and piercing, men in both business suits and dresses, gray-haired punk-rock grandmas carrying bags of groceries, and homeless people walking their dogs. While the chances are good that you'll be panhandled by street kids or get an eyeful of someone's pierced nipples, there's nothing particularly threatening about this in-your-face pageant. Suits and spikes intermingle with, usually, precious little tension. It's all just part of the spectacle.

Equally thronging with people, especially chic young nightlife seekers, is the Pike–Pine Corridor, a stretch of aging brick warehouses and former 1950s car dealerships. The 'Corridor' doesn't look like much in the daylight, but after dark the area becomes party central. This was once a predominantly gay- and lesbian-oriented area and it's still the location of most of the good queer clubs, but sexual orientation has taken a back seat lately to catwalk fashions and sleek concept bars. At any rate, being straight here certainly won't make you feel unwelcome.

There seem to be a few bars on every block, but there's more to do here than just drink and dance. Late-night coffeehouses feature live music, poetry readings or pool tables. Here and there are antique stores and more unusual shops, including Babeland (p115) and Beyond the Closet Bookstore (p115), with a good collection of gay, lesbian and transgender books. This area is also the center of the city's tattoo culture: what better way to capture the Seattle experience than to buy a double espresso and head into a body piercing salon?

The sense of urban disenfranchisement along 15th Ave E isn't nearly as strong as on Broadway and the crowds aren't as thick. Instead, with an organic grocery store and a couple of mellow bars as its anchors, 15th Ave feels like an ex-hippie enclave and a real, settled-in community. One of Seattle's favorite places for brunch and lunch, Coastal Kitchen (p131), is here.

It should come as no surprise that most of the things to see and do on Capitol Hill are rather artsy, whether they're galleries, museums, literary hangouts or music-related. This is also just a great neighborhood for wandering around and people-watching. The street theater can't be beaten.

SEATTLE ASIAN ART MUSEUM
Map p82

☎ 206-654-3100; www.seattleartmuseum.org; 1400 E Prospect St, Volunteer Park; adult/student & senior/child $5/3/free; ⏰ 10am-5pm Tue-Sun, 10am-9pm Thu

For almost 60 years the Seattle Art Museum occupied a prestigious Carl Gould–designed space in Volunteer Park. When it moved downtown in the early 1990s, the Seattle Asian Art Museum moved in. The museum now houses the extensive Asian art collection of Dr Richard Fuller, who donated this severe art moderne–style gallery to the city in 1932. Admission is free on the first Thursday and first Saturday of each month.

VOLUNTEER PARK CONSERVATORY
Map p82

☎ 206-684-4743; 1400 E Galer St; admission free; ⏰ 10am-7pm Jun-Aug, 10am-4pm Dec-Feb

The conservatory is a classic Victorian greenhouse built in 1912. Filled with palms, cacti and tropical plants, it features five galleries representing different world environments. Check out the creepy corpse flower.

JIMI HENDRIX STATUE Map p82
1600 Broadway

Guitar genius of the last century and Seattle's favorite son, Jimi Hendrix rocks out eternally in this bronze sculpture by local artist Daryl Smith, made in 1997. Hendrix fans have been known to leave flowers, candles and notes at the base of the kneeling statue.

RICHARD HUGO HOUSE Map p82
☎ 206-322-7030; 1634 11th Ave

Established in honor of famed Northwest poet Richard Hugo (see p159), this 1902 Victorian house, a former mortuary, is now the center of an active segment of Seattle's literary life. The house contains a library, conference room, theater and café with a small stage. It hosts readings and performances, writer-in-residence programs, reading groups and writing classes.

ST MARK'S CATHEDRAL Map p82
☎ 206-323-0300; 1245 10th Ave E, cnr 10th Ave E & E Galer St; performances ⏰ 9:30pm Sun

Go north on Broadway (as the chaos turns to well-maintained houses with manicured lawns) until it turns into 10th Ave E and you're within a block of Volunteer Park. At the neo-Byzantine St Mark's Cathedral, a choir performs Gregorian chants on Sundays, accompanied by a 3700-pipe Flentrop organ. The performance is free and open to the public.

LAKEVIEW CEMETERY Map p82

One of Seattle's oldest cemeteries and the final resting place of many early settlers, Lakeview Cemetery borders Volunteer Park to the north. Arthur Denny and his family, Doc and Catherine Maynard, Thomas Mercer and Henry Yesler are all interred here. This is also the gravesite of Princess Angeline, the daughter of Duwamish Chief Sealth, after whom Seattle was named.

Most people, however, stop by to see the grave site of martial arts film legends Bruce Lee and Brandon Lee. Flowers from fans are usually scattered around Brandon's red and Bruce's black tombstones, which stand side by side in a tiny part of the cemetery. The graves are not so easy to find: enter the cemetery at 15th Ave E and E Garfield St; follow the road in and turn left at the Terrace Hill Mausoleum. At the crest of the hill you'll see the large Denny family plot on your left. Look a little further along the road, and you'll find the Lees. Even if you're not usually into graveyards, you'll at least enjoy the beautiful views at this one.

LOUISA BOREN LOOKOUT Map p82
15th Ave E at Garfield St

Outside the Volunteer Park boundaries, the Louisa Boren Lookout provides one of the

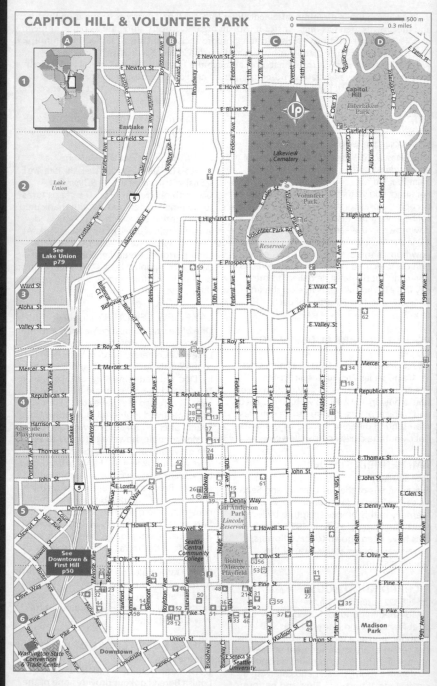

CAPITOL HILL & VOLUNTEER PARK

CAPITOL HILL & VOLUNTEER PARK

best views over the university and Union Bay. The small park is named after the longest-surviving member of the party that founded Seattle in 1851.

WATER TOWER OBSERVATION DECK
Map p82

1400 E Prospect St
Keen seekers of views can climb 107 steep steps to the top of Volunteer Park's 75ft water tower. Built in 1907, it provides wonderful vistas of the Space Needle and over Elliott Bay.

SEATTLE MUSEUM OF THE MYSTERIES Map p82

☎ 206-328-6499; 623 Broadway E; adult/child $3/2; ⊗ 11:30am-9pm Mon-Thu, 11:30am-midnight Fri & Sat, 1-8pm Sun
More a cache of obscure and alternative knowledge than a museum in the traditional sense, this odd but fascinating den in Capitol Hill has a number of treasures that reveal themselves to those with the patience to explore. It's kitschy, but it's fun. There's also an oxygen bar ($5 for a five-minute treatment).

U DISTRICT

Drinking p145, Eating p132, Shopping p116, Sleeping p181

The U District, named for the 'U Dub' (what locals call the University of Washington), feels like its own little college town. The streets are full of tiny, cheap eateries, thrift stores, record stores, second-hand bookshops, tattoo parlors and a couple of bars. Everyone on the sidewalks around here seems to be between the ages of 18 and 24. There used to be a thriving drug trade along the main drag (University Way NE, called 'the Ave'), which could make nighttime strolling unpleasant, but the city has cracked down and the number of down-and-outers has decreased dramatically.

The number of cheap places to eat, especially Indian and Asian, make the Ave the best place to find an inexpensive meal. Coffeehouses grow like weeds in this area and owners are used to students buying one coffee and sitting around for three hours. The absolutely cavernous University Bookstore (p116) takes up an entire city block. It has an excellent selection of general books and more scholarly tomes, along with a giant section of yellow and purple Huskies clothing.

At University Way and NE 50th St, the Grand Illusion Cinema (p160), an excellent though tiny theater, shows interestingly chosen programs of foreign and art films. The coffee shop next door is a popular place to have a latte and settle into a novel. At 25th Ave NE you'll find the University Village, an upscale, semi-outdoor mall geared more toward the parents of the UW students than the students themselves, with highbrow chains such as Anthropologie, Eddie Bauer and Pottery Barn. Along NE 45th St, east of the Ave, are some of UW's sorority and frat houses.

The University of Washington campus, sitting at the edge of this busy commercial area, is beautiful and lends itself to leisurely, tranquil walks. A campus-wide smoking ban took effect in February 2007 but there are designated smoking areas scattered around campus, including along walking trails and near park benches.

A great way to explore the campus is on a bicycle. The Burke-Gilman Trail follows the south side of campus, providing an excellent arterial for getting to and from the university.

The University of Washington campus is a pretty one, with a couple of excellent buildings worth checking out as well as one of the city's finest galleries and a great museum. The student population lends the area a youthful, unpretentious feeling.

HENRY ART GALLERY Map p85

☎ 206-543-2280; 15th Ave NE & NE 41st St on campus; adult/senior/student $10/6/free; Thu free; ☯ 11am-5pm Tue-Sun, 11am-8pm Thu

The university's sleek fine-art gallery mounts some of the most intelligent exhibits and installations in Seattle and serves as a touchstone for the arts community. There are dedicated spaces for video and digital art, and a small permanent collection, as well as rotating shows (35 a year). Part of the permanent collection is *Skyspace*, by James Turrell, an artist whose medium is light. Turrell's installation over the sculpture garden will alter the way you look at the ever-changing Seattle sky. If you pay $1 extra for a ticket here, you can get into the Burke Museum on the same day for free.

BURKE MUSEUM Map p85

☎ 206-543-5590; 16th Ave NE & NE 45th St; adult/senior/student $8/6.50/5, 1st Thu of month free; ☯ 10am-5pm, 1st Thu of month 10am-8pm

This museum of natural history and anthropology is located on the University of Washington's campus. There's a good collection of dinosaur skeletons, but the real treasures here are the North Coast Indian artifacts, especially the collection of cedar canoes and totem poles. On the ground level of the museum is the pleasant Museum Café (☎ 206-543-9854), a high-ceilinged, atmospheric place with warm pine paneling and wooden tables. The Burke/Henry Dollar Deal applies (see Henry Art Gallery, left).

UNIVERSITY OF WASHINGTON
Map p85

Visitors center ☎ 206-543-9198; 4014 University Way; ☯ 9am-5pm

Established in 1861, the University of Washington was first built downtown on the site of the present Fairmont Olympic Hotel. The university moved to its present location along Lake Washington's Union Bay in 1895. Much of the 639-acre site constituted the grounds of the 1909 Alaska-Yukon-Pacific Exposition. Dozens of new buildings were constructed for this World's Fair–like gathering.

U DISTRICT

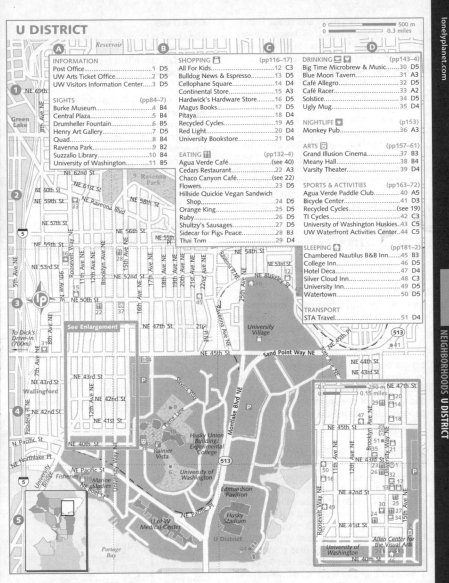

0 — 500 m
0 — 0.3 miles

INFORMATION	(pp116–17)
Post Office	1 D5
UW Arts Ticket Office	2 D5
UW Visitors Information Center	3 D5

SIGHTS	(pp84–7)
Burke Museum	4 B4
Central Plaza	5 B4
Drumheller Fountain	6 B5
Henry Art Gallery	7 D5
Quad	8 B4
Ravenna Park	9 B2
Suzzallo Library	10 B4
University of Washington	11 B5

SHOPPING 🛍	(pp116–17)
All For Kids	12 C3
Bulldog News & Espresso	13 A3
Cellophane Square	14 D4
Continental Store	15 A3
Hardwick's Hardware Store	16 D5
Magus Books	17 D5
Pitaya	18 D4
Recycled Cycles	19 A5
Red Light	20 D4
University Bookstore	21 D4

EATING 🍴	(pp132–4)
Agua Verde Café	(see 40)
Cedars Restaurant	22 A3
Chaco Canyon Café	(see 22)
Flowers	23 D5
Hillside Quickie Vegan Sandwich Shop	24 D5
Orange King	25 D5
Ruby	26 D5
Shultzy's Sausages	27 D5
Sidecar for Pigs Peace	28 B3
Thai Tom	29 D4

DRINKING 🍺 🎵	(pp143–4)
Big Time Microbrew & Music	30 D5
Blue Moon Tavern	31 A3
Café Allegro	32 D5
Café Racer	33 A2
Solstice	34 D5
Ugly Mug	35 D4

NIGHTLIFE 🎭	(p153)
Monkey Pub	36 A3

ARTS 🎨	(pp157–61)
Grand Illusion Cinema	37 B3
Meany Hall	38 B4
Varsity Theater	39 D4

SPORTS & ACTIVITIES	(pp163–72)
Agua Verde Paddle Club	40 A5
Bicycle Center	41 D3
Recycled Cycles	(see 19)
TI Cycles	42 C3
University of Washington Huskies	43 C5
UW Waterfront Activities Center	44 C5

SLEEPING 🛏	(pp181–2)
Chambered Nautilus B&B Inn	45 B3
College Inn	46 D5
Hotel Deca	47 D4
Silver Cloud Inn	48 C3
University Inn	49 D5
Watertown	50 D5

TRANSPORT	
STA Travel	51 D4

Today, the university is the largest in the Northwest, with around 35,000 students, 211 buildings and 4000 faculty members. Noted programs include law and medicine; it's also highly regarded for computer science and liberal arts. More than half of its students are in graduate programs. The university publishes its own paper, aptly named the *Daily*. In it, you'll find out about whatever's currently causing the angst around campus, details about campus events and U District classifieds.

The collective name given to all the U Dub sports teams is the Huskies. They compete in 25 intercollegiate sports, most notably basketball and football. Most teams play at Husky Stadium and the Edmundson Pavilion, both on the east side of campus. To find out about athletic events and tickets, call ☎ 206-543-2200.

The university's main arts venue is the 1200-seat Meany Hall. Live dance, theater and musical performances also take place at U Dub's other three theaters – the Penthouse, Playhouse and the Studio. For information and tickets, call or stop by the UW Arts Ticket Office (☎ 206-543-4880; cnr University Way NE & NE 40th St).

The university is a lovely, lively place; it is definitely worth touring, especially in spring when bulbs and azaleas paint the verdant campus with brilliant colors. Maps are available from the UW Visitors Information Center (☎ 206-543-9198; 4014 University Way NE). The center also offers free 90-minute campus tours that start at its offices at 10:30am weekdays.

SUZZALLO LIBRARY
Map p85

Those architecturally minded will be interested in the University of Washington's Suzzallo Library. Designed by Carl Gould around 1926, this bibliophile's dream was inspired by Henry Suzzallo, UW's president at the time. Suzzallo wanted it to look like a cathedral, because 'the library is the soul of the university.' Unfortunately for him, his bosses disagreed; on reviewing the building, they deemed it too expensive and fired Suzzallo for his extravagance. Gould was the founder of the university's architecture program; he created the plans for 18 campus buildings.

CENTRAL PLAZA (RED SQUARE) Map p85
The center of campus is more commonly referred to as Red Square because of its base of red brick. It's not the coziest, but it fills up with students cheerfully sunning themselves on nice days and it looks impressive at night. *Broken Obelisk,* the 26ft-high stainless-steel sculpture in the square, was made by noted color-field painter Barnett Newman. Just below Red Square is a wide promenade leading to lovely Rainier Vista, with spectacular views across Lake Washington to Mt Rainier.

DRUMHELLER FOUNTAIN
Map p85

Drumheller Fountain sits inside of what was originally known as Geyser Basin (now 'Frosh Pond'), one of the few remaining pieces leftover from the 1909 expo that beefed up the university.

QUAD Map p85
The Quad is home to many of the original campus buildings. When the ivy turns red in the fall, the effect is more reminiscent of New England than the Northwest.

RAVENNA PARK Map p85
Just north of the U District is Ravenna, a residential neighborhood that's home to a lot of professors and university staff. At its heart is Ravenna Park, a lush and wild park with two playgrounds on either side of the mystery-drenched ravine carved by Ravenna Creek.

U DISTRICT
Walking tour
1 Burke Museum Start this tour at the Burke Museum (p84), which you may choose to visit now (this will add at least an hour to the tour time) or simply note to check out later. Its collection of Northwest native art is definitely not to be missed. From here, walk along NE 45th St to Memorial Way – take a right and amble into campus through the university's north gate.

WALK FACTS

Start **Burke Museum**
End **Henry Art Gallery or the Ave**
Distance **2 miles**
Duration **One hour**
Fuel stops **Ruby, Flowers, Schultzy's Sausages**

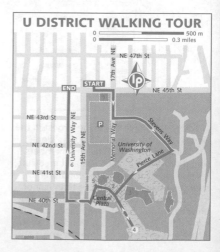

U DISTRICT WALKING TOUR

2 Central Plaza (Red Square) Stroll along Stevens Way to Pierce Lane which leads to the center of campus, Red Square (opposite).

3 Suzzallo Library From Red Square you'll see the gorgeous, cathedral-like Suzzallo Library (opposite). Admire it from the inside and out, then take a sharp left when you exit the library.

4 Drumheller Fountain Descend the stairs and walk straight ahead toward Drumheller Fountain (opposite), which spews out of the circular pool known as 'Frosh Pond.' On the way, along the pathway leading to the fountain, you'll be stunned (if it's a clear day) by the views from what is appropriately named Rainier Vista.

5 Henry Art Gallery Head back toward Red Square, and bear left at the library. This will lead you to the Henry Art Gallery (p84), one of the best galleries in Seattle. The café downstairs is a good place for coffee and a panini. Or press on to 'The Ave,' bustling University Way NE, where there's a string of affordable coffeeshops and ethnic restaurants to kick back in (see the Eating chapter, p132).

6 The Ave Wander up the Ave, peeking in shops and cafés along the way. The tour concludes when you reach the busy intersection with NE 45th St; this is the core of the U District.

FREMONT

Drinking p147, Eating p134, Shopping p117

Historically the most fun-loving of the northern neighborhoods, Fremont is known for its unorthodox public sculpture, junk stores, summer outdoor film festivals and general high spirits. In the evenings, the pubs, restaurants and coffeehouses fill with a lively mix of old hippies, young professionals and gregarious students. Except for the odd glitch, chain stores stay away from Fremont. Unlike the flashy urban disenfranchisement that gives Capitol Hill its spirit, life in Fremont is conducted with humor and a sense of community well-being. Fremont's motto 'De Libertas Quirkas' gives it the 'Freedom to be Peculiar,' and its residents happily live up to that proclamation. Though some of its quirks have been smoothed over recently by an influx of deep-pocketed real-estate investors, this district is still one of the more entertaining to visit.

Named by its first claim-holders after Fremont, Nebraska, the area was logged with the aid of oxen in the late 1890s. Once a working-class town, filled with employees of the Stimson shingle mill in Ballard, Fremont didn't really flourish until the building of the Fremont Bridge in 1916. The Hiram M Chittenden Locks opened a year later, allowing boat traffic to travel from the lakes to Puget Sound via the ship canal.

Fremont wasn't always cool and, like a child who lacks natural talent, had to work hard to get where it is. The completion of the high-flying Aurora Bridge (officially known as the George Washington Memorial Bridge, a fact unknown even to most Seattleites) in the 1930s meant people didn't need to come through Fremont anymore, which sent its commercial district into a sharp decline. Through the 1950s and '60s, Fremont experienced a tragic architectural blight, when many of the old mill-workers' houses were converted into cookie-cutter duplexes and cheaply built apartment buildings. Through the 1960s, Fremont had more vacant stores than occupied ones and it lacked neighborhood necessities, such as a grocery store or pharmacy. The low-rent buildings attracted a rather dowdy and rowdy bunch who didn't have much energy for making Fremont a better place.

In the 1970s things started to change. The first Fremont Fair danced its way along the neighborhood streets in 1972. The Fremont Public Association, today the envy of every neighborhood association, was created in 1974 to provide shelter, food and help to disadvantaged residents. The association did (and still does) wonders for Fremont, although it has recently changed its name to Solid Ground (www.fremontpublic.org). Its formation spawned a number of other thriving community associations, including the Fremont Arts Council (www.fremontartscouncil.org).

Public art, often wacky and unconventional, famously decorates neighborhood streets, and blatant eccentricity is encouraged. In 1994, Fremont citizens declared that they had seceded from Seattle, and the neighborhood was thenceforward the 'Republic of Fremont, Center of the Known Universe.'

Today, Fremont thrives economically, but it's got other problems. Like a teenager who suddenly becomes popular, everyone wants to hang out with it. Rents have skyrocketed here, stores and restaurants are pricier, and prime real estate is being sold to people who can afford it – generally not Fremont locals. The U-Park lot behind the former Redhook Brewery long held the infamous Fremont Almost-Free Outdoor Cinema, where movies played on a building wall and filmgoers brought couches from home, sat back in the parking lot and watched movies. That lot was bulldozed in 2001. The ever-expanding Lake Union Center, which houses software giant Adobe among others, brought more than 500,000 sq ft of office space to the once building-free Fremont waterfront.

One great Fremont must-do is the Fremont Fair (www.fremontfair.com), a colorful, musical and beer-filled event that takes place on the weekend nearest the summer solstice in June. The fair kicks off with the Solstice Parade, where human-powered floats traipse through the neighborhood in a lively tribute to quirkiness. Another annual event, Trolloween, features a candlelight procession of costumed locals on Halloween night (October 31), followed by a dance. Throw a costume on and join the fun. But be warned: don't even think about parking in Fremont during either of these events.

Fremont's changed a lot over the years, but it hasn't stopped thinking of itself as the center of the universe. And despite the influx of normality lately, the funky little corner of Seattle still has plenty going for it. Where else can you see dinosaurs, tour a chocolate factory, walk underneath a rocket and get your photo taken with Lenin, all in the space of a couple of blocks?

FREMONT SUNDAY MARKET Map p89

☎ 206-781-6776; www.fremontmarket.com; Stone Way & N 34th St; ⏰ 10am-5pm Sun Jun-Aug, 10am-4pm Sun Dec-Feb

Fremont is an especially great place to be during the Fremont Sunday Market, featuring fresh fruits and vegetables and an incredible variety of artists and people selling junk. In summer the market is held outdoors in the parking lot; in winter, it moves inside. Fremont's market has joined forces with its sister market in Ballard, which also runs every Sunday but is more a traditional farmers market.

FREMONT BRIDGE Map p89

Look across Fremont Ave N and you'll see the Fremont Bridge, not exactly a spectacular structure or piece of art, but interesting nonetheless. The bridge was built in 1916 when construction of the Washington Ship Canal sliced a gully between Fremont and the northern reaches of Queen Anne. The bridge went up, providing a vital link across the canal. It was painted industrial green – after all, this was long before Fremont became so colorful. When the revitalization of the neighborhood began in 1972, the bridge was to be repainted with the same shade of green. In the process, a coat of orange primer was painted on the bridge and a few people thought, 'Hey, that orange isn't bad!' Of course just as many people thought the orange was awful, but it won out and the bridge stayed orange until the mid-1980s, when it needed yet another repainting. The orange-haters were

NEIGHBORHOODS FREMONT

still adamant and the decision about what color to repaint the bridge was put to a vote. Orange wasn't even on the ballot, and an acceptable shade of blue won. But the orange-lovers were still adamant and a group of Fremont rebels went out in the middle of the night and painted orange accents on the blue bridge. This orange-and-blue combination stuck and is now the official color scheme every time the bridge gets repainted.

FREMONT ROCKET Map p89
Evanston Ave N off N 36th St
Fremont has adopted this phallic and zany-looking rocket as its community totem. Constructed in the 1950s for use in the Cold War, the rocket was plagued with difficulties and never actually went anywhere, leaving the engineering team with the unfortunate problem of 'not being able to get it up.' Before coming to Fremont, the rocket was affixed to an army surplus store in Belltown. When the store went out of business, the Fremont Business Association snapped it up. Beneath the rocket you'll find a coin box affixed to the building. Drop in 50 cents and the rocket will 'launch' by blowing a bunch of steam, but true to its under-performing nature, it won't go anywhere.

STATUE OF LENIN Map p89
N 36th St & Fremont Pl N
This is the latest and most controversial addition to Fremont's collection of public art. This bronze, 16ft statue of former communist leader Vladimir Lenin weighs 7 tons. It was brought to the USA from Slovakia by an American, Lewis Carpenter, who found the statue in a scrap pile after the 1989 revolution. Carpenter spent a

fortune to bring it over, sure that some crazy American would want to buy it. No-one did, so here it stands biding its time in Fremont, allegedly still on sale for $250,000.

WAITING FOR THE INTERURBAN
Map p89
N 34th St & Fremont Ave N
Seattle's most popular piece of public art, this lively sculpture in recycled aluminum depicts people waiting for a train that never comes. The train that once passed through Fremont stopped running in the 1930s, and the people of Seattle have been waiting for a new train – the Interurban – ever since. Finally, in 2001, Sound Transit trains started once again to connect Seattle with Everett, much like the original train did. The sculpture is prone to regular 'art attacks,' where locals lovingly decorate the people in outfits corresponding to a special event, the weather, someone's birthday, a Mariners win – whatever. Rarely do you see the sculpture 'undressed.' Take a look at the human-faced dog peeking out between the legs of the people. That face belongs to Armen Stepanian, one of the founders of today's Fremont and its excellent recycling system. Sculptor Richard Beyer and Stepanian had a disagreement about the design of the piece, which resulted in Beyer's spiteful yet humorous design of the dog's face.

THEO CHOCOLATE FACTORY Map p89
☎ 206-632-5100; www.theochocolate.com; 3400 Phinney Ave N; ⏰ 11am-5pm, tours 1 & 3pm daily plus 11am Sat; tour $5
What, perhaps you wonder, could possibly take the place of the free beer that came

---

ROCKETS, RUSSIANS & TROLLS, OH MY!

There's a good chance that one of the first things you'll hear about from any Seattle resident is the Fremont Troll. People get a little weird about the troll. Understandably, of course. It's an unlikely attraction to find in a city, or rather, it *would* be unlikely anywhere but in Fremont. But keep in mind, this is the corner of Seattle that's also home to topiary dinosaurs (see opposite), an inoperative rocket sticking out of a building (above), a statue of Lenin brought over from Slovakia and still available for purchase (above), and a statue of people waiting for a train that's never passed the spot (above). In that context, the Fremont Troll makes perfect sense.

The troll is easy enough to find; it lurks beneath the north end of the Aurora Bridge (not the Fremont Bridge) at N 36th St. It's an 18ft-high cement figure, made of 2 tons of ferro-concrete, and it's in the process of consuming a whole Volkswagen Beetle. The troll's creators – artists Steve Badanes, Will Martin, Donna Walter and Ross Whitehead – won a competition sponsored by the Fremont Arts Council in 1990. The team took seven weeks to complete the troll, whose menacing chrome eye keeps watch over Fremont.

at the end of a Redhood Brewery tour? How about free chocolate? That's right – the old Redhood Brewery that's been empty for years since the company moved operations to Woodinville, has reopened as a chocolate factory, and it does tours. Enough said.

DELUXE JUNK Map p89
☎ 206-634-2733; 3518 Fremont Pl N; ☯ 11:30am-5:30pm Wed-Mon
Stop in and look around one of Seattle's most kitschy secondhand shops. Located in a former funeral parlor, Deluxe Junk sells everything from retro sundresses and fluffy feather boas to home wares and furniture from the 1950s.

APATOSAURS Map p89
Along the banks of the ship canal, Fremont Canal Park extends west following the extension of the Burke-Gilman Trail. Right at the start of the park, at the bottom of Phinney Ave N, you'll see two giant, life-sized 'apatosaurs.' These are the world's largest known topiaries, given to Fremont by the Pacific Science Center.

HISTORY HOUSE Map p89
☎ 206-675-8875; 790 N 34th St; admission $1; ☯ noon-5pm Wed-Sun
The History House contains rotating exhibits focused on the history of Seattle neighborhoods. It's a good place to see photos of early Seattle. The building's colorful metal fence is another piece of public art, built by blacksmith and welder Christopher Pauley. The fence features brightly colored houses with open doors, a reflection of Fremont's welcoming attitude.

FUN IN FREMONT
Walking Tour
1 Fremont Rocket Exploring Fremont can take as much or as little time and energy as you want. Start the walk on Evanston Ave N between N 35th and N 36th Sts at the rather conspicuous Fremont Rocket (opposite), Fremont's community totem.

2 Vladimir Lenin Walk north (away from the water) up Evanston Ave N to N 36th St. Take a right onto Fremont Place N. On N 36th St at Fremont Place N, you'll see a controver-

sial addition to Fremont's collection of public art. It's a bronze, 16ft statue of former communist leader Vladimir Lenin (opposite) weighing 7 tons. Brought to the USA from Slovakia, it's for sale and still waiting for a buyer.

3 Deluxe Junk Walk half a block east along Fremont Place N. Stop at one of Seattle's most kitschy secondhand shops, Deluxe Junk (left), located in a former funeral parlor.

Continue east along Fremont Place N, cross Fremont Ave N and go east on N 35th St, which you'll follow to Aurora Ave N. You should now be underneath the Aurora Bridge. Turn left and head for the dark, shadowy space where the bridge meets the ground.

4 Fremont Troll Watch out! It's the Fremont Troll (opposite). This incredible piece of public art is a must-see for anyone interested in the peculiar things in life. He's an 18ft cement figure busily munching on a VW bug, a reference to the children's story of the Three Billy Goats Gruff.

Back away slowly, then head back down Aurora Ave N to N 34th St. Turn right.

WALK FACTS
Start Fremont Rocket
End Theo Chocolate Factory
Distance ¾ mile
Duration One hour
Fuel stops Triangle Lounge, Baguette Box

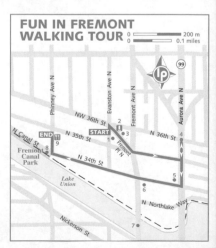

FUN IN FREMONT
WALKING TOUR

5 History House On your right, you'll see the colorful metal fence of the History House (p91). The fence features colored houses with open doors. Inside are exhibits about the history of Seattle neighborhoods.

6 Waiting for the Interurban Follow N 34th St west, toward the Fremont Bridge. Here you'll find Seattle's most popular piece of public art, Waiting for the Interurban (p90), showing people waiting for a train that never comes. Their clothes change regularly, as locals like to decorate them.

7 Fremont Bridge Continue west and look left down Fremont Ave N, and you'll see the Fremont Bridge (p89), with an orange-and-blue color scheme that seems to fit perfectly in this slightly wacky neighborhood.

8 Apatosaurs From the bridge, go west along N 34th St for two blocks until you get to Phinney Ave N. Along the banks of the ship canal, Fremont Canal Park extends west following the extension of the Burke-Gilman Trail. Right at the start of the park, at the bottom of Phinney Ave N, you'll see two giant, life-sized apatosaurs (p91), giant topiaries given to Fremont by the Pacific Science Center.

9 Theo Chocolate Factory Near the corner of Phinney Ave N and N 35th St is the building that used to house the Redhook Brewery and the Trolleyman Pub. The brewery has moved, and been replaced by the only thing that could possibly be better: a chocolate factory (p90). Which means it's time for you to get your sugar fix – officially the end of our tour.

Drinking p147, Eating p134, Shopping p117

Wallingford has blossomed from an old working-class neighborhood into a pleasant district of interesting shops, bookstores and inexpensive eateries, all just across the I-5 freeway from the University of Washington. The best thing about Wallingford is that it's not built upon a gimmick or tourist draw. This is as real as a neighborhood gets. The people who hang out here live here; you can still find an old-fashioned hardware store and a locals' pub among the espresso shops. Some excellent ethnic restaurants line N 45th St, along with some fun local bars and cool shops you don't want to miss.

Teahouse Kuan Yin (p147) is a great place to stop for a pot of exotic tea and a wireless internet session. Seattle's best travel bookstore is Wide World Books (p117). Another bookstore worth noting is Open Books (p117), which is devoted entirely to poetry; call to ask about readings and events. If you're not up for shopping, the Guild 45th St Theater (☎ 206-781-5755; 2115 N 45th St) shows mainstream movies as well as artsy flicks.

Wallingford is a quiet, mostly residential area, nice for a wander even though it doesn't have too many tourist attractions. The Burke-Gilman Trail comes through here near Gas Works Park, which itself is a great spot to hang out, watch kayakers go by and admire the Seattle skyline.

GAS WORKS PARK off Map p93
Meridian Ave at N Northlake Way

Urban reclamation has no greater monument in Seattle than Gas Works Park. The former power station here produced gas for heating and lighting from 1906 to 1956. The gas works was thereafter understandably considered an eyesore and an environmental menace. But the beautiful location of the park – with stellar views of downtown over Lake Union, sailboats and yachts sliding to and from the shipping canal – induced the city government to convert the former industrial site into a public park in 1975. Rather than tear down the factory, landscape architects preserved much of the old plant. Painted black and now highlighted with rather joyful graffiti, it looks like some odd remnant from a former civilization. It also makes a great location for shooting rock album covers and music videos.

The soil and groundwater beneath the park still contain chemical contamination. Though this apparently poses no health risks to humans, state government and environmental agencies occasionally close the park to complete various cleanup and research projects, primarily to avoid further contamination of Lake Union.

Despite its toxic history, this is still one of Seattle's best-loved parks. People come

WALLINGFORD

0 — 500 m
0 — 0.3 miles

INFORMATION		
45th St Community Clinic......1 B2		

SIGHTS	(pp93–4)
Wallingford Center.............2 C2	

SHOPPING	(pp117–18)
Bottleworks Inc................3 B2	
City Cellars.....................4 B2	

Comics Dungeon..................5 D2	
Erotic Bakery.....................6 D2	
Open Books.......................7 D2	
Wide World Books & Maps......8 B2	

EATING	(pp134–5)
Bizzarro...........................9 B2	
Boulangerie......................10 C2	
Kabul..............................11 C2	

Rancho Bravo Taco Cart.......12 D2	
Tilth...............................13 B2	

DRINKING	(p147)
Bungalow Wine Bar & Café....(see 7)	
Murphy's Pub....................14 C2	
Teahouse Kuan Yin.............15 C2	

ARTS	(p93)
Guild 45th St Theater..........16 C2	

here to fly kites, picnic near the lake, or simply to take in the view. And it *is* like nothing else you've ever seen. Be sure to climb the small hill in order to see the sun-dial at the top. This is notorious as one of the best places from which to photograph Seattle's skyline, especially at sunset when you can see the sun glistening in the windows of downtown buildings.

Before the trail was extended to Fremont and Ballard, the Burke-Gilman Trail started in Gas Works Park. This is still a great spot

to pick up the trail that you can then follow east to the University of Washington.

WALLINGFORD CENTER Map p93
Wallingford Ave N & N 45th St
This boutique and restaurant mall, inhabit-ing the nearly-condemned, refurbished old Wallingford grade school, is the hub of the area. Out front, the *Wallingford Animal Storm Sculpture,* created by artist Ronald Petty, depicts wildlife found in and around the neighborhood.

GREEN LAKE & PHINNEY RIDGE

Drinking p147, Eating p135, Shopping p118

Just north of Fremont and Wallingford and closely tied to both is Green Lake, a small natural lake that's the hub of a large park complex and a pleasant low-key neighborhood. The lake is packed with crowds in summer, but it's even better in fall, when the leaves are changing, or on a rare rain-free day in winter. Any time of the year, it's a great spot for a walk or a run or to sit back on a bench and watch the rowers on the water. People circling the lake seem pretty serious about getting their exercise – if you just show up for a stroll in your street clothes, you might get some funny looks.

If you want to get away from the lakefront crowds, the small but serviceable business district, just to the east along NE Ravenna Blvd, offers the requisite coffee shops and restaurants.

Below Green Lake, the Woodland Park Zoo is absolutely a must-see. And don't neglect to head further up to Phinney Ridge, the hilltop neighborhood north of the zoo along Phinney Ave N, as it also has some good pubs (p147) and restaurants (p135).

This is a tree-heavy, outdoorsy part of town, with its centerpiece, Green Lake Park, being the obvious favorite among local bodies of water circumnavigated by soccer moms, rollerbladers, joggers and babysitters.

GREEN LAKE PARK Map p95

One of the most popular spots in the city for recreationalists and sunbathers, scenic Green Lake Park surrounds Green Lake, a small natural lake created by a glacier during the last ice age. In the early 1900s, city planners lowered the lake's water level by 7ft, increasing the shoreline to preserve parkland around the lake. After the lowering, however, Ravenna Creek, which fed the lake, no longer flowed through. Green Lake became stagnant and filled with stinky green algae. Massive dredging efforts to keep Green Lake a lake (instead of a marshy wetland) continue. The lake is prone to algae blooms, which can cause an unpleasant condition

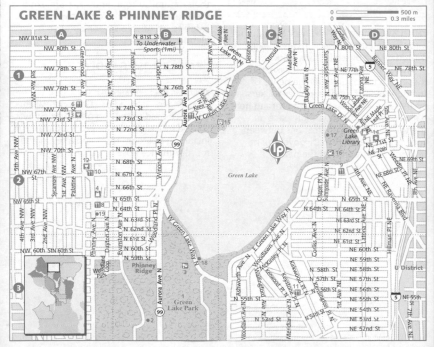

GREEN LAKE & PHINNEY RIDGE

GREEN LAKE & PHINNEY RIDGE

called 'swimmer's itch' to anyone venturing into the water. Warning signs are usually posted on the beach if this is a risk.

Two paths wind around the lake, but these aren't enough to fill the needs of the hundreds of joggers, power-walkers, cyclists and in-line skaters who throng here daily. In fact, competition for space on the trails has led to altercations between speeding athletes; the city government now regulates traffic on the paths.

Green Lake also has a soccer field, bowling green, baseball diamond, basketball and tennis courts, and boat, bike and in-line skate rentals. Two sandy swimming beaches line the north end of the lake, but on sunny days the entire shoreline is massed with gleaming pale bodies.

BATHHOUSE THEATER Map p95

The Bathhouse Theater, on the west side of the lake, is a 1928 bathing pavilion that was converted to a live-performance venue in 1970.

WOODLAND PARK ZOO
Map p95

☎ 206-684-4800; 5500 Phinney Ave N; adult/child $10.50/7.50 Oct-Apr, $15/10 May-Sep; ⏰ 9:30am-4pm Oct-Apr, 9:30am-6pm May-Sep; Ⓟ $4

In Woodland Park, up the hill from Green Lake Park, the Woodland Park Zoo is one of Seattle's greatest tourist attractions, consistently rated as one of the top 10 zoos in the country. It was one of the first in the nation to free animals from their restrictive cages in favor of ecosystem enclosures, where animals from similar environments share large spaces designed to replicate their natural surroundings. Feature exhibits include a tropical rain forest, two gorilla exhibits, an African savanna and an Asian elephant forest.

SEATTLE ROSE GARDEN
Map p95

admission free; ⏰ 7am-dusk

The 2.5-acre Seattle Rose Garden, near the entrance road to the zoo off N 50th St, was started in 1924 and contains 5000 plants, including heirloom roses and a test garden for All-America Rose selections.

Drinking p148, Eating p136, Shopping p118

Ballard, settled by Scandinavian fishermen in the early 20th century, at first feels like your average lutefisk-flavored blue-collar neighborhood. Once a seedy district where people spilled out of bars at 6am only to puke on the sidewalk and go back in, Ballard has learned how to hold its own. Unlike other former lowbrow-turned-fashionable neighborhoods, such as Belltown or Fremont, Ballard still attracts folks looking for no-nonsense venues, where they can eat a greasy breakfast, drink $3 beers and listen to good down-home folk or rock and roll. How long historic Ballard's well-guarded seediness lasts in the face of the current hipster invasion is anyone's guess.

Though just a bridge away, Ballard seems distant from urban Seattle. Settled principally by Swedes, Norwegians and Danes (incorporated in 1890 and annexed to Seattle in 1907), this area has long been a Scandinavian enclave. Early Nordic settlers came to work sawmills – Ballard held the Seattle area's largest – and to fish. These seafaring immigrants were instrumental in establishing greater Seattle's fishing fleet. Today, boats no longer leave Ballard to fish the high seas; they depart from Fishermen's Terminal (p99), just across the shipping canal.

Ballard still maintains a decidedly Nordic air, though only about a third of today's population is of Nordic descent. Along NW Market St, you can pop into Olsen's Scandinavian Foods and buy some fresh *lefsa* (potato pancakes), or shop for trinkets at Norse Imports. Most of the names on local businesses' signs are of Scandinavian origin, and many of the older folks on the streets and in the shops still speak with distinct accents, if they're not actually speaking their mother tongue.

The heart of old Ballard stretches along Ballard Ave NW, which seems to have hardly changed, at least architecturally, since the 1890s. Seven blocks here have been named a Historic Landmark District, but fortunately the buildings have not been thoughtlessly glamorized; the structures in this district are old, not 'olde.' Some are still hardware stores or meat markets, while others are brewpubs and bars. This is where you'll find Ballard's notable concentration of live music venues.

The 'Historic' designation helps protect Ballard from overcommercialization or other undesirable growth. Any proposed development has to be approved by a board of locals, and the locals are pretty picky about who they let in. Ballard is fun and casual; here you can let your proverbial hair down, do shots with a fisherman, eat cheap food, get a tattoo or sit in a bar and get drunk all day – in Ballard, you won't be the only one.

The Historic Landmark District along Ballard Ave NW extends seven blocks, starting from its intersection with Market St. Pick up a copy of the *Historic Ballard Ave Walking Tour* pamphlet for background on the buildings. The Ballard Historical Society (www.ballardhistory.org) also gives occasional tours.

Discovery Park is 534 acres of urban wilderness northwest of downtown Seattle and just southwest of the mouth of Chittenden Locks. Locals love to come here to escape the ever-present manicure of city gardens and get windswept along the park's many trails. Though it's easy to reach, it feels utterly remote. There are good walking trails, long beaches, picnic areas and a helpful visitors center.

The park was originally Fort Lawton, an army base established in 1897 to protect Seattle from unnamed enemies. Fort Lawton didn't see much activity until WWII, when it was used as barracks for troops bound for the Pacific. Over the course of the war it held up to 1400 German and Italian prisoners. When the fort was declared surplus property in the 1960s, the City of Seattle decided to turn it into a park (although significant areas of the park are still used for military housing). The fort was finally proclaimed public parkland in 1972.

For a map of the park's trail and road system, stop by the visitors center (☎ 206-386-4236; ◷ 8:30am-5:30pm) near the Government Way entrance. The park runs educational programs including Saturday nature walks, day camps for children and bird-watching tours.

BALLARD

NORDIC HERITAGE MUSEUM Map p98
☎ 206-789-5707; 3014 NW 67th St; adult/senior/child/child under 5 $6/5/4/free; ◷ 10am-4pm Tue-Sat, noon-4pm Sun

This museum preserves the history of the northern Europeans who settled in Ballard and the Pacific Northwest, as well as bringing in special exhibits of new work by contemporary Scandinavian artists. It's the only museum in the USA that

BALLARD & DISCOVERY PARK

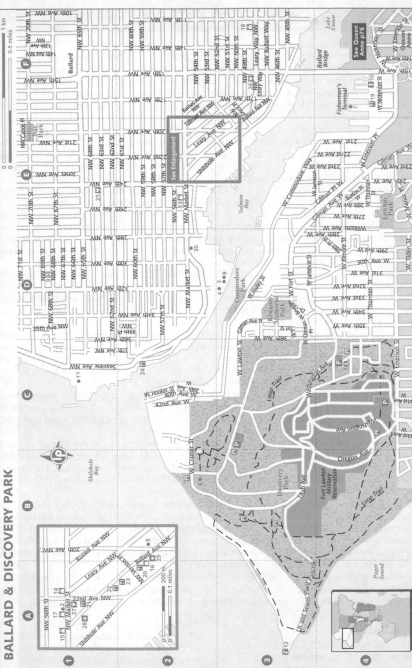

BALLARD & DISCOVERY PARK

commemorates the history of settlers from all five Scandinavian countries. A permanent exhibit, with one room for each country, features costumes, photographs and maritime equipment, while a second gallery is devoted to changing exhibitions. The museum also offers Scandinavian language instruction, lectures and films.

To get here, take bus 17 from downtown at 4th Ave and Union St, get off at 32nd Ave NW and walk one block east on NW 67th St.

HIRAM M CHITTENDEN LOCKS Map p98
Visitors center ☎ 206-783-7059; 3015 NW 54th St; ⏰ 24hr; 🚌 17 from downtown at 4th Ave & Union St
These locks, also known as the Ballard Locks, are about a half mile west of Ballard off NW Market St. Watching boats cross the two locks on the Lake Washington Ship Canal holds a strange attraction for locals and tourists alike. The process takes between 10 and 30 minutes, depending on tides and lake levels and on whether the large or the small lock is used. Walkways along the locks allow an intimate look at the workings of these water elevators and a chance to see the vessels coming and going from Puget Sound to Lakes Union and Washington.

BALLARD FISH LADDER Map p98
3015 NW 54th; ⏰ **ladder & gardens 7am-9pm, visitors center 10am-6pm**
On the southern side of the Hiram M Chittenden Locks, the fish ladder was built in 1976 to allow salmon to fight their way to spawning grounds in the Cascade headwaters of the Sammamish River, which feeds Lake Washington. Visitors can watch the fish from underwater glass-sided tanks or from above (there are nets to keep salmon from over-leaping and stranding themselves on the pavement). Sea lions munch on the salmon while the fish attempt to negotiate the ladder. Just what to do about the sea lions has stymied environmentalists, anglers and the local Fish & Wildlife Department. The best time to visit is during spawning season, from mid-June to September.

On the northern entrance to the lock area is the Carl English Jr Botanical Gardens, a charming arboretum and specimen garden. Trails wind through gardens filled with mature trees that are labeled and flower gardens.

Flanking the gardens is a small museum and visitors center documenting the history of the locks. Free tours are offered at 1pm and 3pm daily mid-May to mid-September, with an added tour of the locks at 11am on weekends. The rest of the year, tours are offered at 2pm Thursday to Monday.

FISHERMEN'S TERMINAL Map p98
19th Ave & W Nickerson St; 🚌 **15, 17 or 18**
Seattle's fishing fleet resides at Fishermen's Terminal, in a wide recess in the ship canal called Salmon Bay on the south side of the Ballard Bridge at 19th Ave and W Nickerson St. Fishermen's Terminal is a popular moorage spot because the facility is in freshwater, above the Chittenden Locks. Freshwater is much less corrosive to boats than saltwater.

It's great fun to wander the piers, watching crews unload their catch, clean boats and repair nets. Many of these fishing boats journey to Alaska in summer and return to dry dock while they wait out winter. Outdoor interpretive displays explain the history of Seattle's fishing fleet, starting with the native inhabitants who first fished

top picks

CHEAP FUN IN SEATTLE *BABYMONKEY*

Bar hopping
Pioneer Square (p55) in Downtown Seattle is the place to be. Paying a cover charge at one club will automatically get you in to all the others for free. Friday and Saturday nights are best, but Thursdays have great drink specials.

Quiet night out
One bus to the Seattle area of Fremont (p88) is all you need for a good night out any day. The main strip is littered with small clubs and bars, often with live music. A nice alternative to the large crowds of downtown.

Daytime fun
Gas Works Park (p92) by Lake Union is a great place. From the park you can see the skyline – especially beautiful at sunset – and watch the boats drift about on the lake. A great place for a picnic, flying a kite, or taking a romantic walk.

BLUELIST[1] **(blu list)** *v.*
to recommend a travel experience.
What's your recommendation? www.lonelyplanet.com/bluelist

these waters in canoes, to the Slavs and Greeks, who dominated salmon fishing in the early 1900s. A statue, the bronze Seattle Fishermen's Memorial at the base of the piers, commemorates Seattle fishers lost at sea. This memorial is also the site of the ceremonial blessing of the fleet, held annually on the first Sunday in May.

In the two terminal buildings are some good restaurants specializing in the freshest seafood in Seattle, a tobacconist, a ship chandler and a charts and nautical gifts store. Stop at the Wild Salmon Fish Market (p118) to buy the freshest pick of the day's catch.

CENTER ON CONTEMPORARY ART
Map p98

COCA; ☎ 206-728-1980; www.cocaseattle.org; 6413 Seaview Ave NW; ☽ Mon-Fri 10am-5pm, to midnight Thu; entry free
This gallery has been a force in Seattle's contemporary art scene for two decades. After moving around a lot, it has opened a new branch in Belltown (2721 1st Ave) as well as this primary space in the Shilshole Bay Beach Club.

BALLARD BUILDING Map p98
2208 NW Market St
Built in the 1920s by the Fraternal Order of Eagles, this imposing structure is the only major terra-cotta building in Ballard. It once held a community hospital and now houses the *Ballard News-Tribune* offices.

CORS & WEGENER BUILDING Map p98
5000-5004 20th Ave NW
Once a wine bar and the offices of the early local broadsheet, the *Ballard News*, this grand building was one of the first in the area to be revitalized. It's now mostly shops, apartments and office space.

GOLDEN GARDENS PARK Map p48
8498 Seaview Pl NW
Golden Gardens Park, established in 1904 by Harry W Treat, is a lovely 95-acre beach park with sandy beaches. There are picnic facilities, restrooms, basketball hoops, volleyball nets, gangs of Canadian geese, lots of parking and plenty of space to get away from all the activity. Rising above Golden Gardens is Sunset Hill Park (NW 77th St and 34th Ave), a prime perch for dramatic sunsets and long views.

SHILSHOLE BAY MARINA Map p98
Seaview Ave NW
The Shilshole Bay Marina, about 2 miles west of the locks along Seaview Ave, offers nice views across Puget Sound and, as Seattle's primary sailboat moorage, a glittery collection of boats. Inside the marina, you can rent sailboats or take classes at Windworks (☎ 206-784-9386; 7001 Seaview Ave NW).

DISCOVERY PARK

DAYBREAK STAR INDIAN CULTURAL CENTER Map p98
W Cramer St
In 1977, Native American groups laid claim to the land in this area, and 17 acres of parkland were decreed Native American land on which now stands the Daybreak Star Indian Cultural Center, a community center for Seattle-area Native Americans. Discovery Park has over 7 miles of hiking trails, several of which lead to the Daybreak Star Center. Except for a small art gallery, there are few facilities for outside visitors. The vista point in front of the center affords beautiful views of the Sound, and several

steep trails lead down through the forest to narrow, sandy beaches.

WEST POINT LIGHTHOUSE Map p98
About a mile off from the 3-mile paved loop that circles the park, a trail skirts the water's edge all the way to the still-functioning West Point Lighthouse. It's a great spot for panoramic views of the Sound and mountains to the west.

DISCOVERY PARK
Walking tour
1 Discovery Park visitors center Bring a picnic lunch, plenty of water and good walking shoes for this tour. You might also want to dress in layers and be prepared for rapid weather changes. Start the tour at the East Parking Lot of the Discovery Park visitors center (see p97), at the intersection of W Government Wy and 36th Ave W. Ask for a map at the visitors center's front desk.

2 West Point lighthouse As this is a loop tour (the main trail is called the Loop Trail, good to remember if you start to feel lost), you have several options. If it's a sunny day, don't miss the chance to see the West Point lighthouse (left) over Shilshole Bay. To get to it, head south when you leave the visitors center parking lot. This southern loop will take you past the South Parking Lot and onto the South Beach Trail. Follow signs to the lighthouse.

3 Daybreak Star Indian Cultural Center If you'd rather see the Daybreak Star Indian Cultural Center (opposite), start with the northern route on the Loop Trail. Aim for the North Parking Lot, then follow the paved road to the cultural center then return to the East Parking Lot or pick up the Loop Trail where you left it and head west.

From here simply complete the loop and head back to the visitors center, or branch off and see the lighthouse first.

> ### WALK FACTS
> **Start** Discovery Park Visitors Center
> **End** Daybreak Star Indian Cultural Center
> **Distance** Two to 11 miles
> **Duration** One to six hours
> **Fuel stops** Picnic

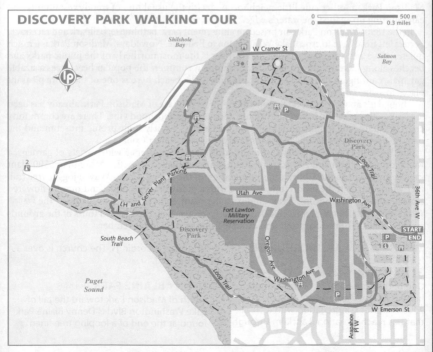

DISCOVERY PARK WALKING TOUR

0 — 500 m
0 — 0.3 miles

Shilshole Bay

W Cramer St

Salmon Bay

Discovery Park

Loop Trail

Utah Ave

Washington Ave

36th Ave W

LH and Server Plant Parking

Fort Lawton Military Reservation

Oregon Ave

South Beach Trail

Discovery Park

Loop Trail

Washington Ave

START END

Puget Sound

W Emerson St

Arapahoe PI W

NEIGHBORHOODS BALLARD & DISCOVERY PARK

lonelyplanet.com

101

CENTRAL DISTRICT, MADRONA & MADISON PARK

Eating p136

Running down the east slope of First Hill to the upscale neighborhoods that flank Lake Washington, the Central District – sometimes called 'the CD' – represents the heart of Seattle's African American community. Few blacks lived in Seattle until WWII, when they moved to the area in large numbers to work in the shipyards and contribute to the war effort. Today the CD is overrun with empty storefronts, which is ironic considering the high price of real estate in nearby Capitol Hill and First Hills. Despite the lack of a business buzz, the CD is a friendly place, where you can find some great soul food and barbecue joints and, more recently, an increasing number of Ethiopian restaurants (p136).

Madrona is one of Seattle's more ethnically diverse neighborhoods, blending elements of the CD's African American community to the west with the predominantly white neighborhoods that ring Lake Washington proper. Once a relatively unheard-of neighborhood, Madrona has been gentrified recently and now draws crowds from around the city, notably at one of the most popular brunch places in Seattle, the Hi Spot Café (p137).

If you follow Madison St from downtown (or take bus 11), you're following the old trolley line that once served the eastern side of Capitol Hill and the amusement park and beach at Madison Park. Today these tranquil neighborhoods are quietly upscale, home to little commercial hubs lined with understated shops and good restaurants. When it gets hot in the summer, locals make the pilgrimage to Lake Washington to sprawl out on the small sandy-grassy beaches. Just driving or cycling around is a good respite – the houses along Lake Washington Blvd boast old money or new corporate wealth.

The first neighborhood you come to is Madison Valley, where the biggest attractions are two notable restaurants: Rover's (p136), considered one of the best restaurants in Seattle, and Café Flora (p137), a vegetarian's dream restaurant. Continue toward Lake Washington to reach Madison Park, another cute little neighborhood with the usual hub of trendy restaurants and cafés butting up against the water's edge.

In the 1890s Madison Park comprised an amusement park, bathhouse, ballpark and racetrack. Ferries left from here to cross Lake Washington to Bellevue. Nowadays, Madison Park is a much quieter place and very genteel. The park proper is the most northerly of the public parks and beaches along Lake Washington's western shore. In summer, the popular beach sees a sizable gay male contingent mixed in with local families. The beach here is one of the more pleasant places to swim and sunbathe.

Though it's about to be severely gentrified – or, in the case of Madison Park, already has been for years – this area still has a comfortable, unfancy neighborhood vibe. There are community churches, barbecue joints and family parks, as well as a fairly high-profile museum and the park that serves as a pilgrimage site for fans of Nirvana's Kurt Cobain.

The Washington Park Arboretum is a wild and lovely park that offers a wide variety of gardens, a wetlands nature trail and 200 acres of mature forest threaded by paths. More than 5500 plant species grow within the arboretum's boundaries. In the spring Azalea Way, a jogger-free trail that winds through the arboretum, is lined with a giddy array of pink- and orange-flowered azaleas and rhododendrons. Trail guides to the plant collections are available at the Graham Visitors Center & Gift Shop (Map opposite; 2300 Arboretum Dr E; ☽ 10am-4pm). Free guided tours of the grounds are available at 1pm on Saturday and Sunday from January to November.

MOUNT ZION BAPTIST CHURCH
Map p103

☎ 206-322-6500; 1634 19th Ave at E Madison St
One of the cornerstones of this neighborhood is Mount Zion Baptist Church, a 2000-member congregation with a choir that has reached national acclaim through its gospel recordings. The church is over a century old.

DENNY BLAINE PARK Map p103

South of Madison Park toward the tail of Lake Washington Blvd is Denny Blaine Park, found at the end of a looping tree-lined

SEATTLE FROM THE SOUND

Seeing Seattle from the water is one of the best ways to fall in love with the city. A number of places rent kayaks and canoes (see p167), or you can arrange a guided tour through the Northwest Outdoor Center (p166), the University of Washington's Waterfront Activities Center (p167) or the Moss Bay Rowing Club (p166). The Center for Wooden Boats (p167) offers sailing lessons as well as sailboat rentals.

lane. This predominantly lesbian beach is surrounded by an old stone wall, which marked the shoreline before the lake level was dropped 9ft during construction of the ship canal. Just a little further south on your right-hand side, you'll find the two-tiered Viretta Park, from which you can see the mansion once owned by Nirvana's Kurt Cobain and Courtney Love (it's the house on the north, or left, side of the benches if you're facing the water). Cobain took his life with a shotgun in the mansion's greenhouse in April 1994. The greenhouse is long gone and Love no longer owns the house, but Nirvana fans still make the pilgrimage to this small park to pay tribute to the angst-ridden king of grunge, and scribble messages on the benches in the lower part of the park.

HOWELL PARK Map p103
Just south of Viretta Park is a small beachfront called Howell Park. It is usually less crowded due to the lack of parking. If you're on foot, look for a small sign and trailhead that leads to the beach.

COLMAN PARK Off Map p103
Continue south along the Lake Washington Blvd E through the very upscale Madrona Park neighborhood and you'll end up at Colman Park. The entire lakefront stretch between here and Seward Park is parkland. This is an especially good area for bike riding. On the weekends the boulevard is closed to cars.

MADRONA PARK BEACH Map p103
Madrona Park Beach, down from the business district in Madrona Park, is one of the nicest along the lake. In clear weather the

views of Mt Rainier are fantastic. Swimming is only for hardy souls, however, as the water's icy cold, even in summer. Further south, past the yacht moorage, is Leschi Park, a grassy green space with a children's play area.

MUSEUM OF HISTORY & INDUSTRY
Map p103
Mohai; ☎ 206-324-1126; 2700 24th Ave E; adult/senior & student $7/5; ☼ 10am-5pm Fri-Wed, 10am-8pm first Thu of month
This museum at the northwest corner of Washington Park Arboretum documents the history of Seattle and the Puget Sound in regard to its lumber, fishing and shipping industries. There's also a big Boeing presence, including a 1920s mail plane. Usually called by its acronym, Mohai has an entertaining collection of historic photos, old planes, memorabilia from the Great Fire and artifacts and lore from Seattle's great seafaring era.

JAPANESE GARDEN Map p103
☎ 206-684-4725; adult/senior & student $5/3; ☼ 10am-7 or 8pm Mar-Sep, 10am-dusk Oct-Mar
At the southern edge of Washington Park Arboretum, this 3½-acre formal garden has koi pools, waterfalls, a teahouse and manicured plantings. Granite for the garden's sculptures was laboriously dragged in from the Cascades. Tea ceremony demonstrations are frequently available. Call for a schedule.

FOSTER ISLAND WETLANDS TRAIL
Map p103
The northern edge of Washington Park Arboretum includes this wonderful trail around Foster Island in Lake Washington's Union Bay, a picnic spot that once was a burial ground for Union Bay Indians. The waterfront trail winds through marshlands and over floating bridges to smaller islands and reedy shoals. Bird-watching is popular here, as is swimming, fishing and kayaking (for kayak rentals, see p167). It's just too bad that the busy, elevated Hwy 520 roars above the island. The nature trail is best accessed from the Mohai parking lot (see above).

WEST SEATTLE

Drinking p148, Eating p138, Shopping p118

West Seattle is the nose of land across Elliott Bay to the west of downtown Seattle, beyond the Port of Seattle and Harbor Island. West Seattle hasn't succumbed to gentrification and still feels working class. Although access to downtown is good, it seems removed from the rest of the city. From here the views can be stellar, both of the city center and of the islands to the west.

Alki Point, the westernmost point of the peninsula, initially attracted the Denny party, who landed in the schooner *Exact* in 1851, establishing the village that would grow to become Seattle. Although the settlers only spent one winter here before moving across the bay to what is now Seattle proper, there's a monument to the pioneers on the beach. For some reason, there's a chip of Plymouth Rock embedded in its base.

The main reason to visit West Seattle, especially in good weather, is to go to Alki Beach Park. The sober and purposeful settlers who landed here wouldn't recognize the place today. This 2-mile stretch of sandy beach is a madhouse in summer. As if in imitation of southern California, the volleyball nets go up, sunbathing occupies the strand and teens in souped-up cars prowl the streets. It's Seattle's only real beach scene and the views of Seattle from Duwamish Head, at the northern end of the beach, are spectacular. The claustrophobic might want to avoid Alki on summer weekends, but good beachside cafés, quaint fish-and-chips joints, the miniature replica of the Statue of Liberty on the beach (currently removed for repair and replaced by a copy) and the Alki Point Lighthouse make this area a nice getaway most other times.

The main commercial strip on West Seattle is along California Ave SW, centering at the junction of SW Alaska St. There's nothing particularly compelling about the shops here, except that they seem at least a generation and 200 miles removed from the rest of Seattle. Old five-and-dime stores slumber next to old diners, neither having changed much since the 1950s.

If you're interested in a ferry ride, follow Fauntleroy Way SW down through West Seattle to Fauntleroy Ferry Terminal at Henderson St SW, south of Lincoln Park. Here you can take a half-hour ferry ride to Vashon Island, a semirural island that also serves as a bedroom community to Seattle.

It doesn't take long to reach West Seattle, but it feels like you've left the state – this part of town has a beachy, resorty atmosphere that screams 'instant vacation.' And the fact that it's the historical birthing ground of the city doesn't mean you can't stroll the waterfront and eat cotton candy.

DUWAMISH HEAD Map p106
Popular for its views of Elliott Bay and downtown, this is the former site of Luna Park. In its days as an over-the-top amusement center, the park covered more than 10 acres and boasted the 'longest bar on the bay'. This grand assertion unfortunately led to claims of debauchery and carousing, and the park was eventually closed in 1913 by the conservative powers-that-were.

ALKI BEACH PARK Map p106
Alki Beach has an entirely different feel from the rest of Seattle; this 2-mile stretch of sandy beach could almost fool you into thinking it's California, at least on a sunny day. There's a bike path, volleyball courts on the sand, and rings for beach fires. Look for the miniature Statue of Liberty, donated by the Boy Scouts. A pylon marking Arthur Denny's landing party's first stop in 1851 now contains a shard of Massachusetts' Plymouth Rock in its base.

ALKI POINT LIGHTHOUSE Map p106
☎ 206-217-6123; btwn Beach Dr & Point Pl, Alki Beach
The US Coast Guard maintains this lighthouse. It has limited public hours and you can't just walk up to it, but tours are available by appointment. Call for a current schedule and more information.

FAUNTLEROY FERRY DOCK off Map p106
☎ 206-464-6400; Fauntleroy Way SW & Henderson St
Washington State Ferries to Vashon Island leave daily from this dock.

HIGH POINT Map p106
SW Myrtle St & 35th Ave
This intersection marks the highest point in Seattle, 518ft above sea level.

WEST SEATTLE

SIGHTS	(pp105–6)
Alki Beach Park	1 B2
Alki Point Lighthouse	2 A2
Duwamish Head	3 C1

SHOPPING	(p118)
Easy Street Records & Café	4 C3

EATING	(p138)
Alki Bakery	(see 5)
Alki Café	5 B2
Phoenicia at Alki	(see 5)
Salty's on Alki	6 C1
Spud Fish & Chips	(see 5)
Sunfish	(see 5)

DRINKING	(p148)
Elliott Bay Brewery & Pub	7 C3
West 5	(see 7)

SPORTS & ACTIVITIES	(p171)
West Seattle Municipal Golf Course	8 D3

SOUTH OF SEATTLE

MUSEUM OF FLIGHT Map p48

☎ 206-764-5720; 9494 E Marginal Way S, Boeing Field, about 10 miles south of downtown; adult /senior/youth/child $14/13/7.50/free, free 5-9pm 1st Thu each month; ☷ 10am-5pm Fri-Wed, 10am-9pm Thu; 🚌 174 from downtown

Aviation buffs wholeheartedly enjoy the Museum of Flight, while others traipse through suppressing yawns, so be choosy about who you come with. The museum presents the entire history of flight, from da Vinci to the Wright Brothers to the NASA space program. More than 50 historic aircraft are displayed, including a recently acquired British Airways Concorde. The restored 1909 Red Barn, where Boeing had its beginnings, contains exhibits and displays. The six-story glass Great Gallery has 20 airplanes suspended from its ceiling. Vintage fliers reside on the grounds outside the buildings. There's also a hands-on area where visitors get to work the controls and sit in the driver's seat. Films about flight and aircraft history are shown in the small theater, and there's a gift shop and café.

To get here by car, take I-5 south from downtown to exit 158, turn west and follow East Marginal Way north.

top picks

- **Elliott Bay Book Company** (p112)
- **Uwajimaya** (p112)
- **DeLaurenti's** (p113)
- **Metsker Maps** (p113)
- **Babeland** (p115)

SHOPPING

Seattle has the best of both worlds: you can power-shop at the big-name stores in the malls – Barney's in Pacific Place, Tiffany – and you can seek out the quirky, one-of-a-kind shops hidden away in some back alley with a spray-painted sign on the door.

The city also has some of the greatest bookstores in the country, and a lot of them. Given Seattle's rich music culture, record stores are also a good bet, although the owners tend to know what they have and charge accordingly.

Naturally, any shopping excursion in Seattle must include Pike Place Market. From stacks of crabs to used books to spiced teas to goth toys, the selection here pretty much runs the gamut. And browsing this historic labyrinth is just as much fun as buying.

SHOPPING AREAS

Downtown dominates Seattle's retail scene with big-name shopping malls. But take a look in the corners of Pioneer Square for art and antique shops, or in the many nooks and crannies of Pike Place Market for everything from embroidered tea towels to lollypop condoms. Make the Waterfront your stop for obligatory souvenirs. For fashion or novelties, browse on Capitol Hill.

OPENING HOURS

Most stores are open every day, typically 9am or 10am to 5pm or 6pm. Malls and department stores often stay open until 8pm or 9pm. Exceptions are noted in the reviews.

CONSUMER TAXES

An 8.8% sales tax is added to all purchases except food to be prepared for consumption (ie groceries). Unlike the European VAT or Canadian GST, the sales tax is not refundable to tourists.

DOWNTOWN & FIRST HILL

The main shopping area in Seattle is downtown between 3rd and 6th Aves and between University and Stewart Sts. If you're anywhere nearby, you can't miss it.

CAMERAS WEST Map p50 · Cameras
☎ 206-622-0066; 1908 4th Ave
The foremost selection of film and photographic supplies (including cameras) in Seattle is Cameras West, right downtown.

CLOTHING SIZES

Women's clothing

Aus/UK	8	10	12	14	16	18
Europe	36	38	40	42	44	46
Japan	5	7	9	11	13	15
USA	6	8	10	12	14	16

Women's shoes

Aus/USA	5	6	7	8	9	10
Europe	35	36	37	38	39	40
France only	35	36	38	39	40	42
Japan	22	23	24	25	26	27
UK	3½	4½	5½	6½	7½	8½

Men's clothing

Aus	92	96	100	104	108	112
Europe	46	48	50	52	54	56
Japan	S		M	M		L
UK/USA	35	36	37	38	39	40

Men's shirts (collar sizes)

Aus/Japan	38	39	40	41	42	43
Europe	38	39	40	41	42	43
UK/USA	15	15½	16	16½	17	17½

Men's shoes

Aus/UK	7	8	9	10	11	12
Europe	41	42	43	44½	46	47
Japan	26	27	27½	28	29	30
USA	7½	8½	9½	10½	11½	12½

Measurements approximate only, try before you buy.

BON-MACY'S
Map p50 · Clothing
☎ 206-344-2121; 3rd Ave & Pine St
Seattle's oldest and largest department store, the 'Bon' – formerly Bon-Marché, but renamed in August 2003 when it was bought by Macy's – is still a classic.

NIKETOWN Map p50 — Clothing
☎ 206-447-6453; 1500 6th Ave
The ridiculously huge Niketown has its
roots in the Northwest. It sells all kinds of
Nike clothing, shoes and accessories.

NORDSTROM
Map p50 — Clothing
☎ 206-628-2111; Pine St btwn 5th & 6th Aves
Born and raised in Seattle, this chain department store occupies a giant space in
the former Frederick and Nelson Building.
Closer to Pike Place Market, Nordstrom Rack
(☎ 206-448-8522; 1601 2nd Ave) offers closeouts
and returns from the parent store.

NORTH FACE Map p50 — Clothing & Outdoors
☎ 206-622-4111; 1023 1st Ave
For hardcore camping, climbing and hiking
clothing and equipment, go to the North
Face, downtown toward the Waterfront.

PACIFIC PLACE Map p50 — Mall
☎ 206-405-2655; 600 Pine St
Seattle's newest boutique mall ranks at the
top. Clothiers include J Crew (☎ 206-652-9788),
Club Monaco (☎ 206-264-8001) and BCBG (☎ 206-
447-3400). The large stores of Restoration
Hardware (☎ 206-652-4545) and Williams-Sonoma
(☎ 206-621-7405) are fun to look around in.
Take a moment to gape in the window at
Tiffany & Co (☎ 206-264-1400), or saunter inside
for a special gift. The mall's top level features a movie theater, a pub and a couple
of restaurants.

WESTLAKE CENTER
Map p50 — Mall
☎ 206-467-3044; 4th Ave & Pine St
This 'boutique mall' – also the starting
point for the Monorail – has turned into a
landmark, partly because of location and
the fact that its concrete patio and steps
make a nice gathering point. It's somehow
heartening to see ragtag groups of anti-war
protesters (and an inordinate number of
cops) rallying in front of such a monument
to the big American dollar. Inside you'll find
shops like Fossil watches (☎ 206-652-2332), LUSH
(☎ 206-624-5874) and Nine West (☎ 206-343-9663).
Local stores include an outlet of Fireworks
(☎ 206-682-6462), which offers inexpensive
arty products by regional craftspeople –
they make great gifts.

top picks

SHOPPING STRIPS
- Pike Place Market (p112)
- Downtown (opposite)
- Broadway (p115)
- Pioneer Square (below)
- The Ave in the U District (p116)

PIONEER SQUARE

Not surprisingly, given its historic importance
to the city, Pioneer Square is where to shop
for antiques. It's also a good place to find
reasonably priced artwork and crafts by local
artists, particularly blown glass and traditional
art by coastal Native American artists. And,
of course, you can't miss a chance to browse
through Elliott Bay Book Company (p112).

ELLIOTT BAY ANTIQUES
Map p57 — Antiques
☎ 340-0770; 165 S Jackson St
Features Asian furniture and art.

JACKSON STREET GALLERY
Map p57 — Antiques
☎ 206-447-1012; 322 1st Ave S
Find all manner of antiques and collectibles
here. Jean Williams and Elliott Bay Antiques
are also nearby.

JEAN WILLIAMS ANTIQUES
Map p57 — Antiques
☎ 622-1110; 115 S Jackson St
Sells English and French period antiques.

PIONEER SQUARE ANTIQUE MALL
Map p57 — Antiques
☎ 206-624-1164; 602 1st Ave
This Antique Mall is a warren of little shops
right across from the Pioneer Square pergola;
it's actually part of the Seattle 'underground'
and can be somewhat claustrophobic.

FOSTER/WHITE GALLERY
Map p57 — Art
☎ 206-622-2833; 123 S Jackson St
The famed Foster/White Gallery features
glassworks, paintings and sculpture by
mainstream Northwest artists.

GLASSHOUSE STUDIO Map p57 Art

☎ 206-682-9939; 311 Occidental Ave S
The Seattle area is known for its Pilchuck School of glassblowing art, and this is the city's oldest glassblowing studio. Stop by to watch the artists in action and pick up a memento right at the source.

LEGACY LTD GALLERY
Map p57 Arts & Crafts

☎ 206-624-6350; 1003 1st Ave
Legacy Ltd is an internationally known and widely respected source of Northwest Coast Indian and Inuit art and artifacts, including baskets and jewelry. Good for a browse even if you don't happen to be a museum curator or a millionaire.

TRADITIONS & BEYOND
Map p57 Arts & Crafts

☎ 206-621-0655; 113 Cherry St
Affordable and authentic Native American crafts are available from this store. Part of the proceeds goes to Native American programs and education.

ELLIOTT BAY BOOK COMPANY
Map p57 Books

☎ 206-624-6600; 101 S Main St
One of the best general bookstores in the Northwest is this rambling bookstore, which takes up an entire block of historic storefronts in Pioneer Square. The interior, all exposed red brick and high ceilings, is absolutely stuffed full of new books and browsing customers. Downstairs is a popular café (p124). Elliott Bay is the local leader in author appearances, with some writer appearing at a reading or signing almost nightly – pick up a schedule near the entrance to see who's coming up.

FLORA & FAUNA BOOKS Map p57 Books

☎ 206-623-4727; 121 1st Ave S
Seattle has some great theme bookstores. Flora & Fauna, a longstanding underground favorite for nature-lovers, has books on natural history and local field guides.

SEATTLE MYSTERY BOOKSHOP
Map p57 Books

☎ 206-587-5737; 117 Cherry St
The name gives it away – Seattle Mystery Bookshop is a specialty store for page-turners and whodunits.

BUD'S JAZZ RECORDS Map p57 Music

☎ 206-628-0445; 102 S Jackson St; ☉ 11am-5:30pm Mon-Sat, noon-6pm Sun
Whether you're looking for recordings of Coltrane or the Duke, you'll have a good chance of finding them here. Bud specializes in vintage vinyl recordings of early and hard-to-find jazz. Hours aren't always strictly kept, but it's worth checking back to catch the shop when it's open.

INTERNATIONAL DISTRICT

In addition to the behemoth Uwajimaya (below), it's worth exploring nooks and crannies in this neighborhood for odd shopfronts and imported wares.

KINOKUNIYA Map p60 Books

☎ 206-587-2477; 525 S Weller St; ☉ 10am-9pm Mon-Sat, 10am-8pm Sun
A great source for hard-to-find imported books and magazines in Asian languages, and in English about Asian culture, this bookstore inside Uwajimaya Village is also one of the few shops in the country where you can buy the films of Kinji Fukasaku and other masters of Asian cinema on DVD.

UWAJIMAYA Map p60 Groceries & Gifts

☎ 206-624-6248; 600 5th Ave S; ☉ 9am-10pm Mon-Sat, 9am-9pm Sun
Dried squid? Check. Sheets of seaweed? Check. Dumpling steamers, teapots, chopsticks? Check, check, check. The enormous Uwajimaya, anchoring an eponymous shopping center, has everything needed to prepare Thai, Japanese, Chinese and other Asian foods. You'll find fresh and frozen meat and fish, canned and dried produce, and intriguingly labeled treats of all kinds, as well as cooking tools, spices, cookbooks, toiletries and gift items. It also has a deli and bakery.

PIKE PLACE MARKET & WATERFRONT

For the compulsive browser, amateur chef, hungry traveler on a budget or student of the human condition, Seattle has no greater attraction than Pike Place Market. This is shopping central in Seattle: dozens of market food stalls hawk everything from geoduck clams to fennel root to harissa. (For suggestions on where to eat in the market, see p125.) We list a few shops here, but do explore on your own.

For the full gamut of souvenirs, simply stroll up and down the boardwalk along the Waterfront.

TENZING MOMO
Map p64 | Apothecary

☎ 206-623-9837; Economy Market Bldg, Pike Place Market

One of the coolest shops in Pike Place Market, Tenzing Momo, in the Economy Market Building, is an old-school natural apothecary, with shelves of mysterious glass bottles filled with herbs and tinctures to cure any ailment.

LEFT BANK BOOKS Map p64 | Books

☎ 206-622-0195; Pike Place Market, cnr 1st & Pike

This legendary bookstore and distributor is small but fierce, with an essential collection of political theory, off-center fiction and surrealist literature. A sign in the anarchist section humbly requests that, if you're going to steal books, you do it from a corporate chain store, not a workers-run collective.

PETER MILLER ARCHITECTURE & DESIGN BOOKS Map p64 | Books

☎ 206-441-4114; 1930 1st Ave

This store, whose window arrangements can make a bibliophile or a design fiend drool, specializes in luxurious architecture books.

SUR LA TABLE Map p64 | Cookware

☎ 206-448-2244; 84 Pine St

It's hard to miss this gigantic cookware store. It's a chain, but a good one, with books, gear and gadgets to entice any foodie, gourmand or gourmet.

DELAURENTI'S Map p64 | Food

☎ 206-622-0141; SW cnr 1st & Pike

DeLaurenti's is a mandatory market stop for the Italian chef or continental food enthusiast. Not only is there a stunning selection of cheese, sausages, hams and pasta, but there's also the largest selection of capers, olive oil and anchovies that you're likely to find this side of Genoa. The wine selection is also quite broad.

JACK'S FISH SPOT
Map p64 | Food

☎ 206-467-0514; Pike Place Market

Perhaps the gift that says 'I heart Seattle' the most is a whole salmon or other fresh seafood from the fish markets. All the markets will prepare fish for transportation on the plane ride home, or you can just call and have them take care of the overnight shipping.

METSKER MAPS
Map p64 | Maps

☎ 206-623-8747; 1511 1st Ave

In its new, high-profile location on 1st Ave, this legendary map shop sells all kinds of useful things for the traveler, from maps to guidebooks to various accessories.

MADE IN WASHINGTON
Map p64 | Souvenirs

☎ 206-467-0788; 1530 Post Alley

If you're looking for something more authentically Northwest than most souvenir shops offer, head to Made in Washington.

YE OLDE CURIOSITY SHOP
Map p64 | Souvenirs

☎ 206-682-5844; Pier 54; ☻ 9am-9:30pm Jun-Aug, 10am-6pm Sun-Thu & 9am-9pm Fri & Sat Sep-May

This landmark shop, on Pier 54, now has a lesser sibling, Ye Olde Curiosity Shoppe Too – but never mind that. The original shop is where you'll find cabinets of shrunken heads, piglets in jars and dried puffer fish – not for sale, of course, just for atmosphere. Also not for sale are the famous black diamond, Chief Seattle's hat, a variety of stalagmites and 'tites, and some pretty cool fortune-telling machines. The funniest souvenir available for purchase is a Mt St Helens 'snowglobe' – instead of snow, it has little gray particles meant to look like ash from the volcano's eruption.

SOUK
Map p64 | Spices

☎ 206-441-1666; Pike Place Market

Supplies here include Middle Eastern and North African spices and foods. Named after the Arabic word for marketplace, the shop sells everything you'll need to get from cookbook to curry – including cookbooks and curries.

GOLDEN AGE COLLECTIBLES
Map p64   Toys
☎ 206-622-9799; downstairs, Pike Place Market
A haven for geeks, kids and, especially, geeky kids, this shop has comic-book–inspired toys, novelty items (hopping nuns etc), costumes and loads of goth-friendly knickknacks.

GREAT WIND UP
Map p64   Toys
☎ 206-621-9370; North Arcade, Pike Place Market
This kids' heaven in the market has every wind-up toy and gizmo known to human-kind, and then some.

MARKET CELLAR WINERY
Map p64   Wine
☎ 206-622-1880; 1432 Western Ave
Located at the southern end of the market, Market Cellar Winery makes its own wine and sells do-it-yourself home brew kits.

PIKE & WESTERN WINE SHOP
Map p64   Wine
☎ 206-441-1307; 1937 Pike Pl
A good selection of regional wine and friendly service make this shop at the northern end of Pike Place Market a great place to get introduced to the wines of the Northwest.

BELLTOWN
Belltown's shopping runs the gamut from a punk-rock record store to the polar-fleece-happy Patagonia (below). Be prepared for any-thing, and you'll probably find something.

ELLIOTT BAY BICYCLES
Map p69   Bicycles
☎ 206-441-8144; 2116 Western Ave
This place aims more at pro or hardcore cyclists who are prepared to slap down big bucks for bikes. Custom-made bikes are a renowned specialty.

PATAGONIA Map p69   Clothing & Outdoors
☎ 206-622-9700; 2100 1st Ave
The fashionable outdoor clothing at Pat-agonia may seem to be only for the very adventurous, but experience a sodden winter in Seattle and you'll understand why this is where the locals shop for rain gear and outdoor apparel.

SINGLES GOING STEADY Map p69   Music
☎ 206-441-7396; 2219 2nd Ave; ⏰ 11am-7pm Mon-Sat, noon-6pm Sun
Singles Going Steady specializes in punk, hip-hop and ska, mostly in the form of 7-inch vinyl singles, as well as posters, patches and other accessories.

SEATTLE CELLARS Map p69   Wine
☎ 206-256-0850; 2505 2nd Ave
A good source for regional wines, Seattle Cellars can help you find gifts to take back home. Ask about open tastings on Thurs-day nights and some Saturday afternoons.

SEATTLE CENTER & QUEEN ANNE

QUEEN ANNE BOOKS Map p76   Books
☎ 206-283-5624; 1811 Queen Anne Ave N
This quiet little nook is a charming neigh-borhood bookstore, with special events and a nice selection of children's materials.

MOUNTAINEERS Map p76   Outdoors
☎ 206-284-6310; 300 3rd Ave
For outdoor activities guides, the Moun-taineers in Lower Queen Anne has one of the best selections anywhere. In addition to books, it has CDs, videos, maps and technical manuals. It also offers a range of outdoor courses; see p164.

CHANNEL 9 STORE Map p73   Toys
☎ 800-937-5387; 401 Mercer St
In the lobby of KCTS TV, this cool shop is filled with educational videos and games that educate as much as they entertain. It also benefits public broadcasting.

LAKE UNION

FEATHERED FRIENDS Map p79   Outdoors
☎ 206-292-2210; 119 Yale Ave N
Near REI, Feathered Friends stocks high-end climbing equipment, made-to-order sleep-ing bags and backcountry ski gear. Prod-ucts made with down are the specialty.

PATRICK'S FLY SHOP Map p79   Outdoors
☎ 206-325-8988; 2237 Eastlake Ave E
Located near Lake Union, this shop has been around as long as anyone can re-

member. It offers workshops on fly-fishing, sells equipment and gives advice.

REI Map p79 — Outdoors
☎ 206-223-1944; 222 Yale Ave N
The state-of-the-art REI store is right by I-5 south of Lake Union. This outdoor recreation megastore has become a tourist destination: it has its own climbing wall, and you can check out the rain-proofing of various brands of gear by entering a special rainstorm shower, or road-test hiking boots on a simulated mountain trail. It has practically every kind of outdoor equipment and gear, from hiking boots to kayaks, pitons to bicycle tires. Also see p164.

CAPITOL HILL & VOLUNTEER PARK

Shopping on Capitol Hill makes you instantly hipper; even just window-shopping is an education in cutting-edge popular culture. This is the place to find great record stores, unusual bookstores, vintage clothing shops and risqué toy stores.

BABELAND Map p82 — Adult
☎ 206-328-2914; 707 E Pike St; 🕙 11am-10pm Mon-Sat, noon-7pm Sun
Opened in 1993 as Toys in Babeland, this sex-positive toy store for women has since abbreviated its name and expanded its business to include shops in New York and Los Angeles.

CRYPT Map p82 — Adult
☎ 206-325-3882; 113 10th Ave E
A cheesy but fun place to browse, the Crypt sells clubwear, leather and novelties for folks just slightly too grown-up to buy them at Hot Topic (the Wal-Mart of goth-punk fashion).

VELO STORES Map p82 — Bicycles
☎ 206-325-4526; 1535 11th Ave
Velo Stores has a good selection of road and mountain bikes, along with helpful staff.

BAILEY/COY BOOKS Map p82 — Books
☎ 206-323-8842; 414 Broadway E; 🕙 10am-10pm Mon-Sat, 10am-8pm Sun
This is a general bookstore with a good gay and lesbian section and a really classy, well-chosen supply of literary fiction.

top picks
SEATTLE BOOKSTORES

- Elliott Bay Book Company (p112) Drenched in atmosphere.
- Bailey/Coy Books (left) Smaller but well-chosen selection.
- Magus Books (p116) Used treasures in the U District.
- Twice Sold Tales (below) Don't be insulted when the cats ignore you.
- Left Bank Books (p113) A light in the darkness.

BEYOND THE CLOSET BOOKS
Map p82 — Books
☎ 206-322-4609; 518 E Pike St
Beyond the Closet is the city's primary gay-focused bookstore. It also holds readings and book signings; check local papers for a schedule.

TWICE SOLD TALES
Map p82 — Books
☎ 206-324-2421; 905 E John St; 🕙 10am-10pm, 24hr Fri
Twice Sold Tales' Capitol Hill location has shrunk to a cozy den full of used books; it stays open late most nights and 24 hours on Friday; be alert for steep discounts at midnight. A bunch of aloof cats roam the shop, actively ignoring everybody.

DILETTANTE CHOCOLATES
Map p82 — Chocolate
☎ 206-329-6463; 416 Broadway E
If you have a sweet tooth to satisfy, try the confection truffles here. Great selection of desserts, too. You can taste chocolates in the shop, along with good coffee and other snacks, or pick up a box to take home. The European-style chocolates are made in-house.

APRIE
Map p82 — Clothing
☎ 206-324-1255; 310 Broadway E
A small boutique with a well-curated selection of trendy tops, dresses and skinny jeans from brands too hip to list here (I mean, if you don't know, I'm not gonna tell you). Aprie is a miniparadise for fashionistas.

CROSSROADS TRADING CO

Map p82   Clothing

☎ 206-328-5867; 325 Broadway E
This place is less expensive than Red Light
but also generally less hipster-chic.

RED LIGHT Map p82   Clothing

☎ 206-329-2200; 312 Broadway E
Red Light carries stylish, painstakingly
selected vintage clothing, organized by decade. Red Light also has a store in the U District
(Map p85; ☎ 206-545-4044; 4560 University Way NE).

URBAN OUTFITTERS Map p82   Clothing

☎ 206-322-1800; 401 Broadway E
Urban Outfitters in the Broadway Market
sells clothing geared toward young folks
looking to score points on the hip scale.

SONIC BOOM Map p82   Music

☎ 206-568-2666; www.sonicboomrecords.com;
514 15th Ave E; ☀ 10am-10pm Mon-Sat, 10am-
7pm Sun
A local institution, Sonic Boom now has
several locations, including branches at
Fremont (3414 Fremont Ave N) and Ballard (2209
NW Market St), and has just added a 'general
store' next door to its Fremont shop. Ask
about in-store performances by bands
coming through town.

WALL OF SOUND Map p82   Music

☎ 206-441-9880; 315 E Pine St; ☀ 11am-7pm
Mon-Sat, noon-6pm Sun
One of the coolest record stores in town,
this smart shop stocks music you've never
heard of, from obscure noise artists to
gypsy folksongs, but nothing the owners
and staff wouldn't listen to at home. The
wall of magazines, comics and small-press
books is top-notch too.

U DISTRICT

Bookstores and record stores are the main thing
here, although everyone should make time to
explore the bins at Hardwick's Hardware Store
(right). University Way NE, called 'the Ave,' is the
main drag in the U District, lined with shops
and a wild variety of cheap eateries.

RECYCLED CYCLES Map p85   Bicycles

☎ 206-547-4491; 1007 NE Boat St
Recycled Cycles, at the bottom of the
U District along Lake Union, sells used and

consignment bikes. It also has a wide selection of parts including cranks, forks, pedals,
tires and tubes. Staff members are candid
with their advice and know what they're
talking about.

ALL FOR KIDS Map p85   Books

☎ 206-526-2768; 2900 NE Blakely St
Near the University District, All For Kids has
one of the largest selections of children's
books in town and also stocks a lot of
children's music.

MAGUS BOOKS Map p85   Books

☎ 206-633-1800; 1408 NE 42nd St
Magus is a great used-book store that –
fittingly, given the neighborhood –
specializes in scholarly books.

UNIVERSITY BOOKSTORE

Map p85   Books

☎ 206-634-3400; 4326 University Way NE; ☀ 9am-
9pm Mon-Fri, 10am-7pm Sat, noon-5pm Sun
University Bookstore is vast and all-
purpose, though lacking in the time-worn
atmosphere of many of Seattle's other
bookstores. It does have absolutely everything, though.

HARDWICK'S HARDWARE STORE

Map p85   Cool Junk

☎ 206-632-1203; 4214 Roosevelt Way NE;
☀ 8am-6pm Mon-Fri, 9am-6pm Sat
Locals in the know come to Hardwick's
to explore the rows and rows of buckets
filled with bizarre little gadgets and gizmos.
Some people probably know what these
objects are for, but most shoppers are look-

top picks

RECORD STORES

- Easy Street Records & Café (p118) A fun place to
  hang out and browse.
- Wall of Sound (left) Obscurities, as well as great
  publications.
- Sonic Boom (left) Alt-rock and indie rock
  essentials.
- Singles Going Steady (p114) Totally punk rock.
- Cellophane Square (opposite) Used records on the
  cheap.

ing for things to use in their art projects. It's a hive of a place that's fun just to explore.

PITAYA Map p85 — Clothing
☎ 206-548-1001; 4520 University Way NE
This is a cute little clothing boutique with carefully selected dresses, hipster jeans and cool accessories.

CONTINENTAL STORE Map p85 — Food
☎ 206-523-0606; 5014 Roosevelt Way NE
By 'the continent,' they mean Germany; here's where to pick up imported foods, books and knickknacks. There's also a great deli.

BULLDOG NEWS & ESPRESSO
Map p85 — Newsstand
☎ 206-632-6397; 4208 University Way NE
The newsstand of choice at the university, this place has pretty much every magazine or newspaper you might want, from imports and big glossies to stapled-together zines. Good coffee, too.

CELLOPHANE SQUARE Map p85 — Music
☎ 206-634-2280; 4538 University Way NE;
☽ 10am-10pm Sun-Thu, 10am-11pm Fri & Sat
Locally based chain Cellophane Square has rack after rack of used CDs to flip through and can special-order anything.

FREMONT

Once a warren of junk shops and craft-supply stores frequented by granola crunchers, Fremont has become a bit more of a soccer-mom neighborhood. Still, it's a fun place to browse regardless of whether you're in the mood to spend money.

FREMONT PLACE BOOK CO
Map p89 — Books
☎ 206-547-5970; 621 N 35th St
This is a friendly little place with a relatively small but interesting collection of new fiction and nonfiction. Ask about in-store author readings and monthly discussion groups.

DELUXE JUNK Map p89 — Cool Junk
☎ 206-634-2733; 3518 Fremont Pl N
A local landmark, Deluxe Junk carries a deeply weird assortment of, well, junk. But some of it is pretty nice junk, retro and glitzy and sometimes fabulous.

EVO
Map p89 — Sporting Goods
☎ 206-973-4470; 122 NW 36th St; ☽ 10am-8pm Mon-Sat, 11am-7pm Sun
Skateboards, skis and snowboards, funky gear and a tuning service are all to be found at this huge new space, which also includes a small art gallery.

WALLINGFORD

Some of the city's most interesting bookstores are in this area – don't miss Wide World Books & Maps (below), for travelers, and Open Books (below) for anyone interested in poetry.

OPEN BOOKS
Map p93 — Books
☎ 206-633-0811; 2414 N 45th St; ☽ noon-6pm Tue-Sun
Open Books in Wallingford is devoted totally to poetry; call to ask about readings and events.

WIDE WORLD BOOKS & MAPS
Map p93 — Books & Maps
☎ 206-634-3453; 4411 Wallingford Ave N;
☽ 10am-9pm Mon-Sat, 11am-6pm Sun
Travelers will want to make a pilgrimage to Wide World Books & Maps. In addition to a great selection of travel guides, this pleasant store offers a full array of travel accessories and a staff of seasoned globetrotters. Ask for a calendar of events such as slideshows and author readings.

COMICS DUNGEON
Map p93 — Comic Books
☎ 206-545-8373; 250 NE 45th St
Nestled right between the U District and Wallingford, Comics Dungeon stocks a good selection of comics and graphic novels plus the usual accompaniments of gothy dolls, toys and action figures.

EROTIC BAKERY
Map p93 — Novelty
☎ 206-545-6969; 2323 N 45th St
Kind of worn-out and vaguely icky in a not-all-that-hilarious way, the Erotic Bakery nevertheless clings to its 'local landmark' status with boob cookies, penis cakes and other baked goods shaped like body parts. Send one anonymously to your boss on his or her birthday.

CITY CELLARS

Map p93   Wine

☎ 206-632-7238; 1710 N 45th St

There's no snobbery at City Cellars, just great wines at reasonable prices. In the adjoining storefront, check out Bottleworks Inc (☎ 206-633-2437; Suite 3, 1710 N 45th St), which sells mostly imported bottled beer.

GREEN LAKE & PHINNEY RIDGE

GREGG'S CYCLES Map p95   Bicycles

☎ 206-523-1822; 7007 Woodlawn Ave NE

This is Seattle's largest bicycle dealer. Near Green Lake, it has a huge stock of all kinds of bikes and accessories and a very helpful staff. Gregg's also hires out bicycles; see p168.

FROCK SHOP

Map p95   Clothing

☎ 206-297-1638; shopfrockshop.com; 6500 Phinney Ave N

Flirty little dresses in an attractive space make this shop fun to visit.

BALLARD & DISCOVERY PARK

Ballard is a fun place to browse. Make sure to allow plenty of time for Archie McPhee (right), especially if you have kids or enjoy pretending to be one. You can also pick up Scandinavian foods and knickknacks at several shops in the area.

WILD AT HEART

Map p98   Adult

☎ 206-782-5538; 1111 NW Leary Way

This women-owned shop sells sex toys, fetish-wear, clubwear, lingerie and DVDs.

SECRET GARDEN BOOKSHOP

Map p98   Books

☎ 206-789-5006; 2214 NW Market St

The children's collection, especially the fiction selection, is excellent here, and the staff will order you anything they don't have.

ARCHIE MCPHEE Map p98   Cool Junk

☎ 206-297-0240; 2428 NW Market St

Famous for its mail-order catalog, Archie McPhee is the source for all your weird gift items. It's a browser's heaven, and you'll almost certainly wind up buying something you never realized you needed – like bacon air fresheners or a ninja lunchbox.

OLSEN'S SCANDINAVIAN FOODS

Map p98   Food

☎ 206-783-8288; 2248 NW Market St

If you've had a hankering for authentic *lefse* (Norwegian flatbread), black licorice or Kalle's Kaviar in a squeeze tube – and who hasn't? – this is the place to cure it. Olsen's also stocks Nordic-flavored knickknacks and gift items.

SECOND BOUNCE Map p98   Outdoors

☎ 206-783-1967; 5221 Ballard Ave NW

Second Bounce sells used outdoor gear, clothing, boots, backpacks and camping equipment. This is a good way to save some money if you've decided on an impromptu hiking trip but didn't pack any gear.

WILD SALMON SEAFOOD MARKET

Map p98   Seafood

☎ 206-283-3366, 888-222-3474; 1900 W Nickerson St

At Wild Salmon Seafood Market – in the Fishermen's Terminal on the south side of the Ballard Bridge – you can buy fresh salmon and shellfish directly from the fisherman who caught it. The market will also ship fresh fish at reasonable prices.

WEST SEATTLE

EASY STREET RECORDS & CAFÉ

Map p106   Music

☎ 206-938-3279; 4559 California Ave SW

This place has everything: rock-and-roll, coffee, beer, food…and an open, airy place to hang out while enjoying all of the above. Any place where you can shop for new import records, have a beer and then kick back on the couch for a while is bound to attract attention, and you might have to elbow some hipsters out of your way to grab that coveted album – just try not to spill.

top picks

- **Dahlia Lounge** (p121)
- **Steelhead Diner** (p126)
- **Coastal Kitchen** (p131)
- **Tilth** (p134)
- **Salumi** (p123)
- **House of Hong** (p125)
- **Pho Bac** (p125)

EATING

It's easy to become food-obsessed in Seattle. The city's focus on locally produced, fresh, organic ingredients, whether from nearby farms or the bounteous sea, means dinner is never just dinner – it's a sociopolitical act. Guilt-free indulgence is the rule – upscale restaurants that *don't* emphasize sustainable fishing and farming are the exception. The biggest brag a Seattle restaurant can make these days is that the chef helped reel in the day's catch, is lifelong pals with the farmer who grew your salad, and can name the chicken who laid the egg that's now beside your toast.

'Northwest cuisine' is a fairly inclusive term in the sense that it can mean anything from surf-and-turf to pasta to sushi and pad Thai; what defines it is an insistence on showing off the best of what the region produces: seafood so fresh it squirms, fat berries freshly plucked, mushrooms dug out of the rich soil and cornucopias of fruits and vegetables.

Going hand in hand with the regional emphasis on sustainable, organic, unfussy food is the prevalence of vegan and vegetarian restaurants here. This is the kind of city where it's automatically understood that vegan cupcakes are sexier than the regular kind. The city has won attention and praise in the national press for its combination of healthy gourmet restaurant options, sustainable farming and cooking practices, inventive use of ingredients and overall quality of life. Of course, Seattle also loves a good steak – especially one that's led a happy, grass-fed life on a farm just outside of town.

The restaurant world is an ever-shifting one, and the metaphorical kitchen-of-the-moment award is definitely a traveling trophy. Check the dining sections of the local papers for new developments, and ask around – practically everyone in town is a food expert and most will be quite happy to recommend their favorite spot.

One interesting new development in Seattle dining is the popularity of underground supper clubs. These are usually set-menu meals served family-style in a location that remains secret until you've made a reservation. For an example, check out Caché (www.cacheseattle.com), which hosts themed dinners for $50 to $60 a person in a commercial space in the Belltown area. Keep in mind that these events tend to sell out a couple of months in advance.

Food-related internet forums such as eGullet (www.egullet.org, click on the Pacific Northwest division) or Chowhound (www.chowhound.com/boards/4) can be helpful in tracking down the latest news about which restaurants are hot, which have fallen off their game, and which places local foodies are hoping to keep all to themselves.

There are also several new companies that cater to Seattleites' desire to eat more healthfully and responsibly in the home. EatLocal (☎ 206-328-3663; eatlocalonline.com; 2400 Queen Anne Ave N) is a company that delivers organic prepackaged meals made with ingredients from local or regional farms, frozen and packaged with cute Nikki McClure artwork. And Surfin' Seafood (☎ 425-821-1303; www.surfinseafood.com) buys fresh seafood, flash-freezes and vacuum-packs it, and delivers it right to your door.

OPENING HOURS

Specific opening hours are listed in reviews only if they differ from the norm; otherwise we simply note which meals each restaurant serves. Breakfast is typically served from 7am to 11am; brunch from 7am to 3pm; lunch from 11:30am to 2:30pm; and dinner from 5:30pm to 10pm.

HOW MUCH?

The range of eateries in Seattle means it's possible to find dining options that suit most budgets, whether that's a $2 taco from a

PRICE GUIDE	
$$$$	over $30
$$$	$15-30
$$	$10-15
$	under $10

These guides reflect the cost of an average main dish. Prices are per person, not including drinks or tip.

parking-lot stand, a $5 bowl of noodles in the U District or a $30 wedge of hazelnut-encrusted line-caught wild salmon with organic field greens served in a chic converted warehouse. Typically, breakfast and lunch fall in the $8-to-$10 range per person, and dinner can be anywhere from $6 to $60 or more, depending on extras like wine or cocktails and how much buzz the restaurant's been getting. That may seem like a wide price range, but most restaurants make it just as easy to scrimp by ordering from the appetizer or bar menu as to splash out on a full three-course meal.

BOOKING TABLES

Most Seattle restaurants don't require advance bookings but the hot new places fill up quickly, so it's best to call ahead if you want to be sure to avoid disappointment. Many restaurants also have a bar section where you can wait for a table to open up if you don't have reservations. In the listings below, where reservations are recommended or mandatory it's noted in the review.

TIPPING

Tips are not figured into the check at a restaurant. In general, 15% is the baseline tip, but 20% is usually more appropriate, and 25% if you enjoyed the service. If you're just ordering coffee at a counter, tip with change, but if someone makes you a specialty drink, leave 10% to 20%. There's also a 9.3% tax on food and beverages purchased in restaurants and bars.

DOWNTOWN & FIRST HILL

You might have to empty your pockets to fill your belly in the central downtown area, where a majority of the restaurants are designed with business meetings and expense accounts in mind. But this is the place to find classic Northwest food in old-fashioned oyster bars and cavernous steakhouses, as well as a couple of celebrity chef Tom Douglas's flagship restaurants (see boxed text, p122) and the posh dining rooms of some of the city's finest hotels.

GEORGIAN Map p50   Continental $$$-$$$$
☎ 206-621-7889; 411 University St; starters $15-20, mains $20-35; ☽ breakfast & lunch daily, dinner Tue-Sat
A treat above treats, the Georgian at the Fairmont Olympic Hotel is one of the most imposing restaurants in the city – the ornate high ceilings and dripping chandeliers, shiny silver and gilt details will have you swooning. The food is equally eye-catching and inspired by regional ingredients, such as scallops with truffles or roasted sea bass. Service is tops here, and it's one of the few places where Seattleites tend to be sharply dressed; jackets aren't required, but they're certainly not discouraged. Reservations are recommended.

DAHLIA LOUNGE
Map p50   Northwest $$-$$$$
☎ 206-682-4142; 2001 4th Ave; lunch $6-22, dinner starters $9-13, mains $22-36; ☽ lunch & dinner Mon-Fri, dinner until 11pm Sat & Sun
Owner Tom Douglas (see boxed text, p122) started fusing flavors at this Seattle institution in the late 1980s and single-handedly made Seattleites more sophisticated; his empire has grown a lot since then, but the flagship restaurant remains a local favorite. There's a bakery next door where you can pick up one of the Dahlia's fabulous desserts to go. Reservations are recommended.

HUNT CLUB Map p50   Northwest $$-$$$$
☎ 206-343-6156; Sorrento Hotel, 900 Madison St; starters $8-10, mains $21-38; ☽ breakfast, brunch & dinner daily, lunch Mon-Fri
The Hunt Club ought to be on the shortlist if you're looking for a special-occasion, top-end restaurant. The setting is ultra posh and absolutely beautiful: an intimate mahogany-paneled dining room shimmering with candles and decked with flowers. The food is equally stellar, featuring local lamb, fish and steaks from sustainable farms, accentuated with inventive sauces and regional produce. Reservations are recommended.

METROPOLITAN GRILL
Map p50   Steak & Seafood $$-$$$$
☎ 206-624-3287; 820 2nd Ave; starters $9-18, steaks $35-45; ☽ lunch 11am-3pm Mon-Fri, dinner 5-10:30pm Mon-Thu, 5-11pm Fri, 4-11pm Sat & Sun
This handsome and atmospheric business favorite fills up with stock analysts and bankers who pour out of nearby office towers. Though you can get fish, 'portabella mushroom mignon' or even Beluga caviar, beef's the big thing here; steaks are custom-aged and grilled over mesquite charcoal. Locals usually name the Met as the top chophouse in the city.

TOM DOUGLAS

A fixture in the Seattle foodie scene, chef Tom Douglas helped define what people mean when they talk about Northwest cuisine. He opened his first restaurant, Dahlia, in 1989; it was followed by Etta's Seafood, Palace Kitchen and, more recently, Lola and Serious Pie. Douglas won the 1994 James Beard Award for Best Northwest Chef, and the James Beard Foundation named *Tom Douglas' Seattle Kitchen* the Best American Cookbook in 2001. Douglas also battled Masaharu Morimoto in an episode of *Iron Chef America* – and won.

Clearly, the guy knows his way around a dinner plate. So when we asked him to describe his perfect Seattle afternoon, naturally there was food on the menu. Including dessert.

Douglas starts his trek at his favorite local landmark, Pike Place Market. 'I would stop for lunch first at the Pink Door (p126), out on their deck, which overlooks Elliott Bay there and the market itself,' Douglas says. 'There's something about being outdoors in the market. When it's nice out and you can sit outdoors and eat, there's nothing quite like it. So I love sitting up there.

'When I'm at the Pink Door I'll have the lasagne verde, which is just this perfect little lasagne that my wife and I had there for our wedding reception 24 years ago, and they still have it. That's our date food. And we have a little pink prosecco to go with it, to "put you in the mood." Then we kinda stroll through and head down the Pike Place Hillclimb, and by the time you're down the Hillclimb, I'm ready for dessert. I go down to that little Procopio (p128) and have a little canteloupe or coconut sorbet or gelato.

'And then we stroll over to the ferry, and if you've never been on one of the Washington State Ferries here, it's the best way to see Seattle. I think it's even better than the Space Needle because of the water and the movement and the sea life. It's just so grand on the top deck of the ferries. We pack refreshments in a brown paper bag and just go to and from the city. If you have time you can stop in Bainbridge, but I like just riding the ferry back and forth. It's just an hour and 10-minute ride, cheap.

'And then my favorite thing to do from there is walk over to the stadium and get an early baseball game. You can get the Ichi-roll in center field, there's a good little sushi bar. Safeco Field is awesome.'

There you have it.

PALACE KITCHEN Map p50 Northwest $$-$$$
☎ 206-448-2001; 2030 5th Ave; salads $7-9, mains $12-25; ✷ dinner until 1am

Owned by the Dahlia's Tom Douglas, the Palace is a see-and-be-seen hotspot that really picks up for the late-night cocktail scene. Daily dinner specials present such wonders as spaetzle-stuffed pumpkin or traditional pork loin. Snack on appetizers – including a smoked-salmon-and-blue-cheese terrine or a sampler plate of regional cheeses – or go for the whole shebang with grilled trout, leg of lamb or roasted chicken with blackberries and nectarines. After 10pm there's a 'late-night breakfast' that includes a king crab omelet ($14).

MCCORMICK'S FISH HOUSE & BAR
Map p50 Steak & Seafood $$
☎ 206-682-3900; 722 4th Ave; starters $8-14, mains from $12; ✷ lunch & dinner

A mainstay of traditional Seattle dining and the flagship of a small Northwest chain, this classy, wood-lined place is a network of cubbyholes that looks like an old-boys club (it was built as a hotel in 1827). The food is consistently good, with daily fresh fish specials, mostly grilled with zesty sauces, and a fine selection of local oysters, chops and steak. Try the crab cakes or the seared *ahi* (tuna), or just ask your server what's fresh. The bar menu is awesome, with a number of substantial snacks for less than $2.

WILD GINGER Map p50 Asian $-$$
☎ 206-623-4450; 1401 3rd Ave; satay $3-6, lunch $8-12, dinner $10-25; ✷ lunch Mon-Sat, dinner until 11pm Sun-Thu, to midnight Fri & Sat

Seattle was more or less introduced to the satay bar by this popular Indonesian restaurant, where throngs of diners sit and sample bite-size, skewered bits of fiery grilled chicken, vegetables or scallops, luscious soups and daily specials. More substantial dishes include Burmese curry crab and cinnamon-and-anise-spiced duck. The bar is a happening place, and there's a live music venue, the Triple Door, downstairs.

FARESTART RESTAURANT
Map p50 Northwest $-$$
☎ 206-443-1233; farestart.org; 700 Virginia St; starters $3-5, sandwiches $6-8, mains $8-12, 3-course dinner $25; ✷ 11am-2pm Mon-Fri, dinner Thu

Now in an attractively designed and much larger new space, FareStart continues to serve substantial meals that benefit the community. The constantly changing lunch menu is pretty darn gourmet for the price – try the veggie reuben, or a flatiron steak in blue-cheese sauce. All proceeds from lunch and the popular Thursday-night Guest Chef dinners – when FareStart students work with a famous local chef to produce outstanding meals – go to support the FareStart program, which provides intensive job training, housing assistance and job placement for disadvantaged and homeless people. Reservations are recommended for dinner.

CYBER-DOGS Map p50   Vegetarian $
☎ 206-405-3647; 909 Pike St; dogs $2-5; ⏱ 10am-midnight; 🚹 Ⓥ
One of those all-things-to-some-people places, like Easy Street in West Seattle, Cyber-Dogs is an all-veggie hot-dog stand, espresso bar, internet café (internet free for first 20 minutes, then $6 per hour); and youngster hangout/pickup joint. Its advertising campaign is based on miniature hand-scribbled-and-stapled chapbooks with cute indie-rock–style cartoons. But the best thing about the place is trying out the weird, insanely imaginative non-meat 'not-dogs' with tastes-better-than-it-sounds toppings (eggplant, potatoes, hummus).

TOP POT DONUTS
Map p50   Coffee & Doughnuts $
☎ 206-728-1966; 2124 5th Ave; doughnuts $1-3; ⏱ breakfast, lunch & dinner
At Top Pot it's all about the doughnuts, and no, it is not wrong to eat them three meals a day. The doughnuts here are hand-forged as quickly as the little Seattleites can gobble them up, and this huge store (there's also one on Capitol Hill) means you can down them twice as often. They're also available at various coffee shops around town, but it's best to go to the source. Krispy what?

PIONEER SQUARE

Pioneer Square is the ideal place to be if you're looking for a meal in an old-school steak and seafood restaurant with loads of atmosphere and traditional service. It also has a good range of budget-friendly options that are inexpensive without lacking character.

FX MCRORY'S STEAK, CHOP & OYSTER HOUSE
Map p57   Steak & Seafood $$-$$$$
☎ 206-623-4800; 419 Occidental Ave S; oyster sampler $12, starters $6-11, lunch $9-25, dinner mains $16-35; ⏱ lunch until 4pm daily, dinner 4-7pm Sun, 4-9pm Mon-Thu, 4-10pm Fri & Sat
This vast Pioneer Square landmark across from the sports stadiums is a weird blend of class and ass – it's a majestic old space with a bar on one side, fancy dining room on the other and an oyster bar in between, but the ball-cap/jock quotient gets high on days when the Seahawks or Mariners play. McRory's claims to have the largest selection of bourbon in the world – believable when you ogle the pyramid of booze behind the bar. Tuck into classic fare like prime rib or Dungeness crab, or share a seafood platter of raw oysters on the half-shell, smoked salmon, prawns, crab, Penn Cove mussels and scallops.

SALUMI Map p57   Sandwiches $-$$
☎ 206-621-8772; 309 3rd Ave S; sandwiches $7-10, plates $11-14; ⏱ 11am-4pm Tue-Fri
Sure, you'll have to wait in line. This is Mario Batali's dad's place, after all. But the line to get a Salumi sandwich is like its own little community. People chat, compare notes, talk about sandwiches they've had and loved…it's nice. When you finally get in the door of this long, skinny shop front, you're further teased by display cases of hanging meats and cheeses. Sandwiches come with any of a dozen types of cured meat and a handful of fresh cheese on a hunk of bread – you can't go wrong. There's only a couple of seats, so be prepared to picnic. On Tuesdays, 'Aunt Izzy' makes gnocchi in the window.

NEW ORLEANS CREOLE RESTAURANT
Map p57   Southern $-$$
☎ 206-622-2563; 114 1st Ave S; lunch $5-6.50, gumbo $7-9, mains $10-12; ⏱ lunch & dinner; 🚹
Enjoy some live Dixieland jazz with your homemade gumbo or jambalaya in one of the coolest spaces in Pioneer Square. This bourbon-heavy institution serves unpretentious food in an attractive space (warm lighting, exposed brick walls decorated with portraits of jazz greats) that's kid-friendly until 10pm. There's live music most nights.

top picks

WORTH THE WAIT

Some of the most popular restaurants in Seattle are not only worth the wait, but also actually make it fun to hang out and kill time before your meal.

- **Salumi (p123)** Chat with hungry fellow meat-seekers in Seattle's friendliest and possibly longest line. Why aren't these people crankier? Because they know what awaits them at the end of that line.
- **Steelhead Diner (p126)** Stake out a spot at the bar and score an awesome view of the bay.
- **La Carta de Oaxaca (p136)** The fun bar here, stocked with premium tequilas, makes the inevitable wait for a table pass quickly.
- **Thai Tom (p133)** Cram into the storefront of this tiny place with everybody else, and watch the spicy, steamy cooking action.

ZAINA Map p57 Middle Eastern $

☎ 206-624-5687; 108 Cherry St; sandwiches $4-7, plates $9; ⏱ 10am-9pm Mon-Fri, 11am-9pm Sat

This friendly café, bejeweled with a mish-mash of sparkly decorations and pulsing with Middle Eastern pop, dishes out juicy falafel sandwiches stuffed to overflowing, as well as shawarma, tabbouleh, hummus, great baklava and freshly squeezed lemonade. On weekend nights the vibe goes clubbish, with hookahs and belly dancers in the house.

ELLIOTT BAY CAFÉ
Map p57 Soup & Sandwiches $

☎ 206-682-6664; 101 S Main St; breakfast $3-4, salads $6.50, sandwiches $6-8; ⏱ breakfast, lunch & dinner

This cozy crypt underneath Elliott Bay Book Co is a clean well-lit place to settle in with a book and a bowl of soup or salad, or a Bukowski's Ham on Rye sandwich (named for the grisly old barfly poet), and browse the book-lined walls while you eat.

GRAND CENTRAL BAKING CO
Map p57 Soup & Sandwiches $

☎ 206-622-3644; 214 1st Ave S; sandwiches $5-9; ⏱ 7am-5pm Mon-Fri, 8am-4pm Sat

This artisan bakery in the Grand Central Arcade builds sandwiches on its own peasant-style loaves and baguettes, with soups, salads, pastries and other treats.

BAKEMAN'S Map p57 Diner $
☎ 206-622-3375; 122 Cherry St; sandwiches $4-6; ⏱ 10am-3pm Mon-Fri

Legendary for its theatrical counter service and its roasted-fresh-daily turkey-and-cranberry sandwich, this subterranean diner demands that you know what you want and aren't afraid to ask for it.

INTERNATIONAL DISTRICT

The International District (ID) is a great neighborhood for cheap eats, or you can go all-out on a sumptuous eight-course dinner banquet. It's also a good place to seek out decent food after the bars close. The many Vietnamese, Thai and Chinese restaurants that line Jackson St between 6th and 12th Aves give you plenty of options. East of 8th Ave S and I-5, Little Saigon takes over and the flavor becomes decidedly Vietnamese.

Locals argue fiercely over which place does the best *pho* and, especially, the best dim sum, so ask around and try a bunch.

SHANGHAI GARDEN
Map p60 Chinese $-$$$

☎ 206-625-1688; 524 6th Ave S; lunch $6.95, dinner mains $8-18; ⏱ lunch & dinner; ♿

Hand-shaved green barley noodles are the specialty of Shanghai Garden, and the sugar-pea vines are also a favorite. If you're used to heavy, greasy Chinese food, you're in for a revelation.

JADE GARDEN Map p60 Chinese $-$$

☎ 206-622-8181; 424 7th Ave S; mains $8-12; ⏱ dim sum, lunch & dinner, 10am-10pm daily

Dumplings to die for and a vast array of interesting dim sum make this a good choice for a brunch in the ID. You can nibble on a chicken foot or play it safe with familiar-looking noodle and rice concoctions, but the more things you try, the more fun you'll have. The Jade Garden's hot pots have also been recommended.

CHINA GATE Map p60 Chinese $-$$

☎ 206-624-1730; 516 7th Ave S; starters $3.50-12, mains $6-12; ⏱ 10am-2am; ♿

Like House of Hong, the China Gate now has all-day dim sum. The Hong Kong-style menu offers a couple hundred choices, and the building is interesting in its own right – it was built in 1924 as a Peking Opera house.

PURPLE DOT CAFÉ
Map p60   Macao-style $-$$
☎ 206-622-0288; 515 Maynard Ave S; mains $5-12; ☯ breakfast, lunch & dinner, open until 3:30am Fri & Sat

The Purple Dot looks like the inside of an '80s videogame (it is actually purple) and draws a late-night drunken-disco crowd on weekends, but most of the time it's a calm, quiet place to get dim sum and Macao-style specialties (meaning you can feast on spaghetti and toast along with your Hong Kong favorites).

HOUSE OF HONG Map p60   Chinese $-$$
☎ 206-622-7997; 408 8th Ave S; dim sum $2-3 per item; ☯ 9am-2am Mon-Sat, 9am-midnight Sun; ☕

This giant yellow mainstay of the neighborhood now serves dim sum from 10am until 4:30pm every day – handy if your craving hits in the middle of the day.

TAMARIND TREE
Map p60   Vietnamese $
☎ 206-860-1414; 1036 S Jackson St; starters $2.50-7, pho $4-8, mains $6-10; ☯ 10am-10pm

Serving upscale food in a beautiful dining room but at lowbrow prices, this elegant place has a HUGE menu including everything from satays and salad rolls to big bowls of pho and a tasty version of the traditional scallop-prawn-pork-mushroom

fried crepe. It also donates some of its profits to the Vietnam Scholarship Foundation. Reservations are recommended on weekends.

GREEN LEAF
Map p60   Vietnamese $
☎ 206-340-1388; 418 8th Ave S; mains from $5; ☯ lunch & dinner

A tiny nook with shiny black tables, this cozy joint is known for inexpensive noodle dishes packed with flavor, as well as huge bowls of traditional or vegetarian pho and a swoon-inducing version of bahn xeo – sort of a cross between a pancake and an omelet.

PHO BAC Map p60   Vietnamese $
☎ 206-568-0882; 1240 Jackson St; mains from $5; ☯ brunch, lunch & dinner

You can get three sizes of pho at this well-established restaurant on the edge of 14th Ave and Jackson St, with its huge windows gazing onto Little Saigon, as well as excellent spring rolls wrapped in fresh herbs and other classic Vietnamese dishes.

PIKE PLACE MARKET & WATERFRONT

For a wide selection of fresh produce, bakery products, deli items and takeout ethnic foods, head to Pike Place Market. Explore the market on an empty stomach and commit to a few hours of snacking; you'll be full by the time you leave, and it doesn't have to

NOT SO FAST!

It sounds downright un-American, this idea of sitting still and patiently waiting for who knows how long, while someone prepares your sustainably farmed, hand-selected, all-organic food from scratch. There's a reason every intersection in the US has a fast-food outlet and every fast-food outlet has a drive-through window. This is not a patient nation. When we order a burger and fries, we'd like them now, please.

But what many Americans are just starting to think about is how our food managed to get so fast in the first place. Those french fries weren't born stick-shaped at the bottom of a deep fryer. Along with the popularity of Eric Schlosser's best-selling book Fast Food Nation and similar high-profile examinations of the fast food industry has come greater attention for the handful of folks who have, for years, been going against the fast-food grain: the Slow Food movement.

Begun in Italy in 1986, the Slow Food idea has gradually spread to other countries and expanded its mission. The Pacific Northwest is home to several Slow Food chapters, including six in western Washington.

One of the Seattle area's biggest priorities in terms of Slow Food is, no surprise, seafood. Increasing demand and better means of transportation mean that, for example, those fresh oysters you're slurping up might not be local at all. And some of them may be locally grown representatives of non-native species.

Urging people to take the time to find out as much as they can about the origins of what they're eating is a key part of the Slow Food movement, in Seattle and elsewhere.

To find out more about the Slow Food movement and how you can help, visit slowfoodseattle.org.

cost you much. And if you're looking for serious dining, you can find that here, too; some of Seattle's favorite restaurants are tucked in mysterious corners in the market district.

For a full directory and map of everything in the market, be sure to pick up a copy of the pamphlet *Welcome to the Pike Place Market* from the market information booth on 1st Ave at Pike St, in front of the main entrance.

CAMPAGNE Map p64 French $$$-$$$$
☎ 206-728-2800; 86 Pine St; starters $9-24, bar menu $6-21; mains $23-29; 5:30-10pm
You have to love a place that cut off part of its building to save the one tree in the market, as the bar at Campagne did. Nestled in the courtyard of the Inn at the market, this is a favorite among Seattle's traditional French restaurants. Try the pan-roasted sea scallops or the free-range beef tenderloin. Reservations are recommended. The lounge is open until midnight.

CHEZ SHEA Map p64 Mediterranean $$$-$$$$
☎ 206-467-9990; 94 Pike St, Ste 34; starters $8-11, mains $20-35; dinner Tue-Sun
Another treasure hidden in one of the market's many corners (upstairs in the Corner Market Building), Chez Shea has great views over Puget Sound that combine with spectacular multicourse meals to make this one of the city's most romantic restaurants. The chef's tasting menu (eight courses, $72) makes the rounds of basically every edible thing to be found in the Pacific Northwest, depending on season. The attached Shea's Lounge now has a three-course menu ($25), if you're not quite ready to commit.

IL BISTRO Map p64 Italian $$$-$$$$
☎ 206-682-3049; 93 Pike St, Ste A; starters $9-14, mains $22-42; dinner
At this atmospheric Italian café, the best and freshest of the market is incorporated into daily specials. Il Bistro's red lighting gives it a gangster-movie feel; the Godfather would no doubt kill for the roasted chicken or the *saltimbocca alla romana* (veal cutlets with prosciutto and sage).

STEELHEAD DINER
Map p64 Southern/Diner $$-$$$$
☎ 206-625-0129; steelheaddiner.com; 95 Pine St; starters $9-14, sandwiches $9-13, mains $15-33; lunch & dinner Tue-Sat, 10am-5pm Sun
'Highbrow diner' sounds like an oxymoron, but the Steelhead does it right – hearty, homey favorites like fish-and-chips, grilled salmon or braised short ribs and grits become fine cuisine because they're made with the best of what Pike Place Market has to offer. The awesome gumbo features Uli's sausage from the market; 'Squimbled Eggs' come poached over Dungeness crab on toast; a fried-chicken sandwich is fall-apart moist and lemony; and the crab cakes have been making local foodies swoon. The place is all windows, which is great considering it's perched right over the market and Elliott Bay, and decorations include tied flies in glass. Reservations are recommended.

PINK DOOR RISTORANTE
Map p64 Italian $$-$$$
☎ 206-443-3241; 1919 Post Alley; mains $15-23; lunch Mon-Sat, dinner daily
Beloved for its atmosphere at least as much as its food, the Pink Door is an old-school

---

LATE-NIGHT EATS

Seattle is the kind of city that rolls up the streets and turns out the lights at 2am, and it doesn't matter how long it's been since dinner. But there are a handful of places where you can still get a snack – or even a proper, decent meal – late at night.

Caffe Minnie's (p129) is open all night long and serves hearty food in portions big enough to soak up whatever liquid damage you've inflicted upon yourself. Experienced bar-hoppers know that a 3am breakfast is a pretty reliable way to stave off a mean hangover. Same goes for Beth's (p135), in which people who might've been standing next to you at the dive-bar jukebox serve dauntingly huge omelets all hours of the night.

Several locals have raved about the black-bean crab at the Sea Garden (☎ 206-623-2100; 509 7th Ave S), open until 3am Friday and Saturday night (and until 2am the rest of the week). Also in the International District, the Purple Dot (p125) sees a lively late-night dinner crowd after the bars close.

Though it doesn't quite qualify as after-hours, Palace Kitchen (p122) offers a so-called 'late-night breakfast' after 10pm.

But there's really nothing better for a post-barcrawl snack than cheap Mexican food consumed in a parking lot, which is why Rancho Bravo taco cart (p135) gets our vote for number-one choice in late-night dining.

favorite – on a nice evening, stopping for dinner and drinks on the deck overlooking the market is hard to beat. The menu is traditional Italian; the vegetarian lasagne comes highly recommended.

ETTA'S SEAFOOD

Map p64   Seafood $$-$$$

☎ 206-443-6000; 2020 Western Ave; brunch $8-12; mains $12-25, ⊗ brunch 9am-3pm Sat & Sun, lunch & dinner daily

Famous for its gourmet seafood brunch, including such mouth-waterers as poached eggs with Dungeness crab and chipotle hollandaise, Etta's is a reliable and classy place with a fish-focused dinner menu – you can never go wrong with the king salmon.

CAFÉ CAMPAGNE Map p64   French $$-$$$

☎ 206-728-2233; 1600 Post Alley; lunch mains $12-21, lunch set menu $15, dinner mains $16-19, dinner set menu $29; ⊗ lunch & dinner daily, brunch 8am-4pm Sat & Sun

At this casual younger sibling of the up-scale Campagne (opposite), the quality of the French-style cooking is what you'd expect from such a talented kitchen; the prices are more manageable, and you don't have to dress up for dinner.

IVAR'S ACRES OF CLAMS

Map p64   Seafood $-$$$

☎ 206-624-6852; Pier 54, 1001 Alaskan Way; outdoor counter snacks $4-7, dinner mains $12-20; ⊗ lunch & dinner; ♿

Ivar Haglund was a beloved local character famous for silly promotional slogans ('Keep clam!'), but he sure knew how to fry up fish-and-chips. Ivar's is a Seattle institution that started in 1938. Forgo the dining room for the outdoor lunch counter; the chaotic ordering system involves a lot of yelling, but it seems to work, and then you can enjoy your clam strips and chips outdoors on the pier.

LE PICHET Map p64   French $-$$$

☎ 206-256-1499; 1933 1st Ave; snacks $4-12, lunch $6-12, dinner $9-19; ⊗ breakfast, lunch & dinner, until 2am Sat & Sun

This tiny French café, bistro and wine bar is elegant and tasteful, and yet it's casual enough to quickly become a favorite haunt. The menu features traditional French cuisine without the aorta-clogging heaviness

that this often implies. Breakfast is simple and delicious, and small snack plates of olives, almonds or various *rillettes* (potted meats) are available all day. For a treat, order the roasted chicken with celery and potatoes ($34); it's made only on request and takes an hour, but is worth the wait.

MATT'S IN THE MARKET

Map p64   Northwest $-$$$

☎ 206-467-7909; www.mattsinthemarket.com; 94 Pike St, ste 32; lunch $6-16, starters $9-14, dinner mains $23-28; ⊗ lunch & dinner Mon-Sat

A beloved spot that's been closed for renovations, the expanded Matt's was due to reopen as this guide was being researched; check the website for updates.

ATHENIAN INN

Map p64   Diner $-$$

☎ 206-624-7166; 1517 Pike Place Market; mains $8-12; ⊗ 6:30am-6:30pm Mon-Sat

There's nothing fancy about the Athenian, but it's a landmark and a bastion of unpretentious, frontier-era Seattle, a holdover from the days before Starbucks and Grand Central Bakery (*way* before – it opened in 1909). It's been a bakery and a lunch counter and now seems to have settled in as a diner-bar combination where, especially in the off hours, you can snuggle into a window booth and gaze over Elliott Bay with a plate of fried fish.

LOWELL'S RESTAURANT

Map p64   Diner $-$$

☎ 206-622-2036; 1519 Pike Pl; mains $6-12; ⊗ breakfast, lunch & dinner

If you want a sit-down meal but nothing fancy, head to Lowell's, well loved by shoppers, businesspeople and fellow market operators for its classic, eye-opening breakfasts and cheap-and-cheerful lunches. Order up eggs Benedict, salmon omelets or fish-and-chips from the chalkboard menu, lunch cafeteria style, then take it over to a window seat and enjoy the view.

MEE SUM PASTRIES

Map p64   Asian $

☎ 206-682-6780; 1526 Pike Pl; bao $2; ⊗ breakfast, lunch & dinner

This little storefront window is famed for its giant *hum bao* – eminently portable meat- or vegetable-filled steamed buns that make a great snack or small meal.

LE PANIER Map p64 · Bakery $
☎ 206-441-3669; 1902 Pike Pl; pastries $2-5;
⏱ breakfast, lunch & dinner
A great place to grab a coffee and croissant and watch the market action, Le Panier calls itself a 'very French bakery' and tends to live up to the name.

PROCOPIO GELATI Map p64 · Gelato $
☎ 206-622-4280; 1501 Western Ave; gelato $1-4;
⏱ 9am-6pm;
If the Pike Place hill-climb wears you out – or even if it doesn't – stop for an authentic Italian-style gelato. The owner learned his trade from a Milanese gelato maker, and he uses only super-fresh ingredients for completely undiluted flavors.

BELLTOWN

Formerly scruffy, now condo-clean and safe for yuppie families, Belltown makes it easy to either spend a little or spend a lot and still get a fabulous meal. Peppering its rows of bars and cocktail lounges is a great variety of cafés, delis, top-of-the-line restaurants and low-budget noodle huts frequented by arty musicians and starving students. The other advantage of Belltown is that you're more likely to be able to find late-night dining, thanks to an active cocktail scene that encourages many restaurants to serve at least a bar menu until 2am.

FLYING FISH Map p69 · Seafood $$-$$$$
☎ 206-728-8595; 2234 1st Ave; lunch $7-15, dinner small plates $7-14, mains $18-38; ⏱ lunch Mon-Fri, dinner daily until midnight, bar menu until 2am
Still the reigning king of fish dishes in Seattle, or at least in Belltown, Flying Fish is a reliable spot for seafood. Combine several small plates, share a platter of oysters, or go with a main dish, such as yellowtail with eggplant and soy ginger sauce, or monkfish in coconut peanut sauce. The dining room is bustling and energetic, the service friendly and top-notch. The menu changes daily depending on what's fresh.

QUEEN CITY GRILL Map p69 · Seafood $$-$$$$
☎ 206-443-0975; 2201 1st Ave; starters $9-17, salads $6, mains $12-33; ⏱ dinner until 2am
This longtime Belltown favorite specializes in grilled seafood from its daily menu and a solid selection of meats and chicken from its seasonal menu. The goat-cheese appetizer and the grilled *ahi* with red-pepper sauce are divine, and warm lighting makes the room feel cozy yet sophisticated. Reservations are recommended.

RESTAURANT ZOE Map p69 · Northwest $$$
☎ 206-256-2060; 2137 2nd Ave; small plates $6-19, mains $18-28; ⏱ dinner Mon-Sat
Chef-owner Scott Staples' sleek, attractive restaurant still has people lining up for dinner. The menu depends on the freshness of the ingredients; there's a lot of barely seared fish and seasonal vegetables. Starters include a rabbit and foie gras 'mosaic' with Granny Smith apples, beet risotto and a horseradishy tuna tartare, and the mains – wild boar, sea scallops – reveal a knack for doing interesting things to meat. Reservations are recommended.

BUENOS AIRES GRILL Map p69 · Meat $$$
☎ 206-441-7076; 2000 2nd Ave; sides $7-14, steaks $16-30; ⏱ dinner daily, until midnight Fri & Sat
Tucked into a Belltown side street, this Argentinean steakhouse serves minty fresh cocktails, unusual salads (like hearts of palm) and huge portions of well-prepared steak. The cooking aromas will lure you in; the fun vibe and the staff's tendency to tango on request will make you linger.

MARCO'S SUPPERCLUB
Map p69 · International $$-$$$
☎ 206-441-7801; 2510 1st Ave; starters $8-13, mains $17-24; ⏱ brunch Sun, lunch Mon-Fri Jun-Aug, dinner Mon-Sat
Marco's travels the globe with its ever-shifting multi-ethnic menu, including such items as Jamaican jerk chicken and eggplant masala; the deep-fried sage leaves are mandatory.

SHIRO'S SUSHI RESTAURANT
Map p69 · Japanese $-$$$
☎ 206-443-9844; 2401 2nd Ave; mains $20-21, specials $9-13, sushi $2-9; ⏱ 5:30-9:45pm
Kyoto-born sushi master Shiro Kashiba ran Seattle's first sushi restaurant, Nikko, for 20 years. He spends a lot of time shopping for the freshest ingredients, hence his reputation as the go-to guy for raw fish in Seattle. He's a cheerful looking fellow but takes his sushi very seriously – get a seat at the bar if you can, and watch him work.

BELLTOWN PIZZA Map p69   Pizza $-$$$

☎ 206-441-2653; 2422 1st Ave; starters $7-8, sandwiches $9, pizzas $11-22; ☽ dinner

Pizza and beer is great, but pizza and hard liquor works quicker. Started as a tiny bar serving New York-style pizza, Belltown Pizza has expanded a lot since then but maintains its original mission of good food and good fun at grownup hours (the bar's open until 2am). A large pie is enough to feed four hungry people. You can also get salads, pasta and sandwiches.

CAFFE MINNIE'S Map p69   Diner $-$$

☎ 206-448-6263; 101 Denny Way; mains $5-11; ☽ 24hr; ⊛

At the northern end of Belltown, almost in Lower Queen Anne, is this appealingly worn-in 1950s-style diner, a blessing for insomniacs, bar-crawlers, truckers, fugitives or those with the munchies after 2am. You can have breakfast all day while looking out the window at a little cake shop and a chintzy costume-rental store.

BLACK BOTTLE Map p69   Northwest $

☎ 206-441-1500; blackbottleseattle.com; 2600 1st Ave; mains $8-9; ☽ 4:30pm-1:30am

The huge crowd congregating outside the front door of this new Belltown restaurant is your first clue that something interesting is happening inside. The menu has a lot more clues: octopus carpaccio, lemon-squid salad, saffron risotto cakes. It's a spartanly decorated but warm-looking space, with friendly service and a chic atmosphere. Plus, you can't beat a Belltown menu where nothing tops $9.

NOODLE RANCH Map p69   Asian $

☎ 206-728-0463; 2228 2nd Ave; curries $8-10; ☽ lunch & dinner Mon-Sat; Ⓥ

In the same block as Mama's, this old standby looks like a modernized greasy diner but serves pan-Asian noodle dishes, many of them vegetarian. The tofu spring rolls, green curries and pad Thai are worth trying if you need some cheap, effective stomach-padding before (or after) your bar crawl.

MAMA'S MEXICAN KITCHEN

Map p69   Mexican $

☎ 206-728-6262; 2234 2nd Ave; starters $4-6, burritos $6-8; ☽ lunch & dinner

Wildly popular, California-style Mama's Mexican Kitchen is always packed. But that's no surprise for a place that serves scrumptious burritos, huge combination plates and killer margaritas (cheapest during happy hour from 4pm to 6pm Monday to Saturday). It's in a great location for people-watching, but the kitsch Mexican artifacts plastering the walls are equally absorbing. Velvet Elvises!

MACRINA Map p69   Bakery $

☎ 206-448-4032; 2408 1st Ave; snacks $1-5; ☽ breakfast, lunch & dinner

You might have to wait in line, especially if you want to sit at a table, but as soon as you bite into your breakfast roll or panini sandwich, you won't care. Macrina makes some of the city's best artisan bread and decadent snacks.

SEATTLE CENTER & QUEEN ANNE

Many of the dining options in Lower Queen Anne, just west of Seattle Center, are geared toward the pre- or post-game crowd attending games at Key Arena. Up on top of the hill, in Upper Queen Anne, restaurants have more of the neighborhood's quiet, grownup, family-friendly atmosphere.

CANLIS Map p76   Northwest/American $$$$

☎ 206-283-3313; 2576 Aurora Ave N; starters $9-18, mains $35-70; ☽ dinner Mon-Sat

This place is old-school enough for either prom night or your grandma's birthday dinner. The traditional, classic food and service are both top-notch, and you can rest assured that none of the style is affected. Canlis has been around since 1950 and its authenticity shows. The view is lovely, too. Reservations are recommended, especially for weekends.

SKY CITY

Map p73   Northwest $$$$

☎ 206-905-2100; 219 4th Ave N; starters $15-25, mains $34-54; ☽ brunch Sat & Sun, lunch Mon-Fri, dinner daily; ⊛

You don't really go to this revolving restaurant atop the Space Needle for the food. The view's the thing, and it is tremendous from 500ft up in the air. The elevator ride is free if you have meal reservations.

PARAGON BAR & GRILL

Map p76   American $$-$$$

☎ 206-283-4548; 2125 Queen Anne Ave N; brunch $7-10, starters $8-11, dinner mains $19-24; ☾ brunch Sun, lunch Mon-Sat, dinner daily

The Paragon is a bastion of American regional cooking, with a specialty in grilled fish and updated classics. Try the avocado shrimp cakes, either as a starter or in a sandwich, or go with a classic cheeseburger. There's an open fireplace, a lively bar scene (the bar's open until 2am) and live music most nights.

SAPPHIRE KITCHEN & BAR

Map p76   Mediterranean $$-$$$

☎ 206-281-1931; 1625 Queen Anne Ave N; mains $10-18; ☾ brunch Sun, dinner until midnight Sun-Wed, until 2am Thu-Sat

A groovy spot for nightlife in Upper Queen Anne, the Sapphire has a well-stocked bar and serves Spanish-influenced Mediterranean fare in a chic dining room with sapphire, red and purple walls. The black-painted facade and the neon sign outside might not fit with Queen Anne's style, but don't let it turn you off.

5 SPOT

Map p76   Northwest $-$$

☎ 206-285-7768; 1502 Queen Anne Ave N; breakfast scrambles $8-9, lunch $7-10, dinner mains $10-14; ☾ breakfast, lunch & dinner until midnight; ⓖ

In Upper Queen Anne, everyone's favorite breakfast and hangover diner is the 5 Spot. Good strong coffee keeps the staff ultraperky. Try a local legend, like the red flannel hash, or get crazy with the wild-salmon cakes. On weekends, go early to avoid the lines snaking out the door – or go for lunch or dinner; this is an excellent place for a quiet meal featuring good American cooking.

QUEEN ANNE CAFÉ

Map p76   Northwest $-$$

☎ 206-285-2060; 2121 Queen Anne Ave N; sandwiches $8, mains $10-12; ☾ breakfast, lunch & dinner Mon-Fri, brunch Sat & Sun

Locals flock to this trendy neighborhood spot for traditional comfort food, including broiled pork chops and various sandwiches, but the place really shines at breakfast. Expect a bit of a wait for weekend brunch.

LAKE UNION

The area around Lake Union might not benefit from the kind of hype that surrounds other more traditionally foodie-friendly neighborhoods, but it does have a couple of eateries that are well worth your time seeking out.

CHANDLER'S CRABHOUSE & FRESH FISH MARKET

Map p79   Seafood $$$-$$$$

☎ 206-223-2722; 901 Fairview Ave N; starters $10-15, salads $6-9, mains $27-47; ☾ lunch Mon-Fri, dinner daily, brunch Sat & Sun

All windows, with a great view of Lake Union, Chandler's may feel a bit like a chain restaurant (because it is) but it's the reliable place to go if you want to sit near the water and dine on ocean-fresh seafood. You can also buy fish or crab to ship home.

SERAFINA

Map p79   Italian $$-$$$

☎ 206-323-0807; www.serafinaseattle.com; 2043 Eastlake Ave E; starters $8-13, mains $17-25, prix fixe lunch $13.95; ☾ brunch Sun, lunch Mon-Fri, dinner daily (until 1am Fri & Sat)

This lovely neighborhood restaurant in Eastlake specializes in Tuscan-style cooking, with simply prepared meat and fish as well as pastas that can be ordered as a first or a main course. Reservations are recommended.

SITKA & SPRUCE

Map p79   Northwest $-$$$

☎ 206-324-0662; www.sitkaandspruce.com; 2238 Eastlake Ave E; lunch $5-11, dinner $5-18; ☾ lunch Mon-Fri, dinner Wed-Sat

Despite its unlikely location – in a strip mall next door to a Subway – this small green restaurant has won acclaim for its casual vibe, constantly changing tapas-style menu, good wine selection and involved chef-owner (he'll be the guy who brings bread to your table). All the ingredients are obtained from local producers, and the idea is to assemble a meal out of a bunch of different taster-size dishes. Reservations are only accepted for groups of five people or more, and the wait can be long, so grab yourself a beer and spend some time studying the chalkboard menu until it's your turn.

WHAT IS NORTHWEST CUISINE?

A lot of Seattle's gourmet restaurants describe their style of cuisine as 'Northwest.' But what does that actually mean? Besides the high quality of the raw materials found naturally in this region, the thing that distinguishes Northwest cuisine from standard US food is the influence of Asian cooking traditions. Pan-Asian cooking, often referred to as Pacific Rim cuisine or fusion food, is the blending of American or European standards with ingredients from Asia. It results in some unusual combinations – don't be surprised if you get wasabi on your French fries.

Not surprisingly, seafood is a cornerstone of Northwest cuisine. Crab, often Dungeness fresh from the boat, is available almost everywhere – you'll see stacks and stacks of crabs at Pike Place Market. In restaurants, crab is usually served in salad or with garlic butter, but you can also get crab cakes, crab bisque or even crab burgers. The better seafood restaurants print a new list of what's freshly caught each day; you might love seared *ahi*, but if it's the (very limited) season for native coho salmon, for example, you'd be silly not to choose that instead, and a good restaurant will tell you so.

Locally caught fish include red snapper, flounder, sole, tuna, halibut and cod. Shrimp is another major catch. For most of the year, salmon, still a menu staple, is as likely to be from Alaska as from the Northwest. Local trout is also found in fish markets and on menus: try the vibrantly yellow golden trout.

The chilly waters of the Pacific produce sweet-tasting, delicately tangy oysters, causing oyster farms to spring up all along the coast. In the best places, discerning diners can choose which Northwestern bay their oysters on the half-shell hail from. Clams, usually steamed in broth or seawater, and mussels, which cover practically every rock along the Pacific Coast, are common as appetizers, frequently in combination. The elongated, delicately flavored razor clam, in particular, gets nobility status on the West Coast.

The Northwest offers an incredibly rich diversity of fruit, which the best chefs sprinkle like jewels all over their creations, or whip into decadent sauces to drizzle over meat and fish. Blueberries thrive in the acidic soil, and they appear in pies, breads, muffins and scones. The mild climate is also good for strawberries and raspberries. Washington is the nation's largest producer of apples, and other notable orchard crops include pears, cherries and peaches. Blackberry brambles, which snag clothing and grab at the legs of hikers, are a great annoyance until late summer and early fall, when they produce a heady abundance of purple-black fruit. A favorite of black bears, wild huckleberries are found high up in mountain meadows. Washington state is also a major producer of tart, bright-red cranberries, which appear frequently in local dishes.

Rainy Washington is also a mushroom lover's paradise. The best chefs use wild mushrooms gathered in the forest that morning. Don't miss a chance at the saffron-colored chanterelles, whose brief season, intense hue and unique flavor make them a sought-after commodity. Other mushrooms that grow in Northwest forests include the oyster, morel, porcini and shiitake, which are shipped worldwide.

No discussion of food from the Northwest would be complete without mentioning nuts. Filberts (hazelnuts) grow profusely here, as do walnuts. For that special Northwest touch, look for hazelnut gift packs (some jazzed up in smoke house- or jalapeno-style) or hazelnuts served in baked goods or with meat.

CAPITOL HILL & VOLUNTEER PARK

The scene on Capitol Hill is almost as much about style as food; it's no use enjoying a fabulous dinner if no one can see how chic you look while you're eating it. Then again, ambience hardly detracts from a fine dining experience, so who's complaining? The restaurants along Broadway and 15th Ave and the Pike-Pine Corridor offer the full range of Seattle dining options.

COASTAL KITCHEN

Map p82   Northwest $$-$$$

☎ 206-322-1145; 429 15th Ave E; lunch mains $8-12, starters $8-10, dinner mains $14-20; ✇ breakfast 8am-3pm, lunch & dinner until 11pm

This longtime favorite turns out some of the best food in the neighborhood – it has an eclectic mix of Cajun, Mayan and Mexican inspirations, and an Italian-language instruction tape running in the bathroom, if that gives a clue toward influences. Menus rotate by theme; a recent Catalan ensemble included fish stew and pan-seared chicken in Amontillado-sherry-mushroom sauce. If there is a pasta lunch special, do not hesitate: get it! There's also a great 'blunch' ($8.75) between 8:30am and 3pm on weekdays.

CAFÉ SEPTIEME   Map p82   Northwest $$-$$$

☎ 206-860-8858; 214 Broadway E; breakfast & lunch mains $7-9, starters $5-9, dinner mains $15-18; ✇ breakfast, lunch & dinner

The fact that Septieme has gone from super-trendy to warmly familiar probably

top picks

DINING ROOMS WITH A VIEW

- Athenian Inn (p127)
- Chez Shea (p126)
- Sky City (p129)
- Ivar's Acres of Clams (p127)
- Chandler's Crab House (p130)
- Ray's Boathouse (p136)
- Salty's on Alki (p138)

says as much about the changing neighborhood as the place itself. A pretty, Euro-style restaurant-bar with red walls and white-clothed tables, Septieme serves filling but sophisticated burgers, salads, pastas and fish dishes; the bacon-provolone cheeseburger is great. In nice weather, outdoor tables provide first-rate people-watching. It's equally comfortable as a morning coffee shop or a classy late-night cocktail bar.

KINGFISH CAFÉ

Map p82   Southern $-$$

☎ 206-320-8757; 602 19th Ave E; mains $10-15; ☻ lunch Wed-Sun, dinner Mon-Sat

The Coaston sisters' café, opened in 1997, turns out fried chicken that has locals lined up for miles, every night. Don't forget to save room for the sweet-potato pie and Red Velvet Cake.

SIX ARMS PUB & BREWERY

Map p82   American $-$$

☎ 206-223-1698; 300 E Pike St; sandwiches $7-10, specials $7-12; ☻ lunch & dinner

Part of the Portland-based McMenamins chain, this charming old tavern is resplendent with high ceilings, cool antique lighting fixtures, friendly staff and funky art, like the crazy twisted-pipe sculpture over the bar. There's a good selection of sandwiches and burgers and a few specials, such as pasta or halibut-and-chips. And, of course, there's a selection of the McMenamins' microbrewed beer.

GLOBE CAFÉ & BAKERY

Map p82   Vegan $

☎ 206-324-8815; 1531 14th Ave; breakfast $4-9.50, lunch mains $6-9; ☻ 9am-3pm; Ⓥ

We're not even vegetarian and we'd still go miles out of our way for the Globe's incredibly rich vegan food, especially the tempeh-and-yam gyros dripping with onions and tahini sauce. It's an industrial gallery-type space with a huge comic-book panel on the ceiling, giant Plexiglas bookplates hanging like curtains between low booths, funky art on the walls, and a ragtag clientele of workmen, young punks, homeless people and middle-aged intellectual poets. Hipster boys in an open kitchen churn out tofu scrambles, french toast and sandwiches to die for.

HONEYHOLE Map p82   Sandwiches $

☎ 206-709-1399; 703 E Pike St; sandwiches $5-10; ☻ 10am-2am

Cozy by day, irresistible at night, the Honeyhole has a lot to recommend it: big stuffed sandwiches with cute names (Luke Duke, the Texas Tease), greasy fries, a full bar, DJs and a cool cubbyhole atmosphere at night.

BIMBO'S BITCHIN' BURRITO KITCHEN

Map p82   Mexican $

☎ 206-329-9978; 506 E Pine St; tacos $2.95, burritos $5.50-7.50; ☻ lunch, dinner until 2am

A godsend for anyone prowling Capitol Hill late at night, Bimbo's slings fat tacos, giant burritos and juicy quesadillas until closing time. The tiny space is crammed with kitschy knickknacks, including velvet matador portraits, oil paintings with neon elements, and a hut-style thatched awning. Have a margarita with your meal or check out the adjoining Cha-Cha Lounge.

U DISTRICT

This is one of the best districts in Seattle for cheap and authentic ethnic food, and it's easy to find vegan and vegetarian options. When you're browsing for lunch or dinner, don't be put off by unappetizing-looking storefronts; some of the most interesting food comes from places that have the outward appearance of rundown five-and-dime stores. The adventurous will be rewarded.

CEDARS RESTAURANT

Map p85   Indian & Middle Eastern $-$$

☎ 206-527-5247; 4759 Brooklyn Ave NE; starters $4-8, lunch mains $7-10, dinner mains $7-13; ☻ 11:30am-10pm Mon-Sat, 1-9pm Sun; Ⓥ

Cedars serves enormous curries and vindaloos so smooth and creamy you want to dive into them. Eat here just once and you will dream about it later. There's also a great selection of Mediterranean specialties like shish kebabs, falafel and gyros, much of which is vegetarian. The covered wooden patio is a cool hangout in nice weather.

FLOWERS
Map p85   Eclectic $-$$

☎ 206-633-1903; 4247 University Way NE; lunch buffet $8, mains $5-12; ☼ lunch, dinner until 2am; Ⓥ

One of the most stylish places in the U District, Flowers has a vegetarian buffet served until 5pm, and dinners include meat choices. The lunch menu includes 20 sandwiches, each around $5. After hours, it becomes an inviting place to sip a cocktail, munch on an appetizer and 'do homework' with a promising study partner.

RUBY Map p85   Eclectic $

☎ 206-675-1770; 4241 University Way NE; sandwiches $6; ☼ breakfast, lunch, dinner until 2am

The menu at this attractive space next to Flowers reflects the room's Casablanca feel, with fragrant jasmine rice bowls ($8 to $9), a ginger-onion-chili breakfast omelet ($6) and soups like yellow dhal with tofu; spinach, lemon, garlic and ginger; or lemongrass miso with shiitake mushrooms. The bar is hopping at night, and drinks are large and well crafted.

THAI TOM Map p85   Thai $

☎ 206-548-9548; 4543 University Way NE; mains $6-8; ☼ lunch & dinner

First you notice the delicious aroma wafting down the street. Then you see the crowd of hungry people crammed into the doorway of this teeny storefront. It's an open-kitchen lunch counter in a long narrow nook decorated with elephant heads on dark brown walls. There's minimal seating, and the menus are written in gold on wooden blocks. Accepts cash only.

AGUA VERDE CAFÉ
Map p85   Mexican $

☎ 206-545-8570; 1303 NE Boat St; 3 tacos $6.50; ☼ 11am-9pm Mon-Sat, takeout window 7:30am-2pm Mon-Fri

On the shores of Portage Bay at the southern base of University Avenue, Agua Verde Café is a little gem that overlooks the bay and serves fat tacos full of lemony cod, shellfish or portabella mushrooms, plus other Mexican favorites. There's usually a wait for a table, but you can have a drink and wait on the deck, or order from the walkup window. You can rent kayaks in the same building, in case you want to work off your dinner (see p167).

CHACO CANYON CAFÉ
Map p85   Vegan $

☎ 206-522-6966; 4761 Brooklyn Ave NE; juices $3-5, mains $5-10; ☼ 8am-8pm Mon-Fri, 9am-4pm Sat, 10am-4pm Sun; Ⓥ

Just below Cedars is this comfy Southwestern-style nook with a menu that's all vegan, 90% organic and almost half raw-food. If you're a newbie to the raw-food movement (it's pretty much what it sounds like), try the spicy Thai grinder or the gluten-free kiwi lime tart. There's also a long list of vegan sandwiches, smoothies and juices, coffee and tea, and a little window by the entrance where you can pick up vegan, gluten-free, wheat-free baked treats from Flying Apron organic bakery on your way in or out.

HILLSIDE QUICKIE VEGAN SANDWICH SHOP Map p85   Vegan $

☎ 206-632-3037; 4106 Brooklyn Ave NE; sandwiches $7-9; ☼ 11am-9pm Mon-Sat; Ⓥ

This organic vegan Jamaican sandwich shop has annoyingly erratic hours (it's supposed to be open until 9pm but seems to close early a lot) but also has indisputably delicious vegan sandwiches and wraps. The Hillside Quickie educates U-Dub students about the glories of tofu, tempeh and seitan. There's usually only one person working, but guilt-free indulgences like the fake steak or the spicy tofu wrap are worth the wait.

SCHULTZY'S SAUSAGES
Map p85   Meat $

☎ 206-548-9461; 4142 University Way NE; brats $7-8; ☼ lunch & dinner; ♿

This former hole-in-the-wall has doubled in size, which serves as a warning to all who overindulge in Schultzy's meaty goodness. Its claim to fame is straightforward and simple: bratwurst, burgers and beer. There are also veggie dogs, but come on, seriously.

SIDECAR FOR PIGS PEACE
Map p85   Vegan Deli $

☎ 206-523-9060; www.sidecarforpigspeace.com;
5270B University Way NE; snacks $1-6; ⏱ 10am-
8pm Tue-Sun; Ⓥ

This one qualifies for the 'only in Seattle'
tag: an all-vegan deli and store whose
profits go entirely to support a nearby
sanctuary for pigs rescued from their otherwise grisly fates. Pick up vegan sandwiches,
spirulina cookies, organic wine, vegan
cupcakes and meat-free pet food, and ask
the volunteers who work there about the
'board of directors.'

ORANGE KING Map p85   Burgers $
☎ 206-632-1331; 1411 NE 42nd St; burgers $2-5;
⏱ lunch & dinner, closed Sun

At this old-fashioned greasy spoon, miracu-
lously, you can still get a burger and fries
for less than $4. It's not gourmet, but it's
fast and cheap.

DICK'S DRIVE-IN
off Map p85   Burgers $

☎ 206-632-5125; 111 NE 45th St; meals $1-5;
⏱ breakfast, lunch & dinner; ♿

Sometimes you don't want gourmet. Sometimes you just want a big, greasy burger at
2am, with fries and a shake, and you want it
all for less than $5. At Dick's, you can have
it – plus a bonus sideshow of parking-lot
hijinks that peak right after the bars close.
It's not just fast food; it's an institution. There
are other locations around town; their bright
orange signs are hard to miss. The most
theatrically rewarding, of course, is in Capitol
Hill (Map p82; ☎ 206-323-1300; 115 Broadway Ave E).

FREMONT & WALLINGFORD

Fun-loving Fremont is changing fast, but it's
still known for its lively mix of old hippies,
young professionals and gregarious students
who fill the neighborhood's pubs, restaurants
and coffeehouses every evening.

TILTH Map p93   Organic $$-$$$
☎ 206-633-0801; 1411 N 45th St; small plates
$6-14, large plates $10-29; ⏱ brunch Sat & Sun,
dinner Tue-Sun

The only ingredients on chef Maria Hines's
menu that aren't organic are those found

in the wild, like mushrooms and seafood.
Everything else, from asparagus to cheese,
is carefully selected to meet certified-
organic standards, and prepared in a manner that preserves its essence. Try the Duck
Three Ways, made with the first organically raised ducks in Washington. Servers
in the small restaurant are unpretentious
and friendly, and will gamely answer any
questions about the food or wine. Diners
generally order more than one plate. Reservations are recommended; there's also a
small bar in the corner.

BIZZARRO Map p93   Italian $$-$$$
☎ 206-545-7327; 1307 N 46th St; mains $12-18;
⏱ dinner

With a name like Bizzarro you'd never guess
that this Wallingford hotbed is an excellent neighborhood Italian café. When you
learn that it's actually someone's garage
crammed with kitschy art and weird antiques, the name makes sense. Deliciously
buttery pasta dishes, a good wine list and
frequent live music add to the experience.

KABUL Map p93   Afghani $$
☎ 206-545-9000; 2301 N 45th St; mains $12-15;
⏱ dinner Mon-Sat; Ⓥ

You don't find the cuisine of Afghanistan
on every street corner – if you'd like to give
it a try (it's like a blend of Pakistani and
Middle Eastern cooking, with lots of yogurt
and stewed eggplant, grilled lamb kebabs,
and korma, a mild and creamy curry), head
to Kabul. Vegetarians have plenty of great
options here.

TRIANGLE LOUNGE Map p89   American $-$$
☎ 206-632-0880; 3507 Fremont Pl N; starters
$2-10, sandwiches $5-9, pizzas $10-12; ⏱ lunch &
dinner until 2am

Good old American pub food kicked up a
notch – like pizza with garlic sauce, grilled
chicken, red peppers and fresh mozzarella,
or a goat-cheese-and-apple salad – as
well as a cool red-neon 'Prescriptions' sign
above the bar are the trademarks of this
arrowhead-shaped hangout.

BAGUETTE BOX Map p89   Sandwiches $
☎ 206-632-1511; 626 N 34th St; sandwiches $5-8;
⏱ 11am-8pm

Handy when you just want to grab a quick
lunch on the way to the Fremont Troll
(see p90), but don't want corporate fast

food, this new sub shop makes a dozen sandwiches on fresh baguette. The choices range from the decadent drunken chicken or leg-of-lamb to heart-healthy options like squash-and-eggplant or crispy tofu.

BOULANGERIE
Map p93   Bakery $

☎ 206-634-2211; 2200 N 45th St; pastries $2-5; ☻ 7am-2.30pm
One of Seattle's best neighborhood bakeries, Boulangerie whips up French-style pastries and bread loaves delivered with a smile.

RANCHO BRAVO
Map p93   Mexican $

211 NE 45th St; mains $2-5; ☻ varies, open until 2:30am Fri & Sat
A taco stand in the parking lot of Winchell's Donuts, Rancho Bravo serves cheap, filling tacos and burritos that are pretty good anytime and *awesome* at 2am.

GREEN LAKE & PHINNEY RIDGE

This area has an everybody-knows-each-other neighborhood feel to it, and the restaurants consequently tend to be welcoming and casual.

NELL'S
Map p95   Continental $$-$$$

☎ 206-524-4044; 6804 E Green Lake Way N; mains $18-22, 5-course menu $52; ☻ dinner
For fine dining near Green Lake, Nell's serves up classic European dishes with Northwestern flair. It inhabits the space formerly occupied by Saleh al Lago, and it actually maintains one of that beloved eatery's dishes – the calamari with aioli – to widespread critical acclaim. Opt for seafood dishes, and don't skip dessert.

TANGLETOWN PUB
Map p95   Northwest $-$$

☎ 206-547-5929; 2106 N 55th St; mains $7-12; ☻ breakfast Sat & Sun, lunch & dinner daily
This outpost of the Elysian Brewing Company quickly made friends in the neighborhood, despite having taken over the space that was once the worshipped Honey Bear Bakery. It's a more child-friendly space

than Elysian's Capitol Hill brewery, and the building itself is gorgeous: when afternoon sunlight comes streaming into the leaded-glass windows and hits those burgundy walls, look out! Glorified pub food (chicken wings, an eggplant panini) and Elysian beer carry the day.

74TH STREET ALE HOUSE
Map p95   American $

☎ 206-784-2955; 7401 Greenwood Ave N; mains $6-10; ☻ lunch & dinner
This favorite neighborhood pub has a wide selection of beers and a friendly, casual vibe. It also serves good food – locals are particularly enthusiastic about the spicy gumbo and the substantial quesadillas.

MAE'S PHINNEY RIDGE CAFÉ
Map p95   American $

☎ 206-782-1222; 6412 Phinney Ave N; mains $5-10, cinnamon rolls $2.50; ☻ breakfast daily, lunch Mon-Fri; ☻
Breakfast is heavenly, and the tasty milkshakes make it a worthwhile trip any time. Not that there's anything wrong with having a milkshake for breakfast, mind you. Mae's famous cinnamon rolls are now available in stores, but they're inevitably best here in the homey little café.

BETH'S CAFÉ
Map p95   Breakfast $

☎ 206-782-5588; 7311 Aurora Ave N; omelets $6-9; ☻ 24hr
The best – or at least biggest – hangover breakfast in the world is at Beth's, and you can get it all day long. Key words: all-you-can-eat hash browns. You can't smoke in here any more, which, depending on your view, either ruins everything or makes it possible to enjoy Beth's infamous 12-egg omelet while breathing. Feel free to contribute a piece of scribbled artwork to the wall, preferably one that's strongly pro- or anti-pirate.

RED MILL BURGERS
Map p95   Burgers $

☎ 206-783-6362; 312 N 67th St; burgers $4-6; ☻ lunch & dinner
This place is constantly collecting accolades for grilling up the best burger in town, and it also fries up the fattest, yummiest onion rings. There's usually a line out the door but it moves along quickly.

EATING GREEN LAKE & PHINNEY RIDGE

BALLARD & DISCOVERY PARK

An old Scandinavian fishing town that's suddenly hip, Ballard has a number of reputable places to eat and drink. It's an ever-changing scene, so don't hesitate to ask around and check local papers for the latest recommended places.

RAY'S BOATHOUSE
Map p98   Seafood $$-$$$

☎ 206-789-3770; 6049 Seaview Ave NW; mains $25-38, kids' menu $5-8; ⏱ dinner; ⓗ

OK, so it's a cliché, but Ray's offers views over the Olympics, nautical decor and an exhaustive fresh-fish menu. It offers tourists everything they imagine when they think about a nice dinner out in Seattle. Reservations are required; if you can't get in for dinner, at least come for a drink on the sundeck: the bar's open until midnight. Ray's is about a mile west of the Ballard Locks.

CHINOOK'S AT SALMON BAY
Map p98   Seafood $-$$$

☎ 206-283-4665; 1900 W Nickerson St; mains $8-30; ⏱ breakfast Sat & Sun, lunch Mon-Sat, dinner daily

Across the Ballard Bridge in the Fisherman's Terminal, Chinook's is where fish practically leap out of the water and into the kitchen. You can't get it much fresher than this, and the selection of fish and range of preparations is vast. Another plus is watching the fishing fleet coming in or fishers mending their nets from the massive restaurant windows or the sundeck in summer.

MADAME K'S
Map p98   Italian $-$$$

☎ 206-783-9710; 5327 Ballard Ave NW; starters $6-7, pasta $10-12, pizza $12-20; ⏱ lunch Sat & Sun, dinner daily

An elegant red-and-black pizza parlor with an old bordello feel (the building was once a brothel), this small, chic place is packed out for dinner. It's also a popular place for drinks and desserts. There's a really nice patio out back, or you can let history repeat itself in the upstairs dessert room with a decadent 'Chocolate Chip Orgasm.'

OLD TOWN ALE HOUSE
Map p98   American $

☎ 206-782-8323; 5233 Ballard Ave NW; starters $3-6, sandwiches $8-10; ⏱ lunch & dinner

This cavernous, warmly lit, red-brick pub serves giant sandwich 'wedges,' stacks of delicious fries and microbrewed beer in a convivial atmosphere.

HATTIE'S HAT
Map p98   American $

☎ 206-784-0175; 5231 Ballard Ave NW; mains $6-10; ⏱ breakfast, lunch, dinner until 2am

This might be the best place in town to make that ever-so-delicate transition from weekend breakfast to dinner and drinks – you can get coffee with eggs and toast all day long, and nobody will find it odd when you switch to beer, even if it's not quite noon yet. The dinner menu is, unsurprisingly, not super ambitious, but the food is plenty filling and better than your average greasy spoon.

LA CARTA DE OAXACA
Map p98   Mexican $

☎ 206-782-8722; www.lacartadeoaxaca.com; 5431 Ballard Ave NW; mains $3-9; ⏱ lunch Tue-Sat, dinner Mon-Sat

This lively place near the Ballard Locks serves the cuisine of Oaxaca, particularly black *mole* sauce – try the *mole negro Oaxaqueno,* the house specialty. You can sample the same stuff on tamales, or go for a combination of various small plates. Seating is mostly picnic-style, and there's a full bar – handy considering there's usually a wait for a table.

CENTRAL DISTRICT, MADRONA & MADISON PARK

This area has everything from some of the city's best barbecue joints to upscale French cuisine and a long-standing vegetarian restaurant.

ROVER'S
Map p103   French $$$-$$$$

☎ 206-325-7442; 2808 E Madison St; mains $8-24, lunch set menu $35, dinner set menu $80-130; ⏱ lunch Fri, dinner Tue-Sat; Ⓥ

Many locals consider this Seattle's best restaurant. Chef Thierry Rautureau ('the Chef in the Hat') offers three prix-fixe menus a day (one vegetarian), as well as á-la-carte items. The food is upscale French with a Northwest twist – Oregon quail, for example, or Copper River salmon with morels. The cozy space is one of the few in Seattle where you'll want to dress up, and reservations are definitely advised.

MADISON PARK CAFÉ
Map p103   American $$-$$$

☎ 206-324-2626; 1807 42nd Ave E; brunch $8-10, starters $6-8, mains $18-28; ☑ dinner Tue-Sat, brunch Sat & Sun

Down in Madison Park, in a converted house at the end of Madison St just before you hit Lake Washington, the Madison Park Café is a favorite breakfast and lunch spot. It's a cute little space with blue-and-white checked tablecloths, an extremely cheery feel and welcoming owners. The menu is half old-school (filet mignon, duck confit) and half new-school (foie gras, baby octopus confit) – no need to decide, really, just try some of each.

CAFÉ FLORA
Map p103   Vegetarian $$-$$$

☎ 206-325-9100; 2901 E Madison St; starters & sandwiches $7-10, mains $15-17; ☑ brunch Sat & Sun, lunch Mon-Fri, dinner daily; Ⓥ

A longtime favorite for vegan and vegetarian food, Flora has a gardenlike feel and a creative menu, with dinner treats like seitan spring rolls and breaded coconut tofu dipped in chili sauce, a portobello French dip, caprese pizza and black-bean burgers. Or go for the hoppin' john fritters or tomato asparagus scrambles at brunch.

CACTUS
Map p103   Tapas/Mexican $-$$$

☎ 206-324-4140; 4220 E Madison St; lunch $7-10, dinner $10-17; ☑ lunch & dinner Mon-Sat, 4-10pm Sun

Instantly cheery, this Mexican-Southwest restaurant – with branches in Kirkland and Alki Beach – is a fun place to go and pretend you're on a sunny vacation even if it's pouring rain. A margarita and a king salmon torta or butternut squash enchilada will scare off the grayest clouds, and the jaunty waitstaff and fun music do the rest.

R & L HOME OF GOOD BAR-B-QUE
Map p103   Southern $-$$

☎ 206-322-0271; 1816 E Yesler Way; dinner $10-13, sandwiches $7; ☑ lunch & dinner Tue-Sat

You can't get within a block of this little neighborhood joint without drooling from the smell of barbecue. The storefront looks a little unpromising, but inside there's a wood-paneled cafeteria with curtained windows, a few tables and a counter for takeout orders.

HI SPOT CAFÉ
Map p103   Breakfast $-$$

☎ 206-325-7905; 1410 34th Ave; pastries $1-3, breakfast & lunch $7-10, mains $10-12; ☑ breakfast, lunch & dinner

The cinnamon rolls here are bigger than your head, and that's no exaggeration. It's a comfy little space on multiple levels, where you can either get a sit-down meal or a quick espresso and pastry on the go.

ATTIC ALEHOUSE & EATERY
Map p103   American $

☎ 206-323-3131; 4226 E Madison St; burgers $7-9; ☑ daily, breakfast Sat & Sun, until 2am Thu-Fri

The Attic is a friendly neighborhood pub and a good spot for a beer 'n' burger.

EZELL'S FRIED CHICKEN
Map p103   Southern $

☎ 206-324-4141; 501 23rd Ave; meals $6-8; ☑ lunch & dinner

There's fast food and then there's fast food. This is the good kind. Ezell's dishes out crispy, spicy chicken and equally scrumptious side dishes like coleslaw and sweet-potato pie. This place experience a boom after Oprah Winfrey hyped the fried chicken here as some of the best in the country.

CATFISH CORNER
Map p103   Southern $

☎ 206-323-4330; 2726 E Cherry St; meals $4-10; ☑ lunch & dinner Mon-Sat

For traditional, inexpensive Southern-style fare, head to this no-frills corner hangout. Catfish strips are the specialty, and you can accessorize them with all the trimmings, including collard greens or red beans and rice, while meeting the neighbors and catching up on all the local gossip.

WEST SEATTLE

Most of the action in West Seattle is found along a short strip across from Alki Beach or along California Ave SW.

SALTY'S ON ALKI

Map p106   Steak & Seafood $$$

☎ 206-937-1600; 1936 Harbor Ave SW; starters $12, mains from $20; ⏱ lunch & dinner daily, brunch 9am-2pm Sun

While many restaurants afford views onto Alki Beach and its strutting revelers, most people drive to West Seattle for the view at Salty's on Alki. This steak and seafood house looks across Elliott Bay onto downtown Seattle; at sunset, the spectacle of lights, shining towers and the rising moon is amazing. The food is secondary, but still good.

PHOENICIA AT ALKI

Map p106   Mediterranean $$-$$$

☎ 206-935-6550; 2716 Alki Ave SW; mains $12-20; ⏱ lunch & dinner

Mediterranean and Middle Eastern food is the focus at Phoenicia. The owner is Lebanese, but the flavors are pulled from as far afield as Italy and Morocco and combined with a bounty of fresh local seafood.

ALKI CAFÉ

Map p106   Northwest $-$$

☎ 206-935-0616; 2726 Alki Ave SW; breakfast & lunch $9-11, dinner $12-17; ⏱ breakfast until 2pm, lunch, dinner until 8:30pm

One of Seattle's favorite spots for breakfast and brunch, the Alki serves fresh baked goods, seafood or vegetable-filled omelets and hotcakes. Once the beach crowd goes home, come here for a relaxed dinner of grilled fish, meats or pasta.

SPUD FISH & CHIPS

Map p106   Seafood $

☎ 206-938-0606; 2666 Alki Ave SW; fish & chips $5-7; ⏱ lunch & dinner; 👶

The competition is fierce over which Alki institution has the best fish-and-chips, here or Sunfish (below). (Why not try both?) Spud gets the tourist vote, with its crisp, beachy interior, friendly staff and large portions of fried fish, clam strips and oysters.

SUNFISH

Map p106   Seafood $

☎ 206-938-4112; 2800 Alki Ave SW; fish & chips $5-7; ⏱ lunch & dinner; 👶

Locals swear by this fish-and-chips institution. Options include cod, halibut or salmon and chips, fried oysters, clam strips, or combinations thereof. Sit at one of the outdoor tables and enjoy the boardwalk feel.

ALKI BAKERY

Map p106   Bakery $

☎ 206-935-1352; 2738 Alki Ave SW; snacks $1-3; ⏱ breakfast & lunch

This is a great place to grab a coffee and pastry, then sit down at a window seat to partake of the bakery's free wi-fi connection while digging your beachfront view. Cinnamon rolls and cookies reign supreme, but you can also get takeout sandwiches and salads to eat on the beach.

DRINKING

top picks

- Brouwer's (p147)
- Mecca Café (p143)
- Café Racer (p146)
- Shorty's (p142)
- Zeitgeist (p140)

What's your recommendation? www.lonelyplanet.com/seattle

DRINKING

It's hard to complain too much about Seattle's crappy weather when the two best forms of rainy-day solace, coffee and beer, are available in such abundance. No doubt about it, Seattle's an inviting place to get a buzz on, caffeine or otherwise. Hearty, European-style craft-brewed beers are one of the city's trademarks, and you can try them in burly brick alehouses or sleek cocktail lounges, whichever you prefer. And as for coffee, well, this is the birthplace of Starbucks, and the espresso epidemic hasn't let up since then.

Serious bean freaks will be pleased to know that the small but internationally acclaimed coffee-roasting company Stumptown, based in Portland, now has a branch in Seattle: Stumptown Coffee Roasters (☎ 206-323-1544; 1115 12th Ave). Next door is a new café run by the owners of the cute French bistro Le Pichet (see p127), called Café Presse (☎ 206-709-7674; 1117 12th Ave; ☻ 7am-2am).

Coffee shops are generally open from about 7am (9am Sundays) until 6pm or 7pm. Bars usually serve from lunchtime until 2am (when state liquor laws demand they stop selling booze), although some don't open until 5pm and others start as insanely early as 6am. Variations from the norm are noted in the individual reviews below.

PIONEER SQUARE

Though it lends itself more to frenzied clubbing than casual pint-sipping, Pioneer Square is home to some of the city's oldest – and consequently most atmospheric – bars. If you prefer a saloon to a salon, this historic part of town is your best bet. See the Nightlife chapter (p152) for more ambitious forms of entertainment here.

J&M CAFÉ Map p57   Pub
☎ 206-292-0663; 201 1st Ave S; ☻ 11am-2am
A lot of places claim to be the oldest bar in Seattle, but this is the most charming of the bunch. It's right in Pioneer Square but avoids the screeching party throngs that roam these streets on weekend evenings. Food is reasonably priced, and there's a patio out front that's great for people-watching.

PYRAMID ALE HOUSE Map p57   Brewpub
☎ 206-682-3377; 1201 1st Ave S
South of Pioneer Square by Safeco Field, this brewpub has the cleaned-up-in-dustrial feel – all bricks and brass and designer lighting – that defines the typical Pacific Northwest brewpub. It's a nice, mainstream, but still appreciably Seattle-ish place to take your parents or tenderfoot visitors. But don't even try on a game day, unless you want to squeeze into the standing-room-only beer tent outdoors.

ZEITGEIST Map p57   Coffee Shop
☎ 206-583-0497; 171 S Jackson St; sandwiches $5.75, salads $4.50; ☻ 6am-7pm Mon-Fri, 8am-7pm Sat & Sun
One of the prettiest coffee shops around, this converted warehouse space serves coffee, pastries and sandwiches that have locals lined up all the way out the door in the morning and lunchtime rushes. But its blond-wood tables, picture windows, brick walls and wrought-iron accents make it an aesthetically pleasing place to work or read when it's quiet.

INTERNATIONAL DISTRICT

The lounges inside many of the restaurants in the ID are good haunts for hiding away with a cocktail any time of day; many of them have afternoon happy-hour food specials, too. The ID is also the place to come for things like bubble tea and unusual herbal tea concoctions. Hipster cachet roams the area freely, so explore on your own to find the current coolest spot.

PANAMA HOTEL TEA & COFFEE HOUSE Map p60   Teahouse
☎ 206-515-4000; 607 S Main St
Housed in a historic 1910 building that contains the only remaining Japanese bathhouse in the US (tours are available), this beautifully restored space doubles as a memorial to the neighborhood's Japanese

residents who were forced into internment camps during WWII. The owners found trunks full of left-behind belongings in the basement of the old hotel and have put them on display. Historical photos line the walls, and a glass window in the floor offers a peek at the building's secrets.

PIKE PLACE MARKET & WATERFRONT

There are some extremely romantic and very cozy drinking spots tucked away among the warrenlike market buildings in this area, and many of them have incredible views across the water.

ALIBI ROOM Map p64   Cocktail Lounge
☎ 206-623-3180; 85 Pike Pl; ⏰ 4pm-2am
The perfect place to hide from the perfect crime, the Alibi provides entertainment as well as a hideout, with regular DJ nights, art installations, standup performances and experimental-film screenings. Good eats, too.

KELLS Map p64   Irish Pub
☎ 206-728-1916; 1916 Post Alley; ⏰ 11:30am-2am
Part of a small West Coast chain of Irish pubs, this location is the most atmospheric, with its exposed-brick walls, multiple nooks and crannies, and small patio, situated in timeless Post Alley. As with the best pubs, you might go in alone but you aren't likely to leave that way.

OWL & THISTLE Map p64   Irish Pub
☎ 206-621-7777; 808 Post Ave; ⏰ 11:30am-2am
You can choose a room to suit your mood at this multilevel Irish pub. Feeling bookish? Settle into a red booth by the fireplace in the library room. Aiming for a pool game? There's a room for that, too, as well as a large dining area and the usual murky bar section. The happy hour here is great, and food is a notch above the usual pub grub.

PIKE PUB & BREWERY Map p64   Brewpub
☎ 206-622-6044; 1415 1st Ave; ⏰ 11:30am-2am
The hilarious '80s-industrial decor and abundance of nooks and crannies make this market-side brewpub feel like a Chuck E Cheese for grownups. Mammoth burgers, inventive vegetarian specials and Pike's signature beers (try the Kilt Lifter) add function to the fun.

SHEA'S LOUNGE Map p64   Cocktail Lounge
☎ 206-467-9990; 94 Pike St
Good for a romantic drink, this intimate lounge beside Chez Shea restaurant (p126) has views over Pike Place Market and Puget Sound. There are only a few tables, so you'll want to arrive early.

VIRGINIA INN TAVERN Map p64   Pub
☎ 206-728-1937; 1937 1st Ave
Near Pike Place Market is one of Seattle's most likable bars. Lots of draft beers, a nice brick interior and friendly staff make this a good rendezvous point for forays elsewhere.

BELLTOWN

For many folks, this is the pinnacle of Seattle nightlife. Others say it's been completely ruined by an influx of hipsters who then departed, leaving frat boys in their wake.

MACRO AMOUNTS OF MICROBREWS

The microbrew explosion rocked the Northwest around the same time as the gourmet coffee craze – not coincidentally, Seattle's Redhook brewery was cofounded in 1981 by Gordon Bowker, one of the guys who founded Starbucks. Redhook is no longer brewed in Seattle itself, but in two other breweries, one in Woodinville, 20 miles east of Seattle, and the other in New Hampshire.

Most local microbreweries started out as tiny craft breweries that produced European-style ales. Many of these small producers initially lacked the capital to offer their brews for sale anywhere but in the brewery building itself, hence the term brewpub – an informal pub with its own on-site brewery.

Though you can find microbrews at practically every bar in town, brewpubs often feature signature beers and ales not available anywhere else. It's worth asking about specialty brews or seasonal beers on tap. Most of the brewpubs listed in this chapter offer a taster's selection of the house brews. The brewpubs listed are generally open 11am to midnight daily; exceptions will be noted. Pints range in price from $3 to $5.

Whichever view you hold, Belltown is definitely not the sketchy grungeville it once was, but it still has the advantage of numerous bars lined up in tidy rows that lend themselves to all-night barhopping.

CHERRY STREET COFFEE HOUSE
Map p69   Coffee Shop
☎ 206-441-7176; 2121 1st Ave; ☻ breakfast, lunch & dinner
Relaxing and friendly, this high-ceilinged coffee shop (part of a small local chain) will make you feel like you live in the neighborhood. Curl up in the bay-window seat with a yummy salad, a sandwich ($4 to $6) or a smoothie, or start your day here with coffee and a bagel (bagels $1 to $3). Beer is also served and drinks are priced from $1 to $3.

FIVE POINT CAFÉ Map p69   Dive
☎ 206-448-9993; 415 Cedar St; ☻ 24hr, bar 6am-2am
Not 'retro,' just old and endearingly grim, the Five Point Café in Tillicum Square has been around since 1929, and so have many of its patrons. Half diner, half bar and too worn-in to be mistaken for hip, it's where seasoned barflies and young punks go to get wasted, any time of day. Check out the men's bathroom – allegedly there's a periscope view of the Space Needle from the urinal.

FRONTIER ROOM Map p69   Hipster Hangout
☎ 206-441-3377; 2203 1st Ave
Once an old-school holdover from Belltown's gritty whiskey-drinkin' days, the Frontier Room has recently been colonized by frat boys and par-tay-ers – sort of a microcosm of Belltown as a whole. It still looks cool in here, but enter at your own risk.

LAVA LOUNGE Map p69   Hipster Hangout
☎ 206-441-5660; 2226 2nd Ave
This tiki-themed dive has games of all kinds and over-the-top art on the walls (can't miss the Mt St Helens mural). High-backed booths encourage all-night lingering.

NITELITE LOUNGE Map p69   Dive
☎ 206-443-0899; 1926 2nd Ave; ☻ noon-2am
This little place attached to the Moore Hotel (p179) has an outsize charm, thanks mostly

to the seen-it-all-and-liked-most-of-it bartender and the unpretentious regulars. It can get crowded with hipsters on weekends, but most of the time it's a comfy place to hang out, have a cheap drink and shoot some pool. The sign out front is cool but misleading: alas, the Nitelite's no longer open 24 hours.

RENDEZVOUS Map p69   Hipster Hangout
☎ 206-441-5823; 2320 2nd Ave
This classy place has a curved bar upfront and a small theater in the back room. Emblematic of the chic makeover of Belltown, Rendezvous' theater, named the Jewel Box Theater (p160) was once a slightly grubby venue for punk bands but now sparkles enough to live up to its name. It hosts a variety of music, film and performances.

SHORTY'S Map p69   Pinball Bar
☎ 206-441-5449; 2222A 2nd Ave
If you hate what's happened to Belltown, you'll love Shorty's, a lowbrow, punk-rock holdout amid rows of sleek and chic lounges. The game-themed dive has cheap beer and hot dogs, cool blue slushy drinks, and a whole back room of pinball heaven.

TWO BELLS TAVERN Map p69   Pub
☎ 206-441-3050; 2313 4th Ave
Flee the white belt/skinny jeans crowd and seek refuge in the Two Bells, a neighborhood pub with the friendliest barkeeps in town and a familiar crew of regulars whose intense discussions of the previous night's adventures are portable enough to be taken out back to the patio for a smoke. The house special is a meaty burger stacked thigh-high. Show up Sundays at 1pm for help with the Times crossword.

VICEROY Map p69   Cocktail Lounge
☎ 206-956-8423; 2332 2nd Ave
A proper cocktail lounge, the Viceroy is dignified yet comfortable – there's a long, dark bar and sophisticated touches like cologne in the restroom, but there's also puffy wallpaper, squishy leather couches and a boar's head and antlers on the wall. Cocktails here cost $8 and wine is $6 to $9.

SEATTLE CENTER & QUEEN ANNE

When it comes to drinking, this neighborhood is all over the map. There's the nexus of fun that is Seattle Center, and then there's generally sleepy Queen Anne, with everything from traditional beer halls and dives to swank jazz bars.

FUNHOUSE Map p73 — Dive
☎ 206-374-8400; 206 5th Ave N

This is the punk-rock dive of choice for some of the best local and touring bands that play smallish venues. Try not to slip on beer and fall down, or you'll stick to the checkered floor.

HILLTOP ALE HOUSE Map p76 — Pub
☎ 206-285-3877; 2129 Queen Anne Ave N

Hilltop is a comfy neighborhood hang-out on Queen Anne Hill, sister to the 74th Street Ale House (p147). It has a friendly vibe and a large selection of microbrews.

MECCA CAFÉ Map p76 — Dive
☎ 206-285-9728; 526 Queen Anne Ave N; ☯ 7am-2am

The Mecca has been called – by folks who know – the best bar in Seattle. Half of the long, skinny room is a diner, but all the fun happens on the other side, where decades' worth of scribbles on beer mats line the walls, the jukebox still works the way a jukebox should, the bartenders know the songs on it better than you do and you can get waffles with your beer until 3pm or so.

PARAGON BAR & GRILL
Map p76 — Jazz Club
☎ 206-283-4548; 2125 Queen Anne Ave N

Though it doubles as an upscale restaurant and a jazz venue, this Queen Anne classic is a sophisticated and fun place to sip a cocktail.

REVOLUTION BAR & GRILL
Map p73 — Cocktail Lounge
☎ 206-770-2777; Experience Music Project, 325 5th Ave N; ☯ 11:30am-10pm Sun-Thu, to 11pm Fri & Sat

The renamed and redesigned bar inside the Experience Music Project (see p72) makes for a good excuse to check out the EMP building without forking out the cash for a ticket, if you're feeling cheapish. There's good music

top picks

BEST SEATTLE BARS *JADERS82*

Rosebud (☎ 206-323-6636; 719 E Pike St; ☯ 5-10pm Mon-Fri, Sat-Sun 9am-2pm)
Cheap drinks. Cheap and good food. Super comfortable and a little romantic. Fabulous!

Linda's (p145)
The neighborhood hangout...cross section of the city. Great patio. Yummy comfort food. You will love it.

Sitting Room (☎ 206-285-2830; 108 W Roy St; ☯ 5pm-12am Tue, Wed & Sun, 5pm-2am Thu, Fri & Sat)
Feels like you are in Paris. Cozy little place. Great food and drinks. Hidden gem.

Sambar (☎ 206-781-4883; 425 NW Market St; ☯ 5:30pm-12am Mon-Thu, 5:30pm-2am Fri-Sat)
Hidden in Ballard 'hood. Small. Awesome drinks! Great patio.

Baltic Room (p154)
Capitol Hill club. Grrrreat music! Very hip.

Crocodile Café (p153)
True Seattle. Live music.

Showbox (p154)
Live music venue. Always seems to have fantastic live acts. Check out the Green Room next door.

Owl & Thistle (p141)
Comfy joint. Good brew. Good food. Great happy hour. Soccer/football games on TV. Great place to meet people.

BLUELIST[1] (blu list) v.
to recommend a travel experience.
What's your recommendation? www.lonelyplanet.com/bluelist

playing, a good happy hour (4:30pm to 6:30pm daily), and 50 beers on tap!

SAPPHIRE KITCHEN & BAR
Map p76 — Cocktail Lounge
☎ 206-281-1931; 1625 Queen Anne Ave N

A groovy spot for nightlife in Upper Queen Anne, the Sapphire has a well-stocked bar and serves Spanish-influenced Mediterranean fare in a chic dining room with sapphire, red and purple walls. The black-painted facade and the neon sign outside might not fit with Queen Anne's style, but don't let it turn you off.

TS MCHUGH'S Map p76   Pub
☎ 206-282-1910; 21 Mercer St
Your friendly neighborhood Irish pub, McHugh's has 21 beers on tap (mostly Northwest micros) and is famous for its Irish coffee.

UPTOWN ESPRESSO BAR
Map p76   Coffee Shop
☎ 206-285-3757; 525 Queen Anne Ave N; ☻ 5am-10pm Mon-Thu, 5am-11pm Fri, 6am-11pm Sat, 6am-10pm Sun
This is the place to meet in Lower Queen Anne; it's always crowded with filmgoers from Seattle Center and Uptown Cinemas (Map p76; ☎ 206-285-1022; 511 Queen Anne Ave N), but still has an intimate neighborhood feel.

CAPITOL HILL & VOLUNTEER PARK

Capitol Hill is *the* place to go out for drinks, whether you want a fancy cocktail, a cappuccino or a beer. It's also where most of the gay bars are located.

B&O ESPRESSO Map p82   Coffee Shop
☎ 206-322-5028; 204 Belmont Ave E; ☻ 7am-midnight Mon-Fri, 8am-midnight Sat & Sun
This casually elegant spot has loads of atmosphere and is a nice place to take a date for a leisurely dessert – regulars complain that items on the dinner menu arrive slowly and can be underwhelming. But the dessert case is like a window at Tiffany's, and you can get Turkish coffee here, as well as all kinds of tea, beer, wine and cocktails.

BARÇA Map p82   Cocktail Lounge
☎ 206-325-8263; 1510 11th Ave
Velvet couches, filmy curtains, plush booths, a serpentine bar – this is one sexy, decadent lounge. Settle in among the other pretty people for seduction or quiet conversation.

BAUHAUS Map p82   Coffee Shop
☎ 206-625-1600; 301 E Pine St; ☻ 6am-1am
Bauhaus looks like the most beatnik library in the world, with floor-to-ceiling bookshelves and stylish-looking people of all stripes sitting around reading. Big windows make it a good spot for Capitol Hill people-watching.

CAFFÉ VITA
Map p82   Coffee Shop
☎ 206-709-4440; 1005 E Pike St; ☻ 6am-11pm
Vita is known for small-batch roasts and expertly poured shots. The café also hosts seminars and other educational events, many to do with teaching people about sustainable coffee-growing practices.

CANTERBURY ALE & EATS
Map p82   Pub
☎ 206-322-3130; 534 15th Ave E; ☻ 10am-2am Sat & Sun, 11am-2am Mon-Fri
If you can get past the suit of armor guarding the door, you'll find that everything else about this Old English–style pub in a pretty, black-and-white building makes for a cozy hangout, from the snugs and the tapestried booths to the fireplace and friendly service.

CC ATTLE'S
Map p82   Gay Bar
☎ 206-726-0565; 1501 E Madison St
A self-proclaimed 'drinkin' bar,' CC Attle's is a little cheesy, but it's a longstanding favorite hangout for gay men. The drinks are famously stiff and cheap, and the crowd is pretty well mixed and welcoming. A large outdoor deck adds to the fun in summer.

COMET
Map p82   Dive Bar
☎ 206-323-9853; 922 E Pike St
The diviest dive on Capitol Hill, the Comet's a blessed refuge for anyone allergic to the surrounding plethora of basil-infused cocktails and shimmery clothing. This is the domain of cheap pool tables, tattooed barkeeps and loud rock and roll. Live bands play on the weekends.

ELYSIAN BREWING COMPANY
Map p82   Brewpub
☎ 206-860-1920; 1221 E Pike St
Sort of a factory-outlet shop for microbrews, the Elysian should be cooler than it is. Its beers are metal-sounding, with names like Loki Lager and Dragon's Tooth Stout, but the place itself leans more toward a soccer-mom–sportsbar vibe. Pros: it's large enough to accommodate big groups, it has giant windows that make for good people-watching and it serves a good veggie burger.

ESPRESSO VIVACE ROASTERIA

Map p82   Coffee Shop

☎ 206-860-5869; 901 E Denny Way

Asked what's the best coffee in Seattle, most people will mention Vivace. The main roastery is in a cool space with a checkerboard floor and a curved bar. There's also a tiny walkup window on Broadway (321 Broadway E) where you can get an espresso on the run or stand around and watch the overcaffeinated street theater.

LINDA'S

Map p82   Hipster Hangout

☎ 206-325-1220; 707 E Pine St

The back patio here is an excellent place to observe the nocturnal habits of *Hipsterus Northwesticus*. Linda's is also one of the few joints in town where you can recover from your hangover with an Emergen-C cocktail and a vegetarian brunch while taxidermied moose heads stare at you from the walls.

ONLINE COFFEE COMPANY

Map p82   Coffee Shop

☎ 206-328-3731; www.onlinecoffeeco.com; 1720 E Olive Way; ⏰ 7:30am-midnight

Just because there's wi-fi in every corner of every scraggly soup-kitchen bathroom these days doesn't necessarily mean you brought your laptop with you to Capitol Hill. If you need a quiet place to check your email over a latte, this coffee shop in a renovated house is a good bet. Internet use is 14¢ per minute, and students get an hour for free. There's free wi-fi too, of course. The Pine Street branch (Map p82; ☎ 206-323-7798; 1404 E Pine St) is larger and more office-like.

R PLACE

Map p82   Gay Bar

☎ 206-322-8828; 619 E Pine St

This is an easygoing place to sip a microbrew and check out the Capitol Hill scene. The friendly crowd is primarily gay guys in their mid-20s, but sexual orientation here is secondary to good beer and pool.

SIX ARMS PUB & BREWERY

Map p82   Brewpub

☎ 206-223-1698; 300 E Pike St; ⏰ 11am-1am Mon-Sat, to midnight Sun

One of the classiest of the McMenamins outposts, the Six Arms has lived-in booths

and couches upstairs, tons of antique chandeliers and an elaborate pipe sculpture surrounding the bar. McMenamins' Terminator is a decent stout, and Hammerhead is a perennial favorite.

STUMBLING MONK

Map p82   Belgian Pub

☎ 206-860-0916; 1635 E Olive Way

Across the street from B&O Espresso, this little pub serves strictly Belgian and locally made Belgian-style beers strong enough to justify its name.

WILDROSE

Map p82   Lesbian Bar

☎ 206-324-9210; 1021 E Pike St

This small, comfortable lesbian bar has theme nights (dykes on bikes, drag-king shows) as well as a light menu, pool, karaoke and DJs.

U DISTRICT

Explore 'the Ave' (University Way) and surrounding streets for some of the city's most mellow coffee shops, a literary landmark and some lively watering holes.

BIG TIME MICROBREW & MUSIC

Map p85   Brewpub

☎ 206-545-4509; 4133 University Way NE; ⏰ 11:30am-2am

A fun hang-out in the U District, this expansive brewpub is quiet and casual in the daytime, but gets hopping at night. During the school year, it can be crowded with students still testing their alcohol limits.

BLUE MOON TAVERN Map p85   Pub
☎ 206-633-626; 712 NE 45th St
This legendary home of literary drunks, both famous and infamous, is almost exactly a mile from campus, thanks to an early zoning law. Everyone in the place has a limp and an unlikely story to tell. Hang onto your beer with both hands and be prepared for impromptu recitations of poetry, jaw-harp performances, formless rants and/or halfhearted groping – relax, you'll have made new friends by night's end. If things get too weird, try hiding behind one of the books that line the worn-in wooden booths.

CAFÉ ALLEGRO Map p85   Coffee Shop
☎ 206-633-3030; 4214 University Way NE
This exposed-brick café, tucked in the alley between NE 42nd and NE 43rd Sts, east of University Way, helped launch the Seattle coffee scene. It's full of students scribbling over papers or mooning over professors. Upstairs has a large-windowed smoking area.

CAFÉ RACER Map p85   Pub
☎ 206-523-5282; 5828 Roosevelt Way
Conspicuously friendly to two-wheeled transport, this tiny bar has a rec room

upstairs where you can lounge on couches and watch movies from the bar library on the bar TV. Downstairs there's a short counter, a couple of tables and a microscopic open kitchen, and decor includes the occasional taxidermied gazelle poised above a MotoGuzzi gas tank. Check the bulletin board for community goings-on.

SOLSTICE
Map p85   Coffee Shop
☎ 206-675-0850; 4116 University Way NE
This coffee shop has a nice wooden outdoor patio on the Ave and a comfy organic vibe – lots of vegan and bran-heavy snacks, and so laid-back you have to wonder if anyone here is actually drinking the coffee. The interior is well-worn dark wood and much bigger than it looks from outside. There's also panini, salads, beer and wine.

UGLY MUG
Map p85   Coffee Shop
☎ 206-547-3219; 1309 NE 43rd St
Good soups, sandwiches and the atmosphere of a cozy living room make this coffee shop just off the Ave worth a peek. It also serves excellent coffee, as is standard for any Seattle coffee shop.

COFFEE CULTURE

When the first Starbucks opened in Pike Place Market in 1971, Seattle was suddenly the center of the coffee universe. Standards for coffee quality and strength grew, and soon no one was willing to put up with anything but the best. By the mid-1990s, the craving for a decent cup of joe had seized the nation. These days, Starbucks is both loved and loathed in Seattle.

In addition to creating a new class of high-brow caffeine addicts, the city's coffee fanaticism has also served to revitalize the coffee shop as a social meeting place that offers entertainment in the form of poetry readings, theatrical performances and acoustic music sessions. And it's great for officeless working types, too – coffee and wi-fi go hand in hand, and it's not unusual for a packed coffee shop to be dead silent except for the quiet clattering of laptop keys and occasional screams from the espresso machine.

Still, ordering coffee in one of these places can be a daunting enterprise – particularly if you haven't had your coffee yet. Standing in line at Starbucks or SBC gives you front-row seats in the theater of the absurd. It takes the average customer longer to place an order than it takes the frantic baristas to whip up the concoction. Makes you wonder – someone who's capable of walking up to a counter first thing in the morning and ordering a double-tall extra-hot skinny soy caramel latte on the dry side – well, does that person really *need* coffee?

Here are some tips to help you navigate the surprisingly complicated world of the Northwest coffee-shop menu.

- There's no such thing as small, medium and large. This is America; the tiniest available size is enormous. At Starbucks, a 'small' is a Tall (12oz), a 'medium' is a Grande (16oz) and a 'large' is a Venti (20oz). If you want an 8oz drink, ask for a 'short.'
- Ordering a cappuccino 'dry' means you want more foam than liquid; 'wet' means the opposite.
- 'Skinny' means you want your latte made with nonfat milk.
- When the server looks at you and says 'Room?' it's not a come-on; they're asking if you want them to leave room for cream in the cup.

FREMONT & WALLINGFORD

These low-key residential neighborhoods are home to a nice variety of bars, taverns and brewpubs.

BROUWER'S

Map p89　　　　　　　　　　Belgian Pub

☎ 206-267-2437; 400 N 35th St; ☾ 11am-2am

Shaped like a giant industrial oubliette, this dark cathedral of beer has rough-hewn rock walls and a black metal grate on the ceiling, plus two curved metal balconies, a bunch of cozy, black-leather couches, snug booths and an epic bar behind which are tantalizing glimpses into a massive, expertly stocked beer fridge. A replica *Mannequin Pis* statue at the door and the Belgian crest everywhere clue you in to the place's specialty; yes, you can have framboise. With 47 beers on tap, you can probably have anything you want.

BUNGALOW WINE BAR & CAFÉ

Map p93　　　　　　　　　　Wine Bar

☎ 206-632-0254; 2412 N 45th St

Above the Open Books store in Wallingford, this balcony nook offers a light menu and 2oz tasters of wine (about $4 each).

DAD WATSON'S RESTAURANT & BREWERY

Map p89　　　　　　　　　　Brewpub

☎ 206-632-6505; 3601 Fremont Ave N

This place is Fremont's representative of the McMenamins brewpub chain headquartered in Portland. It's roomy and comfortable, and there's a patio where you can sit and watch the street life at the so-called center of the universe.

HALE'S BREWERY & PUB

Map p89　　　　　　　　　　Brewpub

☎ 206-782-0737; 4301 Leary Way NW

Nestled between Fremont and Ballard, Hale's makes some fantastic beer, most notably its ambrosial Cream Ale. But its flagship brewpub feels a bit like a corporate hotel lobby. It's worth a quick stop, though; ask the friendly staff about the personalized mugs hanging above the bar. There's a miniature self-guided tour in the entryway.

MURPHY'S PUB

Map p93　　　　　　　　　　Pub

☎ 206-634-2110; 1928 N 45th St

This charming, many-windowed Irish pub could almost have been airlifted directly from Ireland to Wallingford. There's live Irish music on weekends; the rest of the time the place is filled with dart players and devotees of the perfect pint.

TEAHOUSE KUAN YIN

Map p93　　　　　　　　　　Teahouse

☎ 206-632-2055; 1911 N 45th St; tea $2-6, snacks $2-8; ☾ 10am-11pm Sun-Thu, 10am-midnight Fri & Sat

For a switch from the coffee shop routine, the Teahouse Kuan Yin has an impressive selection of black, oolong, green and herbal teas, as well as all the paraphernalia you need to enjoy a pot of same. It's open later than most coffee shops and has wi-fi and good desserts.

GREEN LAKE & PHINNEY RIDGE

This area is suddenly all aflutter with new bars and restaurants, which makes it fun to explore. Below are some highlights, but make sure to wander further afield if you have time.

74TH STREET ALE HOUSE

Map p95　　　　　　　　　　Pub

☎ 206-784-2955; 7401 Greenwood Ave N

Some say this traditional ale house serves the best gumbo in town. It also has a couple of nitro taps and plenty of top-notch draught beers.

EL CHUPACABRA

Map p95　　　　　　　　　　Mexican Bar

☎ 206-706-4889; 6711 Greenwood Ave N; ☾ 11am-2am Mon-Fri, 2pm-2am Sat & Sun

The patio is where it's at for sipping margaritas at this kitschy neighborhood hangout. Be warned, service can be slow when the place is crowded.

PROST! Map p95　　　　　　　　Pub

☎ 206-706-5430; 7311 Greenwood Ave N; ☾ 3pm-2am

You can order German beer in liters at this tavern, whose name means 'Cheers!' There are free pretzels on the bar and bratwurst on the menu ($3 to $6). It's a small, usually crowded place with black-and-white photos, deep-red walls, darts in the back, and a sticker behind the bar that says 'My bartender can kick your psychiatrist's ass.'

BALLARD & DISCOVERY PARK

Ballard is probably the city's most buzzing neighborhood to hang out in these days. Some people like that and others mourn the fact but, if nothing else, this type of buzz certainly makes for a diverting nightlife.

COPPER GATE Map p98   Scandinavian Bar
☎ 206-706-3292; 6301 24th Ave NW; ⏱ 5pm-midnight
Formerly one of Seattle's worst dives, the Copper Gate has been converted into a bizarre upscale bar-restaurant focused on meatballs and naked ladies. A Viking longship forms the bar, with a peepshow pastiche for a sail and an assortment of helmets and gramophones as cargo. Barstools arranged two-deep encourage conversation. Food and drinks are Scandi-themed. Try an aquavit or an exotic bottled beer; the Sinebrychoff Porter from Finland pours like motor oil.

FLOATING LEAVES Map p98   Teahouse
☎ 206-529-4268; 2213 NW Market St, Suite 100; ⏱ 11am-10pm Wed-Mon, noon-8pm Sun
Supposedly the first authentic Chinese teahouse in Seattle, Floating Leaves is modeled after the teahouses of the owner's native Taiwan. A contemplative place, it holds classes on tea culture and has occasional live music.

HATTIE'S HAT Map p98   Hipster Hangout
☎ 206-784-0175; 5231 Ballard Ave NW; ⏱ Mon-Fri 11am-2am, Sat & Sun 9am-2am
A classic old divey bar that's been revived with new blood without losing its charm, Hattie's Hat is a perfect storm of stiff drinks, fun-loving staff and cheap greasy-spoon food.

JOLLY ROGER TAPROOM
Map p98   Brewpub
☎ 206-782-6181; 1514 NW Leary Way; pitchers $10, pints $4; ⏱ closed Sun

A secret treasure tucked away off busy Leary, Maritime Pacific Brewing's Jolly Roger Taproom is a tiny, pirate-themed bar with a nautical chart painted onto the floor. Though lately it's gone less scurvy-barnacle and more placid-yachtsman, the beer's still tops – and served in 20-oz pints. The food's not bad either; try a chef's special ($4 to $8) or a mess of clams and mussels ($8.95). There are about 15 taps, all serving Maritime Pacific brews. The strong winter ale, Jolly Roger, is highly recommended.

KING'S HARDWARE
Map p98   Hipster Hangout
☎ 206-782-0027; 5225 Ballard Ave NW
Owned by Linda, of Linda's Tavern (p145), King's Hardware has a hunting-lodge-meets-Old-West-game-room feel. There's pinball and skeeball toward the back, big wooden booths, and taxidermied jackalopes propped between bottles of liquor behind the bar. The spacious hangout also has a good jukebox and, in case you're feeling shaggy, easy access to Rudy's Barbershop (it's attached).

WEST SEATTLE

Though it feels isolated from the rest of the city, West Seattle has the beachy charm of a vacation community and a few good watering holes to explore. It also has a great record store (p118) where you can drink a beer while you browse.

ELLIOTT BAY BREWERY & PUB
Map p106   Brewpub
☎ 206-932-8695; 4720 California Ave SW; ⏱ 11am-midnight Mon-Sat, to 11pm Sun
Long and narrow, with a loft at the back of the room and a beer garden outdoors, this comfortable brewpub makes a nice retreat after a day at Alki Beach. Pub food emphasizes organic, locally sourced ingredients and includes monthly specials. There are always two cask-conditioned beers available.

WEST 5
Map p106   Cocktail Lounge
☎ 206-935-1966; 4539 California Ave SW
A long, skinny space lined with tall, white leather wingback chairs and crowned with neon at the far end, West 5 is an oasis of cool on California Ave. Martinis are the specialty.

OTHER NEIGHBORHOODS

GEORGETOWN

If Ballard's already too 'over' for you, head out to Georgetown to find the preferred drinking holes of those in the know. Georgetown is about 3.5 miles south of Safeco Field. Buses 60, 131 and 134 stop near the cluster of bars reviewed here.

GEORGETOWN LIQUOR COMPANY
Map p149   Hipster Hangout
☎ 206-763-6764; 5501B Airport Way S
This odd mishmash of a bar has an elegant industrial-chic design, a vegetarian menu and an astounding collection of retro video games. Plus, you know, beer and liquor.

JULES MAES SALOON
Map p149   Saloon
☎ 206-957-7766; 5919 Airport Way S
Built in the late 1800s, this traditional saloon now benefits from punk rock and tattoos, a regular schedule of live music, pinball and other vintage games to play, and no need to hide its booze from the authorities (the place operated as a speakeasy during Prohibition).

NINE POUND HAMMER Map p149   Pub
☎ 206-762-3373; 6009 Airport Way S
You can bring your dog to this darkened beer hall. The place is generous with the pours and the peanuts, and the mixed crowd of workers, hipsters, punks and bikers vacillates between energetic and rowdy.

SMARTYPANTS Map p149   Biker Bar
☎ 206-762-4777; 6017 Airport Way; ⏰ 11am-2am Mon-Fri, 10am-2am Sat, 10am-3pm Sun
This giant industrial hangout for scooterists and sportbike riders has vintage motorcycles propped up in the windows, a hearty sandwich menu (plus a weekend brunch) and an obvious fondness for two-wheeled mischief of all types. Ask owner Tim Ptak about ice racing! Wednesdays are Bike Nights, when fans watch the week's recorded MotoGP, SuperMoto and superbike races. The kitchen is open until midnight Monday to Saturday. There's a covered patio outdoors for smokers.

DRINKING IN GEORGETOWN

DRINKING 🥂	(p149)
Georgetown Liquor Company....1	B3
Jules Maes Saloon...................2	B3
Nine Pound Hammer..............3	B3
Smartypants............................4	B3

NIGHTLIFE ✸	(p154)
Studio Seven............................5	A1

SPORTS & ACTIVITIES	(p171)
Jefferson Park Golf Course.........6	C2

top picks

- **Crocodile Café** (p70)
  Birthplace of grunge and still a great indie-rock band venue.
- **Tractor Tavern** (p154)
  Beautiful and comfortable venue for folk-rock shows.
- **Dimitriou's Jazz Alley** (p155)
  The city's most prestigious jazz club.
- **Re-Bar** (p156)
  A nominally gay dance club that's fun for everyone.
- **War Room** (p155)
  Main venue for drum-and-bass and hip-hop nights.

This chapter covers live music, clubbing and other nightlife events that don't fall under the general Arts heading (see p158 for the Arts chapter).

LIVE MUSIC

Most visitors will tend to associate Seattle with a particular era and style of music, depending on their age and interest – whether it's Jimi Hendrix, Nirvana or the Presidents of the United States of America. These days, grunge is little more than a mummified corpse taking up a hefty chunk of the Experience Music Project, and most Seattleites would prefer to forget about the national music media's brief love affair with their city. Nevertheless, grunge's influence was tremendously important to Seattle's live music scene, and many of the clubs it spawned are still around in some form or another, helping local bands to get established and providing some medium-sized venues for touring indie-rock bands. Beyond punk and indie rock, there's also a healthy jazz and blues scene, a strong and growing hip-hop scene, and plenty of places where you can hear techno and electronica.

Seattle's status in the live-music world means most touring bands will make a stop here. On any given night, there's a baffling array of shows and concerts to choose from. As anywhere, the club scene here can be capricious. Name changes and small-venue closures happen frequently, so check music listings and ads in the *Stranger* or *Seattle Weekly* (or their online versions, for the most up-to-date information) before heading out.

The free papers also have club directories that list phone numbers and addresses for local venues, and they're good places to find out about up-and-coming new bands, all-ages shows, house parties and one-off performances in galleries or warehouses, often the best way to get an insider's view of the local music scene.

Look for posters stapled to telephone poles, too, and flyers stacked up around the entrances to most coffee shops and record stores. And, of course, every band and every venue in the modern era keeps a regularly updated calendar on its MySpace page.

Seattle shuts down at 2am, but there are a number of after-hours clubs and unofficial speakeasies. Once you get comfortable in town, start asking around about them.

Typically, live music starts between 9pm and 10pm and goes until 1am or 2am. For most of the venues below, you can pay admission at the door. Larger venues sell advance tickets at their box offices or through Ticket Master (p158) or TicketWeb (www.ticketweb.com), usually tacking on a service fee.

For opera and classical-music listings, see the Arts chapter (p161).

FESTIVALS

Children, hipsters and hippies alike enjoy the Northwest Folklife Festival (☎ 206-684-7300; www .nwfolklife.org). Held at Seattle Center in May on the Memorial Day long weekend, this is a fun event with music, dance, food and crafts.

The absolutely best way to kiss the sweetness of Northwest summer goodbye is at Bumbershoot (☎ 206-281-7788; www.bumbershoot.com). Held in September on the Labor Day long weekend, Bumbershoot brings hundreds of musicians to 25 stages throughout Seattle Center, as well as readings, artwork and other performances.

INDIE ROCK, PUNK, METAL & HIP-HOP

CENTRAL SALOON Map p57

☎ 206-622-0209; 207 1st Ave S; cover charge free-$10

An old-fashioned blues club turned nu-metal, the Central is key to the Pioneer Square party circuit and gets crowded on weekends. Weekly theme nights include Metal Mondays and Punks & Pints.

CHOP SUEY Map p82

☎ 206-860-5155; 1325 E Madison St; cover charge $5-15

With its slightly facetious Asian theme achieved via a giant pagoda-like stage prop and a few Chinese lanterns over the bar, this wide-open, uncluttered space hosts national and local rock bands, DJs and karaoke nights. The crowd and the atmosphere depend on who's playing.

CROCODILE CAFÉ Map p69
☎ 206-441-5611; 2200 2nd Ave; cover charge $5-10

One of the best rock clubs in the country and a Seattle institution, this Belltown space helped launch the grunge and alt-rock scenes and is now home to most of the city's best indie-rock shows, whether local or touring bands. The attached café also serves a decent greasy-spoon break-fast, lunch and dinner.

EL CORAZON Map p79
☎ 206-381-3094; 109 Eastlake Ave E; cover charge $5-10

Formerly Graceland, El Corazon has lots of history echoing around its walls – and lots of sweaty, beer-drenched bodies bouncing off them. Save your clean shirt for another night, and don't expect perfect sound qual-ity at every show. It's also one of the few bars that often has all-ages shows.

EXPERIENCE MUSIC PROJECT Map p73
EMP; ☎ 206-367-5483; 325 5th Ave N; cover charge free-$25

The EMP at Seattle Center boasts a stellar venue: the soaring-ceilinged, acoustically brilliant Sky Church just inside the entrance. It has loads of atmosphere, thanks to laser-light and video mosaics. It's also a cool way to check out the building's weird architec-ture from the inside. See pp72–73 for more.

FUNHOUSE Map p73
☎ 206-374-8400; 206 5th Ave N; cover charge free-$5

A great punk venue near Seattle Center, the Funhouse is where you go to drink cheap beer, check out punk bands like the Trashies and maybe hook up with a Rat City Roller-Derby girl.

LOBO SALOON Map p79
☎ 206-223-9204; 433 Eastlake Ave E; cover charge free-$5

The Lobo is a prime venue for down-and-dirty punk shows full of skater boys, frayed black T-shirts, intentional feedback and beer cheap enough to throw at the bands. The little balcony is a major bonus on hot nights.

top picks

LIVE MUSIC

- Crocodile Café (left) A landmark of the grunge era, still going strong.
- Neumo's (below) A classic punk and indie-rock venue.
- Sunset Tavern (p154) Hipster haunt with garage-rock bands and cult movies.
- Chop Suey (opposite) A well-established venue for touring and local rock bands.
- Tractor Tavern (p154) Classy, amber-lit acoustic theater.

MONKEY PUB Map p85
☎ 206-523-6457; 5305 Roosevelt Way NE; cover charge free-$5

This U-District dive is one of the few places in town where you can slug pitchers of cheap beer, shoot pool and catch a live punk show on a weekend night without having to do any planning whatsoever. If the band sucks, it'll be over soon and did we mention the beer's cheap? Slices from the pizza shop next door are available, or you can pop over for to eat and play video games between sets.

MOORE THEATER Map p69
☎ 206-443-1744; 1932 2nd Ave; cover charge $10-25

Bands love playing this 1500-seat Bell-town venue for its classy style and great acoustics. Attached to a stately old hotel, it exudes battered grace and sophistication whether the act is a singer-songwriter, a jazz phenomenon or a rock band.

NECTAR Map p89
☎ 206-632-2020; 412 N 36th St; cover charge free-$5

A small and comfortable rock venue in Fremont that has grown out of its humble beginnings to become a well-established, scenester-approved club, Nectar hosts everything from reggae and dub to funk to Americana as well as DJ nights.

NEUMO'S Map p82
☎ 206-709-9467; 925 E Pike St; cover charge $5-12

Your classic Northwest midsized rock club, Neumo's has a small stage, a balcony and a new separate bar in the back, Moe's Bar. It books some of the best rock shows in town.

PARAGON BAR & GRILL Map p76
☎ 206-283-4548; 2125 Queen Anne Ave N
When it's not an upscale restaurant and chic martini lounge, this flashy Queen Anne standby hosts live bands and DJs playing everything from indie rock to hip-hop, funk and soul.

SHOWBOX Map p64
☎ 206-628-3151; 1426 1st Ave; cover charge $18-35
This cavernous showroom, hosting mostly national touring acts, ranging from indie rock to hip-hop, reinvents itself every few years. Between sets, hop over to the attached Green Room, the venue's smaller bar and restaurant.

STUDIO SEVEN Map p149
☎ 206-286-1312; 110 S Horton St; cover charge free-$7
This all-ages club is south of Safeco Field, in what is called SODO, just off 1st Ave S one block N of Spokane St. It books local and touring punk and metal shows; recent headliners include Sick of It All, TSOL and the Vibrators. Bring your ID to get in to the bar.

SUNSET TAVERN Map p98
☎ 206-784-4880; 5433 Ballard Ave NW; cover charge free-$7
The Sunset is a Ballard dive that books great dirty-rock shows of local and touring bands and frequently has free movie nights, including a series of B-grade kung-fu films most weeks.

TRACTOR TAVERN Map p98
☎ 206-789-3599; 5213 Ballard Ave NW; cover charge $8-15
The premier venue for folk and acoustic music, the elegant Tractor Tavern also books local songwriters and regional bands such as Richmond Fontaine plus touring acts like John Doe and Wayne Hancock. It's a gorgeous room, usually with top sound quality.

TRIPLE DOOR Map p50
☎ 206-838-4333; 216 Union St
This club downstairs from Wild Ginger (p122) has a liberal booking policy that includes

country and rock as well as jazz, gospel, R & B, world music and burlesque performances. There's a full menu and valet parking; the club is all-ages before 9:30pm.

VERA PROJECT Map p73
☎ 206-956-8372; www.theveraproject.org; 766 Thomas St; cover charge free-$8
An excellent nonprofit community center run by and for teenagers, the Vera Project books exclusively all-ages shows in a smoke-free and alcohol-free environment. It's also dedicated to giving youth a place to learn skills, make art and get involved in the community.

ELECTRONICA

BALTIC ROOM Map p82
☎ 206-625-4444; 1207 Pine St; cover charge free-$12
Classy and high ceilinged, with wood-paneled walls, paper lanterns and an

top picks

SEATTLE'S MUSIC SCENE NORIROLL

Ballard Ave for Music
Grunge is dead (thank God), but take your pick on Ballard Ave, a vestige of Norwegian heritage and fishing lore. Up the street you'll find great venues and bars – Sunset Tavern (left), Tractor Tavern (left) and Hattie's Hat (p148), where King Crab (framed over the bar) reigns!

Crocodile Café (p153), Belltown
An REM member's wife owns the place, so they get the best shows, bands that are going to be the greatest new band…tomorrow! A small club, anything you see here will be good. They serve breakfast and late-night food, which can be very key.

EMP Pop Music Conference
In April, the Experience Music Project (a music-history museum, see pp72-73) holds a pop-culture and music conference in its Frank Gehry–designed building. It's an international forum, with panels discussing anything from riot-grrrl rock to Glenn Gould to Bobby Gentry.

BLUELIST[1] (blu list) v.
to recommend a travel experience.
What's your recommendation? www.lonelyplanet.com/bluelist

PIONEER SQUARE PARTY PASS

Designed with the barhopper in mind, this deal gets you into several Pioneer Square nightspots for one flat fee. A joint cover fee of $5 (Sunday to Thursday) or $10 (Friday or Saturday) buys you in-and-out privileges at the following clubs: the hard-rock and metal Central Saloon (p152); the zydeco, blues and jazz New Orleans Creole Restaurant (below); DJ dance tracks at the Last Supper Club (☎ 206-748-9975; 124 S Washington St; lastsupperclub.com); Tiki Bob's Cantina (☎ 206-382-8454; 166 S King St; tikibobsseattle.com); the J&M Café and Cardroom (☎ 206-292-066; 3201 1st Ave S); and the sports bar–dance club Fuel (☎ 206-405-3835; 164 S Washington St; fuelseattle.com). Pay the cover at the first club you visit.

elegant balcony, this Capitol Hill club hosts an excellent mix of local and touring DJs in a range of genres, from reggae and house to DJ Darek Mazzone's monthly global dance party, Juice (see p41).

CONTOUR Map p57

☎ 206-447-7704; 807 1st Ave
This plush venue is open late and has a more extensive food menu than you might expect of a club whose top priority is clearly to keep your booty shaking until dawn. Contour hosts local and visiting DJs, with after-hours dance nights until 4:30am Thursdays through Saturdays.

WAR ROOM Map p82

☎ 206-328-7666; 722 E Pike St
Weekly drum-and-bass and hip-hop nights, an upstairs open-air tiki-themed deck, and hard-to-miss propaganda posters decorating the space make the War Room a unique venue.

CELTIC, FOLK & COUNTRY

KELLS Map p64

☎ 206-728-1916; 1916 Post Alley
Kells is part of a small regional chain of Irish pubs, but it feels completely authentic, with its old wood, nooks and crannies and rosy-cheeked crowd. The perfectly poured Imperial pints of Guinness are divine and there's live Irish (or Irish-inspired) music nightly (no cover charge).

LITTLE RED HEN Map p95

☎ 206-522-1168; 7115 Woodlawn Ave NE; cover charge from $3
This is Seattle's primary venue for authentic, live country music. Nightly entertainment includes country karaoke and good-time honky-tonk bands – or you can make like

Billy Ray Cyrus with weekly line-dancing lessons.

OWL & THISTLE Map p64

☎ 206-621-7777; 808 Post Alley; cover charge free-$5
The schedule here varies, but most nights it books Celtic folk bands or acoustic singer-songwriters. It's also just a comfortable pub to stop in for a pint, if you don't feel like committing to an evening of music.

JAZZ & BLUES

DIMITRIOU'S JAZZ ALLEY Map p50

☎ 206-441-9729; 2033 6th Ave; cover charge free-$15
Hidden in an unlikely spot behind a boring-looking office building is Seattle's most sophisticated and prestigious jazz club. Dimitriou's hosts the best of the locals and many national acts passing through.

NEW ORLEANS CREOLE RESTAURANT Map p57

☎ 206-622-2563; 114 1st Ave S; cover charge free-$10
This old-school hangout in Pioneer Square hosts regular bands playing Dixieland jazz, blues and zydeco. Tuck into a gumbo and soak up the atmosphere of the Big Easy in a mellow brick-walled room lined with photos of jazz greats.

TULA'S Map p69

☎ 206-443-4221; 2214 2nd Ave; cover charge free-$10
Tula's has live jazz seven nights a week, from big bands and Latin jazz to up-and-coming names on tour. It's a non–indie-rock oasis in the booze alley that is Belltown.

DANCE CLUBS

The dance clubs listed below are places you go to shake your booty, not so much to hear the latest experiments in electronica by nationally known techno DJs. However, flexibility reigns in Seattle's clubs; many of the city's live-music venues also have DJ nights that transform them into dance clubs. Check the local weeklies to see what's going on at a given place on a given night.

The best and most fun dance scenes are found in gay discos and nobody much cares if you like boys or girls or both as long as you're out to have a good time. Most of these clubs charge a cover ($5 to $10) Thursday through Saturday nights.

CENTURY BALLROOM Map p82
☎ 206-324-7263; www.centuryballroom.com; 915 E Pine St
Dance lessons followed by an everyone-out-on-the-floor dance free-for-all makes a night at the Century the perfect combination of spectating and participating. Dance nights include everything from the lindy hop to salsa. Check the website for a schedule.

NEIGHBOURS Map p82
☎ 206-324-5358; 1509 Broadway E
Referred to on one occasion as a 'big, soulless, cha cha palace,' Neighbours is ostensibly a gay disco but attracts a varied crowd – even newbie suburbanites come in for its weekly '80s night.

R PLACE Map p82
☎ 206-322-8828; 619 E Pine St
Three floors of dancing to hip-hop and R&B DJs and plenty of sweaty body contact make this club a blast for pretty much everyone who isn't terribly uptight. Keep your outfit small and close-fitting if you plan to keep it attached to your body.

RE-BAR Map p50
☎ 206-233-9873; 1114 Howell St
The Re-Bar hosts everything from hip-hop DJs to drag shows and attracts a lively crowd that comes to boogie on various theme nights. Whether you're gay, lesbian, bi, straight or undecided, you'll have fun at the classic weekly Queer Disco.

top picks

- Globe Café & Bakery (p159)
- Richard Hugo House (p159)
- Annex Theater (p159)
- Intiman Theater Company (p160)
- Northwest Film Forum (p160)

THE ARTS

There's a good range of cultural diversions available in Seattle at any given moment. Author readings, dance, opera, ballet, theater and film are all going strong here. Ranked the most literate city in the nation in 2005, Seattle's a book-loving town. It's home to a number of big-name writers, and the plethora of bookstores and coffee shops here help to fuel its book culture. There's a literary event of one kind or another happening practically every night of the week.

Film is also big news in Seattle these days. The Seattle International Film Festival (p160) is among the most influential festivals in the country, and a thriving independent film scene has sprung up in a handful of underground venues, including the Alibi Room (p141).

Live theater runs the gamut from big productions, such as Ibsen at the Intiman Theater (p160), to staged readings of obscure texts in cobbled-together venues or coffee shops.

The Seattle Symphony (p161) has become nationally known and widely respected, primarily through its excellent recordings.

Some of the city's more interesting cultural events, whether film, music, theater or a combination, occur in makeshift venues, galleries, warehouses and the like. To find a current listing, check the *Stranger* or the *Seattle Weekly*, available free at various points around town as well as online. Most of the venues and arts organizations listed below also have easy-to-find calendar information online.

TICKETS & RESERVATIONS

Tickets for big events are available through Ticket Master (☎ 206-628-0888, 206-292-2787; www.ticketmaster .com) online, by phone or at ticket centers located in retail shops around Seattle; call for locations. Ticket centers are open 8am to 9pm Monday to Saturday and 10am to 6pm Sunday. But if you can buy tickets at the door and there's no risk of the show being sold out, do so; it'll save you the service fee TicketMaster tacks on (usually $6 to $10). Downtown, the TicketMaster discount ticket booth at Westlake Center (Map p50; ☎ 206-233-1111; ⏰ opens 10am) has last-minute seats for a variety of different events.

TicketsWest (☎ 800-992-8499, 800-632-8499; www .ticketswest.rdln.com) is a regional ticketing service, with outlets at Rudy's Barbershops and QFC grocery stores.

Ticket/Ticket (☎ 206-324-2744) offers day-of-performance ticket sales without service charges if you pay cash. You can't get information on ticket availability over the phone, but booths are at the Market Information Booth at Pike Place Market (Map p64; cnr 1st Ave & Pike St; ⏰ noon-6pm Tue-Sun) and on the upper level of the Broadway Market (Map p82; ⏰ noon-6pm Tue-Sun) on Capitol Hill.

READINGS

Maybe it's because of the rain, or maybe it's all that good coffee, but Seattleites read voraciously – whether it's the latest literary novel, an underground comic or a home-stapled zine. A lot of authors live here and there are some important literary landmarks worth checking out. Not the least of them is Blue Moon Tavern (p146), which was the retreat of choice for the great poet Theodore Roethke, who taught at the nearby University of Washington.

The Elliott Bay Book Company is a mandatory stop on any major author's book tour, and people turn out in droves to go to readings there. Several other bookstores host readings on a regular basis; see the Shopping chapter (p110) for a start.

For detailed events schedules and to find offbeat happenings at nonmajor venues, check listings in the *Stranger* or the *Seattle Weekly* or look for events calendars posted in bookstores around town. Most readings and open-mic events are free.

BORDERS BOOKS & MUSIC
Map p50

☎ 206-622-4599; 1501 4th Ave S
Borders stages readings by touring authors, plus occasional live music and children's events, mostly during the day.

ELLIOTT BAY BOOK COMPANY
Map p57

☎ 206-624-6600; 101 S Main St
The greatest bookstore in town also holds the best readings in Seattle, with nation-

ally touring authors as well as a number of local literary stars (such as Tom Robbins, Sherman Alexie, David James Duncan and others). Readings are usually free and most will start at 7pm. Pick up a schedule by the store entrance.

GLOBE CAFÉ & BAKERY
Map p82

☎ 206-547-4585; 1531 14th Ave
The Globe has long held poetry readings and open-mic performances. Stop by and mingle with the pierced Capitol Hill crowd for an all-vegetarian breakfast (see p132) on the weekends.

RICHARD HUGO HOUSE
Map p82

☎ 206-322-7030; www.hugohouse.org; 1634 11th Ave; ⏱ house 10am-9pm Mon-Fri & noon-5pm Sat, zine archive 1-5pm Mon-Sat & 5-9pm most evenings
The nexus of Seattle's literary community, the Hugo House hosts readings, classes and workshops as well as offering various events around town. Writers-in-residence keep office hours at the house, during which they're available for consultation about writing projects free of charge. The extensive zine library invites all-day lingering.

THEATER & COMEDY
Seattle has one of the most vibrant theater scenes on the West Coast, from weird experimental troupes to elaborate productions of Shakespearean classics. Check the local newspapers for openings and reviews.

5TH AVENUE THEATER
Map p50

☎ 206-625-1900; 1308 5th Ave
Built in 1926 with an opulent Asian motif, the 5th Avenue opened as a vaudeville house; it was later turned into a movie theater and closed in 1979. An influx of funding and a heritage award saved it in 1980, and now it's Seattle's premier theater for Broadway musical revivals. It's worth going just for a look at the architecture.

A CONTEMPORARY THEATER (ACT)
Map p50

☎ 206-292-7676; 700 Union St; ⏱ box office noon-7pm Tue-Sun
One of the three big companies in the city, ACT fills its $30-million home at Kreielsheimer Place with excellent performances featuring Seattle's best thespians, and occasionally big-name actors too.

ANNEX THEATER
☎ 206-728-0933; 1621 12th Ave
Seattle's main experimental–fringe theater group is the Annex. It has its offices inside the Capitol Hill Arts Center (see p160) and produces shows and a monthly cabaret at various locations, including the adorable, swanked-up Jewel Box Theater (Map p69; 2320 2nd Ave), which can be found at the Rendezvous (p142) in Belltown.

RICHARD HUGO

Who was Richard Hugo, and why is the literary center of Seattle named after him? Hugo (1923–82) was, like his mentor and fellow Seattle writer Theodore Roethke, a poet and a great teacher of poetry.

Born in White City, a suburb of Seattle, he was raised by his grandparents after his father left the family. In 1943 he volunteered for the Army Air Corps, serving as a bombardier on 35 missions. Afterwards, on the GI Bill, he majored in English at the University of Washington, where he enrolled in Roethke's first two workshops. He earned a bachelor of arts degree from U Dub in 1948.

From 1951 until 1963 Hugo worked for Boeing. In 1965 he left Seattle to teach at the University of Montana.

Hugo was a hard-working, hard-drinking (for most of his life), perpetually self-questioning man. The 1930s Seattle of his childhood was a place he described as having a Scandinavian character, with a reputation for the second-highest number of suicides for a city (after Berlin). He explained this as being due to the fact that people who wanted to run away from either themselves or their life would arrive in Seattle and discover there was nowhere left to run.

He died of leukemia in Seattle on October 22, 1982. *The Real West Marginal Way – A Poet's Autobiography* is a collection of Hugo's essays describing his childhood in Seattle as well as his later teaching career. It's worth seeking out for the picture it paints of a city in flux.

CAPITOL HILL ARTS CENTER Map p82

☎ 800-838-3006; www.capitolhillarts.com; 1621 12th Ave

In a brick-and-timber warehouse from 1917, this arts organization maintains three performance spaces and produces theater as well as supporting various other events around the community.

COMEDY UNDERGROUND Map p57

☎ 206-628-0303; 222 S Main St

As its good deed, this gritty club hosts a weekly nonprofit comedy show, currently on Tuesdays – go and have a laugh for a good cause.

INTIMAN THEATER COMPANY Map p73

☎ 206-269-1900; 201 Mercer St, Seattle Center

Intiman Theater is Seattle's mainstay for classic dramas and heavy-hitting, serious theater (by Henrik Ibsen and Langston Hughes, for example), although artistic director Bartlett Sher, who joined Intiman in 2000, has amped up the edginess of the company's schedule to include striking new work.

MARKET THEATER Map p64

☎ 206-781-9273; 1428 Post Alley

The Market Theater hosts improvisational comedy, called Theater Sports, on Friday and Saturday night; call for the schedule.

SEATTLE REPERTORY THEATER Map p73

☎ 206-443-2222; 155 Mercer St, Seattle Center; adult $15-46, child $10

The Seattle Repertory Theater (the Rep) won a Tony Award in 1990 for Outstanding Regional Theater. The largest nonprofit resident theater outfit in the Pacific Northwest, it's known for elaborate productions of big-name dramas and second-run Broadway hits.

FILM

Although colossal multiscreen cinema complexes are plentiful in Seattle, there are still a number of small independent theaters that go out of their way to feature the unusual and obscure. Some of the first-run houses, including those listed below, also show foreign and smaller independent films alongside mainstream smash hits. To really delve into

Seattle's film culture, though, you have to seek out the tiny independent festivals and screenings.

The biggest event of the year for cinephiles is the Seattle International Film Festival (SIFF; ☎ 206-464-5830; www.seattlefilm.com/siff; tickets $5-10, passes $300-800). Film geeks wait all year for this annual three-week extravaganza of international art films, experimental works and newly unearthed classics.

The festival uses a half-dozen theaters but also has its own dedicated theater, in McCaw Hall's Nesholm Family Lecture Hall (Map p73; 321 Mercer St, Seattle Center), which also runs various film programs throughout the year. SIFF typically starts in mid-May.

The Seattle Lesbian & Gay Film Festival (☎ 206-323-4274; admission $6-8), a popular festival in October, shows new gay-themed films from directors worldwide.

Check film listings in the weekly papers, or ask around at the cinemas listed below. For a full list of theaters, times and locations, check the *Stranger*, or the *Seattle Weekly* or the arts sections of the daily papers.

top picks

MOVIE THEATERS

- Cinerama (Map p69; ☎ 206-441-3653; 2100 4th Ave) One of the very few Cineramas left in the world, it has a fun, sci-fi feel.
- Grand Illusion Cinema (Map p85; ☎ 206-523-3935; 1403 NE 50th St) Antique theater in the U District known for director retrospectives and other cool series.
- Harvard Exit (Map p82; ☎ 206-781-5755; 807 E Roy at Harvard) Seattle's first independent theater, built in 1925.
- Rendezvous Jewel Box Theater (Map p69; ☎ 206-441-5823; 2320 2nd Ave) A restored jewel-box theater tucked away behind a sleek cocktail bar.
- Northwest Film Forum (Map p82; ☎ 206-329-2629; www.wigglyworld.org; 1515 12th Ave) Impeccable programming, from restored classics to cutting-edge independent and international films.
- Varsity Theater (Map p85; ☎ 206-632-3131; 4329 University Way NE) Independent and international films, usually in one-week runs.

MEGAVENUES

Tickets for these major concert and event venues can generally be purchased from TicketMaster (for a fee) or through the box office of the venue at the number listed.

Benaroya Concert Hall (Map p50; ☎ 206-215-4747; 200 University St) The Seattle Symphony's home venue.

Gorge Amphitheater (754 Silica Rd NW, George, WA) A 20,000-person venue for huge concerts (Sting, Aerosmith) and festivals (Sasquatch, the Warped Tour).

McCaw Hall (Map p73; ☎ 206-684-7200; 321 Mercer St) Home of the Seattle Opera.

Meany Hall (☎ 206-543-4880; University of Washington)

WaMu Theater (Map p57; ☎ 206-628-0888; 800 Occidental Ave S) The new venue for music and live entertainment at Qwest Field seats up to 7000 people.

White River Amphitheater (☎ 360-825-6200; 40601 Auburn Enumclaw Rd, Auburn, WA) This giant outdoor arena opened in June 2003 and serves the entire Seattle Tacoma region.

OPERA, CLASSICAL MUSIC & DANCE

Seattle is a sophisticated city with a well-regarded symphony, an everstrengthening opera and a vibrant dance scene. It's hard to go wrong with any of the following options. Keep an eye out for the University of Washington's annual World Series (☎ 206-543-4880, 800-859-5342; www.uwworldseries.org; Meany Hall, University of Washington; tickets $32-45) of music, performance and dance.

PACIFIC NORTHWEST BALLET
Map p73

☎ 206-441-9411; McCaw Hall, Seattle Center

This is the foremost dance company in the Northwest. The ballet does more than 100 performances a season from September through June.

SEATTLE MEN'S CHORUS

☎ 206-323-2992; www.seattlemenschorus.org

The largest community chorus in the USA and the largest gay men's chorus in the world, the Seattle Men's Chorus has nearly

three dozen engagements throughout the year. Its annual Christmas concert is a popular event.

SEATTLE OPERA Map p73

☎ 206-389-7676; McCaw Hall, Seattle Center

The Seattle opera features a program of four or five full-scale operas every season, including Wagner's *Ring* cycle, which draws sellout crowds in summer. It has recently begun offering a number of tickets at the bargain price of $25 each, available from the ticket office (1020 John St) or by phone.

SEATTLE SYMPHONY Map p50

☎ 206-215-4747; Benaroya Concert Hall, 200 University St

Under maestro Gerard Schwartz, the symphony has earned its reputation as the heart of the Seattle classical-music scene. Since Schwartz came aboard in 1984 it has presented several successful series and released a number of recordings to critical acclaim. Worth noting is the symphony's Discover Music! series – concerts designed to introduce children to various aspects of classical music.

SPORTS & ACTIVITIES

top picks

- Seattle Mariners (p165)
- Northwest Outdoor Center (p167)
- Center for Wooden Boats (p167)
- Recycled Cycles (p168)
- Sierra Club (p169)

What's your recommendation? www.lonelyplanet.com/seattle

SPORTS & ACTIVITIES

Never mind the rain – that's why Gore-Tex was invented. When you live this close to the mountains, not to mention all that water and a stunning range of parks, it's just criminal not to get outdoors, rain or shine.

Getting out there is easy, too: the Olympic and North Cascade mountains, Mt Rainier National Park and the fingers of Puget Sound are right outside the door. But Seattle is rare for a large city in that many forms of outdoor recreation (hiking, kayaking, cycling and windsurfing) are available within the city itself. If you'd rather watch other people sweat, there's plenty to do in the way of spectator sports, too.

Sure, they had to put a retractable roof on the stadium to avoid perpetual rainouts, but Seattleites love their sports. It's an active city, for starters. There's a reason people like to preserve their environment here, and it's not so they can sit back and look at it. Numerous urban parks and trails, combined with an eminently walkable downtown core, have helped make Seattle one of the easiest-to-walk big cities in the US. It's also near the top of the list for cycling. And all that water doesn't go to waste, either: locals put it to use for canoeing, kayaking and windsurfing. In the winter, skiing and snowboarding are popular activities close to town.

When they're not out there doing sports themselves, Seattleites love to watch a good game of baseball. The Mariners got a double bonus when the old Kingdome was replaced by fancy new Safeco Field (in 1999) and an outfielder from Japan named Ichiro Suzuki joined the team (in 2001). Starting in 2002, fans turned out in record numbers, with Safeco Field setting Major League records for attendance.

Seattle's National Basketball Association (NBA) team, the SuperSonics, won its sixth division title in the 2004–05 season. In 2004 the Women's NBA team, the Seattle Storm, won the city its first professional sports championship since 1979. Storm games are hugely popular family events that draw enthusiastic crowd participation.

The Seattle Seahawks made it to the Super Bowl in 2006 and, as underdogs, beat the Pittsburgh Steelers for the National Football League (NFL) championship.

The University of Washington, of course, has the full range of college sports going. And with the Seattle Sounders, even soccer is represented. See opposite for details on how to catch a game or a match.

When it comes to finding out where to go, what to do or where to rent equipment, a couple of places deserve special notice. Recreational Equipment Inc, better known as REI (Map p79; ☎ 206-223-1944; 222 Yale Ave N), is a Seattle native and one of the largest sporting and recreational gear and equipment outfitters in the nation. Gearheads go giddy at this flagship store, a wild paean to the outdoor spirit, with a mock mountain-bike trail, a rock gym, a simulated hiking trail (to test boots) and more tents, canoes and rucksacks than you've probably ever seen in one place. The eager staff are very knowledgeable about local recreation, and there are several bulletin boards with information on talks, gatherings, outings, clubs and courses. REI's good selection of books and maps on regional recreation is helpful, especially the topographic maps of nearby mountains. The rental department can rent you most kinds of equipment or tell you where to go to do so. REI Adventures (☎ 800-622-2236) organizes trips.

Upstairs at REI, the Forest Service/National Park Service (Map p79; ☎ 206-470-4060) runs an Outdoor Recreation Center, and its staff can tell you anything you need to know about nearby national parks.

Another Seattle-based travel resource, the Mountaineers (Map p76; ☎ 206-284-6310; www.mountaineers .org; 300 3rd Ave W) in Lower Queen Anne, specializes in Northwest recreation. The organization offers courses in hiking, mountaineering, kayaking, every type of snow sport and other outdoor skills, such as first aid and backcountry travel. Events such as film and slide shows are enough to tickle anyone's adventurous spirit, and the bookstore boasts an unbeatable collection of books, maps and videos about the outdoors, many of which are available for loan through the Mountaineers library. Note that the Mountaineers headquarters are set to move to Magnuson Park in summer 2008.

SPECTATOR SPORTS

With state-of-the-art stadiums and teams that flirt with glory, Seattle is a great town to watch the pros play. College games, too, are hugely popular with locals and a fun way to spend an afternoon.

You can buy tickets for the teams listed here through TicketMaster (☎ 206-628-0888) or Pacific Northwest Ticket Service (☎ 206-232-0150).

BASEBALL

SEATTLE MARINERS Map p57
☎ 206-628-3555; www.mariners.org; admission $7-60

There was a time when Seattle's professional baseball team was nothing but an annoying itch on the upper right shoulder of the USA, but not anymore. The Mariners won a division title in 1995 and promptly moved into the shiny new $417 million open-air Safeco Field. In 2000, the Ms (as they are fondly referred to) missed a World Series berth by a hair, but snagged even more love from their devoted fans. The season runs April to August (October if they make the playoffs), and games usually start at 7:05pm, or 1:05pm on Sundays. There are also occasional midday games during the week; check the website for a full schedule.

BASKETBALL

SEATTLE SUPERSONICS Map p73
☎ 206-283-3865; www.nba.com/sonics; admission $10-235

Seattle's National Basketball Association (NBA) franchise, the Seattle SuperSonics, provides plenty of excitement at Key Arena in Seattle Center. The Sonics' season runs November to late April. Games typically start at 7pm.

FOOTBALL

SEATTLE SEAHAWKS Map p57
☎ 425-827-9777; www.seahawks.com; admission $42-95

The Northwest's only National Football League (NFL) franchise, the Seattle Seahawks has enjoyed both roaring success and dismal slumps, one of which prompted its former owners to put the team on the selling block, which left Seattleites fearing its relocation. In 1997 Microsoft cofounder

Paul Allen saved the day by purchasing the Seahawks franchise, with the stipulation that the Hawks get a new stadium. So the Hawks' former home, the Kingdome, was spectacularly imploded and replaced in 2002 by the new 72,000-seat Seahawks Stadium.

UNIVERSITY OF WASHINGTON HUSKIES Map p85
☎ 206-543-2200; www.gohuskies.com; admission $6-65

The University of Washington Huskies football and basketball teams are another Seattle obsession. The Huskies football team plays at Husky Stadium; you'll find the men's and women's basketball teams at the Edmundson Pavilion, both of which are on campus. The women's basketball team draws massive crowds.

HOCKEY

SEATTLE THUNDERBIRDS
Map p73
☎ 206-448-7825; www.seattlethunderbirds.com; admission $12-20

Also playing at Key Arena, the Seattle Thunderbirds rip around the ice in the Western Hockey League (WHL) from September to March. The games are lively and well attended, and tickets are reasonably priced.

SOCCER

SEATTLE SOUNDERS Map p57
☎ 206-622-3415; www.seattlesounders.net; admission $13-18

Soccer's no stranger in Seattle either. The A-League Seattle Sounders play at Seahawks Stadium, admittedly looking a little lost in the gigantic facility; soccer has yet to become huge in the USA, but those who love it, *really* love it. The soccer season runs May to mid-September.

ACTIVITIES

On the water, on wheels, or on your own two feet – there's plenty of variety in the kind of fun to be had outdoors in and around Seattle. Equipment rental is widely available, too, so here's your chance to try something you've always wanted to do, whether it's golf, rock climbing, rollerblading or paddling a canoe.

ON THE WATER

Rumor has it that one in three people who live in Seattle owns a boat of some sort. It could be a rubber dinghy, a crusty kayak or a salty sailboat, but regardless, the locals here love to play in the water. Whether you learn to windsurf on Green Lake, kayak past the houseboats on Lake Union or hoist the sails on Lake Washington, there are plenty of organizations here that are geared toward having fun on the water.

Sea kayaking can soothe your soul or wake up your adventurous spirit, and it's one of the easiest sports for beginners to pick up. Seattle's many waterways are ideal for kayak exploration, and it doesn't take long before controlling your paddle is as natural as waving your arm. White-water kayaking on area rivers is also popular, though a little more challenging to pick up. But have no fear, many organizations offer excellent lessons or tours led by able instructor-guides.

Despite the flood of water in Seattle, summer sailing isn't that great; in fact, you're lucky if the calm days cough up enough of a breeze to keep you moving. In the spring, fall and winter, however, a soft wind exhales over the Sound and sailing becomes a spectacular way to spend time outside. Even on days when you have to keep the motor running, sailing offers views and perspectives you can only get from the water. More adventurous sailors head out on Puget Sound and along its inland waterways, or all the way up the coast to British Columbia.

Windsurfing is a big sport in Seattle. It's part of that quintessential Seattle mix of being in a band, having a job at an espresso stand and putting your sail up on the lake. As such, windsurfing draws more locals than tourists. Lake Washington is the most popular place to sail – it's big enough to accommodate traffic and out-of-control newbies. The warm waters of Green Lake are good for beginners, but it can get pretty congested in summer. Between the sailboats, floatplanes and motorboat traffic, Lake Union is not good for anyone but expert windsurfers with full control. Usual launch spots are Magnuson and Mount Baker Parks. In summer, the calm waters of Puget Sound are good for experienced windsurfers. Try setting out from Alki Beach (p105) in West Seattle or from Golden Gardens Park (p100) northwest of Ballard.

Some people shy away from plunging into the chilly waters surrounding Seattle, but local divers will tell you that the marine biodiversity in the Northwest beats any tropical clime.

Sure, you're not likely to see colorful tropical fish, but dive sites in Puget Sound and along the Northwest coast offer year-round diving and regular sightings of octopus, huge ling cod, cabezon, cathedral-like white anemones and giant sea stars.

Most of the area's best dive sites are outside of Seattle, in sheltered coves and bays up and down the coast. Popular spots include Alki Cove, on the east side of Alki Point; Saltwater State Park, south of Seattle in Des Moins; and Edmonds Underwater Park near the Edmonds Ferry Dock, north of Seattle. Other popular spots include Port Angeles, Keystone and the San Juan Islands. For more information on area dive sites, look for *Northwest Shore Dives* by Stephen Fischnaller, considered the dive-site bible. It's usually available at most diving shops.

MOSS BAY ROWING & KAYAK CENTER Map p79

☎ 206-682-2031; www.mossbay.net; 1001 Fairview N; ☺ 8am-8pm summer, 10am-5pm Thu-Mon winter

Moss Bay offers rentals, extensive lessons and tours on Lake Union.

NORTHWEST OUTDOOR CENTER
Map p79

☎ 206-281-9694; www.nwoc.com; 2100 Westlake Ave N, Lake Union

The center offers a vast selection of rentals, guided tours and instruction in sea and white-water kayaking.

PUGET SOUND KAYAK COMPANY

☎ 206-933-3008; www.pugetsoundkayak.com

This active organization, which is located on both Bainbridge and Vashon Islands, offers classes, clinics and guided trips; however, the future of the Vashon branch is unclear, as it was up for sale at the time of writing.

UNDERWATER SPORTS Map p48

☎ 206-362-3310; www.underwatersports.com; 10545 Aurora Ave

This is the best place to go for gear repair; it also offers courses in its on-site pool.

WASHINGTON KAYAK CLUB

www.washingtonkayakclub.org

The Kayak Club doesn't have a physical location, but its website acts as a clearing house for both white-water and sea kayaking courses. It's also in the business of educating paddlers about conservation and safety.

Gear Rental

In addition to the above, water-sport equipment rentals are available at the following establishments.

AGUA VERDE PADDLE CLUB Map p85

☎ 206-545-8570; 1303 NE Boat St; single kayak per 1hr/2hr $15/25, double kayak $18/30; ☺ 10am-dusk Mon-Sat & 10am-6pm Sun Mar-Oct

On Portage Bay, near the university, you can rent kayaks from this friendly place right at the edge of the water. When you get back from your paddle, be sure to visit the café upstairs (see p133) to eat fish tacos on the covered deck.

CENTER FOR WOODEN BOATS Map p79

☎ 206-382-2628; www.cwb.org; 1010 Valley St; per hr small sailboat weekday/weekend $20/30, large sailboat $30/45, rowboat $15/25, beginner sailing course $330

This museum offers sailboat lessons and rentals on Lake Union. One person in your party has to know how to sail and must do a checkout ($10 fee) before you'll be permitted to rent. It's pretty straightforward; you need to demonstrate tacking, jibing and docking. The center also offers sailing lessons, including an excellent beginner course that gives you as many lessons as it offers in a four-month period (usually eight to 12 lessons). Seasoned sailors who are a little rusty can take a one-on-one lesson for $50 per hour.

GREEN LAKE SMALL CRAFT CENTER
Map p95

☎ 206-684-4074; 7351 E Green Lake Dr

Green Lake's still waters help keep beginner kayakers calm, though the crowds might also keep you waiting. Run by Seattle Parks & Recreation Department, the center rents kayaks, canoes, rowboats and paddleboats from March to October, and also provides lessons.

SAILING IN SEATTLE Map p79

☎ 206-289-0094; www.sailing-in-seattle.com; 2040 Westlake Ave; lessons per hr $100

On Friday evenings Sailing in Seattle holds races on Lakes Washington and Union.

Anyone can come join a racing crew and, though you should be somewhat fit, no experience is necessary; they'll show you what to do. For information on hiring Sailing in Seattle's 33ft *Whoodat*, see p211.

UW WATERFRONT ACTIVITIES CENTER Map p85

☎ 206-543-9433; canoe & rowboat per hr $7.50; ☺ approx 10am-7pm, closed Nov-Jan

Another good way to explore the waters surrounding the Arboretum is to rent a canoe or rowboat from the University of Washington's facility. You need a current driver's license or passport. The center is in the southeast corner of the Husky Stadium parking lot.

BICYCLING

Despite frequent rain and hilly terrain, cycling is still a major form of both transportation and recreation in the Seattle area. Both bicycle touring and mountain biking are widespread, so whether you're a clipless mudhound or a casual cruiser, you'll find plenty of places to ride.

In the city, commuter bike lanes are continually painted on city streets; city trails are well maintained; and the friendly and enthusiastic cycling community is happy to share the road. The wildly popular 16.5-mile Burke-Gilman Trail winds from Ballard to Log Boom Park in Kenmore on Seattle's Eastside. There, it connects with the 11-mile long Sammamish River Trail, which winds past the Chateau Ste Michelle winery in Woodinville before terminating at Redmond's Marymoor Park. Marymoor Park boasts the only velodrome (☎ 206-957-4555) in the Pacific Northwest. You'll need to be a trained velodrome rider before you can get on the track, but the untrained can watch the exciting races, which are held Monday, Wednesday and Friday mid-May to September. Admission to the amateur races is free Monday and Wednesday; when the pros hit the track on Friday, admission costs $3.

More cyclists than you can imagine peddle the loop around Green Lake, making it downright congested on sunny days. Closer to downtown, the scenic 2.5-mile Elliott Bay Trail runs along the waterfront through Myrtle Edwards and Elliott Bay Parks. The 8-mile Alki Trail in West Seattle makes a pretty ride as it follows Alki Beach before connecting to the 11-mile Duwamish Trail that heads south along W Marginal Way SW.

BIKE RENTALS

The following places are recommended for bicycle rentals and repairs:

Gregg's Cycles (Map p95; ☎ 206-523-1822; 7007 Woodlawn Ave NE) Here since 1932, Gregg's is a higher-end shop with two new storefronts in Bellevue and Lynwood; rentals are still out of the Greenlake shop. Fancy road bikes rent for $30 to $56 per hour, or you can get a more standard model for $18 per hour or $135 per week.

Recycled Cycles (Map p85; ☎ 206-547-4491; 1007 NE Boat St; bike rental per 6hr/24hr $20/40) Also in the U District, toward the water at the lower end of the 'Ave.' It has a friendly, unpretentious vibe – unlike at some other bike shops in town, you'll never get the feeling you're underdressed.

Bicycle Center (Map p85; ☎ 206-523-8300; 4529 Sand Point Way; bike rental per 1hr/24hr $3/15) Another long-standing bike shop that does rentals and repairs; it's right off the Burke-Gilman Trail.

TI Cycles (Map p85; ☎ 206-522-7602; www.ticycles.com; 2943 NE Blakely St; bike rental per 4hr/day $25/40; ⏰ 10am-6pm Mon-Fri, 9am-6pm Sat, 10am-4pm Sun) In the U District, and the Burke-Gilman Trail runs right past its front door.

Though they are not specified trails, the tree-lined roads winding through the Washington Park Arboretum and along Lake Washington Blvd make for lovely road rides. The bike trail around Seward Park gives cyclists the sensation of looping a forested island. The 14-mile Mercer Island Loop is another residential ride along E and W Mercer Way around the perimeter of the island.

Bainbridge and Vashon Islands are popular with cyclists and are just a ferry ride away, offering near-rural isolation on rolling country back roads. Bike stores and the folk who work there are usually gushing fountains of good information. Most shops stock cycling publications and can point you in the right direction for public rides, trails and places to avoid. Anyone planning on cycling in Seattle should pick up a copy of the *Seattle Bicycling Guide Map*, published by the City of Seattle's Transportation Bicycle and Pedestrian Program (☎ 206-684-7583) and available at bike shops. Alternatively you can order the map free of charge over the phone or online at www.cityofseattle.net/transportation/bikemaps.htm.

Cycling Clubs

Seattle's active cycling community thrives in part because of organized clubs.

BACKCOUNTRY BICYCLE TRAILS CLUB

☎ 206-524-2900; www.bbtc.org
Fat-tire riders will want to contact this club, which organizes mountain-biking trail rides and offers bike repair and technical-riding courses.

CASCADE BICYCLE CLUB

☎ 206-522-3222; www.cascade.org
With more than 5500 members, this is the largest cycling club in the USA. It holds organized rides daily as well as various special events, such as races and long-distance rides. It also publishes the *Cascade Corner*, a newsletter that describes what's happening in the cycling world.

HIKING

In Seattle, it's possible to hike wilderness trails without ever leaving the city. Seward Park (Map p48) offers several miles of trails in a remnant of the area's old-growth forest, and an even more extensive network of trails is available in 534-acre Discovery Park (Map p98), northwest of downtown. At the northern edge of Washington Park Arboretum, Foster Island (Map p48) offers a 20-minute wetlands trail winding through marshlands created upon the opening of the Lake Washington Ship Canal. This is a great place for bird-watching, fishing and swimming. The trail begins at the bottom of the Museum of History & Industry (Mohai; p104) parking lot.

Several parks now offer family-friendly hiking activity packs for sale or loan, complete with field guides, binoculars, games and so on. Washington Park Arboretum has one pack for $7 for two hours; they are also available at Discovery, Carkeek and Magnuson Parks.

Outside the city, hiking opportunities are practically endless in the Olympic Range, the north, central and south Cascades and in the Issaquah Alps. For specific trail information, contact REI (p164), the Mountaineers (p164) or the following groups.

SIERRA CLUB
Map p89

☎ 206-378-0114; cascade.sierraclub.org; suite 202, 180 Nickerson St

The Cascade chapter of the Sierra Club is a busy and active group. Its extremely diverse offerings range from beachcombing and botany walks at Alki to weekend day-hiking and car-camping trips along the Pacific Crest Trail. Call for a recorded message of future events. Most day trips are free; longer trips may have fees.

WASHINGTON TRAILS ASSOCIATION
☎ 206-625-1367; www.wta.org

This nonprofit group organizes hiking trips, conservation efforts and trail-building jaunts into local mountains.

RUNNING

With its many parks, Seattle provides a number of good trails for runners. If you're in the downtown area, the trails along Myrtle Edwards Park – just north of the Waterfront along Elliott Bay – make for a nice run, affording views over the sound and of the downtown skyline. Green Lake includes two paths, the 2.75-mile paved path immediately surrounding the lake and a less crowded, unpaved path going around the perimeter of the park. The Washington Park Arboretum is another good choice for running, as the trails lead through some beautiful trees and flower gardens. The trails in the arboretum connect to the Lake Washington Blvd trail system, which extends all the way south to Seward Park, just in case you happen to be training for a marathon. Most of the bicycling routes listed earlier also make good running routes.

Running Clubs

Runners looking to hook up with running mates can contact a number of Seattle's running clubs, most of which offer organized runs that usually turn into social events. Active clubs include the Puget Sound Hash Harriers (☎ 206-528-2050), Seattle Frontrunners (☎ 206-322-7769; www.seattlefrontrunners.org) and the West Seattle Runners (☎ 206-938-2416; www.westseattlerunners.org). Also, check sports stores for *Northwest Runners,* a monthly publication and a good resource for running-related information.

IN-LINE SKATING

Call 'em in-line skaters, rollerbladers or just kickbacks from the disco era, skaters are everywhere in Seattle, wearing everything from Nike's latest trends to groovy pink legwarmers. Seattle's paved paths are perfect except when it rains, which is why you should beware the skating storm on sunny days. Popular skating spots include the Burke-Gilman Trail, around Green Lake, Alki Point, Lake Washington Blvd and the Sammamish River Trail on the Eastside. Gregg's Cycles (opposite) rents in-line skates for $5 per hour, although at time of research the skate-rental facilities were closed for construction.

ROCK CLIMBING

There's plenty of climbing and mountaineering to be had in the Olympics and the Cascades, but even if your travel plans don't allow time for an excursion to the mountains, you can keep in shape by clambering up the faces at Seattle-area rock walls. If the weather is good, head to Marymoor Park in Redmond (on the Eastside), where there's a 45ft outdoor climbing structure for all levels of climbers.

SPORTS & ACTIVITIES   **ACTIVITIES**

CRITICAL CONDITION

If you've ever been stuck behind them, or looking out the window when they roll past, most of them in wildly colorful costumes, you've probably wondered just what Critical Mass cyclists are all about.

Critical Mass' raison d'être could be boiled down to something like this: cycling, fun and provocation, with a purpose. The main agenda is to assert cyclists' right to the road and to promote bicycling as a better alternative to cars (in terms of health, the environment and traffic congestion) – it's hard to argue with that, especially when you're stuck in Seattle gridlock or searching for a parking space.

It's a communal, antiauthoritarian group, so there's no official leadership or bylaws or website – anyone can start a Critical Mass wherever they live, simply by setting a time and a meeting place for the rides and spreading the word. It's easy to find information, goals and manifestos about Critical Mass on the internet.

Seattle's Critical Mass (www.seattlecriticalmass.org) goes on a group ride the last Friday of each month, rain or shine, leaving at 5:30pm from Westlake Center.

REI Map p79
☎ 206-223-1944; 222 Yale Ave N
The REI Pinnacle climbing wall is a 65ft rock pinnacle to the side of the store's entryway. The wall is open for scrambling at various times daily except Tuesday, when it's reserved for private groups. You can climb free of charge, but be prepared to wait your turn.

STONE GARDENS: THE CLIMBERS GYM Map p98
☎ 206-781-9828; 2839 NW Market St

This is a full climbing gym with 14,000 sq ft of climbing surface on more than 100 routes. The gym also has weights, lockers and showers. Courses, from beginner climber to anchoring, are also offered. The drop-in rate is $15.

ULTIMATE FRISBEE
Ultimate Frisbee is hugely popular in the Northwest, and many mixed leagues offer games for players of every level. The Potlatch tournament, held annually in Redmond in July, attracts the West Coast's top players.

SKI SEATTLE Thomas Kohnstamm

While Denver and Salt Lake City are known as America's gateways to skiing, snowboarding and other mountain recreation, Seattle quietly goes about its business as the snow-sports capital of the Pacific Northwest. The resorts may not be as plush as those in Colorado and the snow may not be quite as dry as that in Utah, but western Washington claims a staggering variety of terrain to delight skiers and snowboarders of all skill levels.

Many of Washington's top-notch ski areas remain understated, as they're in protected parklands that forbid extensive hotel and resort development. Therefore Washington snow sports have a decided lack of glitz and ego. Here it is all about the sport, the mountains and having a good time. Après ski is better known here as 'getting a beer.'

Washington skiing has traditionally been as much a blue-collar sport as it has catered to wealthy skiers. Nordic skiing and inner tubing are also available for those who don't care for downhill. This relaxed and inclusive vibe allowed Washington to be one of the first areas in the world to embrace snowboarding in the 1980s and to play a major role in the development of what was to become global snowboarding culture.

Daily adult lift-ticket prices range from the mid-$40s to mid-$50s. Hours of operation and ticket prices vary according to the point in the season and snow and weather conditions; check the appropriate websites or call for updated information.

Crystal (☎ 360-663-2265; www.skicrystal.com; 33914 Crystal Mountain Blvd, Hwy 410) Just off the eastern flank of Mt Rainier National Park, this majestic ski area offers unparalleled views of Mt Rainier, Washington's highest mountain, and some of the best skiing on the West Coast. Located 80 miles from Seattle, Crystal is the largest of the ski areas with the most accessible peak skiing, a solid variety of terrain and a reputation for powder. It is consistently rated by ski magazines as a top North American ski destination.

Mt Baker (☎ 360-734-6771; www.mtbaker.us; East of Bellingham on Hwy 542) Not technically on its namesake, Baker is located on the adjacent Shuksan Arm. It blows the mind with an average annual snowfall of 647in and holds the unofficial world record for seasonal snowfall at an established ski area (1140in during the 1998–99 season). Rightly famous for powder, expert runs and backcountry, Baker is also home to the Legendary Banked Slalom every February. The Slalom started in 1985 and was the first organized snowboarding competition in the world. Baker is about three hours' drive from Seattle, but is worth the longer trip.

Stevens Pass (☎ 206-812-4510; www.stevenspass.com; Summit Stevens Pass, US Hwy 2) Stevens Pass is some 80 miles east, and slightly north, of Seattle. It is known for its surprising variety of terrain with everything on offer from glades to bowls to bumps to an elaborate terrain park. Throw in a huge lift-accessible 'backside' area that gives a backcountry experience without the danger or extra effort and you can't go wrong. Stevens is also good for families and groups that vary in skill level but want something more challenging than the Summit West or Central.

The Summit at Snoqualmie (☎ 425-434-7669; www.summitatsnoqualmie.com; 1001 State Route 906, Snoqualmie Pass) The Summit is a network of four ski areas that lie 50 minutes due east of downtown Seattle on Interstate 90. Alpental is a smaller mountain best for advanced and expert skiers. It is known for its steeps, extensive backcountry and limited but challenging tree skiing. Summit West is the main area of the Summit; it's for beginners and families and has gear rentals and the most developed lodge and dining facilities. It is possible to ski from Summit West over to Summit Central, which is for beginners and intermediates and is home to the Summit's largest terrain park. Summit East is the smallest of the areas and is good for intermediates. It's the location of the Nordic ski center.

Thomas Kohnstamm is a Seattle-based writer who has worked on a number of Lonely Planet guidebooks.

DISC NORTHWEST

☎ 206-781-5840; www.discnw.org

Disc Northwest runs a summer league and a winter league and is the primary resource for ultimate Frisbee in the Seattle area. Check out the website for a detailed schedule of regular pickup games, as well as where they're held and how to get there.

TENNIS

Many of Seattle's public parks have tennis courts, and you don't have to wait long to play. Seattle Parks & Recreation (☎ 206-684-4075) maintains a number of courts in parks throughout the city; most operate on a first-come, first-served basis. You can play tennis on any of the four courts in Volunteer Park on Capitol Hill; the 10 courts in lower Woodland Park, adjacent to Green Lake; or the four courts in Magnolia Playfield on 34th Ave W and W Smith St. For a full listing of public tennis courts, contact Seattle Parks & Recreation.

AMY YEE TENNIS CENTER

off Map p103

☎ 206-684-4764; 2000 Martin Luther King Jr Way; games singles/doubles $20/28

The giant Amy Yee Tennis Center in the Central District has 10 courts indoors and four outside.

GOLF

Seattle Parks & Recreation (☎ 206-684-4075) operates three public golf courses in Seattle, along with a short (nine-hole) pitch-and-putt course located at Green Lake (☎ 206-632-2280; 5701 W Green Lake Way N), a fun spot to go if you're just learning or lack the patience or experience to go a full round. Green fees for city courses are $28 per person on weekdays and $33 on weekends. When they are not booked, the courses also offer reduced rates in the evenings.

JACKSON PARK GOLF COURSE

Map p48

☎ 206-363-4747; 1000 NE 135th St

The most popular municipal course, Jackson Park is on the far northern edge of Seattle. This 18-hole course is best on weekdays, when there are fewer lines at the first tee.

JEFFERSON PARK GOLF COURSE

Map p149

☎ 206-762-4513; 4101 Beacon Ave S

Another convenient tee-off spot, Jefferson Park is an 18-hole course with short fairways and lots of lovely mature (but sometimes troublesome) trees and bushes.

WEST SEATTLE MUNICIPAL GOLF COURSE Map p106

☎ 206-935-5187; 4470 35th Ave SW

With 18 holes and superior views across Elliott Bay, this is one of the area's best public courses.

SWIMMING

When summer temperatures rise, there's no more popular place to be than on one of Seattle's beaches. One of the most popular is Alki Beach (p105) in West Seattle, a real scene with beach volleyball, acres of flesh and teenagers cruising in their cars. Green Lake Park (p95) has two lakefront swimming and sunbathing beaches, as do several parks along the western shores of Lake Washington, including Madison Park (p102), Madrona Park (p104), Seward Park, Magnuson Park and Mt-Baker Park. Lifeguards are on duty at public beaches between 11am and 8pm mid-June to Labor Day (beginning of September).

Swimming is a great way to keep in shape. Many pools host swim clubs or masters programs. The following are public pools that offer a variety of open swim sessions, lessons and lap swimming. Drop-in fees are about $3. For information on other pools, contact Seattle Parks & Recreation (☎ 206-684-4075).

Evans Pool at Green Lake (Map p95; ☎ 206-684-4961; 7201 E Green Lake Drive N)

Medgar Evers Aquatic Center (Map p103; ☎ 206-684-4766; 500 23rd Ave)

Queen Anne Pool (Map p76; ☎ 206-386-4282; 1920 1st Ave W)

HEALTH & FITNESS

Most of Seattle's large hotels have workout facilities available to guests. But if you're looking for more expansive facilities, including group classes and personal trainers, try one of the gyms listed below. Seattle also has plenty of yoga studios, several of which are included here. And for a real treat, try one of the city's posh day spas.

GYMS

24-HOUR FITNESS Map p50

☎ 206-624-0651; 1827 Yale Ave; initial fee about $150, monthly dues $35; ⊙ 24hr

Downtown, with an indoor pool, spa, sauna and steam room, child care, classes and tanning, plus the usual weights and cardio equipment. Ask about specials or check online before you go; free 10-day passes are often available.

DOWNTOWN SEATTLE YMCA Map p50

☎ 206-382-5010; 909 4th Ave; day pass $10-15; ⊙ 5am-9pm Mon-Fri, 7am-6:30pm Sat, 11am-6:30pm Sun

The Y is notably traveler-friendly, and this location has clean, classy, updated equipment including a pool, free weights, cardio equipment and child care.

GOLD'S GYM Map p50

☎ 206-583-0640; 825 Pike St; day pass $10-15; ⊙ 5:30am-10pm Mon-Fri, 8am-8pm Sat & Sun

The downtown Seattle branch of this chain has first-rate facilities for cardio and strength training, plus classes in aerobics, yoga, pilates, dance, kickboxing and karate. Massage, personal training, a sauna and a women-only section are also available.

SOUND MIND & BODY Map p89

☎ 206-547-3470; 437 N 34th St; ⊙ 5:30am-10pm Mon-Thu, to 9pm Fri, 8am-7pm Sat, 9am-7pm Sun

You'll find this Fremont gym vast but quiet. It has close to 40,000 sq ft of weight training and cardio equipment, plus basketball and volleyball courts. It has a sauna and steam room. There are also group classes in yoga, pilates and kickboxing, and a ski-conditioning class. Most unusual is that there's hardly a blaring TV or stereo to be found (viewers must wear headphones while working out).

YOGA

8 LIMBS YOGA CENTER Map p82

☎ 206-523-9722; 500 E Pike St; classes $8-15; ⊙ 6:30am-8:30pm

This Capitol Hill yoga studio emphasizes a supportive, noncompetitive environment and integrating yoga with the rest of life.

PUNK ROCK YOGA Map p82

punkrockyoga.com/seattle/schedule.php; various locations including Home Alive, 1415 10th Ave; drop-in rate $10

An open-minded, stereotype-defying approach to yoga defines this group, which holds all kinds of classes in a number of locations. Though not at all irreverent, it is a bit unorthodox in the best sense. Check the website for the latest schedule.

DAY SPAS

SACRED SKIN THERAPY Map p95

☎ 206-229-7176; www.sacredskintherapy.com; 6306 Phinney Ave N; ⊙ 11am-7pm Tue-Fri, to 5pm Sat

Owner Fauzia Morgan uses organic ingredients and a personal approach to create decadent facials in this gracefully remodeled Phinney Ridge home.

SPA BLIX Map p79

☎ 206-274-5681; 213 Yale Ave N, Alley 24; ⊙ 9am-7pm Mon-Sat, 10am-7pm Sun

Get pampered with a manicure, pedicure, seaweed face wrap, haircut and a full-body exfoliation at this South Lake Union day spa. Charities receive 10% of its monthly profits.

SPA DEL LAGO Map p103

☎ 206-322-5246; 1929 43rd Ave E, Ste 100; ⊙ 11am-5pm Mon, 9am-8pm Tue-Thu, 9am-6pm Fri, 9am-4pm Sat, 10am-5pm Sun

A salon up front with private rooms in the back for facials and massages, this cute place is right by the water in Madison Park.

SPA NOIR Map p69

☎ 206-448-7600; 2231 2nd Ave; ⊙ 10am-8pm Tue-Sat

Looking more like a chic cocktail lounge than a spa, with its deep red walls and heavy velvet curtains, this place caters to the funkier Belltown set. The last Tuesday of the month is bargain day.

SLEEPING

top picks

- **Moore Hotel** (p179)
- **College Inn** (p182)
- **Hotel Monaco Seattle** (p176)
- **Ace Hotel** (p179)
- **Hotel Max** (p176)

SLEEPING

As in many large cities, sleeping options are plentiful and varied in Seattle. Want to drive up to a motor inn and park your beater where you can see it through the window from your mauve-and-blue synthetic-covered bed? You can do that. Rather slink up in a limo and look down your nose as a bellhop lugs your bags to the penthouse suite? You can do that too, as well as pretty much everything in between.

Now that Seattle's central Hostelling International (HI) facility has closed, ultracheap options in the downtown core are more limited, but deals can still be found, even at midrange and upscale hotels. It's best to shop around and plan ahead, as bargains go quickly.

Average hotel rooms cost about $150. The rates listed in the price guide below are what you can expect to pay in peak season – generally May through August. Be aware, though, that prices can vary wildly depending on whether there are festivals or events going on in town. Seattle hotel rooms are also subject to a room tax of 15.6% (less for most B&Bs and historic properties) that will be tacked on to the final bill.

Finding a downtown hotel with free parking is like finding an extra $20 in your pocket while doing laundry. It's been said half the population of Portland, Oregon, consists of people who couldn't find a place to park in Seattle and, searching in ever-widening circles, eventually wound up in Portland and stayed. Many hotels downtown don't offer parking but can direct you to paid lots nearby. There's usually an extra fee for parking (if it is offered), ranging from about $10 to $20. Our reviews note whether parking is provided; if there's a fee, it appears after the ⓟ icon. If there's no ⓟ icon in the review, you're on your own. Look for street meters and paid parking garages downtown, or off-street parking elsewhere.

There are some 10,000 hotel rooms in downtown Seattle, ranging from budget digs with bath and shower down the hall to huge posh suites with everything you could imagine right at your fingertips. Booking ahead is essential to get the best deals, particularly during the summer months (June to August) and around the more popular festival times (see Getting Started, p16).

Check-out times vary, but are usually 11am or noon, and check-in is usually between 2pm and 4pm. Most places, however, are flexible if notified ahead of time.

Washington state recently passed a law banning smoking in public buildings, but hotels are exempt from this; therefore, in the reviews below, the nonsmoking icon ⊠ means a hotel is 100% nonsmoking. Virtually every hotel will offer at least some nonsmoking rooms.

From mid-November through March 31, most downtown hotels offer Seattle Super Saver Packages. These rates are generally 50% off the rack rates, and they come with a coupon book that offers savings on dining, shopping and attractions. To obtain a Super Saver Package, or to get help finding a hotel when Seattle is booked up, call the Seattle Hotel Hotline (☎ 800-535-7071). You can also get information or make reservations any time of year on its website at www.seattlesupersaver.com.

The Seattle B&B Association (☎ 206-547-1020, 800-348-5630; www.lodginginseattle.com) has a searchable list of B&Bs affiliated with the association. The following websites can help with bookings:

Expedia (www.expedia.com)

Lonely Planet Hotels & Hostels (lonelyplanet.com/hotels)
Book Lonely Planet author–approved rooms.

Orbitz (www.orbitz.com)

Travelocity (www.travelocity.com)

PRICE GUIDE

$$$$	more than $200 a night
$$$	$151-200 a night
$$	$80-150 a night
$	under $80 a night

Prices in this chapter are for one standard double room, not including tax or extra fees such as parking. Reviews are divided by neighborhood and listed in order of price, from highest to lowest, based on the cheapest room normally available in high season (May to August).

DOWNTOWN & FIRST HILL

Some of the city's coolest, most character-ful hotels are downtown, and getting from here to any other part of the city on foot or by public transport is a cinch. If you have a car, things get more complicated: driving on hilly one-way streets is maddening, and you'll need to factor the parking fees in to the cost of accommodations. Most of the following downtown hotels offer some kind of parking program with in-and-out privileges, usually for $12 to $20 a day.

FAIRMONT OLYMPIC HOTEL

Map p50   Historic Hotel $$$$

☎ 206-621-1700; www.fairmont.com/seattle; 411 University St; s/d from $419/429; P valet; 🕱 🖵
Built in 1924, the historic Fairmont Olympic is listed with the National Register of Historic Places, so it's not too surprising that it feels like a museum of old money. Over the years, remodels to the bathrooms and the main lobby have kept the place functional without destroying the period glamour of its architecture. With 450 rooms and every imaginable service, this place is out of reach for most, but it's worth exploring even if you can't stay here – have an oyster at Shuckers, the oak-paneled hotel bar. The palpable decadence of the place has been mitigated lately by new, earth-friendly policies such as free parking for hybrid cars.

SORRENTO HOTEL

Map p50   Historic Hotel $$$$

☎ 206-622-6400, 800-426-1265; www.hotelsorrento .com; 900 Madison St; r from $339; P $19; 🕱 🖵
William Howard Taft, 27th US president, was the first registered guest at the Sorrento, an imposing Italianate hotel known since its birth in 1909 as the jewel of Seattle. The combination of luxurious appointments, over-the-top service and a pervasive sense of class add up to a perfect blend of decadence and restraint. The hotel's award-winning restaurant, the Hunt Club, is worth a stop whether you're staying here or not.

HOTEL MONACO SEATTLE

Map p50   Boutique Hotel $$$$

☎ 206-621-1770, 800-945-2240; www.monaco -seattle.com; 1101 4th Ave; r from $325; P $26-36; 🕱 🖵

The hip Hotel Monaco is housed in the old Seattle Phone Building, which sat vacant before the Kimpton group from San Francisco converted it. The suite-style rooms have stripy wallpaper and heavy curtains; leopard-print bathrobes are part of the deal. If you're lonely for your pet, you can borrow a goldfish for the length of your stay. The hotel's restaurant, Sazerac, is a popular New Orleans–style joint with a following of its own.

WESTIN HOTEL SEATTLE

Map p50   Business Hotel $$$$

☎ 206-728-1000, 800-228-3000; 1900 5th Ave; r $260-290; P $20; 🕱 🖵 🖴
This impossible-to-miss, two-cylinder luxury business hotel has almost 900 rooms, some of which contain Jacuzzis, CD players, or a range of workout equipment. There's a heated pool, an exercise room, a gift shop, internet access and a business center – not to mention great views and a popular restaurant.

ALEXIS HOTEL

Map p50   Boutique Hotel $$$$

☎ 206-624-4844, 888-850-1155; www.alexishotel .com; 1007 1st Ave; r from $249, ste from $349; P valet; 🕱 🕱 🖵
Each of the 109 rooms in this Kimpton hotel is decorated with original artwork. Some suites include fireplaces and jetted tubs. Ask about the 'Miles Davis Suite,' which contains art, biographies and CDs by the jazz legend. There's wine tasting in the lobby each evening. Even your dog gets

top picks

PET-FRIENDLY HOTELS

- **Sorrento Hotel** (left) Your pet gets the same classy treatment you do.
- **Alexis Hotel** (above) They'll offer to walk your dog for you.
- **Hotel Monaco Seattle** (left) If you brought a dog, he gets to wear a monogrammed dog jacket; if you didn't, you can borrow a goldfish from the front desk.
- **Hotel Vintage Park** (p176) Pooch gets his own dog tags, plus doggie treats during afternoon wine tastings.

distilled water in its bowl on arrival, along with a complimentary doggie bed and the canine equivalent of a pillow mint. The attached Library Bistro and Bookstore Bar are cozy nooks. You can also get room-service facials from the nearby Aveda spa.

HOTEL VINTAGE PARK
Map p50   Boutique Hotel $$$$
☎ 206-624-8000, 800-624-4433; www.hotel vintagepark.com; 1100 5th Ave; r from $239; P $28; 🖳

The rooms here are a little smaller than at some other downtown hotels and they get a bit of street noise, but it's a pleasant place to stay, especially if you get a west-facing room. The theme is wine; rooms are named after Washington vineyards and wineries, and there's wine tasting in the lobby every afternoon.

HOTEL 1000 Map p50   Design Hotel $$$$
☎ 206-957-1000; www.hotel1000seattle.com; 1000 1st Ave; r from $225, ste from $325; P valet; 🔀 🖳

If you love the clean lines and simple elegance of IKEA, but you happen to have just won the lottery, you might design a hotel like this. Leather-clad egg chairs cuddle around a concrete-and-steel tube fireplace in the lounge; rooms have bedside tables made of chrome and wood; bathrooms have granite counters and freestanding tubs that fill from the ceiling; beds are curtained off in luxurious earth-toned textiles. Each room has art reflecting guests' taste (you tell them what kind of art you like when you book or check-in and they adjust the art in the room) and a 40in HDTV with surround sound. Some have a private bar, and some are pet-friendly. There is also virtual golf.

PARAMOUNT HOTEL
Map p50   Chain Hotel $$$$
☎ 206-292-9500, 800-426-0670; www.paramount hotelseattle.com; 724 Pine St; r from $215; P $20 valet; 🔀 🖳

The Paramount has 146 large rooms that, like the lobby areas, are furnished with heavy antiques perhaps meant to give the relatively new hotel an old-world feel. The downstairs restaurant-bar, Dragonfish, has a 'sushi happy hour' and is a convenient place to meet for a drink before hitting the town.

MAYFLOWER PARK HOTEL
Map p50   Hotel $$$$
☎ 206-623-8700, 800-426-5100; www.may flowerpark.com; 405 Olive Way; r from $209, ste from $229; P valet; 🔀 🔀 🖳

If you're coming to Seattle to shop, this is the hotel for you. Next door to the Westlake Center, it's also a good choice if you're going to take the monorail out to Seattle Center for an event.

RENAISSANCE MADISON HOTEL
Map p50   Hotel $$$-$$$$
☎ 206-583-0300, 800-468-3571; 515 Madison St; r $199-339; P $23-25; 🔀 🖳 🔁

With a calming green-and-brown color scheme, this gigantic, 553-room tower, part of the Marriott chain, is one of the city's nicest hotels. Rooms are large, all have views and windows that open, and pets are welcome (nominal fee). Other features include an indoor pool, two restaurants, a bar-lounge, a beauty shop and a spa.

HOTEL MAX Map p50   Art Hotel $$$
☎ 206-441-4200, 800-426-0670; www.hotelmax seattle.com; 620 Stewart St; s/d from $179/199; P $15; 🖳

There's something mildly obnoxious about a place (or a person) that describes *itself* as hip and artistic, but in the case of Hotel Max, the description fits. Original artworks by local and national artists hang in the (small but cool) guest rooms and public areas of the hotel, and it's tough to get any hipper than the place's supersaturated color scheme – not to mention special package deals like the Grunge Special or the Gaycation. Rooms include not only a pillow menu, but also one for spirituality. Best of all: for $50,000 or so, you can buy your entire hotel room and have it delivered to your home.

EXECUTIVE HOTEL PACIFIC
Map p50   Boutique Hotel $$$
☎ 206-623-3900, 800-426-1165; www.pacific plazahotel.com; 400 Spring St; r from $169; P $16
Centrally located next to the new public library, this Eurasian-themed hotel has small but stylish rooms, with voice mail and data ports, in-room coffee and tea, and windows that open. A business center has free high-speed internet, and the room fee includes a big breakfast. Small dogs are welcome.

RAMADA INN DOWNTOWN

Map p50   Chain Hotel $$

☎ 206-441-9785, 800-272-6232; 2200 5th Ave; r from $149; Ⓟ $12; ▢

This conveniently located hotel is close to Belltown, downtown and Seattle Center. It's also within the Ride Free Area for buses, although most of this area is within easy walking distance. Some of the rooms have views of the Space Needle or downtown, and all have the basic amenities such as in-room coffee and cable TV.

INN AT VIRGINIA MASON

Map p50   Inn $$-$$$

☎ 206-583-6453, 800-283-6453; www.innatvirginia mason.com; 1006 Spring St, First Hill; d/ste from $125/185; Ⓟ $13; ✕

On First Hill, just above the downtown area near a complex of hospitals, this nicely maintained older hotel caters to families needing to stay near the medical facilities. It also offers a number of quiet rooms for other visitors and has a nice rooftop garden with a view from First Hill overlooking the rest of the city. There are discounts if you are staying at the hotel for family medical reasons.

SIXTH AVENUE INN

Map p50   Motel $$

☎ 206-441-8300, 800-627-8290; www.sixth avenueinn.com; 2000 6th Ave; s/d from $119/129; Ⓟ $10; ✖ ▢

Situated just a five-minute walk north of the downtown shopping frenzy, this motor inn possesses an old-fashioned glamour, mostly thanks to its clubby, low-lit bar and lounge area, full of big comfy chairs and a fireplace. Spacious rooms feature vehemently '80s-style brass beds and square lamps – if unironi retro is your thing, you're in luck. There's room service and a fitness room, and free wi-fi is available in the lobby and the lounge.

EIGHTH AVENUE INN

Map p50   Motel $$

☎ 206-624-6300, 800-578-7878; www.eighth avenueinn.com; 2213 8th Ave; r from $116; Ⓟ ✕ ✖ ▢

Formerly a Travelodge, this basic motor inn offers free parking and a handy location, as well as frequent discounts. The rooms are basic but clean and spacious, with free breakfast and friendly staff.

LOYAL INN BEST WESTERN

Map p50   Chain Hotel $$

☎ 206-682-0200; www.bestwestern.com/ prop_48062; 2301 8th Ave; s/d from $110/129; Ⓟ $5; ▢

More plush than other similarly priced options in the area, this chain hotel is in a great location and has a Jacuzzi and sauna, a small exercise room and free continental breakfast. Beds are enormous and rooms are relatively spacious; some include mini-refrigerators and microwaves.

GREEN TORTOISE HOSTEL

Map p50   Hostel $

☎ 206-340-1222; www.greentortoise.net; 105 Pike St; dm $24-29, r $77-80; ▢

Newly situated around the corner from its old home, this hostel is one of the few budget options in the city and has an unbeatable location right across the street from Pike Place Market. Once pretty crusty, the place has moved to the Elliot Hotel Building and now offers 30 bunk rooms and 16 European-style rooms (shared bath and shower). Free breakfast includes waffles and eggs. The hostel offers a free dinner three nights a week and there are weekly events such as open-mic nights.

PIONEER SQUARE

BEST WESTERN PIONEER SQUARE HOTEL
Map p57   Historic Hotel $$$-$$$$

☎ 206-340-1234, 800-800-5514; 77 Yesler Way; r $179-259; Ⓟ $15; ✕ ▢

Rooms and common areas at this historic hotel feature period decor and a comfortable atmosphere. The only hotel in the historic heart of Seattle, it can't be beaten for location – as long as you don't mind some of the saltier characters who populate the square in the off hours. Nightlife, restaurants and shopping are just steps from the door.

PIKE PLACE MARKET & WATERFRONT

The Waterfront and Pike Place Market areas are prime real estate, and hotels here consequently tend to be on the expensive side, but you can't beat the location – or the views. A warning to shoestring travelers hoping to stay in this neighborhood: what used to be among the best budget-friendly options in town, HI Seattle, has closed.

HOTEL EDGEWATER
Map p64   Legendary Landmark $$$$

☎ 206-728-7000, 800-624-0670; www.edgewater hotel.com; 2411 Alaskan Way, Pier 67; r with city/ water views from $299/439; **P** $26 valet

Perched over the water right *in* Elliott Bay, the Edgewater is one of the few places that lives up to its storied past. The timber-lodge theme, with its rock fireplaces and rough-hewn pine furniture, is pure Pacific Northwest, but a seriously classed-up version thereof. Half of the 223 rooms have bay views and the rest overlook the Seattle skyline; many contain gas fireplaces. OK, so you can't fish out the windows anymore, but that's probably just about the only wish this place won't fulfill.

INN AT THE MARKET
Map p64   Hotel $$$-$$$$

☎ 206-443-3600, 800-446-4484; www.innatthe market.com; 86 Pine St; r $175-300, r with water views $230-400; **P** $20

Right in the thick of things, the Inn at the Market is an elegant and architecturally interesting hotel and the only lodging in the venerable Pike Place Market. This 70-room boutique hotel has large rooms, many of which enjoy grand views onto market activity and Puget Sound. Its two restaurants, Campagne and Cafe Campagne, are renowned for their excellent French cuisine.

PENSIONE NICHOLS
Map p64   B&B $$

☎ 206-441-7125; www.pensionenichols.com; 1923 1st Ave; s/d $98/125, ste $230; **P** $12; 🖫

In a town with few cheap hotels and hardly any B&Bs right downtown, Pensione Nichols is a treat. Right in the urban

thick of things between Pike Place Market and Belltown, this charmingly remodeled European-style pensione has 10 rooms that share four retro-cool bathrooms, two large suites, and a spacious common area that overlooks the market. Rooms come with a complete and tasty breakfast. Parking is in a nearby garage.

BELLTOWN

Some of the city's best budget- and hipster-friendly accommodations can be found in Belltown, which is handy when you're finished with your pub crawl and need to make your way back to your room for the night. This area is also an easy walk from downtown, Pike Place Market and the Seattle Center. It can get a little loud at night, though, so light sleepers beware.

HOTEL ÄNDRA
Map p69   Design Hotel $$$$

☎ 206-448-8600, 877-448-8600; hotelandra.com; 2000 4th Ave; r from $219, ste $249-309; **P** valet; ⌧ 🅿 🖫

Wild fabric patterns and vivid colors combine with sleek Scandinavian-influenced design to give this hotel (formerly the Claremont) a calming yet sharply modern feel. Its 119 rooms have a sense of luxury without being claustrophobically overfurnished with the usual trappings of decadence. The trappings here, in fact, are quite unusual: alpaca headboards, anyone? There are blue-glass wall sconces, brushed-steel fixtures, gigantic walnut work desks – even the fitness room has spartan prints and flat-screen TVs on the walls. Some of the suites have plasma-screen TVs. Bathroom toiletries come from Face Stockholm. The hotel is attached to chef Tom Douglas' Greek-via-Northwest restaurant, Lola.

GREEN HOTELS

Nearly all hotels these days have little notes placed on the bed and in the bathroom advising guests that, in an effort to conserve water and energy, sheets and towels will not be washed every day unless requested. But some hotels in Seattle go beyond these basics. The city's three Kimpton hotels – the Alexis Hotel (p175), the Hotel Monaco Seattle (p175) and the Hotel Vintage Park (p176) – all benefit from the chain's EarthCare program, which emphasizes sustainable, ecofriendly practices without sacrificing luxury. These include recycling, using soy ink and recycled paper, serving organic or fair-trade coffee in the lobby, and using environmentally friendly cleaning products. The luxurious Fairmont Olympic (p175) has added ecofriendly policies as well, such as free parking for hybrid cars, compact fluorescent light bulbs, recycling containers in rooms, and composting facilities.

INN AT EL GAUCHO

Map p69   Luxury Hotel $$$-$$$$

☎ 206-728-1133, 866-354-2824; inn.elgaucho
.com; 2505 1st Ave; ste $195-295; Ⓟ valet;
✕ ✖ ▣

In 18 suites decorated '50s-style, above the type of anachronistic steakhouse that harks back to the good ol' days when vegetarians were eaten by the wealthy as snacks between meals, the Inn at El Gaucho offers a particularly outsized, swaggering American luxury. Plasma-screen TVs, Bose stereo systems, 'Rain System' showers and buttery leather couches grace all the suites. And if it's too much to leave for even a moment, El Gaucho restaurant will serve you steak in bed.

ACE HOTEL

Map p69   Design Hotel $$-$$$

☎ 206-448-4721; www.acehotel.com; 2423 1st Ave;
r without/with bathroom $99/190; Ⓟ $15; ▣

Each of the Ace's 28 hospital-tidy rooms is unique and so stylish you quickly get the feeling you're the star of an art film. Ranging from European style with shared bathrooms to deluxe versions with private bathrooms, CD players and enough mirrors to make you paranoid, the rooms are stocked with condoms and, where your average Midwestern motor inn would place the Gideon Bible, a copy of the *Kama Sutra*. Obviously this isn't the place for the uptight – it's also bad for light sleepers, as the always-hopping Cyclops bar and restaurant is just downstairs. Rock-and-roll hipsters have it made.

MOORE HOTEL

Map p69   Hotel $-$$

☎ 206-448-4851, 800-421-5508; 1926 2nd Ave;
s/d $52/64, s/d with private bathroom $67/79, ste
$104-156; ✕ ▣

The once grand Moore Hotel offers 135 bedrooms, small and not fancy but refurbished with an understated elegance. The early-20th-century lobby, with its molded ceiling and marble accoutrements, speaks of the building's long history, which is echoed in the better rooms (ask for one with a view of the Sound). Don't miss the great little lounge next door, the Nitelite (p142), whose clientele is a mix of young hipsters and regulars at least as old as the hotel. There's free internet in the lobby.

SEATTLE CENTER & QUEEN ANNE

Staying around Seattle Center makes sense for a number of reasons: it's only five minutes from downtown on the monorail or bus (and just slightly more to walk), and room prices are often lower than those downtown (except when big concerts or festivals are on at Seattle Center). You can also park your vehicle free of charge at most hotels, and that's no small matter – it'll save you the cost of a nice dinner out.

Most of the hotels around here are fairly anonymous, motor-court type lodgings from the 1960s, and many of them cater to business travelers – so they're efficient and have all the amenities you might need, but generally not a lot of character.

Immediately to the west of Seattle Center is Lower Queen Anne. It's only a five-minute walk from here to the opera house or Key Arena and a 10-minute walk to the Space Needle.

HAMPTON INN

Map p73   Chain Hotel $$-$$$

☎ 206-282-7700; 700 5th Ave N; standard r from
$199; Ⓟ $9; ✖ ▣

A couple of blocks north of Seattle Center, the Hampton Inn has 198 rooms, most of which have balconies. There's a wide variety of rooms, from standards to two-bedroom suites with fireplaces, and a cooked breakfast is included.

MARQUEEN HOTEL

Map p76   Hotel $$$

☎ 206-282-7407, 888-445-3076; 600 Queen Anne
Ave N; r from $190; Ⓟ $16; ▣

Another old (1918) apartment building, the MarQueen Hotel has hardwood floors throughout and a variety of rooms, all with kitchenettes leftover from their days as apartments. There's a free courtesy van that takes guests to nearby sights.

BEST WESTERN EXECUTIVE INN

Map p73   Chain Hotel $$$-$$$$

☎ 206-448-9444, 800-351-9444; 200 Taylor Ave N;
r from $189-209; Ⓟ $5; ✕ ✖ ▣

In the shadow of the Space Needle, the Executive Inn has an exercise spa and a complimentary shuttle to downtown. Pillowtop beds, in-room coffee and tea, microwaves and refrigerators, room service, a fitness room and a sports lounge are also available.

TRAVELODGE BY THE SPACE NEEDLE
Map p73   Chain Hotel $$

☎ 206-441-7878, 800-578-7878; 200 6th Ave N; r from $139; P ⌗ ▣ ▨
Quieter than anything on Aurora Ave N, this hotel offers amenities including a year-round Jacuzzi, outdoor pool (open in summer), in-room coffee makers and a free continental breakfast (though it's fairly skimpy).

INN AT QUEEN ANNE
Map p76   Inn $$

☎ 206-282-7357, 800-952-5043; www.innat queenanne.com; 505 1st Ave N; r standard/deluxe $89/109; P $10; ⌗ ▣
This place is a 1929 apartment building-turned-hotel. Rooms come with kitchen-ettes and continental breakfast; or grab a complimentary apple from the bowl in the lobby. The only difference between stand-ard and deluxe is that deluxe rooms have air-conditioning.

LAKE UNION

MARRIOTT RESIDENCE INN
Map p79   Residence Hotel $$$$

☎ 206-624-6000, 800-331-3131; 800 Fairview Ave N; studio ste from $259, 2-bedroom ste from $369; P $19; ⌗ ⌗ ▣ ▨
A convenient place to settle in for a length-ier stay, the Residence Inn has work-friendly studio suites and family-size two-room suites, all with kitchens. There's a lap pool, exercise room and spa, free breakfast and evening desserts in the lobby. Rooms on the west side of the hotel have good views of Lake Union – rates vary depending on whether you get a view or not.

SILVER CLOUD INN LAKE UNION
Map p79   Chain Hotel $$$-$$$$

☎ 206-447-9500, 800-330-5812; 1150 Fairview Ave N; r from $189, ste from $209; P ⌗ ⌗ ▣ ▨
This hotel has 184 rooms, some of which have stunning views of Lake Union. There's also a gym, indoor and outdoor pools, laun-dry facilities and complimentary breakfast, plus a free shuttle service to downtown, a handy amenity in this area.

COURTYARD MARRIOTT
Map p79   Chain Hotel $$$

☎ 206-213-0100, 800-321-2211; 925 Westlake Ave N; r from $179; P $17; ⌗ ⌗ ▣ ▨
Over on the southwest side of Lake Union, the Courtyard Marriott has all the big hotel amenities, including an indoor pool and a restaurant. It's set up to suit the business traveler, but is comfy enough to justify not getting any work done. There's a small convenience store on-site for impromptu snacks.

CAPITOL HILL & VOLUNTEER PARK

Beyond its nightlife-oriented main drags, Capitol Hill is full of beautiful, well-maintained homes on quiet, tree-lined resi-dential streets. Lucky for the traveler, many of them have been converted into plush B&Bs. These are friendly, welcoming places where you can start your day with a giant breakfast, hear a local's advice on what to see and usu-ally park free of charge on the street. (Note, however, that parking becomes much more difficult on weekend evenings as you approach Broadway and the Pike–Pine Corridor.)

SALISBURY HOUSE B&B
Map p82   B&B $$-$$$

☎ 206-328-8682; www.salisburyhouse.com; 750 16th Ave E; s $119-139, d $129-149, ste $179; ⌗ ▣
Salisbury House, in a quiet, tree-lined neighborhood near Volunteer Park, is a 1904 home with four elegant corner rooms and one suite, all equipped with private bathrooms, phone with voice mail, and wireless internet access. It's comfortably modern, not the floral overload of a typical B&B. The full breakfast is vegetarian and served family-style. Downstairs there's a library with a fireplace. Two cats roam the grounds, and children over 12 are welcome.

HILL HOUSE B&B Map p82   B&B $$-$$$

☎ 206-720-7161, 800-720-7161; www.seattlehill house.com; 1113 E John St; r $99-199; P ⌗ ▣
Close to the hub of Capitol Hill, the guestrooms in this 1903 home feature queen beds, down comforters, fluffy robes and a range of moods, from over-the-top lacy to English gentleman. Some rooms

have private bathrooms, and two are large suites with garden and patio access.

BACON MANSION B&B
Map p82   B&B $$-$$$$
☎ 206-329-1864, 800-240-1864; www.bacon mansion.com; 959 Broadway E; r $89-209; &
A 1909 mansion that's imposing at first glance and very welcoming, this four-level B&B on a quiet residential street just past the Capitol Hill action has a grand piano in the main room that guests are invited to play. The 11 rooms come in a variety of configurations, including a carriage house that's wheelchair-accessible, and include TV and voice mail. One large suite has a view of the Space Needle, one has a fireplace, and another has an Italian fountain as a backdrop.

GASLIGHT INN B&B Map p82   B&B $$-$$$
☎ 206-325-3654; www.gaslight-inn.com; 1727 15th Ave; r $88-158; ☒ ☲
The Gaslight Inn has 15 rooms available in two neighboring homes, 12 of which have private bathrooms. In summer, it's refreshing to dive into the outdoor pool or just hang out on the sun deck. No pets; the B&B already has a cat and a dog.

U DISTRICT
This area is another good place to find good-value rates at hotels and B&Bs. Accommodations here are also more likely to include free parking, as real estate is less limited than it is downtown.

WATERTOWN Map p85   Hotel $$$-$$$$
☎ 206-826-4242, 866-944-4242; www.watertown seattle.com; 4242 Roosevelt Way NE; s $165-175, d $175-185, ste $185-265; ℗ ☒ ☲
Easy to miss because it looks like one of those crisp new modern apartment buildings, the Watertown has more of an arty-industrial feel than its sister hotel, the University Inn (right). Bare concrete and high ceilings in the lobby make it seem stark and museum-like, but that translates to spacious and warmly furnished rooms, with giant beds, swivel TVs and huge windows. Thematic 'Ala Carts' – for example a Relaxation Cart, a Seattle Cart or a Game Cart – are delivered free to your room. Guests can borrow bicycles or use the hotel's free shuttle to explore the area.

HOTEL DECA Map p85   Design Hotel $$$-$$$$
☎ 206-634-2000, 800-899-0251; www.hotel deca.com; 4507 Brooklyn Ave NE; r $160-290; ℗ ☒ ☲ ☲
Formerly the University Tower, and before that the Meany Tower Hotel, the Deca is currently enjoying its fanciest incarnation so far after a $2 million renovation. The same architect who designed the Old Faithful Lodge in Yellowstone National Park built this hotel in 1931. Its 16 stories offer rooms with either a Cascade view or a downtown view. Rooms also feature flat-screen TVs with DVD players and iPods so you can listen to your own music. Breakfast is included, and there's a 24-hour workout room, a bar and a restaurant, plus a Tully's coffee shop in the building.

SILVER CLOUD INN
Map p85   Chain Hotel $$$
☎ 206-526-5200, 800-205-6940; 5036 25th Ave NE; s from $159, d from $179; ℗ ☒ ☲ ☲ ☲
Just a little nicer and a little friendlier than it has to be, the Silver Cloud is ideal for business travelers or those staying long enough to want to make use of the kitchenettes in each suite. In-room coffee and tea, data ports, flat screen TVs, plush couches and huge beds add to the comfort, and the free breakfast, guest laundry, indoor pool, spa and fitness room don't hurt, either. The Burke-Gilman Trail abuts the parking lot, and a free hotel shuttle will drop you anywhere in town within 3 miles.

UNIVERSITY INN Map p85   Hotel $$
☎ 206-632-5055, 800-733-3855; www.university innseattle.com; 4140 Roosevelt Way NE; standard s/d from $109/119, deluxe s/d from $129/139, premier s/d from $145/155; ℗ ☒ ☲ ☲
What pushes this spotless, modern, well-located place over the edge into greatness is, believe it or not, the waffles served at the complimentary breakfast. They're amazing. The hotel is three blocks from campus, and its 102 rooms come in three levels of plushness. All of them offer such basics as a coffee maker, hair dryer and wi-fi; some have balconies, sofas and CD players, and some are pet-friendly ($20 fee). There's a Jacuzzi, an outdoor pool, laundry facilities and a guest computer in the lobby. Attached to the hotel is the recommended Portage Bay Cafe, and there's a free shuttle to various sightseeing areas.

AIRPORT HOTELS

If you're flying in to Sea-Tac late at night or out early in the morning, you might want to stay near the airport for the sake of convenience. The following hotels all offer complimentary airport shuttles and do a good job of getting you to and from the airport on time.

Days Inn at Sea-Tac Airport (☎ 206-244-3600, 800-325-2525; 19015 International Blvd S; r from $67; P ✂ 🖥) Some of the 86 rooms at this hotel have Jacuzzis and some have kitchenettes. There's also a small gym, free continental breakfast and a 24-hour airport shuttle.

Radisson Hotel Seattle Airport (☎ 206-244-6000, 800-333-3333; 17001 Pacific Hwy S; r $109-165; P ✂ 🖥) One of the fancier options around here, the Radisson has 300-plus rooms, a restaurant, lounge, outdoor pool, gym and sauna. The free shuttle will also take you to nearby restaurants or car-rental agencies.

Wyndham Seattle-Tacoma Airport (☎ 206-244-6666; 18118 Pacific Hwy S; r $95-189; P ✂ 🖥 🐾) A 10-minute walk (or even quicker shuttle ride) from the airport, this large hotel has business-friendly rooms with data ports (some with high-speed internet connections), CD players and in-room coffee. There's a pool, Jacuzzi, exercise room and a restaurant-bar, plus a fireplace in the lobby.

CHAMBERED NAUTILUS B&B INN
Map p85   B&B $$-$$$

☎ 206-522-2536, 800-545-8459; 5005 22nd Ave NE; r $94-169, ste $104-199; ✂ 🖥
The 1915 Georgian-style Chambered Nautilus has six guestrooms that are decorated with authentic British antiques, as well as an annex with one- and two-bedroom suites. All B&B rooms here come with private baths, down comforters, handmade soaps and a teddy bear. The communal living room has a welcoming fireplace, and the full gourmet breakfast is reason enough to stay here. It's found in a handy but quiet location, tucked into the forested hillside that lies between the university and Ravenna Park.

COLLEGE INN
Map p85   Hostel/B&B $-$$

☎ 206-633-4441; www.collegeinnseattle.com; 4000 University Way NE; s/d from $55/75; ✂ 🖥
The College Inn is a great budget option. Built for the 1909 Alaska-Yukon Exposition, the building has 27 European-style guestrooms with shared bathrooms down the hall. There's no TV, but there's a ton of atmosphere, and some of the rooms have a view of the Space Needle. South-facing rooms get the most light. Rates include a continental breakfast served in the communal lounge. Downstairs there's a coffee shop that serves full meals, a convenience store, and a lively pub. Note that the building lacks elevators, and the 'front desk' is four flights up a narrow stairway.

EXCURSIONS

EXCURSIONS

Seattle's location makes it ideal for getting out of the city with ease and exploring the natural beauty of its surroundings. With very little effort, you can trade that caffeinated urban buzz for a tranquil island retreat, an orchard-strewn valley or a rugged mountain peak – even all three.

Puget Sound (p187), the sparkling jewel that surrounds Seattle, is dotted with tiny islands once dismissed as agricultural backwaters but now among the most popular tourist destinations in the area. Visiting the islands does take some planning in the summer months, when everybody else wants to be there too, but you'll understand why as soon as you start paddling your rented kayak or sailboat out on the water. The sparse population of many of the islands makes them ideal places for bicycle fiends. Or, if you prefer, you can always sit at a dockside pub and sip a microbrew while you watch active people do their thing. Most of the hotels, B&Bs and restaurants in island towns are open all year, so if you'd like to avoid the crowds, plan on an off-season visit. For the purposes of ferry schedules and seasonal business hours, 'summer' refers to mid-June through September.

Those looking to take their minds off city life with a serious physical challenge also have a couple of options. The most tempting is Mt Rainier (p193), mostly because its pointy peak beckons from the horizon almost everywhere you go in Seattle. Reaching the summit is no picnic, but the whole Mt Rainier National Park area has an abundance of hikes at all skill levels and distances.

Climbing the summit of Mt St Helens (p195) is another option for serious hikers. Or, for peace and quiet, enjoy your lunch along the shores of Coldwater Lake at the base of the dramatically scarred mountain.

Drive a bit further and feel infinitely more distant from urban chaos by visiting the Olympic Peninsula (p197). This remote area feels steeped in mystery – partly because of its thick, misty, moss-laden forests and partly because there is only one major road going through it. Combine the wild nature of the Hoh River Rain Forest (p197) with the charm of Victorian-era Port Townsend (p197) and you might just accidentally forget to catch that flight home.

For those with less time and energy, the Snoqualmie Valley (p194) makes a quick and easy escape from the city. Its pastoral landscape, dotted with orchards and imbued with an eerie feel, is a lovely place for a leisurely drive. In winter it offers some of the area's best skiing.

Just a short ferry ride away is Victoria (p195), the Olde English–style capital of British Columbia. Its high teas, B&Bs and famed botanical garden make it a pleasantly quiet retreat.

ISLANDS

It's almost criminal to be in Seattle and not get out on the water. Puget Sound (p187) has some of the most gorgeous islands in the country, and it's a great area to explore by ferry. An outing on the sound makes a relaxing day trip, whether you're going by car or bike or just on foot.

Bainbridge Island (p187) makes an easy day or half-day trip from downtown Seattle. Explore the island's main town, Winslow, with a stop at the local winery. Rent bicycles to pedal around the easily accessible island.

If you have time for a longer island-hop, start with Lopez Island (p191), the closest and most agricultural, full of pastoral charm. Then press on toward Shaw Island (p193), where the traffic-free roads are a cyclist's paradise. And don't miss San Juan Island (p190) itself. Its fetching Friday Harbor (p190) is hard not to love;

this is a fairly substantial town, so there are plenty of options for dining and sleeping. The picturesque farmlands just outside the town are close enough to reach on foot.

NATURE

Seattle has the advantage of being one of the few major cities in the US with easy access to wilderness right outside its back door. Nature wild enough to get lost in is as close as Discovery Park (p97), and there's plenty more where that came from.

It's even easier to get lost on the Olympic Peninsula, where misty trails meander through the regal forests of the Hoh River Rain Forest (p197). At the end of your hike, play on the rugged beach and sleep in a working farmhouse (p198).

To see what happens when nature has a bad day, visit the Mt St Helens Visitors Center (p195). The

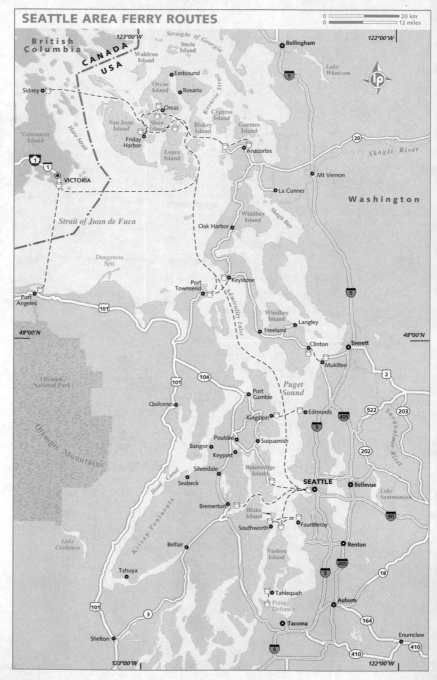

SEATTLE AREA FERRY ROUTES

MAKING SENSE OF SEATTLE FERRIES

Ferries are by far the most fun means of travel in the Seattle area, and a handy way to get to the surrounding islands, but it's not always easy to figure out how to use the system. Schedules are pretty chaotic at first glance – not every ferry goes to every island every day – and the payment system can be confusing, too.

The clearinghouse for information on Washington State Ferries (☎ 206-464-6400, in Washington 800-808-7977, automated information 800-843-3779; www.wsdot.wa.gov/ferries; main office Pier 52, Alaskan Way, Marion St, Seattle) which serve most of the destinations we review, can be found online. From here, links take you to online or downloadable schedules for all possible routes. There are also notes about delays or service interruptions. A complicated code, explained in the page's margins, tells you the name of the boat that will be making each run, as well as whether it has disabled access, and specifies that certain routes are only on weekends or only on weekdays.

Then there's a link to the fare information. Fares depend on the length of the route and the size of your vehicle, if you have one. Also, each route seems to have a different way of collecting the fares; some collect on departure, some mid-trip, and some when you arrive. These are specified on the website's trip planner. Note that there's no charge for journeys back toward Seattle from Friday Harbor; the full round-trip fare will have been collected on your way out.

Transportation details are described under each island's listing. Between the islands, transportation is by inter-island ferries, which travel a circular route exclusively between the four main islands. There is a fee for vehicles (by length) and drivers traveling west-bound only; there is no charge for walk-ons or bicycles.

site does an amazing job of displaying the terrifying power of a volcano. Dramatically situated observation points put you practically inside the crater that was blown out of the side of the mountain more than 20 years ago. The adventurous (and fit) can hike up to the crater's edge, though you'll need to book in advance.

OUTDOOR ACTIVITIES

It's hard to resist a visit to majestic Mt Rainier (p193); after all, you've probably been gazing wistfully at it through restaurant and hotel windows throughout your stay in Seattle. Tackle the summit and linger in Paradise (p193) to mingle with the wildlife.

There's also great hiking around the infamously volcanic Mt St Helens (p195). For adventures on a flatter scale, the islands of Puget Sound (right), as well as the San Juan Islands (p189), have leisurely but spectacular cycling routes. The islands are also great for water sports such as canoeing and sea kayaking. For downhill skiing and snowboarding, haul your gear over to Snoqualmie Valley (p194). See p165 for more about outdoor activities.

TIME TRAVEL

The well-preserved historic buildings lining the streets of Port Townsend (p197), many of them housing shops filled with antiques and Victorian knickknacks, make it easy to believe you've taken the ferry to another era. Fort Worden State Park (p197), where the 2002 movies

The Ring and *An Officer and a Gentleman* were filmed, enhances the illusion.

PUGET SOUND

The islands of Puget Sound make a fantastic escape from the city. Aside from their scenic beauty – very different from the natural landscapes you'll find in and around Seattle, despite their proximity – two activities draw people here: rest and relaxation. These come in many forms, from berry picking or leisurely cycling to wine sampling or lolling on beaches. Reset your internal clock to 'slow' while you take in the gorgeous views of the city and mountains during the ferry ride over, and you'll make the most of a vacation from your vacation.

BAINBRIDGE ISLAND

When it comes to visiting Bainbridge Island, getting there really is half the fun. It's a popular destination with locals and visitors alike, largely because it's the quickest and easiest way to get out on the water from Seattle. It's also one of the loveliest. The ferry ride alone provides enough stunning views of Seattle and the Sound to make the trip worthwhile. Once you get to the island, prepare to stroll around lazily, tour some waterfront cafés, taste unique wines at the Bainbridge Island Winery, maybe rent a bike and cycle around the invitingly flat countryside, and generally relax until it's time to ferry back.

The family-owned Bainbridge Island Winery (☎ 206-842-9463; ☽ tastings 11am-5pm Fri-Sun) near Winslow is a good destination for cyclists, or for wine-lovers who don't mind a walk – the winery has moved to a place at the edge of its vineyards, about 4 miles north of town on Hwy 305. On Sundays at 2pm there's a winegrower's tour of the vineyards.

Information

Chamber of Commerce (☎ 206-842-3700; www.bainbridgechamber.com; 590 Winslow Way E)

Classic Cycle (☎ 206-842-9191; 310 Winslow Way NE; rentals 2hr/2 days/1 week $25/60/150; ☽ 10am-6:30pm Mon-Fri, 10am-5pm Sat, noon-4pm Sun) This bike shop, part vintage-cycle museum, also rents bicycles.

Eating

Café Nola (☎ 206-842-3822; 101 Winslow Way; lunch mains $11-16, dinner mains $16-23; ☽ brunch, lunch & dinner) One highlight of a visit to Bainbridge is a meal at this popular bistro, serving a classy blend of Mediterranean and Northwest cooking.

Harbour Public House (☎ 206-842-0969; 231 Parfitt Way; starters $6-12, mains $10-16) After your bike ride, sit back and quaff microbrews at this public house. Seafood dishes, including the grilled salmon sandwich ($12.95) and a calamari appetizer ($7.95), are recommended.

Mora Iced Creamery (☎ 206-855-1112; www.moraicedcreamery.com; 139 Madrone Lane; ♿) Luscious ice creams and sorbets made locally on Bainbridge Island come in cones, cups or pints – and, as a bonus, it's all low-fat.

TRANSPORTATION: BAINBRIDGE ISLAND

Distance from Seattle 9 miles

Direction West

Travel time 35 minutes

Ferry Vehicle ferries to Bainbridge Island board at the Washington State Ferries main terminal at Pier 52. Ferries run from 5:30am until about 1:30am, hourly in summer and several times a day in winter. Round-trip fares for an adult are $6.70 and for a child $5.40, and for a car and driver it's $28.95. Cyclists pay an extra $1. Passenger and vehicle fares are collected at Seattle Pier 52, while vehicle-only fares are collected at Bainbridge Island. No reservations accepted.

VASHON ISLAND

More rural and countercultural than Bainbridge Island to the north, Vashon Island has resisted suburbanization – a rare accomplishment in Puget Sound. Much of the island is covered with farms and gardens, and its little towns double as commercial hubs and artists' enclaves. Vashon Island also provides unencumbered vistas of the Cascades mountain range, with views from Mt Rainier in the south to Mt Baker in the north. Vashon is a good island to explore by bicycle or car, stopping here and there to pick berries or fruit at a 'u-pick' garden or orchard along the way. Plan a hike in one of the county parks.

Note that the ferry from Seattle deposits you in the north of the island, distant from the centers of Vashon commerce and culture, so you'll need to bring a bike or car, or have a lift arranged.

Eating & Sleeping

Back Bay Inn (☎ 206-463-5355; 24007 Vashon Hwy SW; mains from $12; r $110-115; ☽ dinner Wed-Sat) Local home-style cuisine with an elegant touch is served a few nights a week – in summer only – in this delightful inn. For guests of the four rooms, the daily breakfast is a real treat.

Emily's Café and Juice Bar (☎ 206-463-6404; Vashon Hwy SW at Bank Rd SW; mains $8-10; Ⓥ) Serves light vegetarian fare.

HI Seattle/Vashon AYH Ranch (☎ 206-463-2592; www.vashonhostel.com; 12119 SW Cove St; dm $17-20, r $55-65 summer, r/cabin $80/300 winter) Budget travelers will be glad of this great hostel with bunk beds, teepee camping and rooms available in the summer; during the winter it operates as a lodge with private rooms. It also has bicycles for rent ($6 per hour).

TRANSPORTATION: VASHON ISLAND

Distance from Seattle About 8 miles

Direction Southwest

Travel time 20 minutes

Ferry There are daily departures from Fauntleroy in West Seattle. Passenger and vehicle fares (adult/child/car and driver $4.30/3.35/18.50) are collected at Fauntleroy; no fares are collected at Vashon Island.

BLAKE ISLAND

Blake Island is a state park and can be approached only by boat. This made it a safe place to host the 1993 APEC conference, where former President Bill Clinton met with 14 Asia-Pacific leaders. Most people, however, go to the island to visit Tillicum Village (☎ 206-443-1244; Pier 55, Seattle; tours adult/senior/child $79/72/30), which features the Northwest Coast Indian Cultural Center & Restaurant. A popular tour package includes a traditional Indian salmon bake, dancing and a film about Northwest Native Americans. After the meal, there's time for a short hike or a bit of shopping. You can also get there on your own boat and explore without the formal tour, or opt to watch the performances and skip dinner or vice versa.

TRANSPORTATION: BLAKE ISLAND

Distance from Seattle About 8 miles

Direction Southwest

Travel time Four hours (entire tour)

Ferry Departures from Pier 55 in Seattle daily in summer, weekends only from October to March. Fares are adult/child/senior $79/30/72.

SAN JUAN ISLANDS

The San Juan archipelago contains 457 islands sprawled across 750 sq miles of Pacific waters in the area where Puget Sound and the straits of Juan de Fuca and Georgia meet. About 200 of the islands are named and only a handful are inhabited. Washington State Ferries (see boxed text, p187) provides service to the four largest islands – San Juan, Orcas, Shaw and Lopez – while others are accessible only by private boat or plane.

San Juan itself is also known as the Pig War Island. The so-called Pig War of 1859 was sparked when an American settler in San Juan shot and killed a hog belonging to Bellevue Farm, which supported the Hudson's Bay Company's controversial fur-trapping operations. The settler, Lyman Cutler, said he killed the hog because it kept invading his garden. British troops then tried to arrest Cutler, and, because the boundary between Canada and the US at the time was hazy, US troops went in to confront the British. All of this, absurdly enough, nearly led to a battle; British warships popped up off the coast of San Juan, and things grew tense. But reason won out; the two governments agreed to a joint occupation of the San Juans until the boundary dispute could be settled. The joint agreement lasted 12 years until, in 1872, Kaiser Wilhelm of Germany settled the dispute in favor of the United States. That decision ended the last territorial conflict between the US and Great Britain and made San Juan Island the last bit of American soil occupied by Great Britain.

Until about 30 years ago the islands were considered inaccessible and backward. Their patchwork fields, forests, lakes, sheep pastures and fishing boats setting sail from tiny rock-lined harbors were ignored by all but the fishers and farmers inhabiting them. Today, however, tourism is the mainstay of local economies: the islands are a major holiday destination without enough lodging to handle the crowds during the summer high season. And yet, despite the inevitable adulteration that 'discovery' brings, the islands retain their bucolic charm and make for a restful retreat.

Although many people come to the San Juan Islands for rest and recuperation, the outdoor activities are another reason to visit. The islands are small, largely flat and laced with deserted roads, making this a great getaway for cyclists. Sea kayaking is another favorite sport – the rocky coast and relatively protected waters make for a perfect environment to explore by kayak. Wildlife along the coastline – seabirds, seals and sea lions, otters and even orcas – is also abundant. Most marinas have sailboats for rent. Whale-watching trips are also popular excursions. Tours go all year, but the most sightings of orcas happen from May to September.

Keep in mind that many of the islands' beaches are privately owned, so your best bet for lying on the beach might be at a resort that owns some sandy oceanfront.

Lodging frequently fills up during the summer; don't even think about heading out without reservations during July and August or you may end up having to take the last ferry back to the mainland. Most reservations are made months ahead, and the most attractive places to stay are often booked even further in advance – but if your heart's set on a place, it's worth calling to ask if there have been cancellations. Accommodations are not inexpensive: you'll be hard pressed to find rooms for less than $100 a night during the summer. Maps of the islands are available at the San Juan Islands Visitor Information Center, listed p190.

Information

Island Air (☎ 888-378-2376; www.sanjuan-islandair.com) Provides charter service from SeaTac or Boeing Field/King County Airport

Island Airporter (☎ 360-378-7438; www.islandairporter .com) Daily, non-stop service from SeaTac to San Juan Island (Friday Harbor & Roche Harbor)

Kenmore Air (☎ 800-543-9595; www.kenmoreair.com) Land and seaplanes fly direct daily from Lake Union, Lake Washington, and Boeing Field/King County Airport to San Juan Island, with free shuttle service between SeaTac and the terminals.

San Juan Islands Visitor Information Center (☎ 360-468-3663; www.guidetosanjuans.com; PO Box 65, Lopez, WA 98261) Great website with all sorts of useful info.

Tourist Information (☎ 360-378-6977)

Victoria Clipper (☎ 360-448-5000, 800-888-2535, 206-448-5000; www.victoriaclipper.com) Sails from downtown's Pier 69 to Friday Harbor

Washington State Ferries From the mainland, car ferries leave from Anacortes (see p192) and depart for the four busiest islands; not all ferries go to all islands, so read the ferry schedule carefully. See boxed text, p187.

TRANSPORTATION: SAN JUAN ISLAND

Travel time 70 minutes

Ferry Anacortes (see p192) to San Juan Island (Friday Harbor) costs $13.15/10.55/51.20 adult/child/car and driver via Washington State Ferries.

SAN JUAN ISLAND

Most visitors find that San Juan, of all the islands, offers the most hospitable blend of sophisticated amenities, rural landscapes and bustling harbors. It's the most developed and most visited of the four main San Juan islands. A large part of the island's draw is Friday Harbor – with a population of about 2000, it's the only real town in all the San Juan Islands. Even so, it's small enough to navigate on foot. Legend has it that when the early European explorers first arrived, one of them said, 'What bay is this?' and was misheard as asking 'What day is this?' But the harbor is, in fact, less colorfully named for an early settler from the 1800s called Joe Friday.

Most of the hotels and restaurants are either on or just off the main drag, Spring St, which runs uphill half a block over from the ferry landing. But follow any of the streets out of Friday Harbor and you're soon on a central plateau where small farms, dairies and lakes fill the verdant landscape.

The only other community of any size is Roche Harbor, on a beautiful bay to the northwest. It was originally a company town built to support the Tacoma and Roche Harbor Lime Company, set up in 1886. The surrounding structures included lime kilns, a grand hotel, a private estate, workers' cottages, a small railway, a company store, a chapel and a shipping wharf. The lime factory closed in the 1950s and the extensive buildings are now part of the Roche Harbor Resort. There's also a huge, busy marina here, thanks to the strategically sheltered nature of the harbor.

Eating

Friday Harbor House (☎ 360-378-8455; 130 West St; mains $19-35) This small, modern, comfortable hotel overlooks the harbor. The intimate dining room has a fireplace and great views. The menu is brief but tempting, with seasonal Northwest cuisine.

Front St Ale House & San Juan Brewing Company (☎ 360-378-2337; 1 Front St; shared plates $7-12, mains $5-10) The island's only brewery serves up British-style beers in a real pub atmosphere. The food's good, too. Traditional British favorites like steak-and-kidney pie and bangers-and-mash keep good company with standbys such as chili, chowder and hamburgers.

Springtree Café (☎ 360-378-4848; 310 Spring St; meals $15-24) Casual bistro-style dining in a spare but comfortable café. The menu tends toward seafood and vegetarian dishes.

Sleeping

Blair House B&B (☎ 360-378-5907; blairhouse@rockisland .com; 345 Blair Ave; r incl breakfast $115-195, cottage $195) This woodsy, 1909 home has four rooms and a cottage.

Friday Harbor House (☎ 360-378-8455; www.fridayharborhouse.com; 130 West St; r incl breakfast from $250 summer, $150 winter) The most exclusive and whimsically elegant lodging in Friday Harbor, it's a modern boutique hotel with great views over the harbor. All rooms have a fireplace, Jacuzzi tub and other upscale niceties.

Friday's Historic Inn B&B (☎ 800-352-2632; www.friday-harbor.com; 35 1st St; r with bathroom $119-169, with shared bathroom $59-129) This is a historic but recently renovated B&B, with a good range of room styles and prices. Rates vary depending on season.

Elements San Juan Islands Hotel and Spa (☎ 800-793-4756; 410 Spring St; r $99-199, ste $149-369) This sister property of Friday's Historic Inn is a more upscale, sleek and modern spa-and-suites resort hotel.

Lakedale Campground (☎ 360-378-2350; 2627 Roche Harbor Rd; campsites Apr–mid-May/mid-May–Oct $21/26, canvas cabins from $125) This enormous campground is tucked into 50 acres of wilderness dotted with trout-stocked lakes (no license is required to fish, you just pay a fee at the campground). Canoe, paddle-boat and kayak rentals are available. In addition to campsites and log cabins, there are some yurt-like canvas cabins available; there's also a resort attached if you're really not into roughing it.

Roche Harbor Resort (☎ 360-378-2155, 800-451-8910; www.rocheharbor.com; r with shared bathroom from $99, ste from $179, cottages $279; 🐾) Just about the nicest place to stay in all the San Juans, the Roche Harbor Resort incorporates some of the relics of the original lime-company settlement. You can still spend the night at the imposing old Hotel de Haro on the resort's grounds, which has wide, ivy-covered verandas and formal gardens. Refurbished workers' cottages, just a few yards from the swimming pool and playground, fill a grassy meadow above the harbor. Modern condominiums are discreetly tucked behind a stand of trees. In addition to the lodgings, there's a marina with boat rentals, restaurant, lounge and – on the dock – an old general store. You can even land your private jet on the airstrip.

LOPEZ ISLAND

Lopez is the most agricultural of the San Juan Islands and the closest to the mainland. It has resisted the commercialization of its farmland better than the other islands. Here, pastures are for grazing sheep or hay-making – not merely the aesthetic backdrop for quaint country inns and B&Bs. The island has a vineyard and some nice pebbly beaches. If you want quiet, pastoral charm and don't need organized fun, Lopez is hard to beat.

Fields and pastures stretch across the island's central plateau, and the island gets rockier toward the south; near MacKaye Har-

top picks

SCENIC DRIVES

- **101 Loop** The lonesome highway loops around the Olympic Peninsula from Hoquiam through Forks and Sequim, then back down toward Olympia.
- **Mt St Helens (p195)** The 52-mile Spirit Lake Memorial Hwy up the back of the mountain to Windy Ridge is legendary.
- **I-90 Scenic Drive** A 100-mile Byway that starts at Seattle's waterfront and heads east over the Cascade Mountains to end up on the plains of eastern Washington.
- **Mt Rainier National Park (p193)** Yes, you can drive to Paradise – and then, at least in summer, continue north to form a loop that goes over Chinook Pass and back to Enumclaw.

bor, the stony fields and cliff-lined bay look for all the world like the Hebrides.

Don't be surprised if people wave as you drive along – it's a longstanding tradition in this friendly farming community and people do it now out of habit whether they recognize the person they're waving to or not. Take care not to get too distracted; the roads are winding, and a bicycle might be a wiser option. The terrain is relatively flat and uncommonly scenic, making Lopez a top choice for cyclists.

Eating

Nearly all the places to eat on Lopez are in Lopez Village; in fact, they practically constitute the village.

Bay Café (☎ 360-468-3700; 9 Old Post Rd; mains from $12; 🕒 dinner) The most noted restaurant on Lopez occupies an old storefront. Inventive ethnic seafood dishes and locally raised grass-fed beef headline the menu.

Love Dog Café (☎ 360-468-2150; 1 Village Centre; mains from $5; 🕒 8am-8pm Mon-Fri, 8am-9pm Sat & Sun) Sit on the veranda below the grape arbor and watch the boats in the harbor while munching on a hot deli sandwich.

Sleeping

Edenwild Inn (☎ 360-468-3238; www.edenwildinn.com; r incl breakfast $165-185) Built to resemble a Victorian mansion, this eight-room inn is the most eye-catching building on the island, with lovely formal gardens, a wide porch and gables.

Inn at Swifts Bay (☎ 360-468-3636; www.swiftsbay.com; r incl breakfast $110-210) This graceful inn offers a hot tub in addition to easy beach access and 3 acres of surrounding woods for solitude. To get here, go east on Port Stanley Rd and look for mailbox 856 and the banners hanging from the decks.

Lopez Islander Resort (☎ 360-468-2233, 800-736-3434; www.lopezislander.com; 2864 Fisherman Bay Rd; r $100-260, tents $25, RV site $35) South of Lopez Village, this is as close to a bona fide motel as you'll find in the San Juans. Across from the units is a bar and restaurant that gives onto a marina. All rooms have a deck, and there are a lot of nice campsites overlooking the water.

MacKaye Harbor Inn (☎ 360-468-2253; www.mackaye harborinn.com; 949 MacKaye Harbor Rd; r $155-195) Standing stalwart and white at the edge of a shallow bay near the south end of the island, this inn – a sea captain's home in the 1920s – provides bicycles, rowboats and kayaks for guests.

Spencer Spit State Park (☎ 360-468-2251, Reservations Northwest 800-452-5687; www.stateparks.com/spencer_spit .html; campsites $10-22) Five miles southeast of the ferry landing on Baker View Rd.

TRANSPORTATION: LOPEZ ISLAND

Travel time 40 minutes

Ferry Anacortes to Lopez Island costs $13.15/10.55 adult/child and $35.95 for car and driver. Between the islands, transportation is by inter-island ferries, which travel a circular route exclusively between the four main islands. See p187.

Car Get to Anacortes by following I-5 north of Seattle for about 65 miles to exit 230. Take the exit and drive 20 miles west on Hwy 20 to the Anacortes Ferry Terminal.

ORCAS ISLAND

Orcas is the largest of the San Juan Islands and, in terms of rugged physical beauty, it is probably the most fetching. Mt Constitution is, at 2407ft, the highest point in the San Juans, but it is only one of several forested peaks around which the rest of the island folds in steep valleys. Along the rocky coast, narrow cliff-lined inlets serve as harbors for small pleasure boats.

In some ways Orcas Island is the most exclusive of the San Juans: the rocky promontories and isolated harbors look good in real-estate brochures, so retirement homes,

DOWN ON ORCAS

Eddie Bauer, he of the sporting-goods empire, was born on Orcas Island in 1899. As a young man working in an outdoors store he earned a reputation for stringing tennis rackets, even winning a tournament for speed. On a fishing trip on the Olympic Peninsula in 1934, Bauer nearly died of exposure when he took off his wet woolen jacket. Two years later, in Seattle, he invented the down parka. The Skyliner, the quilted down jacket he patented in 1936, became a popular item in the Eddie Bauer store.

resort communities and weekend manses take the place of agriculture.

Orcas Island's tourist attractions include Moran State Park, the San Juans' largest and a favorite of hikers. Its namesake, Robert Moran, was a shipbuilder who owned what is now Rosario Resort at Cascade Bay; he owned thousands of acres on the island and donated a large chunk of it to the state for the park. There are now 30 miles of hiking and mountain-bike trails here, as well as 150 campsites. If you're not up for a hike, and are traveling by car, it's a 6-mile drive to the summit of Mt Constitution and a short climb to the top of the stone watchtower for a panoramic view of the whole San Juan Archipelago.

There isn't really a town on Orcas Island – the charming Eastsound is just a collection of businesses at a crossroads. Life revolves around the resorts, which are scattered around the island. One indication of the pace of life you'll find here: the only traffic light in the county, which hung for years in Eastsound, now sits in the Orcas Island Historical Museum.

Eating & Sleeping

Christina's Restaurant (☎ 360-376-4904; Main St; starters $7-15, mains $26-42) The namesake chef, Christina Orchid, has written a well-loved cookbook and her menu is noted for its sophisticated simplicity. Try the Dungeness crab ravioli or the fiery halibut.

Doe Bay Resort & Retreat (☎ 360-376-2291; www .doebay.com; dm $30, hostel r $7, cabins $130-210) About 18 miles east of Eastsound off the Horseshoe Hwy on Pt Lawrence Rd, this crunchy, mellow vacation spot is by far the cheapest option around. It has a distinctly 'alternative' vibe and a clothing-optional hot tub, so the uptight and narrow-minded might prefer someplace else.

Moran State Park campgrounds (☎ 888-226-7688; campsites $19-26) A huge park with views of the

Olympic mountains, plus 30 miles of trails and several lakes.

Rosario Resort & Spa (☎ 800-562-8820; www.rosarioresort .com; r from $220; 🏊) The Rosario mansion, built in the early 20th century, is the centerpiece of this resort complex about 4 miles south of Eastsound off the Horseshoe Hwy. There are some 130 modern rooms, tennis courts, swimming pools, elaborate tiled spa facilities in the basement, two fine restaurants and a marina.

TRANSPORTATION: ORCAS ISLAND

Travel time **70 minutes**

Ferry Anacortes (see opposite) to Orcas Island $13.15/10.55/43.10 for adult/child/car and driver.

SHAW ISLAND

The smallest of the San Juan Islands with a ferry service, Shaw Island has the fewest facilities for travelers – which is to say, practically none. There are about 200 people on the island at most, and only one small shop and a handful of primitive campsites. But this lack of development is itself a good reason to disembark at Shaw, especially if you're on two wheels: it means the island's roads are mostly free of traffic. The rolling hills are covered with sheep, whose wool plays a large part in Shaw's cottage industries – spinning and knitting. If it's peace and quiet and uninterrupted time outdoors you're looking for, this is the place. Comb the beach, ride around, take long walks, camp out – a few mornings in a row of waking up to a quiet sunrise on a pristine beach and you'll happily forget the meaning of words like 'mall' and 'skyscraper.'

For years the ferry landing at Shaw was operated by Franciscan nuns with fluorescent safety vests over their habits; they also ran the small general store and the gas station at the tiny marina near the ferry landing. Though the nuns all retired in 2004 and the facilities are now run by a local couple, many visitors to the island still ask about the Franciscans. There are still nuns on Shaw Island, however; eight Benedictine nuns (who wear black-and-white habits rather than the brown ones of the Franciscans) live in Our Lady of the Rock Monastery, founded on the island in 1977. The Benedictines raise cattle, sheep, llamas, poultry, vegetables, herbs, and flowers.

Sleeping

South Beach Park (☎ 360-378-1842; campsites $13-16) Run by San Juan County, this is basically the only place to stay on the island, with a dozen primitive campsites. Sites fill up months in advance for summer, so reservations are strongly recommended.

TRANSPORTATION: SHAW ISLAND

Travel time **70 minutes**

Ferry Anacortes (see opposite) to Shaw Island $13.15/10.55/43.10 for adult/child/car and driver.

MT RAINIER NATIONAL PARK

At 14,410ft, Mt Rainier is the highest peak in the Cascades. The main entrance road, Hwy 706 (also known as the Nisqually-Longmire Rd), comes in through the town of Ashford, near the park's southwest corner, and follows the Nisqually River into the park. This route leads up to the Paradise Viewpoint and to the Paradise Inn (p194). Paradise is especially known for its alpine wildflower meadows, which are laced with hiking trails. Follow the Skyline Trail on foot for a good view of the Nisqually Glacier. All other roads to the park close down in the winter, but this route is plowed as far as Paradise, which then becomes the setting-off point for cross-country skiers and snowshoers.

Some of the best views of Mt Rainier – with Emmons Glacier sliding down its face, Little Tahoma Peak in the foreground and the craggy Goat Rocks Wilderness Area off to the southeast – are from Sunrise. Sunrise's open meadows are scattered with trees and linked by hiking trails. Since it's on the mountain's east side, the Sunrise area benefits from Mt Rainier's rain shadow and receives less precipitation than the damp west side.

It doesn't take long for hikers to become enraptured with Sunrise, which usually means you have to deal with crowds. Try to hike on a weekday and hit the trail early in the morning. Park naturalists lead a 1.5-mile hike each Sunday afternoon on a Sunrise Goat Watch from the Sourdough Ridge to explore the mountain goat's habitat. Get to Sunrise by following Hwy 410 east from Enumclaw.

For overnight trips, get a wilderness camping permit (free) from ranger stations or visitors centers. The six campgrounds in the park have running water and toilets, but no RV (recreational vehicle) hookups.

Information

Carbon River Ranger Station (☎ 360-829-9639)

Gray Line (☎ 206-624-5077; www.graylineseattle.com) Runs a 10-hour tour from Seattle at $59.

Jackson Visitors Center (☎ 360-569-2211 ext 2328; ☷ May-Oct)

Longmire Hiker Information Center (☎ 360-569-2211 ext 3317; ☷ summer) Trail information and backcountry permits.

Packwood Ranger Station (☎ 360-494-0600)

Rainier Mountaineering (☎ 253-627-6242, in summer 360-569-2227; www.rmiguides.com; 3-day climb $805) Guided summit climbs.

Rainier Shuttle (☎ 360-569-2331) Runs between Sea-Tac airport and Paradise ($46, once daily).

Road Conditions (☎ 800-695-7623)

Superintendent's Office (☎ 360-569-2211 ext 3314; www.nps.gov/mora; park admission per car/pedestrian/ pedestrian under 17 $15/5/free)

Sleeping

Plenty of accommodations can be found at Ashford, Packwood and Enumclaw. There are also two campgrounds near Longmire at the southwest corner of the park; for information on all of the area's campgrounds, call ☎ 360-569-2211 ext 2304. Reservations (☎ 800-365-2267; www.recreation.gov; reserved campsites on-/off-season $15/12) are strongly advised during summer months and can be made up to two months in advance by phone or online.

Hotel Packwood (☎ 360-494-5431; 104 Main St; r $29-49) A historic landmark, this neat old wooden building has nine clean, charming rooms and a mountain-view veranda.

Paradise Inn (☎ 360-569-2275; www.guestservices .com/rainier; r with/without bathroom from $139/104; ☷ May-Oct) Though closed for renovations at the time of research, the grand Paradise Inn is due to reopen in early 2008. It's a fantastic old log lodge on the mountain's south flank. Huge fireplaces anchor each end of the lobby, massive timbers hold up the ceiling and comfortable leather sofas and chairs face windows with views of the peak. Meanwhile,

the National Park Inn (same contact information) is open year-round.

TRANSPORTATION: MT RAINIER

Distance from Seattle 95 miles

Direction Southeast

Travel time About three hours

Car The park has four entrances: Nisqually, on Hwy 706 via Ashford, near the park's southwest corner; Ohanapecosh, via Hwy 123; White River, off Hwy 410; and Carbon River, the most remote entryway, at the northwest corner. Only the Nisqually entrance is open in winter, when it's used by cross-country skiers.

SNOQUALMIE VALLEY

East of Seattle's Eastside, the Snoqualmie Valley has long been a quiet backwater of dairy farms, orchards and produce gardens. Although suburbs are quickly taking over the valley, there's still enough of a rural, small-town ambience to make for a pleasant drive or bike ride. Snoqualmie is also a popular ski and snowboard resort (see p170).

Up the road, the little town of Snoqualmie has a number of antique stores and shops, including a store devoted to Northwest wines. The Snoqualmie and Tolt Rivers meet at John McDonald Park in Carnation, a great place for a picnic, a swim or a hike along the rivers. Carnation was once the center of the valley's dairy industry, and there are still a number of farms here. Stop by roadside stands for a basket of fruit or vegetables.

Further north, Duvall is far enough from Seattle to retain its rural small-town atmosphere. Wander Main St and check out the small shops and nurseries.

North Bend is Twin Peaks country, the setting for David Lynch's surreal hit TV series from the early 1990s. The former Mar T's Café in North Bend, now called Twede's (☎ 425-831-5511; 137 W North Bend Way; cherry pie $3.39; ☷ 6:30am daily, Mon-Thu to 8pm, Fri-Sat to 9pm, Sun to 7pm;), was the diner with the famous cherry pie and cups of joe; a fire gutted it in 2000, but it has been rebuilt and is still a good place for lunch or a slice of pie.

Salish Lodge and Spa (☎ 425-888-2556, 800-826-6124; r from $280) is a beautiful resort that sits atop 268ft Snoqualmie Falls. *Twin Peaks* fans may recognize the hotel as the Great Northern; the exterior of the lodge was used in a number of scenes, including the opening credits. Visitors can view the falls from the lodge's dining room, or hike to them along a winding trail.

TRANSPORTATION: SNOQUALMIE VALLEY

Distance from Seattle 31 miles

Direction East

Travel time 30 to 40 minutes

Car Follow I-90 east from Seattle. Exit at North Bend (31 miles) and get onto Hwy 202, which follows the Snoqualmie River north.

MT ST HELENS

Thanks to a 1980 eruption that set off an explosion bigger than the combined power of 21,000 atomic bombs, Washington's 87th tallest mountain needs little introduction. What it lacks in height Mt St Helens makes up for in fiery infamy; 57 people perished on the mountain on that fateful day in May 1980 when an earthquake of 5.1 on the Richter scale sparked the biggest landslide in recorded history and buried 230 sq miles of forest under millions of tonnes of volcanic rock and ash.

More recently, in October 2004 magma bubbled up to reach the surface of the volcano, resulting in a new lava dome on the existing dome's south side. This new dome continued to grow throughout 2005 and into 2006, accompanied by (so far) harmless spewings and sputterings. In March 2005 a 36,000ft plume of steam and ash big enough to be seen from Seattle came up; though exciting, the eruption was relatively minor, considered a pressure-release typical of volcanic dome building. The release was accompanied by a magnitude 2.5 earthquake. Steam-releasing activity and small eruptions continue around the dome. To view a webcam from the Johnston Ridge observatory, visit www.spiritoftruth.org /mtsthelenswatch.htm.

Still recovering from the devastation of the 1980 eruption, the 171 sq miles of volcano-wracked wilderness can be visited as a day trip. Although driving from Seattle makes for a long day, the sights here are absolutely unique. For anyone interested in geology and

natural history, this trip is well worth the expenditure of time. The whole experience is even more dramatic for the contrast between the scarred mountainside and the gorgeous, shimmering Coldwater Lake at its foot – an ideal place to picnic.

If you're looking to go hiking on Mt St Helens, you'll need to get a $15 permit (with a $7 service fee charged, making a total of $22), which you must buy online in advance at www .mshinstitute.org/experience/permit-system .html. The climb takes about four hours up and two hours down, though the difficulty of the climb changes, depending on the weather. Be sure to check on conditions before heading up, and be prepared for dramatic changes in temperature.

Information

Coldwater Ridge Visitors Center (☎ 360-274-2131; ☽ 9am-5pm summer, 9am-4pm winter)

Johnston Ridge Visitors Center (☎ 360-274-2131; pass adult/child $8/free; ☽ 10am-6pm) At the end of State Hwy 504, in the heart of the blast zone, this center provides views directly into the mouth of Mt St Helens' north-facing crater.

Monument Headquarters (☎ 360-247-3900) Issues hiking permits.

Mt St Helens Visitors Center (☎ 360-274-2100; ☽ 9am-5pm) Presents an overview of the site's history and geology. Just off I-5 exit 49 near Castle Rock.

TRANSPORTATION: MT ST HELENS

Distance from Seattle 120 miles (to Mt St Helens Visitors Center)

Direction South

Travel time Three hours

Car Take I-5 South to Castle Rock; the Mt St Helens Visitors Center is east along Hwy 504.

VICTORIA, BRITISH COLUMBIA

The nearest you can get to hopping across the pond, Victoria is a pretty, if a bit grandmotherly, town famous for afternoon tea, botanical gardens and little old houses. It's the capital of British Columbia, Canada, and just a short ferry ride across the Strait of

Juan de Fuca from Seattle. With a picturesque crescent-shaped downtown that faces onto the busy Inner Harbour, it makes for a lovely day trip or weekend escape.

Some sights worth a look are the Art Gallery of Greater Victoria (☎ 250-384-4101; www.aggv.bc.ca; 1040 Moss St; adult/senior/child $12/10/4; ☺ 10am-5pm, to 9pm Thu), the Butchart Gardens (☎ 250-652-5256, 866-652-4422; www.butchartgardens.com; 800 Benvenuto Ave; adult/youth/child 5-12 mid-Jun–Sep $25/12.50/3, reduced rest of year; ☺ 9am-10:30pm mid-Jun–Aug, to dusk rest of year), Craigdarroch Castle (☎ 250-592-5323; 1050 Joan Cres; adult/child $11.75/3.75; ☺ 9am-7pm mid-Jun–early Sep, 10am-4:30pm rest of year) and the Royal British Columbia Museum (☎ 250-356-7226, 888-447-7977; www.royalbcmuseum.bc.ca; 675 Belleville St; adult/child 6-18 $25.50/17.50; ☺ 9am-5pm, extended in summer to 6pm Sun-Thurs, 10pm Fri-Sat). Also based here are SpringTide Whale Watching Tours (☎ 250-386-6016; www.springtidecharters.com; 950 Wharf St; tours adult/child $89/59; ☺ 9am-6pm Apr-Oct), which takes people out to spot orcas.

Keep in mind that the prices listed in this section are in Canadian dollars.

Information

Cycling Victoria (www.cyclingvictoria.com)

Tourism Victoria Visitor Information Centre (☎ 250-953-2033, 800-663-3883; www.tourismvictoria.com; 812 Wharf St; ☺ 8:30am-6:30pm mid-Jun–Sep, 9am-5pm Oct–mid-Jun) Activity and accommodation booking services.

Eating

Fairmont Empress Hotel (☎ 250-384-8111, 866-540-4229; 721 Government St) Victoria's 1908 grand dame has a regal, bygone-era opulence that knows no bounds. It's where honeymooners stay and tour groups take high tea.

Pagliacci's (☎ 250-386-1662; 1011 Broad St; lunch $7-10, dinner $12-20; ☺ 11:30am-3pm & 5:30-10pm, to 11pm Fri & Sat) At Pagliacci's, unlimited baskets of fresh focaccia bread are delivered to the marble-topped tables. Generous pasta servings from the cinema-themed menu almost defy devouring; try the Hemingway Short Story (beef-stuffed tortellini).

Reef (☎ 250-388-5375; 533 Yates St; mains $10-15; ☺ 11am-midnight Sun-Wed, 11am-1am Thu-Sat) Delectable Caribbean dishes are served here.

Sam's Deli (☎ 250-382-8424; 805 Government St; sandwiches $6-12; ☺ 7:30am-7pm) Opposite the info centre, Sam's is the perfect spot for a coffee or bottle of beer and a sandwich big enough to feed two.

Strathcona Hotel (☎ 250-383-7137; 919 Douglas St) This multivenue complex includes the rooftop volleyball courts of Sticky Wicket Pub; hillbilly, peanut-shell-on-the-ground haven of Big Bad John's; and touring musical acts at Legends.

Sleeping

Chateau Victoria (☎ 250-382-4221, 800-663-5891; www.chateauvictoria.com; 740 Burdett Ave; r from $145) The hotel's 177 rooms are not particularly remarkable, but they offer excellent value given all of their business-traveler amenities. The Vista 18 (18th floor) lounge unfurls the city's best views.

HI Victoria Hostel (☎ 250-385-4511, 888-883-0099; www.hihostels.ca; 516 Yates St; dm/r $25/60) This hostel is found in a great location, located just up from the Inner Harbour and close to all of the sights. Although it has room for more than 100 people in barrack-style dorms, it's wildly popular with travelers of all ages, so reserve ahead.

James Bay Inn (☎ 250-384-7151, 800-836-2649; www.jamesbayinn.com; 270 Government St; r $109-154) This old-time, dark-wood inn offers well-kept rooms with bay windows; some have kitchens. It's in a quiet location, yet not far from the action.

Ocean Island Backpackers Inn (☎ 250-385-1788, 888-888-4180; www.oceanisland.com; 791 Pandora Ave; 4- to 6-bed dm $20-25, r from $27) Catering more to a younger crowd, this fun, colorful hostel has a licensed lounge as well as helpful staff who are able to plan cheap day trips and nightly group outings.

TRANSPORTATION: VICTORIA, BRITISH COLUMBIA

Distance from Seattle 153 miles

Direction Northwest

Travel time One to three hours

Ferry A passenger-only ferry service between Port Angeles and Victoria (one hour) and from Victoria to Friday Harbor on San Juan Island (2½ to three hours) is provided by Victoria Express (☎ 360-452-8088, victoriaexpress.com). Whale-watching tours are also available.

OLYMPIC PENINSULA

The Olympic Peninsula is a rugged, isolated area characterized by wild coastlines, deep old-growth forests and craggy mountains. The Makah, a tribe of seafaring Native Americans who recently stirred up mild controversy by reinstituting their right to hunt whales, have lived here for thousands of years. Only one road, US 101, rings the Peninsula, and at its outer stretches it can feel very remote indeed. Although the highway is in excellent condition, distances are great, and visitors often find it takes a lot longer than expected to get where they're going. From Seattle, the fastest access to the peninsula is by ferry and bus via Bainbridge Island or on Washington State Ferries from Keystone, Whidbey Island.

PORT TOWNSEND

Ferrying in to Port Townsend, one of the best-preserved Victorian-era seaports in the USA, is like sailing into a sepia-toned old photograph. The city experienced a building boom in 1890 followed by an immediate bust, leaving its architectural splendor largely intact. Beyond just strolling the main street and admiring the handsome town, one highlight is historic Fort Worden State Park (☎ 360-385-4730), which contains the Coast Artillery Museum (admission $2; ☻ 11am-4pm daily Jun-Aug, Sat & Sun Mar-May & Sep-Oct) and the Commanding Officer's Quarters (admission $1; ☻ 10am-5pm daily Jun-Aug, 1-4pm Sat & Sun Mar-May & Sep-Oct). To get to Fort Worden, go west from the ferry dock until you reach Walker St, take a right, and head north as Walker St becomes Cherry St, which takes you into the park (about two miles from the ferry landing).

Information

Peninsula Taxi (☎ 360-385-1872)

Port Townsend Visitors Center (☎ 360-385-2722; 2437 E Sims Way; ☻ 9am-5pm Mon-Fri, 9am-4pm Sat & Sun)

Eating

Landfall Restaurant (☎ 360-385-5814; 412 Water St; breakfast $6-8) This no-nonsense breakfast café, just inches from the Port Townsend marina, is full of locals starting their morning with one of the delicious scrambles.

Sirens (☎ 360-379-1100; 832 Water St; mains $6-8) A dimly lit, romantic upstairs bar with a balcony overlooking the port, this is the perfect spot to have a burger and a beer and to wait for your ship.

Sleeping

HI Olympic Hostel (☎ 360-385-0655; olyhost@olympus.net; 272 Battery Way; dm $17-20) Within Fort Worden State Park in Port Townsend, this hostel has impeccable if spartan quarters in a former barracks; it's up the hill behind the Park Office. Dorms are a good deal, but private rooms are less so.

Manresa Castle (☎ 360-385-5750, 800-732-1281; www .manresacastle.com; 7th & Sheridan Sts; r $99-229) The turreted Prussian-style Manresa Castle, built in 1892, was later expanded to house Jesuit priests. The smallish rooms are decorated in a pretty, old-fashioned style that suits the town. Even if you don't stay here, it's worth taking the self-guided tour; check out the former chapel, truncated to form a breakfast room and a banquet room. The rates depend on size of room, views, number of occupants, and whether or not it's in a tower.

Waterstreet Hotel (☎ 360-385-5467, 800-735-9810; www.waterstreethotelporttownsend.com; 635 Water St; r $50-150) This hotel in the center of town has loads of old-world charm at reasonable rates. The suite has a deck over the water and a kitchen. There's a brewpub on the 1st floor and an art gallery surrounding the front desk. There are all kinds of different rooms and suites; the prices vary by room.

HOH RIVER RAIN FOREST

Isolated by distance and inclement weather, and facing the Olympic Coast National Marine Sanctuary, the Pacific side of the Olympics remains its wildest. Only US 101 offers access to its spectacular rain forests and wild coastline. The Hoh River Rain Forest can get 12ft to 14ft of annual precipitation. And, as remote as it feels, it's relatively easy to get to. Trails from the visitors center and campground, at the end of 19-mile Hoh River Rd, plunge immediately into thick clusters of old-growth trees wearing furry green sweaters of moss. If you want to reenact *Lord of the Rings*, this is the place.

Information

Forks Visitor Information Center (☎ 360-374-2531, 800-443-6757; 1411 S Forks Ave; ☒ 10am-4pm) Suggested itineraries and seasonal information.

Hoh Forest Visitors Center (☎ 360-374-6925; ☒ 9am-4:30pm Sep-Jun, 9am-6pm Jul & Aug)

Sleeping

Hoh Humm Ranch (☎ 360-374-5337; www.olypen.com /hohhumm; 171763 Hwy 101; r from $35) Stay at the Waltons-esque Hoh Humm Ranch, near mile marker 172 about 20 miles south of Forks, 57 miles from Neah Bay and convenient to the Hoh River Rain Forest and the Olympic coastline. It's a B&B (with shared bathrooms) in a working farmhouse, where balconies allow you to gaze over riverside herds of sheep, cattle and llamas. It's great for families. Accepts cash only.

TRANSPORTATION: HOH RIVER RAIN FOREST

Distance from Seattle 140 miles (to Forks)

Direction West

Travel time About four hours (to Forks)

Car Hwy 101 circles the Peninsula.

If the Emerald City's charms have won you over and you're considering a move here, you're not alone. In July 2007 the Seattle *Post-Intelligencer* reported that Seattle had seen more population growth that year than it had in the previous 40 years. Seattle is a popular destination these days, and for good reason: it's been ranked one of the best cities in the US in which to locate a business, and it has a strong high-tech community, a healthy outdoor lifestyle, and a socially and politically open-minded, well-read population. Seattle, in short, is quite a catch. It's no wonder people are storming the gates to get in.

The resulting influx of people has a huge impact on city life, of course, and not all of it is positive. Housing prices and especially property taxes in the Seattle area have rocketed skyward. In some cases, property taxes have risen 40% to 50% in recent years. This tends to skew the average income of city residents upward, which many longtime residents see as a threat to the city's grungy, arty vibe. Population growth also means heavier traffic, something everyone who's ever driven in the city surely dreads.

Still, most economists will tell you that a growing city means a better economy. So let's not rain on the parade. In this section, we cover the fundamentals of moving to Seattle: information on renting versus buying, which areas are the best bet for housing, resources to help get you settled in and some comments from people who have recently moved to town. If you've moved to Seattle recently, go to www.lonelyplanet.com/contact to let us know what worked for you.

WHERE TO LIVE?

Lifestyle is a crucial factor when deciding where to look for a home in a new city, particularly one with neighborhoods as distinct as Seattle's. Do you have kids? Pets? Are you a one-person household, or a couple, or a larger family? Will you own a car? What part of town will you be working in? Do you want a quiet, residential neighborhood with lots of parks and trees, or is a high-density urban area more your style? A house or a condo? And, of course, the ultimate question: how much can you afford?

BUYING & RENTING

Buying property in Seattle may have been cheap once upon a time, but it sure isn't anymore. The median home price is $489,200. Home appreciation for 2006 (the latest figure available at the time of research) was about 12.8%.

The *Seattle Times* has a chart that calculates, among other things, the annual income you'd need in order to afford to buy the median home in a given neighborhood – and it starts at an income of $60,000 to $90,000. For the central area around Capitol Hill, the chart suggests an annual income of about $115,000. Less than that, and you'd better be either very lucky or prepared to rent. To view the chart as well as a number of other useful online housing calculators, go to seattletimes.nwsource.com/homevalues/2007/income/income-houses-king.html.

You can also get a sense of each of Seattle's neighborhoods from the descriptions in the Neighborhoods chapter of this book (p44).

Price is probably the ultimate decision-maker in terms of figuring out where to live. There's a huge range, from $254,900 in Everett ($184 per sq ft) to $1 million in Madison Park ($476 per sq ft). The following are some sample housing price comparisons for 2006:

Neighborhood	Median price ($)
Central Bellvue (Eastside)	622,500 (296 per sq ft)
Central Capitol Hill	475,000 (324 per sq ft)
East Ballard	455,000 (364 per sq ft)
Everett	254,900 (184 per sq ft)
Fremont/Phinney Ridge	494,525 (352 per sq ft)
Green Lake	550,000 (350 per sq ft)
Madison Park	1 million (476 per sq ft)
North Capitol Hill/Montlake	772,000 (387 per sq ft)
Queen Anne	657,000 (415 per sq ft)
Ravenna	479,950 (298 per sq ft)
U District	504,301 (337 per sq ft)
Vashon Island	435,000 (295 per sq ft)
Wallingford	562,500 (360 per sq ft)
West Ballard	441,250 (330 per sq ft)

There's also a fairly tight rental market. In the more popular areas of the city, vacancy rates are approximately 4% to 10%. There's more space on the Eastside and rents are slightly cheaper, but it's a less desirable place to live.

Most of the rental units in Seattle are found in buildings with less than 50 units, and many of the apartments are found in buildings 10 units and smaller.

About 2% of the apartment buildings in Seattle allow dogs, and 40% allow cats. Some put a size or weight limit on dogs. Expect to pay additional deposits or fees.

Following are some typical monthly rent charges at the time of writing (in dollars):

	Seattle	Eastside
studio (approx 400-650 sq ft)	850-1200	800-1000
1 bedroom (approx 550-850 sq ft)	1000-1500	850-1200
2 bedroom (approx 700-1100 sq ft)	1400-2000	1100-1600
rental house (Seattle, approx 900-2800 sq ft; Eastside, approx 1100-3600 sq ft)	1800-3500	1650-3500

The landlord–tenant laws and regulations in Seattle are relatively tenant-friendly. For example, rent increases of 10% or more in any 12-month period require a 60-day notice to the tenant. If a landlord fails to make repairs that are required by law, a tenant may make the repairs and deduct the cost from the rent.

In a rental house, tenants can expect to find basic appliances like a washer and a dryer, refrigerator and a stove. The latter two also apply to apartments, which frequently have laundry facilities in the basement. Fully furnished apartments are less common and would normally include basics like a bed, kitchen table, chairs, a coffee table and a dresser as well.

In a tight rental market like Seattle's, it pays to be prepared. Have cash or a check ready for a deposit when you go to look at an apartment or a house, and have your list of references and previous-address information collected and ready to hand over. (Make sure your references know they are your references.) Some landlords and property management companies will demand to see pay stubs, so consider bringing those along when you check out the apartment. You'll generally have to pay a small fee for a credit check, too.

For details on landlord–tenant regulations specific to Seattle, download the Department of Planning and Development's information sheet at www.ci.seattle.wa.us/dclu/Publications /cam/cam604.pdf.

Extended Stays

A number of resources exist for people who need to relocate to Seattle for a shorter amount of time. Check Craigslist (www.seattle.craigslist.org) under 'housing – sublets/temporary' for short-term rentals, furnished apartments and corporate housing.

Short-term Suites (www.shorttermssuites.com) has lists of available short-term rentals in a number of buildings across town, from upscale condos to comfy houses. The minimum stay is one month and a deposit is required to reserve a suite. Offering a similar service is Short Term Stay Seattle (☎ 888-363-5004; www.shorttermrentalsseattle.com).

Chambered Nautilus (☎ 800-545-8459; p182) is an excellent B&B in the U District that also operates a building of apartment-like suites with kitchen facilities. The suites are available for extended stays from October through April, with weekly or monthly rates, with or without breakfast and limited housekeeping.

There are also plenty of chains like Extended StayAmerica (☎ 206-365-8100) and Residence Inn by Marriott (☎ 206-624-6000). For an updated list of short-term options with an online booking engine, try www.extendedstaynetwork.com.

JOBS

The easiest jobs to get are in food service and retail, particularly if you have any experience in those areas. These are likely to be part time though and don't do much for your ability to live comfortably in an increasingly expensive city (see p18). Check Craigslist.org for a wide variety of job openings.

The aerospace industry is still an important source of employment in the area. Seattle has the highest concentration of aerospace companies in the world. The state is the highest per capita aerospace employer in the country, at 44 jobs per 1000 workers. Aerospace accounts for nearly 25% of Washington's manufacturing employment. Boeing employs 68,993 people in the Seattle and Washington state area.

The University of Washington, with 28,000 employees, is the largest employer in the city. The health-care industry, including hospitals, health-care products and services, training and research, accounts for 96,000 jobs.

The information-technology sector in the Seattle area comprises about 6000 companies and employs 68,000 people, accounting for $10 billion in annual wages. As of 2006 Microsoft employed some 33,220 people in the greater Seattle area and 71,170 worldwide.

WHY I MOVED TO SEATTLE *Matthew Stearns*

I moved to Seattle to go to graduate school at UW. I was shooting for a master's in comparative literature, but soon realized that getting an MA in comp lit would not only look bad on paper and make my family ashamed of me, it was just a bonehead idea all around. So I promptly extricated myself from the situation and started renegotiating with reality.

I find that Seattle can be particularly resistant to reality – the city, especially recently, seems to operate within a bubble of Caucasian-quasi-liberal-privileged-monied professionalism. That the town is engulfed on all fronts by spectacular natural beauty seems to only reinforce this homogeneous, head-in-the-clouds/up-the-ass sensibility.

I remained in Seattle, after bailing on grad school, for the city's vibrant cultural life and the aforementioned natural beauty, but it got a bit hard when I discovered the brutal flipside of Seattle's emerald dreaminess – that is, its skyrocketing, ludicrous housing costs. Renting a room or buying a home here is not for the faint of wallet. If one is considering doing so, one must come armed to the teeth with currency, rare jewels and precious metals.

Not surprisingly, the upshot of this crippling costliness is an influx of yet more mind-bendingly conventional, lame, square white professionals and a rapid decrease in already negligible levels of brown/black people and penniless-but-genuinely-creative bohemians.

All of that being said, I would pay a small fortune to rent space under a dumpster and dwell in cohabitation with miserable junkies, toothless hookers and moody rats if it meant I could live in continued proximity to the shrimp sandwiches at Paseo in Fremont.

Stearns is the author of Daydream Nation *from the 33 and a Third series of books about albums, published in 2007 by* Continuum, *and is a regular contributor to* Resonance *magazine.*

Biotech is also a major and growing source of employment. South Lake Union has become a biotech hub, thanks to the creation of a $15-million biotech incubator, investment by Paul Allen's company Vulcan and proximity to the Fred Hutchinson Cancer Research Center, among other factors.

Other big employers in the area include Costco Wholesalers, Washington Mutual, Weyerhaeuser and AT&T Wireless.

Visas

To work legally in the USA you generally need both a work permit and a working visa. To apply for the correct visa at the US embassy you are usually required to obtain a work permit from the Immigration and Naturalization Service (INS) first. Your prospective employer must file a petition with the INS for permission for you to work, so you will first need to find a company that wants to hire you and is willing to file all the necessary paperwork. You can find more detailed information at the website of the US Department of State (www.travel.state.gov) and in the Directory chapter, p213.

SCHOOLS & STUDY

Parents moving to Seattle will need to consider the quality of various schools when deciding where to live. The *Seattle Times* newspaper produces a guide to Seattle's public and private schools, available online at community.seattletimes.nwsource.com /schoolguide, or in book form at any Bartell Drugs store for $9.95. It's an excellent and impartial resource.

To enroll your child in the Seattle Public School District, you must call or visit a Student Assignment Service Center for registration materials. The regular enrollment period is February for elementary school and March for middle and high school. Enrolling during these months ensures that your child has a better chance of getting into his or her first choice of school.

For enrollment information, contact one of the following:

Student Assignment Information (☎ 206-298-7410, recorded message)

Student Assignment Service Center (North) (☎ 206-729-3370; Room 106, John Marshall Bldg, 520 NE Ravenna Blvd)

Student Assignment Service Center (South) (☎ 206-760-4690; Sharples Bldg, 3928 S Graham St)

A lot of people move to Seattle to attend college or university. If you're one of them, visit the *Seattle Times*' online guide for college students at seattletimes.nwsource.com/html /collegeguide. The school you are enrolling with should also have available orientation materials and resources for getting settled for students, either on their websites or available by mail.

WHY I MOVED TO SEATTLE *Mark Baumgarten*

Basically, I've chosen to live in Seattle because of the city's reputation as an epicenter of music and culture, where institutions like the Seattle Art Museum and the Seattle International Film Festival are shored up by a community of artists who fill the coffee shops with music, art and bodies.

As an editor, my main goal is to find a community that is both creating and consuming its own unique culture and then find a magazine where I can dig into that culture and help direct that culture. I got lucky.

Many would say that the greatest pain in the ass in Seattle is the rain. Pish-tosh, I say. The real pain in the ass is twofold: the antiquated public transit system makes not owning a car difficult, and the hills make riding a bike painful and reserved mainly for the hardcore.

Mark is the editor of Seattle Sound *magazine (seattlesoundmag.com).*

OTHER RESOURCES

The following resources on housing and related topics might be useful to those thinking of a move to Seattle:

Community Home Ownership Center (☎ 206-587-5641; www.choc-wa.org) Resources and down-payment assistance for low- and moderate-income households trying to buy a home.

Fremont Public Association (☎ 206-694-6767; www.fremontpublic.org) Provides information to tenants in Seattle and King County regarding their rights and responsibilities according to local landlord–tenant laws.

King County Dispute Resolution Center (☎ 206-443-9603; www.kcdrc.org) Helps settle tenant–landlord conflicts.

move.com US-wide real-estate listings for people thinking about renting or buying.

Raincityguide.com A chatty, blog-style guide to real estate in the Seattle area.

roomster.net

seattle.craigslist.org A free classifieds forum, listing everything from job openings and apartments for rent to unclassifiable personal requests.

seattlerentals.com

seattletimes.nwsource.com/html/homevalues2007 A detailed state-of-Seattle-housing section produced by the *Seattle Times* newspaper, including neighborhood profiles and house-hunting tips.

www.apartmentinsider.com/index.htm

www.seattle.gov/html/citizen/housing.htm The government's relocation reference page.

Things Change...

The information in this chapter is particularly vulnerable to change. Check directly with the airline or a travel agent to make sure you understand how a fare (and ticket you may buy) works and be aware of the security requirements for international travel. Shop carefully. The details given in this chapter should be regarded as pointers and are not a substitute for your own careful, up-to-date research.

Flights, tours and rail tickets can be booked online at www.lonelyplanet.com/travel_services.

AIR

Airlines

For toll-free numbers of airlines in the US, call ☎ 800-555-1212 or check the websites of individual airlines. Airlines serving Sea-Tac include: Air Canada, Alaska, America West, American, Asiana, British Airways, China Airlines, Continental, Delta, EVA Air, Frontier, Hawaiian, Horizon Air, Jet Blue, Korean Air, Northwest, SAS, SkyWest, Southwest, Sun Country, United, United Express and US Airways.

Buying tickets online in advance has become the norm. Try the following links to find the best deals on airfares into Seattle:

Cheap Tickets (www.cheaptickets.com)

Expedia (www.expedia.com)

Hotwire (www.hotwire.com)

Orbitz (www.orbitz.com)

Priceline (www.priceline.com)

STA Travel (☎ 800-781-4040; www.statravel.com) Discounted airfares for students.

Travelocity (www.travelocity.com)

Airports

Seattle is served by the Seattle-Tacoma International Airport (Sea-Tac; ☎ 206-431-4444, www.portseattle.org/seatac), located 13 miles south of downtown Seattle. The Port of Seattle recently spent $126 million on a makeover of the airport's central terminal, adding an extensive food-and-shops hub called Pacific Marketplace and large windows that provide a sweet view of the runway. There's also a cell-phone parking lot where the poor souls assigned to fetch new arrivals can wait until they're called to the baggage-claim curb. There are baggage storage facilities (kensbaggage.com; duffels & backpacks $5-10 per day) in the airport as well as currency-exchange services (www.thomascook.com, see Directory chapter p210). Car-rental agencies are located in the baggage-claim area. For a map of the

CLIMATE CHANGE & TRAVEL

Climate change is a serious threat to the ecosystems that humans rely upon, and air travel is the fastest-growing contributor to the problem. Lonely Planet regards travel, overall, as a global benefit, but believes we all have a responsibility to limit our personal impact on global warming.

Flying & Climate Change

Pretty much every form of motor transport generates CO_2 (the main cause of human-induced climate change) but planes are far and away the worst offenders, not just because of the sheer distances they allow us to travel, but because they release greenhouse gases high into the atmosphere. The statistics are frightening: two people taking a return flight between Europe and the US will contribute as much to climate change as an average household's gas and electricity consumption over a whole year.

Carbon Offset Schemes

Climatecare.org and other websites use 'carbon calculators' that allow travelers to offset the greenhouse gases they are responsible for with contributions to energy-saving projects and other climate-friendly initiatives in the developing world – including projects in India, Honduras, Kazakhstan and Uganda.

Lonely Planet, together with Rough Guides and other concerned partners in the travel industry, supports the carbon offset scheme run by climatecare.org. Lonely Planet offsets all of its staff and author travel.

For more information check out our website: www.lonelyplanet.com.

airport's ground-transport options, go to portseattle.org/about/maps/ground.shtml.

BICYCLE

Bicycling is still a major form of both transportation and recreation in the Seattle area, despite the mad traffic and hilly terrain. Many streets downtown have commuter bike lanes. Pick up a copy of the *Seattle Bicycling Guide Map*, published by the City of Seattle's Transportation Bicycle and Pedestrian Program (☎ 206-684-7583) and available at bike shops. Alternatively you can order the map free of charge over the phone or online at www.cityofseattle.net /transportation/bikemaps.htm.

Bike fans might want to check out Marymoor Park, which boasts the only velodrome (☎ 206-957-4555; admission $3) in the Pacific Northwest.

Seattle and all of King County require that bicyclists wear helmets. If you're caught without one, you can be fined $30 on the spot. Most places that rent bikes will rent helmets to go with them, sometimes for a small extra fee. It's also important to make sure your bike has sufficient lights and reflectors attached. See p168 for recommended bicycle rental and repair places.

BOAT

Seattle's a watery place and boats are a well-used mode of transport, both for fun and for getting around. But figuring out how to make them take you where you want to go can be a challenge (see the 'Making Sense

of Seattle Ferries' boxed text, p187). Planning ahead is key. Arrive at your ferry dock about 90 minutes ahead of departure time, particularly on weekends or for popular routes. Note that no reservations are taken for the San Juan Islands routes: they're strictly first come, first served.

The following resources can provide helpful information on the Seattle-area boat and ferry network.

Washington State Ferries (☎ 206-464-6400, in Washington 888-808-7977, ferry traffic info 551; www.wsdot .wa.gov/ferries; Seattle-Bainbridge adult/child/car & driver $6.70/5.40/14.45, bicycle surcharge $1) has a website with maps, prices, schedules, trip planners, weather updates and other news, as well as estimated waiting time for popular routes. Fares depend on the route, size of the vehicle and duration of the trip and are collected either for round-trip travel or one-way travel, depending on the departure terminal.

The visitors center section of the website has helpful tips for first-time ferriers: www .wsdot.wa.gov/ferries/visitors_center. Ferries depart from Piers 50 and 52.

Victoria Clipper (☎ 800-888-2535, 206-443-2560; victoriaclipper.com; round-trip adult/child from $117/58) operates several high-speed passenger ferries to Victoria, BC (from two to six daily), and to the San Juan Islands. It also organizes package tours which can be booked in advance through the website. See Excursions for more on visiting Victoria (p196) and the San Juan Islands (p190) with Victoria Clipper.

BUS

A biodiesel bus (☎ 503-502-5750; www.sharedroute.org; Portland-Seattle one-way/round-trip $20/50) runs once daily from Portland and Olympia to Seattle and back on weekends, making an economical and ecofriendly alternative to driving or taking the train. It starts and stops at Union Station in Portland and King Street Station in Seattle.

Greyhound (Map p50; ☎ 800-231-2222, in Seattle 206-628-5561, baggage 206-628-5555; www.greyhound .com; 811 Stewart St; ☺ 6am-midnight) connects Seattle with cities all over the country, including Chicago ($195 one-way, two days, three daily), Spokane ($38, five to seven hours, three daily), San Francisco ($95, 20 hours, four daily), and Vancouver, BC ($25, three to four hours, six daily).

In town, public buses are the main form of public transportation; they are operated by Metro Transit (☎ schedule info 206-553-3000, customer service 206-553-3060; transit.metrokc.gov; fares $1.25-1.75), part of the King County Department of Transportation.

Sound Transit (☎ 800-201-4900, 206-398-5000; www .soundtransit.org) also operates Express buses to regional destinations, including Tacoma, although these are designed for commuters and not as likely to be used by travelers.

Most of the time you pay or show your transfer when you board. For trips on Metro Transit and Sound Transit Express buses that originate in downtown Seattle between 6am and 7pm, you pay when you leave the bus instead. Exceptions to this are Metro Transit routes 116, 118 and 119. For these routes, pay upon boarding when leaving downtown Seattle and traveling south. Pay when you leave when traveling to downtown Seattle. It sounds complicated, but if you follow the lead of the people around you it'll become clear.

Be aware that very few buses operate between 1:30am and 5am, so if you're a long way from home when the bars close, plan on hailing a cab instead. Another option if you plan to travel a lot within the city in a short time is a Visitor Pass ($5), good for one day of unlimited travel on Metro buses throughout King County, including the cities of Seattle and Bellevue and Seattle-Tacoma. It's not sold on buses, so buy it online in advance or at one of the Metro customer-service centers: Transportation Connection (☎ 206-553-3060; 1301 5th Ave, Rainier Sq; ☺ 9am-5:30pm Mon-Fri) or King Street Center (☎ 206-553-3060; 201 S Jackson St; ☺ 8am-5pm Mon-Fri).

CAR & MOTORCYCLE

Driving

Seattle traffic is disproportionately heavy and chaotic for a city of its size, and parking is scarce and expensive. Add to that the city's bizarrely cobbled-together mishmash of skewed grids, the hilly terrain and the preponderance of one-way streets and it's easy to see why driving downtown is best avoided if at all possible. If you are traveling with a car, consider stashing it at your hotel and using public transport to get around within the city center.

Rental

As much of a hassle as it can be in the city, having your own set of wheels can be handy for reaching neighborhoods that are further afield, such as Ballard or Georgetown, and for exploring areas outside of Seattle proper. To rent a car, you need a valid driver's license and a major credit card.

There are rental agencies in Sea-Tac airport, located in the baggage-claim area, with pickup and drop-off service from the 1st floor of the garage. Car-rental agencies within Seattle include the following:

Avis (☎ 800-331-1212; www.avis.com)

Budget (☎ 800-527-0700; www.budget.com)

Dollar (☎ 800-800-3665; www.dollar.com)

Enterprise (☎ 800-261-7331; www.enterprise.com)

Hertz (☎ 800-654-3131; www.hertz.com)

Another good option for those who need only limited use of a vehicle is FlexCar (☎ 206-332-0330; www.flexcar.com; 307 3rd Ave S; membership $35 per year, rates per hr $7-12, per day $65-90). Membership gives you access to a number of car-sharing vehicles distributed throughout the city. Members can make reservations online or by phone for as long as they need the car, then return it to the parking place where they picked it up when they're done. You can drive the borrowed ride as much as you want anywhere within the lower 48 states, as long as you bring it back to its starting point eventually.

TAXI

You can hail a cab from the street, but it's a safer bet to call and order one. All Seattle taxi cabs operate at the same rate, set by King County. At the time of research the rate was

$2.50 at meter drop, then $2 per mile. There may be an extra charge for extra passengers and baggage.

Any of the following offer reliable taxi services:

Graytop Cabs (☎ 206-282-8222)

Orange Cab Co (☎ 206-522-8800; www.orangecab.net)

Redtop Taxi (☎ 206-789-4949; yellowtaxi.net)

STITA Taxi (☎ 206-246-9999)

Yellow Cab (☎ 206-622-6500; yellowtaxi.net)

TRAIN

Sound Transit (☎ 800-201-4900, 206-398-5000; www.sound transit.org) operates trains connecting Seattle to outlying communities. It's set up more for commuters than travelers, but if you happen to want to visit, for example, Everett ($2.50, 40 minutes, several daily), Woodinville ($2.50, one hour, several daily) or, more realistically, Tacoma ($3, one hour, several daily), the trains are new and clean and schedules run smoothly.

Although it doesn't exactly count as a train, the Monorail (☎ 206-905-2600; www.seattlemonorail.com; adult/senior/child $4/2/1.50; ☼ 9am-11pm) was originally intended as public transportation. It only goes one mile, from Westlake Center (p51) straight to Seattle Center and back every 10 minutes, but it's a fun if kitschy way to get there.

Amtrak (☎ 800-872-7245; www.amtrak.com) serves Seattle's King Street Station (303 S Jackson St; ☼ 6am-10:30pm, ticket counter 6:15am-8pm). Three main routes run through town: the Amtrak Cascades (connecting Vancouver, BC, Seattle, Portland and Eugene), the extremely scenic Coast Starlight (connecting Seattle, Oakland and Los Angeles) and the Empire Builder (connecting Seattle, Spokane, Fargo and Chicago).

Examples of one-way ticket prices from Seattle are listed below:

Destination	Cost ($)	Duration (hr)	Frequency
Chicago	from 309	46	daily
Los Angeles	143	35	daily
Oakland	135	23	daily
Portland	28-31	3-4	5 daily
Spokane	95	8.5	daily
Vancouver, BC	28-43	3-4	5 daily

BUSINESS HOURS

Banks are typically open from 9am or 10am until 5pm or 6pm weekdays. Some banks are also open from 10am to 2pm or so on Saturdays. Most businesses generally operate from 9am until 5pm or 6pm from Monday to Friday. Some are also open 10am to 5pm Saturdays. Shops are usually open from 9am or 10am to 5pm or 6pm (or until 9pm in shopping malls) Monday to Friday, as well as noon to 5pm or so (later in malls) on Sunday. Some places, like record stores and bookstores, may keep later hours, such as from noon to 8pm or 9pm.

Restaurants tend to serve breakfast between 7am and 11am, brunch from 7am to 3pm, lunch from 11:30am to 2:30pm and dinner from 5:30pm to 10pm. Meals served and exceptions to the normal opening times are noted in specific listings (see p120).

CHILDREN

Aside from the obvious (Children's Museum, Pacific Science Center, Woodland Park Zoo etc), there are a number of sights and activities in Seattle that are particularly welcoming to and entertaining for the younger set. Many of them are parks, where parents can let the little ones run free and expend some of that excess energy.

Try the following suggestions, collected from several parents in the Seattle area:

5 Spot (p130) A kid-friendly diner in Queen Anne.

Ballard Locks (p99) **and the Fish Ladder** (p99) Watch salmon make their way home to spawn. As exciting as it sounds!

Discovery Park (p97) The visitors center offers parking passes so you can drive to the beach and avoid the long hike down.

Ella Bailey Park (2601 West Smith St) A new park with beautiful views of the city and Mt Rainier, a nice paved loop trail and fun things to play on.

Fremont Troll (p90) Seattle's most endearingly creepy public art.

Pier 69 pool There's a small wading pool at the end of Pier 69 on the waterfront. If there isn't a cruise ship there, you have an unobstructed view. If there is, you get to watch the cranes loading up the ship with all the supplies. For a

list of shoreline public-access points, visit www.portseattle.org/community/resources/publicaccess.shtml.

Shilshole Beach and Park near Shilshole Bay Marina (p100) Another fun beach area to explore.

CLIMATE

It does rain a lot in Seattle, but the temperature stays mild most of the year. For more information see When to Go (p16).

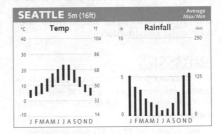

CUSTOMS REGULATIONS

US customs allows each person over the age of 21 to bring 1L of liquor and 200 cigarettes duty-free into the USA. US citizens are allowed to import, duty-free, up to $800 worth of gifts from abroad, while non-US citizens are allowed to import $100 worth. If you're carrying more than $10,000 in US and foreign cash, traveler's checks, money orders etc, you need to declare the excess amount. There is no legal restriction on the amount that may be imported, but undeclared sums in excess of $10,000 will probably be subject to investigation. If you're bringing prescription drugs, make sure they're in clearly marked containers. For updates, check www.customs.gov.

DISCOUNT CARDS

If you're going to be in Seattle for a while and plan on seeing its premier attractions, you might want to consider buying a CityPass (www.citypass.com/city/seattle.html; adult/child $39.50/24). Good for nine days, the pass gets you entry into the Pacific Science Center, Seattle Aquarium, Argosy Cruises' Seattle Harbor Tour, the Museum of Flight and the Woodland Park Zoo. You wind up saving 50% on admission costs and you never have to stand in line. You can buy one at whichever of the six venues you visit first, or online.

Another option is the Go Seattle card (www.go seattlecard.com; adult $55-149, child $39-105), which offers free or discounted admission to a long list of sights and entertainment. Available in one-, two-, three-, five- and seven-day versions, the cards get you in free to a number of the city's top attractions.

ELECTRICITY

The US electric current is 110v to 115v, 60Hz AC. Outlets are made for flat two-prong or three-prong plugs. If your appliance is made for another electrical system, you'll need a US converter, which can be bought from hardware stores and drugstores.

EMBASSIES

If your country does not have a consulate in Seattle, call directory information (☎ 202-555-1212) in Washington, DC , for the number of your national embassy.

Australian Consulate (☎ 206-575-7446; 401 Andover Park E)

Austrian Consulate (☎ 360-466-1100; 1111 3rd Ave)

Belgian Consulate (☎ 206-728-5145; 2200 Alaskan Way)

Bolivian Consulate (☎ 206-244-6696; Ste 100, 15215 52nd Ave S)

Canadian Consulate General (☎ 206-443-1777; Ste 600, 1501 4th Ave)

Cypriot Consulate (☎ 425-827-1700; Ste 200, 5555 Lakeview Dr)

Danish Consulate (☎ 206-230-0888; 6204 E Mercer Way)

Ethiopian Honorary Consulate (☎ 206-364-6401; 12612 Blakely Pl NW)

Finnish Consulate (☎ 425-451-3983; 17102 NE 37th Pl)

French Consulate (☎ 206-256-6184; Ste 490, 2200 Alaskan Way)

German Consulate (☎ 425-638-0347; 1750 112th Ave NE)

Hungarian Consulate (☎ 425-739-0631; PO Box 578)

Japanese Consulate General (☎ 206-682-9107; Ste 500, 601 Union Street)

Korean Consulate General (☎ 206-441-1011; Ste 1125, 2033 6th Ave)

Mexican Consulate (☎ 206-448-3526; 2132 3rd Ave)

Netherland Consulate (☎ 425-637-3050; 40 Lake Bellevue Dr)

Norway Consulate (☎ 206-623-3957; Ste 806, 1402 3rd Ave)

Russian Consulate General (☎ 206-728-1910; Ste 2323, 2001 6th Ave)

EMERGENCY

Community Information Line (☎ 206-461-3200) Information on emergency services, housing, legal advice etc.

Police, Fire and Ambulance (☎ 911)

Seattle Police (☎ 206-625-5011)

Seattle Rape Relief (☎ 206-632-7273)

Washington State Patrol (☎ 425-649-4370)

GAY & LESBIAN TRAVELERS

Seattle is a progressive, left-leaning city with thriving gay and lesbian communities; census data shows that approximately 12.9% of the city's population identifies itself as gay or lesbian, and there doesn't tend to be much sexual orientation–based hostility among the rest of the population.

A good way to get involved in the community is to start with the clearinghouse of information and resources that is the Seattle LGBT Community Center (Map p82; ☎ 206-323-5428; www .seattlelgbt.org; 1122 E Pike St; ☺ 10am-9pm Mon-Sat, 11am-8pm Sun). There's a community calendar, news, classified ads and volunteer opportunities on its website.

Some other resources and events to look for include the following:

Seattle Gay News (www.sgn.org) A weekly newspaper focusing on gay issues.

Seattle Lesbian & Gay Film Festival (www.seattlequeer film.com) Usually held in mid- to late October.

Seattle Pride (www.seattlepride.org) Seattle's popular gay-pride parade occurs in June.

HOLIDAYS

National public holidays are celebrated throughout the USA. On public holidays banks, schools and government offices (including post offices) are closed and public transportation follows a Sunday schedule. Plan ahead if you're traveling during many public holidays. Flights are full, highways are jammed and on Christmas and Thanksgiving, many grocery stores and restaurants close for the day.

New Year's Day January 1

Martin Luther King Jr Day Third Monday in January

Presidents' Day Third Monday in February

Easter Sunday Falls in March or April

Memorial Day Last Monday in May

Independence Day (Fourth of July) July 4

Labor Day First Monday in September

Columbus Day Second Monday in October

Veterans' Day November 11

Thanksgiving Day Fourth Thursday in November

Christmas Day December 25

INTERNET ACCESS

Seattle seems to be one big wi-fi hotspot. It's free nearly everywhere, in almost all hotels, many bars and all but a handful of coffee shops. Some of the main free public wi-fi hotspots include Occidental Park (p56) in Pioneer Square, Seattle Public Library (p52), some Metro buses and Sound Transit buses, the University District (p84), Victor Steinbrueck Park (p67) and some Washington State Ferries.

For laptop-free travelers, there are several good internet cafés (most of which offer 30 minutes free if you buy a coffee or snack), including the Online Coffee Company (☎ 206-328-3731; www.onlinecoffeeco.com; 1720 E Olive Way; also ☎ 206-323-7798; 1404 E Pine St; internet use per min 14c, 1hr for students free; ◷ 7:30am-midnight).

GHOSTBUSTERS

Should things go really awry while you are staying in Seattle and you begin to hear bumps in the night, or glimpse vague and filmy shapes loitering around by the foot of your bed, well, who are you gonna call?

Allow us to suggest Aghost, the Advanced Ghost Hunters of Seattle-Tacoma (☎ 253-203-4383; www.aghost.us). Experts in paranormal activity, the ghost hunters use surveillance equipment like motion detectors and recording devices to check for monsters under your bed, skeletons in the closet and so forth.

They can also tell you all about resident phantoms in Seattle, like the ghosts who lurk in the city's underground or the undead Irishman who sits at the back of the College Inn Pub after closing time.

LEGAL MATTERS

If you're arrested, you have the right to remain silent. There is no legal reason to speak to a police officer if you don't wish to – especially since anything you say 'can and will be used against you' – but never walk away from an officer until given permission. All persons who are arrested have the legal right to make one phone call. If you don't have a lawyer or a family member to help you, call your consulate. The police will give you the number upon request.

MAPS

There are basic, free online maps available via the tourist information office (visit www.visitseattle.org) and at www.see-seattle.com/map.htm, among other places, but for an extended stay it's best to have something more detailed. Good options can be found at any decent bookstore, or ask the experts at Metsker Maps (p113) or Wide World Books & Maps (p117).

MEDICAL SERVICES

Health care is a major problem in this country, as there is no federal law guaranteeing medical care for all citizens, and health insurance is extremely costly. People living below the poverty line are eligible for Medicaid, which covers many costs, and seniors can apply for Medicare, which works in a similar way. As a visitor, know that all hospital emergency rooms are obliged to receive sick or injured patients whether they can pay or not.

Clinics

If you're sick or injured, but not badly enough for a trip to the emergency room, try one of the following options:

45th St Community Clinic (Map p93; ☎ 206-633-3350; 1629 N 45th St, Wallingford) Medical and dental services.

Harborview Medical Center (☎ 206-731-3000; 325 9th Ave) Full medical care, with emergency room.

Health South (☎ 206-682-7418; 1151 Denny Way) Walk-in clinic for nonemergencies.

MONEY

The US dollar is divided into 100 cents. US coins come in denominations of one cent (penny), five cents (nickel), 10 cents (dime), 25 cents (quarter), the practically extinct 50 cents (half-dollar) and the not often seen golden dollar coin, which was introduced in 2000. The latter features a picture of Sacagawea, the Native American guide who famously led the explorers Meriwether Lewis and William Clark on their expedition through the western US. The new coins are often dispensed as change from ticket machines and stamp machines.

Notes come in $1, $2, $5, $10, $20, $50 and $100 denominations.

In recent years the US treasury has redesigned the $5, $10, $20, $50 and $100 bills to foil counterfeiters. The portraits of the presidents on each bill are larger and clearer, and Hamilton in particular looks extra fetching after the makeover.

To check the exchange rate, though it changes daily, see the Quick Reference guide inside this book's front cover.

ATMs

ATMs are easy to find in Seattle. There's practically one per block in the busier commercial areas, as well as one outside every bank. Many bars, restaurants and grocery stores also have the machines, although the service fees for these can be steep. Getting money this way saves you a step – no need to change money from your own currency – and is a safer way to travel, as you only take out what you need as you go.

Changing Money

Banks and moneychangers will give you US currency based on the current exchange rate. See Business Hours (p207) for bank opening hours.

Two other options are as follows:

American Express (Map p50; ☎ 206-441-8622; 600 Stewart St; ☺ 8:30am-5:30pm Mon-Fri)

Travelex-Thomas Cook Currency Services (☎ 206-248-6960; Sea-Tac Airport; ☺ 6am-8pm) The booth at the main airport terminal is behind the Delta Airlines counter. There's also a branch at the Westlake Center (☎ 206-682-4525; Level 3, 400 Pine St; ☺ 9:30am-6pm Mon-Sat, 11am-5pm Sun)

Credit & Debit Cards

Major credit cards are accepted at most hotels, restaurants and shops throughout Seattle, although visitors will find that many smaller cafés and restaurants will tack on an extra 30c or 50c amount for paying with plastic. Places that accept Visa and MasterCard generally also accept (and will often prefer) debit cards, which deduct payments directly from your check or savings account. Be sure to confirm with your bank before you leave that your debit card will be accepted in other states or countries. Debit cards from large commercial banks can often be used worldwide.

If your cards are lost or stolen, contact the issuing company immediately. The following are toll-free numbers for the main credit card companies:

American Express (☎ 800-528-4800)

Diners Club (☎ 800-234-6377)

Discover (☎ 800-347-2683)

MasterCard (☎ 800-826-2181)

Visa (☎ 800-336-8472)

Traveler's Checks

This old-school option offers the traveler protection from theft or loss. Checks issued by American Express and Thomas Cook are widely accepted, and both offer efficient replacement policies. Keeping a record of the check numbers and the checks you've used is vital when it comes to replacing lost checks. Keep this record in a separate place from the checks themselves.

Bring most of the checks in large denominations. Toward the end of a trip you may want to change a small check to make sure you aren't left with too much local currency. Of course, traveler's checks are losing their popularity due to the proliferation of ATMs and you may opt not to carry any at all.

NEWSPAPERS & MAGAZINES

Seattle's newspapers and magazines include the following. For more information, see p40.

Northwest Asian Weekly (www.nwasianweekly.com)
Puget Sound Business Journal (www.bizjournals.com /seattle) Daily.

RealChange Weekly paper focused on the city's homeless community.

Seattle Daily Journal of Commerce (www.djc.com) Focuses on the region's business world.

Seattle Gay News (www.sgn.org) Weekly.

Seattle Magazine (www.seattlemag.com) A slick monthly lifestyle magazine.

Seattle Post-Intelligencer (www.seattlepi.com) The morning daily.

Seattle Times (www.seattletimes.com) The state's largest daily paper.

Seattle Weekly (www.seattleweekly.com) Free weekly with news and entertainment listings.

Stranger (www.thestranger.com) Irreverent and intelligent free weekly, edited by Dan Savage of 'Savage Love' fame.

ORGANIZED TOURS

ARGOSY CRUISES SEATTLE HARBOR TOUR Map p64

☎ 206-623-1445, 800-642-7816; www.argosycruises .com; adult/child $18.61/7.81

One of the major operators, Argosy has a number of different tours departing daily from Pier 55 year-round. Its popular Seattle Harbor Tour is a one-hour narrated tour of Elliott Bay, the Waterfront and the Port of Seattle. This tour is covered in the CityPass (p54). Argosy also offers tours of the Hiram M Chittenden locks, speedboat cruises and a fine-dining cruise.

BILL SPEIDEL'S UNDERGROUND TOUR Map p57

☎ 206-682-4646; 608 1st Ave; adult/senior/child $14/12/7; ☽ 11am-5pm, schedule varies

Speidel was a local historian (he wrote the book Sons of the Profits) who relished stories of Seattle's sordid past: the good old days of hard-drinking politicians and hard-working 'seamstresses,' as the bordello girls were called. This famous 'underground' tour, though it might get a little corny at times, delivers the goods on historic Seattle as a rough and rowdy industrial town (see boxed text, p28). Starting at Doc Maynard's Public House and wandering through the tunnels and sidewalks hidden beneath the streets of Pioneer Square, the tour is massively popular, especially in prime tourist season. No reservations are accepted, so try to arrive half an hour early if you want to be sure you get in.

CHINATOWN DISCOVERY TOURS

☎ 425-885-3085; www.seattlechinatowntour.com; adult/child $16.95/10.95; ☽ 10:30am & 2:30pm

This tour group leads travelers through the International District with stops at historic sites, a fortune-cookie factory and various shops. Options include a daytime tour with a dim-sum lunch and an afternoon tour, as well as student-group tours. Reservations are required: call ahead.

GRAY LINE OF SEATTLE CITY SIGHTS TOUR Map p50

☎ 206-626-5208, 800-426-7532; www.grayline ofseattle.com; 800 Convention Place; tour $32; ☽ 9am & 2pm

Gray Line has a whole catalog of Seattle-area bus tours, but its three hour–plus City Sights Tour is recommended as a quick-hit rundown of the city's highlights in a 20-passenger coach. Gray Line also offers multiday package tours to the San Juan Islands and Victoria, BC. All trips depart from the Gray Line ticket desk at the convention center at 800 Convention Place.

SAILING IN SEATTLE SUNSET CRUISE Map p79

☎ 206-289-0094; www.sailing-in-seattle.com; 2040 Westlake Ave; up to 6 people $250

Sailing in Seattle offers 2½-hour sunset sails around Lake Union on the 33ft Whoodat every evening. There's also a Puget Sound Day Cruise that includes a trip through the Hiram M Chittenden Locks and lasts from eight to 10 hours. Trips meet on Lake Union at Sailing in Seattle's dock behind the China Harbor Restaurant on Westlake Ave.

SEE SEATTLE WALKING TOURS Map p50

☎ 425-226-7641; www.see-seattle.com; per person $20; ☽ 10am Mon-Sat

See Seattle runs a variety of theme tours, from public-art walks to scavenger hunts. While reservations aren't required for the walking tour that starts at the Westlake Center, they are recommended. A Sunday tour will run if at least six people have signed up.

TILLICUM VILLAGE TOURS Map p64

☎ 206-933-8600, 800-426-1205; www.tillicum village.com; adult/senior/child $79/72/30; ☽ Mar-Dec

From Pier 55, take a trip to Blake Island, the birthplace of Seattle's namesake Chief Sealth. The four-hour trip includes a salmon bake, a native dance and a movie at an old Duwamish Indian village.

POST

Rates for sending mail go up every few years, and with increasing frequency. With the latest 2c increase, rates for 1st-class mail within the US are 41c for letters up to 1oz and 26c for postcards. For package and international-letter rates, which vary, check with the local post office or with the online postal-rate calculator (ircalc.usps.gov). For other postal service questions, call ☎ 800-275-8777 or visit the US Post Office website (www.usps.com).

Seattle's most convenient post office locations are the main branch (Map p50; ☎ 206-748-5417; 301 Union St), University Station (Map p85; ☎ 206-675-8114; 4244 University Way NE, U District), Broadway Station (Map p82; ☎ 206-324-5474; 101 Broadway E), Queen Anne (Map p76; 415 1st Ave N) and Belltown (Map p69; Ste 25, 1001 4th Ave).

RADIO

KBKS 106.1 FM Top 40.

KEXP 90.3 FM Legendary independent music and community station.

KPLU 88.5 FM Public radio (NPR) and jazz.

KUOW 94.9 FM NPR news.

KJR 950AM Sports.

KJR 95.7 FM Classic rock.

TELEPHONE

Phone numbers within the USA consist of a three-digit area code followed by a seven-digit local number. If you're calling long distance, dial ☎ 1 + the three-digit area code + the seven-digit number.

Phone numbers in Seattle have a 206 area code. Even local calls made to the same area code require you to dial the full 10-digit number (no need to dial 1 first, though).

All toll-free numbers are prefixed with an 800, 877, 866 or 888 area code. Some toll-free numbers for local businesses or government offices only work within the state or the Seattle region, but most can be dialed from abroad. Just be aware that you'll be connected at regular long-distance rates, which could become a costly option if the line you're dialing regularly parks customers on hold.

Useful numbers include:

Emergency (fire, police, ambulance) ☎ 911

City (area) code ☎ 206

Country code ☎ 1

Directory assistance ☎ 411

International dialing ☎ 0011 + country code + city code + number

Seattle Police (nonemergency) ☎ 206-625-5011

TELEVISION

KCPQ Channel 13; Fox.

KCTS Channel 9; public broadcasting station.

KING Channel 5; NBC.

KIRO Channel 7; CBS.

KOMO Channel 4; ABC.

KSTW Channel 11; UPN.

KTWB Channel 22; WB.

TIME

Seattle is in the Pacific Standard Time Zone. Seattle time is two hours ahead of Hawaii (Hawaii–Aleutian Standard Time), one hour ahead of Alaska (Alaska Standard Time), one hour behind Colorado (Mountain Standard Time), two hours behind Alabama (Central Standard Time) and three hours behind New York (Atlantic Standard Time). In spring and summer, as in most of the time zones in the US, Pacific Standard Time becomes Pacific Daylight Time. Clocks are reset an hour forward in early spring, and reset an hour back in early fall.

TIPPING

Bartenders and wait staff should be tipped 15% to 25% if the service was good. Hotel porters expect $1 to $3 per bag. Tip taxi drivers around 10% to 15%.

TOURIST INFORMATION

The main Seattle visitors center, the Seattle Convention and Visitors Bureau (Map p50; ☎ 206-461-5888; www.seeseattle.org; 7th Ave & Pike St; ☷ 9am-5pm) is inside the Washington State Convention and Trade Center. It also operates the useful Citywide Concierge service.

TRAVELERS WITH DISABILITIES

All public buildings (including all hotels, restaurants, theaters and museums) are required by law to provide wheelchair access and to have restroom facilities available. Telephone companies provide relay operators for the hearing impaired. Many banks provide ATM instructions in braille. Dropped curbs are standard at intersections throughout the city.

Around 80% of Metro's buses are equipped with wheelchair lifts. Timetables marked with an 'L' indicate wheelchair accessibility. Be sure to let the driver know if you need your stop to be called and, if possible, pull the cord when you hear the call. Seeing-eye dogs are allowed on Metro buses. Passengers with disabilities qualify for a reduced fare but first need to contact Metro Transit (☎ 206-553-3060, 684-2029 TTY) for a permit. See the Metro Transit map for wheelchair-accessible stops and stations.

Most large private and chain hotels have suites for guests with disabilities. Many car-rental agencies offer hand-controlled models at no extra charge. Make sure you give at least two days' notice. All major airlines, Greyhound buses and Amtrak trains allow guide dogs to accompany passengers and often sell two-for-one packages when attendants of passengers with serious disabilities are required. Airlines will also provide assistance for connecting, boarding and disembarking the flight. Ask for assistance when making your reservation.

The following organizations and tour providers specialize in the needs of travelers with disabilities:

Access-Able Travel Service (www.access-able.com) Packed full of information, with tips on scooter rental, wheelchair travel, accessible transportation and more.

Easter Seals of Washington (☎ 206-281-5700; 157 Roy St) Provides technology assistance, workplace services and camps, among other things.

Moss Rehabilitation Hospital's Travel Information Service (☎ 215-456-9600, TTY 215-456-9602; 1200 W Tabor Rd, Philadelphia, PA 19141-3099)

Society for Accessible Travel & Hospitality (☎ 212-447-7284; www.sath.org; No 610, 347 Fifth Ave, New York, NY 10016)

VISAS

Foreigners needing visas to travel to the US should plan ahead. There is a reciprocal visa-waiver program in which citizens of certain countries may enter the USA for stays of 90 days or less with a passport but without first obtaining a visa. Currently these countries include Australia, Austria, Denmark, France, Germany, Italy, Japan, the Netherlands, New Zealand, Spain, Sweden, Switzerland and the UK. Under this program you must have a round-trip ticket that is nonrefundable in the USA, and you will not be allowed to extend your stay beyond 90 days.

As of January 2009, citizens of the 27 countries in the US Visa Waiver Program will need to register with the government online (https://esta.cbp.dhs.gov/) three days before their visit. The registration is valid for two years.

Other travelers will need to obtain a visa from a US consulate or embassy. In most countries, the process can be done by mail. Visa applicants may be required to 'demonstrate binding obligations' that will ensure their return home. Because of this requirement, those planning to travel through other countries before arriving in the USA are generally better off applying for their US visa while they are still in their home country, rather than after they're already on the road.

The Non-Immigrant Visitors Visa is the most common visa. It is available in two forms, the first one is the B1 for business purposes and the second is the B2 for tourism or visiting friends and relatives. The validity period for US visitor visas depends on which country you're from. The length of time you'll be allowed to stay in the USA is ultimately determined by US immigration authorities at the port of entry. Non-US citizens with HIV should know that they can be excluded from entry to the USA.

For updates on visas and other security issues, you can visit the US government's visa page (www.unitedstatesvisas .gov), the US Department of State (www.travel .state.gov) and the Travel Security Administration (www.tsa.gov).

VOLUNTEERING

If Seattle's progressive leanings become contagious during your trip and you decide to devote part of your travel time to doing volunteer work, the following resources can help:

Seattle Community Network (www.scn.org/volunteers) Maintains an online list of all kinds of local organizations that are looking for volunteers.

Service Board (☎ 206-324-7771; theserviceboard.org; 2017 E Spruce St) Teaches skill-building and confidence to Seattle-area high-school kids through an active mentorship program.

Seattle Parks and Recreation (☎ 206-684-8028; www .seattle.gov/parks/volunteers/workparty.htm) Frequently organizes work parties in which volunteers gather to help build park equipment, water and weed plants, and clean up public areas.

WOMEN TRAVELERS

Seattle is a generally safe place for women travelers as long as some common-sense practices are observed. Avoid walking alone at night through sketchy-looking or unlit areas. If you're out late bar-hopping, spring for a cab home instead of walking or waiting around for public transit. If you're ever assaulted, call the police (☎ 911).

WORK

To work legally in the USA you generally need both a work permit and working visa. To apply for the correct visa at the US embassy you are usually required to obtain a work permit from the Immigration and Naturalization Service (INS) first.

A prospective employer must file a petition with the INS for permission for you to work, so you will first need to find a company that wants to hire you and will file all the necessary paperwork.

More detailed information is available at the website of the US Department of State (www .travel.state.gov). For more information, see also the Moving to Seattle chapter, pp200–1.

BEHIND THE SCENES

THIS BOOK

This guidebook was commissioned in Lonely Planet's Oakland office, and produced by the following:

Commissioning Editor Heather Dickson

Coordinating Editor Amy Thomas

Coordinating Cartographers Joshua Geoghegan & Valentina Kremenchutskaya

Coordinating Layout Designer Jessica Rose

Managing Editor Bruce Evans

Managing Cartographers Shahara Ahmed & Alison Lyall

Managing Layout Designers Celia Wood & Adam McCrow

Assisting Editors Janice Bird, Penelope Goodes, Charlotte Harrison & Dianne Schallmeiner

Assisting Cartographer Jody Whiteoak

Cover Designer Marika Mercer

Project Managers Craig Kilburn & Eoin Dunlevy

Thanks to Imogen Bannister, Andrea Dobbin, Brice Gosnell, Laura Jane, Lisa Knights, Lyahna Spencer & Wendy Wright

Cover photographs
Space Needle in Seattle, nagelestock.com/Alamy (top); Rowers on Lake Washington in Seattle at dawn, Joel W Rogers/Corbis (bottom).

Internal photographs p5 (#1) Kemp Atwood/Flickr; p4 (#1) Richard Barnes/Seattle Art Museum; p11 (#1 top) Carter 'Rosco' Belleau/Flickr; p11 (#2 bottom) Dave Biddle/Flickr; p9 (#4) Suzanne Brandkamp/Flickr; p7 (#3) Paul Macapia/Olympic Sculpture Park; p7 (#2) Gideon Pertzov/Flickr; p4 (#2) photo courtesy of the Seattle Public Library; p11 (#2 top) photo courtesy of Nordic Heritage Museum. All other photographs by Lonely Planet Images, and by Lawrence Worcester except p12 (#3) Tom Boyden; p5 (#3), p9 (#2), p8 (#2) Ann Cecil; p2, p8 (#3), p8 (#4), p11 (#3 top), p12 (#1) Richard Cummins; p6 (#1), p9 (#3), p11 (#1), p12 (#4) John Elk III.

All images are copyright of the photographer unless otherwise indicated. Many of the images in this guide are available for licensing from Lonely Planet Images: www .lonelyplanetimages.com.

LONELY PLANET: TRAVEL WIDELY, TREAD LIGHTLY, GIVE SUSTAINABLY

The Lonely Planet Story

The story begins with a classic travel adventure: Tony and Maureen Wheeler's 1972 journey across Europe and Asia to Australia. There was no useful information about the overland trail then, so Tony and Maureen published the first Lonely Planet guidebook to meet a growing need.

From a kitchen table, Lonely Planet has grown to become the largest independent travel publisher in the world, with offices in Melbourne (Australia), Oakland (USA) and London (UK). Today Lonely Planet guidebooks cover the globe. There is an ever-growing list of books and information in a variety of media. Some things haven't changed. The main aim is still to make it possible for adventurous individuals to get out there – to explore and better understand the world.

The Lonely Planet Foundation

The Lonely Planet Foundation proudly supports nimble nonprofit institutions working for change in the world. Each year the foundation donates 5% of Lonely Planet company profits to projects selected by staff and authors. Our partners range from Kabissa, which provides small nonprofits across Africa with access to technology, to the Foundation for Developing Cambodian Orphans, which supports girls at risk of falling victim to sex traffickers.

Our nonprofit partners are linked by a grass-roots approach to the areas of health, education or sustainable tourism. Many – such as Louis Sarno who works with BaAka (Pygmy) children in the forested areas of Central African Republic – choose to focus on women and children as one of the most effective ways to support the whole community. Louis is determined to give options to children who are discriminated against by the majority Bantu population.

Sometimes foundation assistance is as simple as restoring a local ruin like the Minaret of Jam in Afghanistan; this incredible monument now draws intrepid tourists to the area and its restoration has greatly improved options for local people.

Just as travel is often about learning to see with new eyes, so many of the groups we work with aim to change the way people see themselves and the future for their children and communities.

THANKS

Becky Ohlsen thanks Maureen O'Hagan and Bob Young, Margo Debeir, Darek Mazzone, Tom Douglas, Cara Egan, Sarah Novotny, Yoram Bauman, Teh Lord Teh, Jason Simms, Alec Scharff, Lynn Bauer, Courtney Nash, Kord Davis, Cathy McCown, Dawn Mucha, Danella Anderson, Thomas Kohnstamm and Heather Dickson for all their help in putting together the guide, and the Sang-Froid Riding Club, Janice Logan, Oregon Motorcycle Road Racing Association, Peter Kahn, Scott Elder, Bradford Duval, Paul Gaudio and all the CB160 folks for providing the best possible means of escaping the office during write-up.

OUR READERS

Many thanks to the travelers who used the last edition and wrote to us with helpful hints, useful advice and interesting anecdotes:

Nick Botham, Ting-Hsu Chen, Neil Chivers, Thatcher Collins, Mario Kischporski, Susan Langsley, Jacqueline Liu, Shirley Low, Jack Miller, Toni Moe, L Mumforr, Brian Richard Peterson, Donna Riegel, Cory Sbarbaro, Bill Turner, William Turner, Keith Unterschute, Peter Vingerhoets, Anne Wallace

SEND US YOUR FEEDBACK

We love to hear from travelers – your comments keep us on our toes and help make our books better. Our well-traveled team reads every word on what you loved or loathed about this book. Although we cannot reply individually to postal submissions, we always guarantee that your feedback goes straight to the appropriate authors, in time for the next edition. Each person who sends us information is thanked in the next edition – and the most useful submissions are rewarded with a free book.

To send us your updates – and find out about Lonely Planet events, newsletters and travel news – visit our award-winning website: www.lonelyplanet.com/contact.

Note: We may edit, reproduce and incorporate your comments in Lonely Planet products such as guidebooks, websites and digital products, so let us know if you don't want your comments reproduced or your name acknowledged. For a copy of our privacy policy visit www.lonelyplanet.com/privacy.

Madona eatey and the house

1138   34th Ave   /E. cnicnst

Jimi
1798 Broadway

INDEX

INDEX

INDEX

INDEX

000 map pages
000 photographs

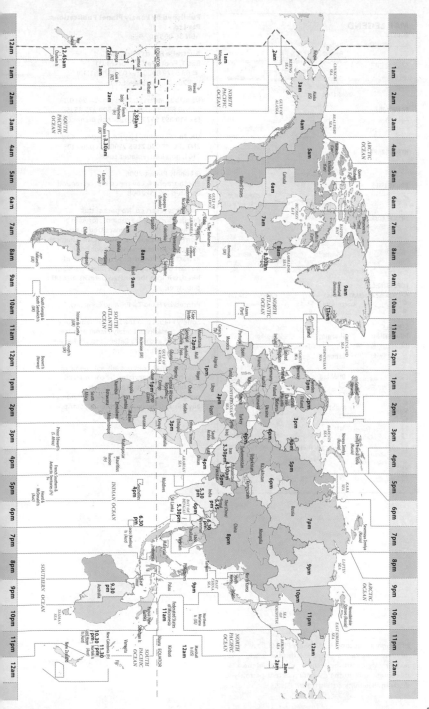

MAP LEGEND

ROUTES

Tollway	Mall/Steps
Freeway	Tunnel
Primary	Pedestrian Overpass
Secondary	Walking Tour
Tertiary	Walking Tour Detour
Lane	Walking Trail
Unsealed Road	Walking Path

TRANSPORT

Ferry	Rail
Monorail	Rail (Underground)
	Tram

HYDROGRAPHY

River, Creek	Canal
Intermittent River	Water

BOUNDARIES

International	Regional, Suburb
Marine Park	Ancient Wall

AREA FEATURES

Airport	Land
Area of Interest	Mall
Beach, Desert	Park
Building	Reservation
Campus	Sports
Cemetery, Christian	Urban

POPULATION

○ **CAPITAL (NATIONAL)**	◉ CAPITAL (STATE)
● Large City	● Medium City
○ Small City	○ Town, Village

SYMBOLS

Information
- Bank, ATM
- Hospital, Medical
- Information
- Internet Facilities
- Police Station
- Post Office, GPO
- Telephone
- Toilets

Sights
- Beach
- Castle, Fortress
- Christian
- Monument
- Museum, Gallery
- Point of Interest
- Ruin
- Zoo, Bird Sanctuary

Shopping
- Shopping

Eating
- Eating

Drinking
- Drinking
- Café

Nightlife
- Nightlife

Arts
- Arts

Sports & Activities
- Point of Interest
- Pool
- Skiing

Sleeping
- Sleeping
- Camping

Transport
- Airport, Airfield
- Bus Station
- Parking Area

Geographic
- Lighthouse
- Lookout
- Mountain, Volcano
- National Park
- Picnic Area
- Waterfall

Published by Lonely Planet Publications Pty Ltd
ABN 36 005 607 983

Australia Head Office, Locked Bag 1, Footscray, Victoria 3011, ☎ 03 8379 8000, fax 03 8379 8111, talk2us@lonelyplanet.com.au

USA 150 Linden St, Oakland, CA 94607, ☎ 510 893 8555, toll free 800 275 8555, fax 510 893 8572, info@lonelyplanet.com

UK 2nd Floor 186 City Rd, London, EC1V 2NT UK, ☎ 020 7106 2100, fax 020 7106 2101, go@lonelyplanet.co.uk

© Lonely Planet 2008
Photographs © Lawrence Worcester and as listed (p215) 2008